Internati
Accounting S
1993

International Accounting Standards 1993

The full text of all International Accounting Standards extant at 1 January, 1993.

International Accounting Standards Committee
167 Fleet Street
London EC4A 2ES
England

No responsibility for loss occasioned to any person acting or refraining from action as a result of any material in this publication can be accepted by the authors or publisher.

© 1992 International Accounting Standards Committee

ISBN 0 905625 15 3

Printed and bound in the United Kingdom by LOC Graphic Services, Hertfordshire, England.

Contents

Revised International Accounting Standard (Effective 1994)

Proposed New International Accounting Standard

Proposed Revised International Accounting Standards

Statement of Intent

Exposure Drafts

Index

Introduction

The International Accounting Standards Committee (IASC) was set up in 1973 to work for the improvement and harmonisation of financial reporting, primarily through the development and publication of International Accounting Standards. IASC develops International Accounting Standards through an international due process that involves the world-wide accountancy profession, the preparers and users of financial statements, and national standard setting bodies. IASC is now established as the only international due process for the development of International Accounting Standards.

The objectives of IASC are:

(a)   to formulate and publish in the public interest accounting standards to be observed in the presentation of financial statements and to promote their world-wide acceptance and observance;

(b)   to work generally for the improvement and harmonisation of regulations, accounting standards and procedures relating to the presentation of financial statements.

The members of IASC are the professional accountancy bodies which are members of the International Federation of Accountants (IFAC). As at December 1992, there are 107 Member Bodies in 81 countries; these Member Bodies represent over one million accountants in industry and commerce, public practice, academic institutions and government.

IASC is funded by the professional accountancy bodies and other organisations on its Board, and IFAC, and by contributions from multinational companies, financial institutions, accounting firms and other organisations.

Board

The business of IASC is conducted by a Board which comprises representatives of accountancy bodies in thirteen countries and up to four other organisations with an interest in financial reporting. Currently the Board includes representatives of accountancy bodies in:

Australia	Jordan
Canada	Netherlands
France	Nordic Federation of Public Accountants
Germany	South Africa
India	United Kingdom
Italy	United States of America
Japan	

and representatives of the International Coordinating Committee of Financial Analysts' Associations.

Consultative Group

The Board meets regularly an international Consultative Group that includes representatives of users and preparers of financial statements and standard setting bodies as well as observers from intergovernmental organisations. The current members of the Consultative Group are:

Federation Internationale des Bourses de Valeurs (FIBV)

International Association of Financial Executives Institutes (IAFEI)

International Chamber of Commerce (ICC)

International Confederation of Free Trade Unions (ICFTU), and World Confederation of Labour

International Organisation of Securities Commissions (IOSCO)

International Banking Associations

International Bar Association (IBA)

International Finance Corporation (IFC)

The World Bank

Financial Accounting Standards Board (FASB)

European Commission

The International Assets Valuation Standards Committee

Organisation for Economic Cooperation and Development (OECD)*

Transnational Corporations and Management Division, United Nations*

*Observer

The Development of International Accounting Standards

Board Representatives, Member Bodies, members of the Consultative Group, other organisations and individuals and the IASC staff are encouraged to submit suggestions for new topics which might be dealt with in International Accounting Standards. From time to time, the staff prepares project proposals which set out the reasons why particular topics should be added to the current work programme. These proposals are considered by the Board.

Once the Board has added a topic to its work programme, it sets up a Steering Committee to develop a Statement of Principles, an Exposure Draft and, ultimately, an International Accounting Standard. Each Steering Committee is chaired by a Board Representative and usually includes representatives of the accountancy bodies in at least three other countries. Steering Committees may also include representatives of other organisations that are represented on the Board or the Consultative Group or which are expert in the particular topic.

The development of every International Accounting Standard includes:

(a) the identification and review of all the accounting issues associated with the topic;

(b) the consideration of the application of IASC's Framework for the Preparation and Presentation of Financial Statements to those issues;

(c) the study of national and regional accounting requirements and practice, and other relevant material on the topic;

(d) a detailed review by the Steering Committee of the issues, national and regional accounting requirements and practice, and other relevant material;

(e) a detailed review by the Board of the Steering Committee's recommendations;

9

(f)   consultation with the Consultative Group, Member Bodies, standard setting bodies and other interested groups and individuals on a worldwide basis;

(g)   public exposure of the draft International Accounting Standard; and

(h)   evaluation by the Steering Committee and the Board of the comments received on Exposure Drafts.

The procedure for the development of an International Accounting Standard is as follows:

(a)   the Steering Committee considers the issues involved and develops a Point Outline;

(b)   after receiving comments from the Board on the Point Outline, the Steering Committee prepares a draft Statement of Principles. The purpose of this Statement is to set out the underlying accounting principles that will form the basis for the preparation of the Exposure Draft. It also describes the alternative solutions considered and the reasons for recommending their acceptance or rejection;

(c)   the draft Statement of Principles is circulated to Member Bodies, members of the Consultative Group and other interested organisations for comment;

(d)   the Steering Committee reviews the comments on the draft Statement of Principles and agrees a final Statement, which is submitted to the Board for approval

(e)   the Steering Committee prepares a draft Exposure Draft based on the Statement of Principles approved by the Board. The draft Exposure Draft is submitted to the Board for approval. After revision and with the approval of at least two-thirds of the Board, the Exposure Draft is published. Comments are invited from all interested parties during the exposure period, usually six months;

(f)   the Steering Committee reviews the comments and prepares a draft International Accounting Standard; and

(g)   the Board reviews the draft International Accounting Standard. After revision and with the approval of at least three-quarters of the Board, the Standard is published.

During this process, the Board may decide that the needs of the subject under consideration warrant additional consultation or would be better served by issuing a Discussion Paper for comment. It may also be necessary to issue more than one Exposure Draft before developing a draft International Accounting Standard. From time to time, the Board may decide to set up a Steering Committee to consider whether to revise an existing International Accounting Standard to take into account developments since the Standard was first approved.

IASC's Work Programme

The Board of the International Accounting Standards Committee (IASC) has issued 31 International Accounting Standards which deal with the substantial majority of topics that affect the financial statements of business enterprises.

The Board has also issued a Framework for the Preparation and Presentation of Financial Statements. The purposes of the Framework include:

(a)   assisting the Board in the development of future International Accounting Standards and in its review of existing International Accounting Standards; and

(b)   assisting the Board in promoting the harmonisation of regulations, accounting standards and procedures relating to the presentation of financial statements by providing a basis for reducing the number of alternative accounting treatments permitted by International Accounting Standards.

In 1987, IASC decided to give a high priority to the reduction or elimination of alternative accounting treatments in existing International Accounting

Standards. Subsequently, it decided to extend the project to deal with other improvements to the Standards.

Comparability of Financial Statements

In January 1989, E32 Comparability of Financial Statements, was published, which represented the culmination of the first important stage of this project. It dealt with 29 issues where existing International Accounting Standards allow a free choice of accounting treatment for like transactions and events. Following reconsideration of each issue, and consideration of the comment letters on E32, the Board approved a Statement of Intent on the Comparability of Financial Statements in June 1990.

The Statement of Intent identified three issues on which the Board decided to make substantive changes to the proposals in E32. It also identified twenty one issues, on which the Board decided to proceed with the E32 proposals unchanged.

Improvements to International Accounting Standards

When it approved the Statement of Intent, the Board recognised that many standards required revision for developments that had taken place since the first standards were issued. These revisions are being dealt with as part of the Improvements project. The implementation of the revisions in the Statement of Intent on the Comparability of Financial Statements created the ideal opportunity to make the necessary revisions. These revisions are being dealt with as part of the Improvements project. The purpose of this project is:

(a)   to revise the Standards for the changes set out in the Statement of Intent on the Comparability of Financial Statements;

(b)   to ensure that the Standards are sufficiently detailed and complete, that their explanations are adequate and that they are consistent with other Standards;

(c)   to review each Standard in the context of the Framework for the Preparation and Presentation of Financial Statements;

(d)   to review the disclosure requirements;

(e)   to revise the format of each Standard

The Board has made significant progress on the Improvements project in the past year with the publication of ten Exposure Drafts of revised standards, (E37-E39 and E41-E47). E37, E38 and E39 deal with the three issues on which the Board decided to make substantive changes to its proposals in E32 and which would, therefore, require re-exposure. All the other revised Standards have been re-exposed in order to allow IASC's constituency to comment on the implementation of the Statement of Intent changes and the other revisions.

The Board intends to approve revised Standards for all the topics covered by the current Exposure Drafts by the end of 1993. This will complete the present phase of the Comparability and Improvements project. The Board is dealing with the Statement of Intent as a package. Therefore, its approval of the revised Standards is subject to its later approval of the revised Standards incorporating the other changes in the Statement of Intent. All the revised Standards will come into effect on the same date.

Other Current Projects

IASC began its review of IAS 12, Accounting for Taxes on Income, in 1988 and published E33, Accounting for Taxes on Income, in 1989. Certain of the proposals in the Exposure Draft attracted a substantial number of adverse comments. Subsequently, a number of national standard setting bodies have reconsidered national requirements on this topic. The Board has placed a high priority on the completion of this project. However, it is likely that the Board will need to issue a further Exposure Draft before proceeding with a revised Standard.

The Board is presently developing Standards on Financial Instruments, Intangibles and Earnings per Share. It has also agreed to carry out a review of IAS 14, Reporting Financial Information by Segment.

The Board is carrying out a project on the Financial Reporting Needs of Developing and Newly Industrialised Countries; many of these countries use International Accounting Standards as, or as the basis for, national accounting requirements.

The Use and Application of International Accounting Standards

International Accounting Standards have done a great deal to both improve and harmonise financial reporting around the world.

The Standards are used:

(a)   as national requirements, often after a national due process;

(b)   as the basis for all or some national requirements;

(c)   as an international benchmark for those countries which develop their own requirements;

(d)   by regulatory authorities for domestic and foreign companies; and

(e)   by companies themselves.

The International Organisation of Securities Commissions (IOSCO) is looking to IASC to provide mutually acceptable International Accounting Standards which are acceptable for multinational securities offerings and other international offerings. Already, a number of stock exchanges require or allow foreign issuers to present financial statements in accordance with International Accounting Standards. As a result a growing number of companies disclose the fact that their financial statements conform with International Accounting Standards.

IASC last published a Survey of the Use and Application of International Accounting Standards in September 1988. The Survey compared International Accounting Standards with the national accounting requirements and practice in member countries. It also described the use of International Accounting Standards by national standard setting bodies and includes examples of the way in which companies disclose that their financial statements conform with International Accounting Standards.

A new Survey will be published during 1993.

Publication of International Accounting Standards

Many of the professional accountancy bodies that are members of IASC have published the texts of International Accounting Standards in their own countries. Such publications usually include national prefaces or other material that explains the application of International Accounting Standards in the country concerned. Copies of these publications are available from the appropriate accountancy body. Further details are available from IASC.

Translation of International Accounting Standards

Various professional accountancy bodies and other organisations have also prepared and published translations of International Accounting Standards. Some or all of the Standards are available in Arabic, Bulgarian, Chinese, Croat, Czech, Danish, Dutch, Flemish, French, Greek, Hebrew, Hungarian, Indonesian, Italian, Japanese, Korean, Malay, Norwegian, Polish, Portuguese, Slovak, Spanish, Thai and Turkish. Copies of these translations are available from the appropriate accountancy body or organisation. Further details are available from IASC.

More Information

More information about the work of IASC, copies of its publications and details of IASC's subscription service may be obtained from:

International Accounting Standards Committee,
167 Fleet Street,
London EC4A 2ES,
England.

| Telephone: | +44 (071) 353-0565 |
| Telefax: | +44 (071) 353-0562. |

Preface to Statements of International Accounting Standards

This Preface is issued to set out the objectives and operating procedures of the International Accounting Standards Committee (IASC) and to explain the scope and authority of the Statements of International Accounting Standards. The Preface was approved in November 1982 for publication in January 1983 and supersedes the Preface published in January 1975 (amended March 1978). The approved text of this Preface is that published by the International Accounting Standards Committee in the English language.

1. The International Accounting Standards Committee (IASC) came into existence on 29 June 1973 as a result of an agreement by accountancy bodies in Australia, Canada, France, Germany, Japan, Mexico, the Netherlands, the United Kingdom and Ireland, and the United States of America. A revised Agreement and Constitution were signed in November 1982. The business of IASC is conducted by a Board comprising representatives of up to thirteen countries and up to four organisations having an interest in financial reporting.

The Objectives

2. The objectives of IASC as set out in its Constitution are:

'(a)　to formulate and publish in the public interest accounting standards to be observed in the presentation of financial statements and to promote their worldwide acceptance and observance, and

(b)　to work generally for the improvement and harmonisation of regulations, accounting standards and procedures relating to the presentation of financial statements.'

3. The relationship between IASC and the International Federation of Accountants (IFAC) is confirmed by the Mutual Commitments into which they have entered. The membership of IASC (which is the same as that of IFAC) acknowledges in the revised Agreement that IASC has full and complete autonomy in the setting and issue of International Accounting Standards.

4. The members agree to support the objectives of IASC by undertaking the following obligations:

'to support the work of IASC by publishing in their respective countries every International Accounting Standard approved for issue by the Board of IASC and by using their best endeavours:

(i) to ensure that published financial statements comply with International Accounting Standards in all material respects and disclose the fact of such compliance;

(ii) to persuade governments and standard-setting bodies that published financial statements should comply with International Accounting Standards in all material respects;

(iii) to persuade authorities controlling securities markets and the industrial and business community that published financial statements should comply with International Accounting Standards in all material respects and disclose the fact of such compliance;

(iv) to ensure that the auditors satisfy themselves that the financial statements comply with International Accounting Standards in all material respects;

(v) to foster acceptance and observance of International Accounting Standards internationally.'

Published Financial Statements

5. The term 'financial statements' used in paragraphs 2 and 4 covers balance sheets, income statements or profit and loss accounts, statements of changes in financial position, notes and other statements and explanatory material which are identified as being part of the financial statements. Usually, financial statements are made available or published once each year and are the subject of a report by an auditor. International Accounting Standards apply to such financial statements of any commercial, industrial, or business enterprise.

6. The management of such an enterprise may prepare financial statements for its own use in a number of different ways best suited for internal management purposes. When financial statements are issued to other persons, such as shareholders, creditors, employees, and the public at large, they should conform to International Accounting Standards.

7. The responsibility for the preparation of financial statements and for adequate disclosure is that of the management of the enterprise. The auditor's responsibility is to form his opinion and to report on the financial statements.

Accounting Standards

8.   Within each country, local regulations govern, to a greater or lesser degree, the issue of financial statements. Such local regulations include accounting standards which are promulgated by the regulatory bodies and/ or the professional accountancy bodies in the countries concerned.

9.   Prior to the formation of IASC there were frequently differences of form and content between the published accounting standards of most countries. IASC takes cognisance of exposure drafts, or of accounting standards already issued on each subject, and in the light of such knowledge produces an International Accounting Standard for worldwide acceptance. One of the objects of IASC is to harmonise as far as possible the diverse accounting standards and accounting policies of different countries.

10.   In carrying out this task of adaptation of existing standards, and in formulating International Accounting Standards on new subjects, IASC concentrates on essentials. It therefore endeavours not to make the International Accounting Standards so complex that they cannot be applied effectively on a worldwide basis. International Accounting Standards issued by IASC are constantly reviewed to take into account the current position and the need for updating.

11.   International Accounting Standards promulgated by IASC do not override the local regulations, referred to in paragraph 8 above, governing the issue of financial statements in a particular country. The obligations undertaken by the members of IASC, as explained in this Preface, provide that where International Accounting Standards are complied with in all material respects, this fact should be disclosed. Where local regulations require deviation from International Accounting Standards, the local members of IASC endeavour to persuade the relevant authorities of the benefits of harmonisation with International Accounting Standards.

The Scope of the Standards

12.   Any limitation of the applicability of specific International Accounting Standards is made clear in the statements of those standards. International Accounting Standards are not intended to apply to immaterial items. An International Accounting Standard applies from a date specified in the standard and unless indicated to the contrary is not retroactive.

Working Procedure – Exposure Drafts and Standards

13.   The agreed working procedure is to select certain subjects for detailed study by Steering Committees. As a result of this work an exposure draft is

prepared on a particular subject for consideration by the Board. If approved by at least two-thirds of the Board, the exposure draft is addressed to accountancy bodies and to governments, securities markets, regulatory and other agencies and other interested parties. Adequate time is allowed for consideration and comment on each exposure draft.

14.   Since the formation of the Consultative Group in 1981, their views are taken into account at each major decision-making stage.

15.   The comments and suggestions received as a result of this exposure are then examined by the Board and the exposure draft is revised as necessary. Provided that the revised draft is approved by at least three-quarters of the Board, it is issued as an International Accounting Standard and becomes operative from a date stated in the standard.

16.   At some stage in the above process, the IASC Board may decide that, in order to promote discussion of a topic, or to allow adequate time for points of view to be put forward, a discussion paper should be issued. A discussion paper requires approval by a simple majority of the Board.

Voting

17.   For the purpose of voting referred to in paragraphs 13 to 16 above, each country and each organisation represented on the Board has one vote.

Language

18.   The approved text of any exposure draft or standard is that published by IASC in the English language. Members are responsible, under the authority of the Board, for preparing translations of exposure drafts and standards so that, where appropriate, such translations may be issued in the languages of their own countries. These translations indicate the name of the accountancy body that prepared the translation and that it is a translation of the approved text.

The Authority attaching to the Standards

19.   Standing alone, neither the IASC nor the accountancy profession has the power to enforce international agreement or to require compliance with International Accounting Standards. The success of IASC's efforts is dependent upon the recognition and support for its work from many different interested groups acting within the limits of their own jurisdiction. In most countries of the world, the accounting profession has a prestige and standing which is of great significance in these efforts.

Conclusion

20.   The members of IASC believe that the adoption in their countries of International Accounting Standards together with disclosure of compliance will over the years have a significant impact. The quality of financial statements will be improved and there will be an increasing degree of comparability. The credibility and consequently the usefulness of financial statements will be enhanced throughout the world.

Framework for the Preparation and Presentation of Financial Statements

Contents

Preface

Financial statements are prepared and presented for external users by many enterprises around the world. Although such financial statements may appear similar from country to country, there are differences which have probably been caused by a variety of social, economic and legal circumstances and by different countries having in mind the needs of different users of financial statements when setting national requirements.

These different circumstances have led to the use of a variety of definitions of the elements of financial statements; that is, for example, assets, liabilities, equity, income and expenses. They have also resulted in the use of different criteria for the recognition of items in the financial statements and in a preference for different bases of measurement. The scope of the financial statements and the disclosures made in them have also been affected.

The International Accounting Standards Committee (IASC) is committed to narrowing these differences by seeking to harmonise regulations, accounting standards and procedures relating to the preparation and presentation of financial statements. It believes that further harmonisation can best be pursued by focusing on financial statements that are prepared for the purpose of providing information that is useful in making economic decisions.

The Board of IASC believes that financial statements prepared for this purpose meet the common needs of most users. This is because nearly all users are making economic decisions, for example, to:

(a)   decide when to buy, hold or sell an equity investment;

(b)   assess the stewardship or accountability of management;

(c)   assess the ability of the enterprise to pay and provide other benefits to its employees;

(d)   assess the security for amounts lent to the enterprise;

(e)   determine taxation policies;

(f)   determine distributable profits and dividends;

(g)   prepare and use national income statistics; or

(h)   regulate the activities of enterprises.

The Board recognises, however, that governments, in particular, may specify different or additional requirements for their own purposes. These requirements should not, however, affect financial statements published for the benefit of other users unless they also meet the needs of those other users.

Financial statements are most commonly prepared in accordance with an accounting model based on recoverable historical cost and the nominal financial capital maintenance concept. Other models and concepts may be more appropriate in order to meet the objective of providing information that is useful for making economic decisions although there is presently no consensus for change. This framework has been developed so that it is applicable to a range of accounting models and concepts of capital and capital maintenance.

Introduction

Purpose and Status

1.   This framework sets out the concepts that underlie the preparation and presentation of financial statements for external users. The purpose of the framework is to:

(a)   assist the Board of IASC in the development of future International Accounting Standards and in its review of existing International Accounting Standards;

(b)   assist the Board of IASC in promoting harmonisation of regulations, accounting standards and procedures relating to the presentation of financial statements by providing a basis for reducing the number of alternative accounting treatments permitted by International Accounting Standards;

(c)   assist national standard-setting bodies in developing national standards;

(d)   assist preparers of financial statements in applying International Accounting Standards and in dealing with topics that have yet to form the subject of an International Accounting Standard;

(e)   assist auditors in forming an opinion as to whether financial statements conform with International Accounting Standards;

(f)   assist users of financial statements in interpreting the information contained in financial statements prepared in conformity with International Accounting Standards; and

(g)   provide those who are interested in the work of IASC with information about its approach to the formulation of International Accounting Standards.

2.   This framework is not an International Accounting Standard and hence does not define standards for any particular measurement or disclosure issue. Nothing in this framework overrides any specific International Accounting Standard.

3.   The Board of IASC recognises that in a limited number of cases there may be a conflict between the framework and an International

Accounting Standard. In those cases where there is a conflict, the requirements of the International Accounting Standard prevail over those of the framework. As, however, the Board of IASC will be guided by the framework in the development of future Standards and in its review of existing Standards, the number of cases of conflict between the framework and International Accounting Standards will diminish through time.

4.   The framework will be revised from time to time on the basis of the Board's experience of working with it.

Scope

5.   The framework deals with:

(a)   the objective of financial statements;

(b)   the qualitative characteristics that determine the usefulness of information in financial statements;

(c)   the definition, recognition and measurement of the elements from which financial statements are constructed; and

(d)   concepts of capital and capital maintenance.

6.   The framework is concerned with general purpose financial statements (hereafter referred to as "financial statements") including consolidated financial statements. Such financial statements are prepared and presented at least annually and are directed toward the common information needs of a wide range of users. Some of these users may require, and have the power to obtain, information in addition to that contained in the financial statements. Many users, however, have to rely on the financial statements as their major source of financial information and such financial statements should, therefore, be prepared and presented with their needs in view. Special purpose financial reports, for example, prospectuses and computations prepared for taxation purposes, are outside the scope of this framework. Nevertheless, the framework may be applied in the preparation of such special purpose reports where their requirements permit.

7.   Financial statements form part of the process of financial reporting. A complete set of financial statements normally includes a balance sheet, an income statement, a statement of changes in financial position (which may be presented in a variety of ways, for example, as a statement of cash flows or a statement of funds flow), and those notes and other statements and explanatory material that are an integral part of the financial statements. They may also include supplementary schedules and information based on or derived from, and expected to be read with, such statements. Such

schedules and supplementary information may deal, for example, with financial information about industrial and geographical segments and disclosures about the effects of changing prices. Financial statements do not, however, include such items as reports by directors, statements by the chairman, discussion and analysis by management and similar items that may be included in a financial or annual report.

8.   The framework applies to the financial statements of all commercial, industrial and business reporting enterprises, whether in the public or the private sectors. A reporting enterprise is an enterprise for which there are users who rely on the financial statements as their major source of financial information about the enterprise.

Users and Their Information Needs

9.   The users of financial statements include present and potential investors, employees, lenders, suppliers and other trade creditors, customers, governments and their agencies and the public. They use financial statements in order to satisfy some of their different needs for information. These needs include the following:

(a) *Investors*. The providers of risk capital and their advisers are concerned with the risk inherent in, and return provided by, their investments. They need information to help them determine whether they should buy, hold or sell. Shareholders are also interested in information which enables them to assess the ability of the enterprise to pay dividends.

(b) *Employees*. Employees and their representative groups are interested in information about the stability and profitability of their employers. They are also interested in information which enables them to assess the ability of the enterprise to provide remuneration, retirement benefits and employment opportunities.

(c) *Lenders*. Lenders are interested in information that enables them to determine whether their loans, and the interest attaching to them, will be paid when due.

(d) *Suppliers and other trade creditors*. Suppliers and other creditors are interested in information that enables them to determine whether amounts owing to them will be paid when due. Trade creditors are likely to be interested in an enterprise over a shorter period than lenders unless they are dependent upon the continuation of the enterprise as a major customer.

(e) *Customers*. Customers have an interest in information about the continuance of an enterprise, especially when they have a long-term involvement with, or are dependent on, the enterprise.

(f) *Governments and their agencies*. Governments and their agencies are interested in the allocation of resources and, therefore, the activities of enterprises. They also require information in order to regulate the activities of enterprises, determine taxation policies and as the basis for national income and similar statistics.

(g) *Public*. Enterprises affect members of the public in a variety of ways. For example, enterprises may make a substantial contribution to the local economy in many ways including the number of people they employ and their patronage of local suppliers. Financial statements may assist the public by providing information about the trends and recent developments in the prosperity of the enterprise and the range of its activities.

10. While all of the information needs of these users cannot be met by financial statements, there are needs which are common to all users. As investors are providers of risk capital to the enterprise, the provision of financial statements that meet their needs will also meet most of the needs of other users that financial statements can satisfy.

11. The management of an enterprise has the primary responsibility for the preparation and presentation of the financial statements of the enterprise. Management is also interested in the information contained in the financial statements even though it has access to additional management and financial information that helps it carry out its planning, decision-making and control responsibilities. Management has the ability to determine the form and content of such additional information in order to meet its own needs. The reporting of such information, however, is beyond the scope of this framework. Nevertheless, published financial statements are based on the information used by management about the financial position, performance and changes in financial position of the enterprise.

The Objective of Financial Statements

12.   The objective of financial statements is to provide information about the financial position, performance and changes in financial position of an enterprise that is useful to a wide range of users in making economic decisions.

13.   Financial statements prepared for this purpose meet the common needs of most users. However, financial statements do not provide all the information that users may need to make economic decisions since they largely portray the financial effects of past events and do not necessarily provide non-financial information.

14.   Financial statements also show the results of the stewardship of management, or the accountability of management for the resources entrusted to it. Those users who wish to assess the stewardship or accountability of management do so in order that they may make economic decisions; these decisions may include, for example, whether to hold or sell their investment in the enterprise or whether to reappoint or replace the management.

Financial Position, Performance and Changes in Financial Position

15.   The economic decisions that are taken by users of financial statements require an evaluation of the ability of an enterprise to generate cash and cash equivalents and of the timing and certainty of their generation. This ability ultimately determines, for example, the capacity of an enterprise to pay its employees and suppliers, meet interest payments, repay loans and make distributions to its owners. Users are better able to evaluate this ability to generate cash and cash equivalents if they are provided with information that focuses on the financial position, performance and changes in financial position of an enterprise.

16.   The financial position of an enterprise is affected by the economic resources it controls, its financial structure, its liquidity and solvency, and its capacity to adapt to changes in the environment in which it operates. Information about the economic resources controlled by the enterprise and its capacity in the past to modify these resources is useful in predicting the ability of the enterprise to generate cash and cash equivalents in the future. Information about financial structure is useful in predicting future borrowing needs and how future profits and cash flows will be distributed among those with an interest in the enterprise; it is also useful in predicting

how successful the enterprise is likely to be in raising further finance. Information about liquidity and solvency is useful in predicting the ability of the enterprise to meet its financial commitments as they fall due. Liquidity refers to the availability of cash in the near future after taking account of financial commitments over this period. Solvency refers to the availability of cash over the longer term to meet financial commitments as they fall due.

17.   Information about the performance of an enterprise, in particular its profitability, is required in order to assess potential changes in the economic resources that it is likely to control in the future. Information about variability of performance is important in this respect. Information about performance is useful in predicting the capacity of the enterprise to generate cash flows from its existing resource base. It is also useful in forming judgements about the effectiveness with which the enterprise might employ additional resources.

18.   Information concerning changes in the financial position of an enterprise is useful in order to assess its investing, financing and operating activities during the reporting period. This information is useful in providing the user with a basis to assess the ability of the enterprise to generate cash and cash equivalents and the needs of the enterprise to utilise those cash flows. In constructing a statement of changes in financial position, funds can be defined in various ways, such as all financial resources, working capital, liquid assets or cash. No attempt is made in this framework to specify a definition of funds.

19.   Information about financial position is primarily provided in a balance sheet. Information about performance is primarily provided in an income statement. Information about changes in financial position is provided in the financial statements by means of a separate statement.

20.   The component parts of the financial statements interrelate because they reflect different aspects of the same transactions or other events. Although each statement provides information that is different from the others, none is likely to serve only a single purpose or provide all the information necessary for particular needs of users. For example, an income statement provides an incomplete picture of performance unless it is used in conjunction with the balance sheet and the statement of changes in financial position.

Notes and Supplementary Schedules

21.   The financial statements also contain notes and supplementary schedules and other information. For example, they may contain additional information that is relevant to the needs of users about the items in the balance sheet and income statement. They may include disclosures about

the risks and uncertainties affecting the enterprise and any resources and obligations not recognised in the balance sheet (such as mineral reserves). Information about geographical and industry segments and the effect on the enterprise of changing prices may also be provided in the form of supplementary information.

Underlying Assumptions

Accrual Basis

22.   In order to meet their objectives, financial statements are prepared on the accrual basis of accounting. Under this basis, the effects of transactions and other events are recognised when they occur (and not as cash or its equivalent is received or paid) and they are recorded in the accounting records and reported in the financial statements of the periods to which they relate. Financial statements prepared on the accrual basis inform users not only of past transactions involving the payment and receipt of cash but also of obligations to pay cash in the future and of resources that represent cash to be received in the future. Hence, they provide the type of information about past transactions and other events that is most useful to users in making economic decisions.

Going Concern

23.   The financial statements are normally prepared on the assumption that an enterprise is a going concern and will continue in operation for the foreseeable future. Hence, it is assumed that the enterprise has neither the intention nor the need to liquidate or curtail materially the scale of its operations; if such an intention or need exists, the financial statements may have to be prepared on a different basis and, if so, the basis used is disclosed.

Qualitative Characteristics of Financial Statements

24.   Qualitative characteristics are the attributes that make the information provided in financial statements useful to users. The four principal qualitative characteristics are understandability, relevance, reliability and comparability.

Understandability

25.   An essential quality of the information provided in financial statements is that it is readily understandable by users. For this purpose, users are assumed to have a reasonable knowledge of business and economic activities and accounting and a willingness to study the information with reasonable diligence. However, information about complex matters that should be included in the financial statements because of its relevance to the economic decision-making needs of users should not be excluded merely on the grounds that it may be too difficult for certain users to understand.

Relevance

26.   To be useful, information must be relevant to the decision-making needs of users. Information has the quality of relevance when it influences the economic decisions of users by helping them evaluate past, present or future events or confirming, or correcting, their past evaluations.

27.   The predictive and confirmatory roles of information are interrelated. For example, information about the current level and structure of asset holdings has value to users when they endeavour to predict the ability of the enterprise to take advantage of opportunities and its ability to react to adverse situations. The same information plays a confirmatory role in respect of past predictions about, for example, the way in which the enterprise would be structured or the outcome of planned operations.

28.   Information about financial position and past performance is frequently used as the basis for predicting future financial position and performance and other matters in which users are directly interested, such as dividend and wage payments, security price movements and the ability of the enterprise to meet its commitments as they fall due. To have predictive value, information need not be in the form of an explicit forecast. The ability to make predictions from financial statements is enhanced, however, by the manner in which information on past transactions and events is displayed. For example, the predictive value of the income statement is enhanced if

unusual, abnormal and infrequent items of income or expense are separately disclosed.

Materiality

29.   The relevance of information is affected by its nature and materiality. In some cases, the nature of information alone is sufficient to determine its relevance. For example, the reporting of a new segment may affect the assessment of the risks and opportunities facing the enterprise irrespective of the materiality of the results achieved by the new segment in the reporting period. In other cases, both the nature and materiality are important, for example, the amounts of inventories held in each of the main categories that are appropriate to the business.

30.   Information is material if its omission or misstatement could influence the economic decisions of users taken on the basis of the financial statements. Materiality depends on the size of the item or error judged in the particular circumstances of its omission or misstatement. Thus, materiality provides a threshold or cut-off point rather than being a primary qualitative characteristic which information must have if it is to be useful.

Reliability

31.   To be useful, information must also be reliable. Information has the quality of reliability when it is free from material error and bias and can be depended upon by users to represent faithfully that which it either purports to represent or could reasonably be expected to represent.

32.   Information may be relevant but so unreliable in nature or representation that its recognition may be potentially misleading. For example, if the validity and amount of a claim for damages under a legal action are disputed, it may be inappropriate for the enterprise to recognise the full amount of the claim in the balance sheet, although it may be appropriate to disclose the amount and circumstances of the claim.

Faithful Representation

33.   To be reliable, information must represent faithfully the transactions and other events it either purports to represent or could reasonably be expected to represent. Thus, for example, a balance sheet should represent faithfully the transactions and other events that result in assets, liabilities and equity of the enterprise at the reporting date which meet the recognition criteria.

34.   Most financial information is subject to some risk of being less than a faithful representation of that which it purports to portray. This is not due to bias, but rather to inherent difficulties either in identifying the

transactions and other events to be measured or in devising and applying measurement and presentation techniques that can convey messages that correspond with those transactions and events. In certain cases, the measurement of the financial effects of items could be so uncertain that enterprises generally would not recognise them in the financial statements; for example, although most enterprises generate goodwill internally over time, it is usually difficult to identify or measure that goodwill reliably. In other cases, however, it may be relevant to recognise items and to disclose the risk of error surrounding their recognition and measurement.

Substance Over Form

35.   If information is to represent faithfully the transactions and other events that it purports to represent, it is necessary that they are accounted for and presented in accordance with their substance and economic reality and not merely their legal form. The substance of transactions or other events is not always consistent with that which is apparent from their legal or contrived form. For example, an enterprise may dispose of an asset to another party in such a way that the documentation purports to pass legal ownership to that party; nevertheless, agreements may exist that ensure that the enterprise continues to enjoy the future economic benefits embodied in the asset. In such circumstances, the reporting of a sale would not represent faithfully the transaction entered into (if indeed there was a transaction).

Neutrality

36.   To be reliable, the information contained in financial statements must be neutral, that is, free from bias. Financial statements are not neutral if, by the selection or presentation of information, they influence the making of a decision or judgement in order to achieve a predetermined result or outcome.

Prudence

37.   The preparers of financial statements do, however, have to contend with the uncertainties that inevitably surround many events and circumstances, such as the collectability of doubtful receivables, the probable useful life of plant and equipment and the number of warranty claims that may occur. Such uncertainties are recognised by the disclosure of their nature and extent and by the exercise of prudence in the preparation of the financial statements. Prudence is the inclusion of a degree of caution in the exercise of the judgements needed in making the estimates required under conditions of uncertainty, such that assets or income are not overstated and liabilities or expenses are not understated. However, the exercise of prudence does not allow, for example, the creation of hidden reserves or excessive provisions, the deliberate understatement of assets or income, or the deliberate overstatement of liabilities or expenses, because

the financial statements would not be neutral and, therefore, not have the quality of reliability.

Completeness

38.   To be reliable, the information in financial statements must be complete within the bounds of materiality and cost. An omission can cause information to be false or misleading and thus unreliable and deficient in terms of its relevance.

Comparability

39.   Users must be able to compare the financial statements of an enterprise through time in order to identify trends in its financial position and performance. Users must also be able to compare the financial statements of different enterprises in order to evaluate their relative financial position, performance and changes in financial position. Hence, the measurement and display of the financial effect of like transactions and other events must be carried out in a consistent way throughout an enterprise and over time for that enterprise and in a consistent way for different enterprises.

40.   An important implication of the qualitative characteristic of comparability is that users be informed of the accounting policies employed in the preparation of the financial statements, any changes in those policies and the effects of such changes. Users need to be able to identify differences between the accounting policies for like transactions and other events used by the same enterprise from period to period and by different enterprises. Compliance with International Accounting Standards, including the disclosure of the accounting policies used by the enterprise, helps to achieve comparability.

41.   The need for comparability should not be confused with mere uniformity and should not be allowed to become an impediment to the introduction of improved accounting standards. It is not appropriate for an enterprise to continue accounting in the same manner for a transaction or other event if the policy adopted is not in keeping with the qualitative characteristics of relevance and reliability. It is also inappropriate for an enterprise to leave its accounting policies unchanged when more relevant and reliable alternatives exist.

42.   Because users wish to compare the financial position, performance and changes in financial position of an enterprise over time, it is important that the financial statements show corresponding information for the preceding periods.

Constraints on Relevant and Reliable Information

Timeliness

43.   If there is undue delay in the reporting of information it may lose its relevance. Management may need to balance the relative merits of timely reporting and the provision of reliable information. To provide information on a timely basis it may often be necessary to report before all aspects of a transaction or other event are known, thus impairing reliability. Conversely, if reporting is delayed until all aspects are known, the information may be highly reliable but of little use to users who have had to make decisions in the interim. In achieving a balance between relevance and reliability, the overriding consideration is how best to satisfy the economic decision-making needs of users.

Balance between Benefit and Cost

44.   The balance between benefit and cost is a pervasive constraint rather than a qualitative characteristic. The benefits derived from information should exceed the cost of providing it. The evaluation of benefits and costs is, however, substantially a judgmental process. Furthermore, the costs do not necessarily fall on those users who enjoy the benefits. Benefits may also be enjoyed by users other than those for whom the information is prepared; for example, the provision of further information to lenders may reduce the borrowing costs of an enterprise. For these reasons, it is difficult to apply a cost-benefit test in any particular case. Nevertheless, standard-setters in particular, as well as the preparers and users of financial statements, should be aware of this constraint.

Balance between Qualitative Characteristics

45.   In practice a balancing, or trade-off, between qualitative characteristics is often necessary. Generally the aim is to achieve an appropriate balance among the characteristics in order to meet the objective of financial statements. The relative importance of the characteristics in different cases is a matter of professional judgment.

True and Fair View/Fair Presentation

46.   Financial statements are frequently described as showing a true and fair view of, or as presenting fairly, the financial position, performance and changes in financial position of an enterprise. Although this framework does not deal directly with such concepts, the application of the principal qualitative characteristics and of appropriate accounting standards normally results in financial statements that convey what is generally understood as a true and fair view of, or as presenting fairly such information.

The Elements of Financial Statements

47.   Financial statements portray the financial effects of transactions and other events by grouping them into broad classes according to their economic characteristics. These broad classes are termed the elements of financial statements. The elements directly related to the measurement of financial position in the balance sheet are assets, liabilities and equity. The elements directly related to the measurement of performance in the income statement are income and expenses. The statement of changes in financial position usually reflects income statement elements and changes in balance sheet elements; accordingly, this framework identifies no elements that are unique to this statement.

48.   The presentation of these elements in the balance sheet and the income statement involves a process of sub-classification. For example, assets and liabilities may be classified by their nature or function in the business of the enterprise in order to display information in the manner most useful to users for purposes of making economic decisions.

Financial Position

49.   The elements directly related to the measurement of financial position are assets, liabilities and equity. These are defined as follows:

(a)   An *asset* is a resource controlled by the enterprise as a result of past events and from which future economic benefits are expected to flow to the enterprise.

(b)   A *liability* is a present obligation of the enterprise arising from past events, the settlement of which is expected to result in an outflow from the enterprise of resources embodying economic benefits.

(c)   *Equity* is the residual interest in the assets of the enterprise after deducting all its liabilities.

50.   The definitions of an asset and a liability identify their essential features but do not attempt to specify the criteria that need to be met before they are recognised in the balance sheet. Thus, the definitions embrace items that are not recognised as assets or liabilities in the balance sheet because they do not satisfy the criteria for recognition discussed in paragraphs 82 to 98. In particular, the expectation that future economic benefits will flow to or from an enterprise must be sufficiently certain to meet

41

the probability criterion in paragraph 83 before an asset or liability is recognised.

51.   In assessing whether an item meets the definition of an asset, liability or equity, attention needs to be given to its underlying substance and economic reality and not merely its legal form. Thus, for example, in the case of finance leases, the substance and economic reality are that the lessee acquires the economic benefits of the use of the leased asset for the major part of its useful life in return for entering into an obligation to pay for that right an amount approximating to the fair value of the asset and the related finance charge. Hence, the finance lease gives rise to items that satisfy the definition of an asset and a liability and are recognised as such in the lessee's balance sheet.

52.   Balance sheets drawn up in accordance with current International Accounting Standards may include items that do not satisfy the definitions of an asset or liability and are not shown as part of equity. The definitions set out in paragraph 48 will, however, underlie future reviews of existing International Accounting Standards and the formulation of further Standards.

Assets

53.   The future economic benefit embodied in an asset is the potential to contribute, directly or indirectly, to the flow of cash and cash equivalents to the enterprise. The potential may be a productive one that is part of the operating activities of the enterprise. It may also take the form of convertibility into cash or cash equivalents or a capability to reduce cash outflows, such as when an alternative manufacturing process lowers the costs of production.

54.   An enterprise usually employs its assets to produce goods or services capable of satisfying the wants or needs of customers; because these goods or services can satisfy these wants or needs, customers are prepared to pay for them and hence contribute to the cash flow of the enterprise. Cash itself renders a service to the enterprise because of its command over other resources.

55.   The future economic benefits embodied in an asset may flow to the enterprise in a number of ways. For example, an asset may be:

  (a)   used singly or in combination with other assets in the production of goods or services to be sold by the enterprise;

  (b)   exchanged for other assets;

(c) used to settle a liability; or

(d) distributed to the owners of the enterprise.

56.   Many assets, for example, property, plant and equipment, have a physical form. However, physical form is not essential to the existence of an asset; hence patents and copyrights, for example, are assets if future economic benefits are expected to flow from them to the enterprise and if they are controlled by the enterprise.

57.   Many assets, for example, receivables and property, are associated with legal rights, including the right of ownership. In determining the existence of an asset, the right of ownership is not essential; thus, for example, property held on a lease is an asset if the enterprise controls the benefits which are expected to flow from the property. Although the capacity of an enterprise to control benefits is usually the result of legal rights, an item may nonetheless satisfy the definition of an asset even when there is no legal control. For example, know-how obtained from a development activity may meet the definition of an asset when, by keeping that know-how secret, an enterprise controls the benefits that are expected to flow from it.

58.   The assets of an enterprise result from past transactions or other past events. Enterprises normally obtain assets by purchasing or producing them, but other transactions or events may generate assets; examples include property received by an enterprise from government as part of a programme to encourage economic growth in an area and the discovery of mineral deposits. Transactions or events expected to occur in the future do not in themselves give rise to assets; hence, for example, an intention to purchase inventory does not, of itself, meet the definition of an asset.

59.   There is a close association between incurring expenditure and generating assets but the two do not necessarily coincide. Hence, when an enterprise incurs expenditure, this may provide evidence that future economic benefits were sought but is not conclusive proof that an item satisfying the definition of an asset has been obtained. Similarly the absence of a related expenditure does not preclude an item from satisfying the definition of an asset and thus becoming a candidate for recognition in the balance sheet; for example, items that have been donated to the enterprise may satisfy the definition of an asset.

Liabilities

60.   An essential characteristic of a liability is that the enterprise has a present obligation. An obligation is a duty or responsibility to act or perform in a certain way. Obligations may be legally enforceable as a consequence

of a binding contract or statutory requirement. This is normally the case, for example, with amounts payable for goods and services received. Obligations also arise, however, from normal business practice, custom and a desire to maintain good business relations or act in an equitable manner. If, for example, an enterprise decides as a matter of policy to rectify faults in its products even when these become apparent after the warranty period has expired, the amounts that are expected to be expended in respect of goods already sold are liabilities.

61.   A distinction needs to be drawn between a present obligation and a future commitment. A decision by the management of an enterprise to acquire assets in the future does not, of itself, give rise to a present obligation. An obligation normally arises only when the asset is delivered or the enterprise enters into an irrevocable agreement to acquire the asset. In the latter case, the irrevocable nature of the agreement means that the economic consequences of failing to honour the obligation, for example, because of the existence of a substantial penalty, leave the enterprise with little, if any, discretion to avoid the outflow of resources to another party.

62.   The settlement of a present obligation usually involves the enterprise giving up resources embodying economic benefits in order to satisfy the claim of the other party. Settlement of a present obligation may occur in a number of ways, for example, by:

(a)   payment of cash;

(b)   transfer of other assets;

(c)   provision of services;

(d)   replacement of that obligation with another obligation; or

(e)   conversion of the obligation to equity.

An obligation may also be extinguished by other means, such as a creditor waiving or forfeiting its rights.

63.   Liabilities result from past transactions or other past events. Thus, for example, the acquisition of goods and the use of services give rise to trade payables (unless paid for in advance or on delivery) and the receipt of a bank loan results in an obligation to repay the loan. An enterprise may also recognise future rebates based on annual purchases by customers as liabilities; in this case, the sale of the goods in the past is the transaction that gives rise to the liability.

64. Some liabilities can be measured only by using a substantial degree of estimation. Some enterprises describe these liabilities as provisions. In some countries, such provisions are not regarded as liabilities because the concept of a liability is defined narrowly so as to include only amounts that can be established without the need to make estimates. The definition of a liability in paragraph 49 follows a broader approach. Thus, when a provision involves a present obligation and satisfies the rest of the definition, it is a liability even if the amount has to be estimated. Examples include provisions for payments to be made under existing warranties and provisions to cover pension obligations.

Equity

65. Although equity is defined in paragraph 49 as a residual, it may be sub-classified in the balance sheet. For example, in a corporate enterprise, funds contributed by shareholders, retained earnings, reserves representing appropriations of retained earnings and reserves representing capital maintenance adjustments may be shown separately. Such classifications can be relevant to the decision-making needs of the users of financial statements when they indicate legal or other restrictions on the ability of the enterprise to distribute or otherwise apply its equity. They may also reflect the fact that parties with ownership interests in an enterprise have differing rights in relation to the receipt of dividends or the repayment of capital.

66. The creation of reserves is sometimes required by statute or other law in order to give the enterprise and its creditors an added measure of protection from the effects of losses. Other reserves may be established if national tax law grants exemptions from, or reductions in, taxation liabilities when transfers to such reserves are made. The existence and size of these legal, statutory and tax reserves is information that can be relevant to the decision-making needs of users. Transfers to such reserves are appropriations of retained earnings rather than expenses.

67. The amount at which equity is shown in the balance sheet is dependent on the measurement of assets and liabilities. Normally, the aggregate amount of equity only by coincidence corresponds with the aggregate market value of the shares of the enterprise or the sum that could be raised by disposing of either the net assets on a piecemeal basis or the enterprise as a whole on a going concern basis.

68. Commercial, industrial and business activities are often undertaken by means of enterprises such as sole proprietorships, partnerships and trusts and various types of government business undertakings. The legal and regulatory framework for such enterprises is often different from that applying to corporate enterprises. For example, there may be few, if any,

restrictions on the distribution to owners or other beneficiaries of amounts included in equity. Nevertheless, the definition of equity and the other aspects of this framework that deal with equity are appropriate for such enterprises.

Performance

69.   Profit is frequently used as a measure of performance or as the basis for other measures, such as return on investment or earnings per share. The elements directly related to the measurement of profit are income and expenses. The recognition and measurement of income and expenses, and hence profit, depends in part on the concepts of capital and capital maintenance used by the enterprise in preparing its financial statements. These concepts are discussed in paragraphs 102 to 110.

70.   The elements of income and expenses are defined as follows:

(a)   *Income* is increases in economic benefits during the accounting period in the form of inflows or enhancements of assets or decreases of liabilities that result in increases in equity, other than those relating to contributions from equity participants.

(b)   *Expenses* are decreases in economic benefits during the accounting period in the form of outflows or depletions of assets or incurrences of liabilities that result in decreases in equity, other than those relating to distributions to equity participants.

71.   The definitions of income and expenses identify their essential features but do not attempt to specify the criteria that would need to be met before they are recognised in the income statement. Criteria for the recognition of income and expenses are discussed in paragraphs 82 to 98.

72.   Income and expenses may be presented in the income statement in different ways so as to provide information that is relevant for economic decision-making. For example, it is common practice to distinguish between those items of income and expenses that arise in the course of the ordinary activities of the enterprise and those that do not. This distinction is made on the basis that the source of an item is relevant in evaluating the ability of the enterprise to generate cash and cash equivalents in the future; for example, incidental activities such as the disposal of a long-term investment are unlikely to recur on a regular basis. When distinguishing between items in this way consideration needs to be given to the nature of the enterprise and its operations. Items that arise from the ordinary activities of one enterprise may be unusual in respect of another.

73.   Distinguishing between items of income and expense and combining them in different ways also permits several measures of enterprise performance to be displayed. These have differing degrees of inclusiveness. For example, the income statement could display gross margin, profit from ordinary activities before taxation, profit from ordinary activities after taxation, and net profit.

Income

74.   The definition of income encompasses both revenue and gains. Revenue arises in the course of the ordinary activities of an enterprise and is referred to by a variety of different names including sales, fees, interest, dividends, royalties and rent.

75.   Gains represent other items that meet the definition of income and may, or may not, arise in the course of the ordinary activities of an enterprise. Gains represent increases in economic benefits and as such are no different in nature from revenue. Hence, they are not regarded as constituting a separate element in this framework.

76.   Gains include, for example, those arising on the disposal of non-current assets. The definition of income also includes unrealised gains; for example, those arising on the revaluation of marketable securities and those resulting from increases in the carrying amount of long term assets. When gains are recognised in the income statements, they are usually displayed separately because knowledge of them is useful for the purpose of making economic decisions. Gains are often reported net of related expenses.

77.   Various kinds of assets may be received or enhanced by income; examples include cash, receivables and goods and services received in exchange for goods and services supplied. Income may also result from the settlement of liabilities. For example, an enterprise may provide goods and services to a lender in settlement of an obligation to repay an outstanding loan.

Expenses

78.   The definition of expenses encompasses losses as well as those expenses that arise in the course of the ordinary activities of the enterprise. Expenses that arise in the course of the ordinary activities of the enterprise include, for example, cost of sales, wages and depreciation. They usually take the form of an outflow or depletion of assets such as cash and cash equivalents, inventory, property, plant and equipment.

79. Losses represent other items that meet the definition of expenses and may, or may not, arise in the course of the ordinary activities of the enterprise. Losses represent decreases in economic benefits and as such they are no different in nature from other expenses. Hence, they are not regarded as a separate element in this framework.

80. Losses include, for example, those resulting from disasters such as fire and flood, as well as those arising on the disposal of non-current assets. The definition of expenses also includes unrealised losses, for example, those arising from the effects of increases in the rate of exchange for a foreign currency in respect of the borrowings of an enterprise in that currency. When losses are recognised in the income statement, they are usually displayed separately because knowledge of them is useful for the purpose of making economic decisions. Losses are often reported net of related income.

Capital Maintenance Adjustments

81. The revaluation or restatement of assets and liabilities gives rise to increases or decreases in equity. While these increases or decreases meet the definition of income and expenses, they are not included in the income statement under certain concepts of capital maintenance. Instead these items are included in equity as capital maintenance adjustments or revaluation reserves. These concepts of capital maintenance are discussed in paragraphs 102 to 110 of this framework.

Recognition of the Elements of Financial Statements

82.   Recognition is the process of incorporating in the balance sheet or income statement an item that meets the definition of an element and satisfies the criteria for recognition set out in paragraph 83. It involves the depiction of the item in words and by a monetary amount and the inclusion of that amount in the balance sheet or income statement totals. Items that satisfy the recognition criteria should be recognised in the balance sheet or income statement. The failure to recognise such items is not rectified by disclosure of the accounting policies used nor by notes or explanatory material.

83.   An item that meets the definition of an element should be recognised if:

(a)   it is probable that any future economic benefit associated with the item will flow to or from the enterprise; and

(b)   the item has a cost or value that can be measured with reliability.

84.   In assessing whether an item meets these criteria and therefore qualifies for recognition in the financial statements, regard needs to be given to the materiality considerations discussed in paragraphs 29 and 30. The interrelationship between the elements means that an item that meets the definition and recognition criteria for a particular element, for example, an asset, automatically requires the recognition of another element, for example, income or a liability.

The Probability of Future Economic Benefit

85.   The concept of probability is used in the recognition criteria to refer to the degree of uncertainty that the future economic benefits associated with the item will flow to or from the enterprise. The concept is in keeping with the uncertainty that characterises the environment in which an enterprise operates. Assessments of the degree of uncertainty attaching to the flow of future economic benefits are made on the basis of the evidence available when the financial statements are prepared. For example, when it is probable that a receivable owed by a enterprise will be paid, it is then justifiable, in the absence of any evidence to the contrary, to recognise the receivable as an asset. For a large population of receivables, however, some degree of non-payment is normally considered probable; hence an expense representing the expected reduction in economic benefits is recognised.

Reliability of Measurement

86.   The second criterion for the recognition of an item is that it possesses a cost or value that can be measured with reliability as discussed in paragraphs 31 to 38 of this framework. In many cases, cost or value must be estimated; the use of reasonable estimates is an essential part of the preparation of financial statements and does not undermine their reliability. When, however, a reasonable estimate cannot be made the item is not recognised in the balance sheet or income statement. For example, the expected proceeds from a lawsuit may meet the definitions of both an asset and income as well as the probability criterion for recognition; however, if it is not possible for the claim to be measured reliably, it should not be recognised as an asset or as income; the existence of the claim, however, would be disclosed in the notes, explanatory material or supplementary schedules.

87.   An item that, at a particular point in time, fails to meet the recognition criteria in paragraph 83 may qualify for recognition at a later date as a result of subsequent circumstances or events.

88.   An item that possesses the essential characteristics of an element but fails to meet the criteria for recognition may nonetheless warrant disclosure in the notes, explanatory material or in supplementary schedules. This is appropriate when knowledge of the item is considered to be relevant to the evaluation of the financial position, performance and changes in financial position of an enterprise by the users of financial statements.

Recognition of Assets

89.   An asset is recognised in the balance sheet when it is probable that the future economic benefits will flow to the enterprise and the asset has a cost or value that can be measured reliably.

90.   An asset is not recognised in the balance sheet when expenditure has been incurred for which it is considered improbable that economic benefits will flow to the enterprise beyond the current accounting period. Instead such a transaction results in the recognition of an expense in the income statement. This treatment does not imply either that the intention of management in incurring expenditure was other than to generate future economic benefits for the enterprise or that management was misguided. The only implication is that the degree of certainty that economic benefits will flow to the enterprise beyond the current accounting period is insufficient to warrant the recognition of an asset.

Recognition of Liabilities

91.   A liability is recognised in the balance sheet when it is probable that an outflow of resources embodying economic benefits will result from the settlement of a present obligation and the amount at which the settlement will take place can be measured reliably. In practice, obligations under contracts that are equally proportionately unperformed (for example, liabilities for inventory ordered but not yet received) are generally not recognised as liabilities in the financial statements. However, such obligations may meet the definition of liabilities and, provided the recognition criteria are met in the particular circumstances, may qualify for recognition. In such circumstances, recognition of liabilities entails recognition of related assets or expenses.

Recognition of Income

92.   Income is recognised in the income statement when an increase in future economic benefits related to an increase in an asset or a decrease of a liability has arisen that can be measured reliably. This means, in effect, that recognition of income occurs simultaneously with the recognition of increases in assets or decreases in liabilities (for example, the net increase in assets arising on a sale of goods or services or the decrease in liabilities arising from the waiver of a debt payable).

93.   The procedures normally adopted in practice for recognising income, for example, the requirement that revenue should be earned, are applications of the recognition criteria in this framework. Such procedures are generally directed at restricting the recognition as income to those items that can be measured reliably and have a sufficient degree of certainty.

Recognition of Expenses

94.   Expenses are recognised in the income statement when a decrease in future economic benefits related to a decrease in an asset or an increase of a liability has arisen that can be measured reliably. This means, in effect, that recognition of expenses occurs simultaneously with the recognition of an increase in liabilities or a decrease in assets (for example, the accrual of employee entitlements or the depreciation of equipment).

95.   Expenses are recognised in the income statement on the basis of a direct association between the costs incurred and the earning of specific items of income. This process, commonly referred to as the matching of costs with revenues, involves the simultaneous or combined recognition of revenues and expenses that result directly and jointly from the same transactions or other events; for example, the various components of expense making up the cost of goods sold are recognised at the same time as the income derived from the sale of the goods. However, the application

of the matching concept under this framework does not allow the recognition of items in the balance sheet which do not meet the definition of assets or liabilities.

96.   When economic benefits are expected to arise over several accounting periods and the association with income can only be broadly or indirectly determined, expenses are recognised in the income statement on the basis of systematic and rational allocation procedures. This is often necessary in recognising the expenses associated with the using up of assets such as property, plant, equipment, goodwill, patents and trademarks; in such cases the expense is referred to as depreciation or amortisation. These allocation procedures are intended to recognise expenses in the accounting periods in which the economic benefits associated with these items are consumed or expire.

97.   An expense is recognised immediately in the income statement when an expenditure produces no future economic benefits or when, and to the extent that, future economic benefits do not qualify, or cease to qualify, for recognition in the balance sheet as an asset.

98.   An expense is also recognised in the income statement in those cases when a liability is incurred without the recognition of an asset, as when a liability under a product warranty arises.

Measurement of the Elements of Financial Statements

99.   Measurement is the process of determining the monetary amounts at which the elements of the financial statements are to be recognised and carried in the balance sheet and income statement. This involves the selection of the particular basis of measurement.

100.   A number of different measurement bases are employed to different degrees and in varying combinations in financial statements. They include the following:

(a)   *Historical cost.* Assets are recorded at the amount of cash or cash equivalents paid or the fair value of the consideration given to acquire them at the time of their acquisition. Liabilities are recorded at the amount of proceeds received in exchange for the obligation, or in some circumstances (for example, income taxes), at the amounts of cash or cash equivalents expected to be paid to satisfy the liability in the normal course of business.

(b)   *Current cost.* Assets are carried at the amount of cash or cash equivalents that would have to be paid if the same or an equivalent asset was acquired currently. Liabilities are carried at the undiscounted amount of cash or cash equivalents that would be required to settle the obligation currently.

(c)   *Realisable (settlement) value.* Assets are carried at the amount of cash or cash equivalents that could currently be obtained by selling the asset in an orderly disposal. Liabilities are carried at their settlement values; that is, the undiscounted amounts of cash or cash equivalents expected to be paid to satisfy the liabilities in the normal course of business.

(d)   *Present value.* Assets are carried at the present discounted value of the future net cash inflows that the item is expected to generate in the normal course of business. Liabilities are carried at the present discounted value of the future net cash outflows that are expected to be required to settle the liabilities in the normal course of business.

101.   The measurement basis most commonly adopted by enterprises in preparing their financial statements is historical cost. This is usually combined with other measurement bases. For example, inventories are usually carried at the lower of cost and net realisable value, marketable securities may be carried at market value and pension liabilities are carried at their present value. Furthermore, some enterprises use the current cost basis as a response to the inability of the historical cost accounting model to deal with the effects of changing prices of non-monetary assets.

Concepts of Capital and Capital Maintenance

Concepts of Capital

102.   A financial concept of capital is adopted by most enterprises in preparing their financial statements. Under a financial concept of capital, such as invested money or invested purchasing power, capital is synonymous with the net assets or equity of the enterprise. Under a physical concept of capital, such as operating capability, capital is regarded as the productive capacity of the enterprise based on, for example, units of output per day.

103.   The selection of the appropriate concept of capital by an enterprise should be based on the needs of the users of its financial statements. Thus, a financial concept of capital should be adopted if the users of financial statements are primarily concerned with the maintenance of nominal invested capital or the purchasing power of invested capital. If, however, the main concern of users is with the operating capability of the enterprise, a physical concept of capital should be used. The concept chosen indicates the goal to be attained in determining profit, even though there may be some measurement difficulties in making the concept operational.

Concepts of Capital Maintenance and the Determination of Profit

104.   The concepts of capital in paragraph 102 give rise to the following concepts of capital maintenance:

(a) *Financial capital maintenance.* Under this concept a profit is earned only if the financial (or money) amount of the net assets at the end of the period exceeds the financial (or money) amount of net assets at the beginning of the period, after excluding any distributions to, and contributions from, owners during the period. Financial capital maintenance can be measured in either nominal monetary units or units of constant purchasing power.

(b) *Physical capital maintenance.* Under this concept a profit is earned only if the physical productive capacity (or operating capability) of the enterprise (or the resources or funds needed to achieve that capacity) at the end of the period exceeds the physical productive capacity at the beginning of the period, after excluding any distributions to, and contributions from, owners during the period.

105.   The concept of capital maintenance is concerned with how an enterprise defines the capital that it seeks to maintain. It provides the linkage between the concepts of capital and the concepts of profit because it provides the point of reference by which profit is measured; it is a prerequisite for distinguishing between an enterprise's return on capital and its return of capital; only inflows of assets in excess of amounts needed to maintain capital may be regarded as profit and therefore as a return on capital. Hence, profit is the residual amount that remains after expenses (including capital maintenance adjustments, where appropriate) have been deducted from income. If expenses exceed income the residual amount is a net loss.

106.   The physical capital maintenance concept requires the adoption of the current cost basis of measurement. The financial capital maintenance concept, however, does not require the use of a particular basis of measurement. Selection of the basis under this concept is dependent on the type of financial capital that the enterprise is seeking to maintain.

107.   The principal difference between the two concepts of capital maintenance is the treatment of the effects of changes in the prices of assets and liabilities of the enterprise. In general terms, an enterprise has maintained its capital if it has as much capital at the end of the period as it had at the beginning of the period. Any amount over and above that required to maintain the capital at the beginning of the period is profit.

108.   Under the concept of financial capital maintenance where capital is defined in terms of nominal monetary units, profit represents the increase in nominal money capital over the period. Thus, increases in the prices of assets held over the period, conventionally referred to as holding gains, are, conceptually, profits. They may not be recognised as such, however, until the assets are disposed of in an exchange transaction. When the concept of financial capital maintenance is defined in terms of constant purchasing power units, profit represents the increase in invested purchasing power over the period. Thus, only that part of the increase in the prices of assets that exceeds the increase in the general level of prices is regarded as profit. The rest of the increase is treated as a capital maintenance adjustment and, hence, as part of equity.

109.   Under the concept of physical capital maintenance when capital is defined in terms of the physical productive capacity, profit represents the increase in that capital over the period. All price changes affecting the assets and liabilities of the enterprise are viewed as changes in the measurement of the physical productive capacity of the enterprise; hence, they are treated as capital maintenance adjustments that are part of equity and not as profit.

110.   The selection of the measurement bases and concept of capital maintenance will determine the accounting model used in the preparation of the financial statements. Different accounting models exhibit different degrees of relevance and reliability and, as in other areas, management must seek a balance between relevance and reliability. This framework is applicable to a range of accounting models and provides guidance on preparing and presenting the financial statements constructed under the chosen model. At the present time, it is not the intention of the Board of IASC to prescribe a particular model other than in exceptional circumstances, such as for those enterprises reporting in the currency of a hyperinflationary economy. This intention will, however, be reviewed in the light of world developments.

International Accounting Standard 1

Disclosure of Accounting Policies

Contents

Introduction

1. This Statement deals with the disclosure of all significant accounting policies which have been adopted in the preparation and presentation of financial statements.

2. The purpose of International Accounting Standards and the authority attaching to them are set out in the Preface to Statements of International Accounting Standards.

3. The definition of *financial statements* as presently set out in the Preface to Statements of International Accounting Standards is repeated here for convenience. The term *financial statements* covers balance sheets, income statements or profit and loss accounts, notes, and other statements and explanatory material which are identified as being part of the financial statements. International Accounting Standards apply to the financial statements of any commercial, industrial, or business enterprise.

4. The management of such an enterprise may prepare financial statements for its own use in a number of different ways best suited for internal management purposes. When financial statements are issued to other persons, such as shareholders, creditors, employees, and the public at large, they should conform to International Accounting Standards.

5. Usually, financial statements are made available once each year and are the subject of a report by an auditor.

Fundamental Accounting Assumptions

6. Certain fundamental accounting assumptions underlie the preparation of financial statements. They are usually not specifically stated because their acceptance and use are assumed. Disclosure is necessary if they are not followed, together with the reasons.

7. The following are recognised by the International Accounting Standards Committee as fundamental accounting assumptions:

(a) Going Concern
The enterprise is normally viewed as a going concern, that is, as continuing in operation for the foreseeable future. It is assumed that the enterprise has neither the intention nor the necessity of liquidation or of curtailing materially the scale of its operations.

(b) Consistency
It is assumed that accounting policies are consistent from one period to another.

(c) Accrual
Revenues and costs are accrued, that is, recognised as they are earned or incurred (and not as money is received or paid) and recorded in the financial statements of the periods to which they relate. (The considerations affecting the process of matching costs with revenues under the accrual assumption are not dealt with in this Statement.)

Accounting Policies

8. Accounting policies encompass the principles, bases, conventions, rules, and procedures adopted by managements in preparing and presenting financial statements. There are many different accounting policies in use even in relation to the same subject; judgment is required in selecting and applying those which, in the circumstances of the enterprise, are best suited to present properly its financial position and the results of its operations.

9. Three considerations should govern the selection and application by management of the appropriate accounting policies and the preparation of financial statements:

(a) Prudence
Uncertainties inevitably surround many transactions. This should be recognised by exercising prudence in preparing financial statements. Prudence does not, however, justify the creation of secret or hidden reserves.

(b) Substance Over Form
Transactions and other events should be accounted for and presented in accordance with their substance and financial reality and not merely with their legal form.

(c) Materiality
Financial statements should disclose all items which are material enough to affect evaluations or decisions.

Explanation

10. Financial statements must be clear and understandable. They are based on accounting policies which vary from enterprise to enterprise, both within a single country and among countries. Disclosure of the significant accounting policies on which the financial statements are based is therefore necessary so that they may be properly understood. The disclosure of these policies should be an integral part of the financial statements; it is helpful to users if they are all disclosed in one place. Sometimes a wrong or inappropriate treatment is adopted for items in balance sheets, income statements or profit and loss accounts, or other statements. Disclosure of the treatment adopted is necessary in any case, but disclosure cannot rectify a wrong or inappropriate treatment.

Users of Financial Statements

11. Financial statements give information which is used by a variety of users, especially shareholders and creditors (present and potential) and employees. Other important categories of users include suppliers, customers, trade unions, financial analysts, statisticians, economists, and taxing and regulatory authorities.

12. The users of financial statements require them as part of the information needed, among other purposes, for making evaluations and financial decisions. They cannot make reliable judgments on these matters unless the financial statements clearly disclose the significant accounting policies which have been adopted in preparing them.

Variations in Accounting Policies and in their Disclosure

13. The task of interpreting financial statements is complicated by the adoption of diverse policies in many areas of accounting. There is no single list of accepted policies to which users may refer and the diverse accounting policies that are presently available for adoption can produce significantly different sets of financial statements based on the same events and conditions. The following are examples of areas in which differing

accounting policies exist and which therefore require disclosure of the treatment selected:

General
Consolidation policy
Conversion or translation of foreign currencies including the disposition of exchange gains and losses
Overall valuation policy (e.g. historical cost, general purchasing power, replacement value)
Events subsequent to the balance sheet date
Leases, hire purchase, or instalment transactions and related interest
Taxes
Long term contracts
Franchises

Assets
Receivables
Inventories (stock and work in progress) and related cost of goods sold
Depreciable assets and depreciation
Growing crops
Land held for development and related development costs
Investments: subsidiary companies, associated companies, and other investments
Research and development
Patents and trademarks
Goodwill

Liabilities and provisions
Warranties
Commitments and contingencies
Pension costs and retirement plans
Severance and redundancy payments

Profits and losses
Methods of revenue recognition
Maintenance, repairs, and improvements
Gains and losses on disposals of property
Reserve accounting, statutory or otherwise, including direct charges and credits to surplus accounts.

14. Accounting policies are not at present regularly and fully disclosed in all financial statements. Considerable variation in format, clarity, and completeness of disclosure exists among and within those countries in which accounting policies are disclosed. In a single set of financial statements some significant accounting policies may be disclosed while other significant policies are not. Even in countries where disclosure of all significant accounting policies is required, guidelines to secure uniformity in the method of disclosure are not always available. The growth of international enterprises and finance has increased the necessity for greater uniformity of financial statements across national boundaries.

15. Financial statements should show corresponding figures for the preceding period. If a change in an accounting policy is made which has a material effect it is necessary to disclose that a change has been made and to quantify the effect. A change in an accounting policy which may not have a material effect in the current year should nevertheless be disclosed if it may have a material effect in subsequent years.

International Accounting Standard 1
Disclosure of Accounting Policies

International Accounting Standard 1 comprises paragraphs 16–23 of this Statement. The Standard should be read in the context of paragraphs 1–15 of this Statement and of the Preface to Statements of International Accounting Standards.

16. **Going concern, consistency, and accrual are fundamental accounting assumptions. Where fundamental accounting assumptions are followed in financial statements, disclosure of such assumptions is not required. If a fundamental accounting assumption is not followed, that fact should be disclosed together with the reasons.**

17. **Prudence, substance over form, and materiality should govern the selection and application of accounting policies.**

18. Financial statements should include clear and concise disclosure of all significant accounting policies which have been used.

19. The disclosure of the significant accounting policies used should be an integral part of the financial statements. The policies should normally be disclosed in one place.

20. Wrong or inappropriate treatment of items in balance sheets, income statements or profit and loss accounts, or other statements is not rectified either by disclosure of accounting policies used or by notes or explanatory material.

21. Financial statements should show corresponding figures for the preceding period.

22. A change in an accounting policy that has a material effect in the current period or may have a material effect in subsequent periods should be disclosed together with the reasons. The effect of the change should, if material, be disclosed and quantified.

23. This International Accounting Standard becomes operative for financial statements covering periods beginning on or after 1 January 1975.

International Accounting Standard 2

Valuation and Presentation of Inventories in the Context of the Historical Cost System

Contents

Introduction

1. This Statement deals with the valuation and presentation of inventories[1] in financial statements in the context of the historical cost system, which is the most widely adopted basis on which financial statements are presented.

2. The Committee is aware of other systems that are proposed or used in financial statements, including systems that are based on replacement costs or other current values. Inventory valuation and presentation in the context of those other systems are beyond the scope of this Statement. International Accounting Standard 1, *Disclosure of Accounting Policies*, requires that the system adopted must be clearly stated.

3. This Statement does not deal with inventories accumulated under long-term construction contracts and with inventory treatment of by-products.

Definitions

4. The following terms are used in this Statement with the meanings specified.

Inventories are tangible property (a) held for sale in the ordinary course of business, (b) in the process of production for such sale, or (c) to be consumed in the production of goods or services for sale.

Historical cost of inventories is the aggregate of costs of purchase, costs of conversion, and other costs incurred in bringing the inventories to their present location and condition.

Costs of purchase comprise the purchase price including import duties and other purchase taxes, transport and handling costs, and any other directly attributable costs of acquisition less trade discounts, rebates, and subsidies.

Costs of conversion are those costs, in addition to the costs of purchase, that relate to bringing the inventories to their present location and condition.

[1]The term "inventories" is used throughout this Statement; in some countries inventories are described as "stock and work in progress."

Net realisable value is the estimated selling price in the ordinary course of business less costs of completion and less costs necessarily to be incurred in order to make the sale.

Explanation

5. Inventories comprise a significant portion of the assets of many enterprises. The valuation and presentation of inventories therefore have a significant effect in determining and presenting the financial position and results of operations of those enterprises.

Determination of Historical Cost

6. In determining historical cost as defined in paragraph 4, different interpretations arise in practice as regards production overhead, other overheads, and the cost formula to be used.

Production Overhead

7. Production overhead is comprised of costs incurred for production other than direct materials and labour. Examples are indirect materials and labour, depreciation and maintenance of factory buildings and equipment, and the cost of factory management and administration.

8. Production overhead requires analysis to determine the portion related to bringing the inventories to their present location and condition and thus to be included in the costs of conversion when determining the historical cost of inventories.

9. Both fixed and variable production overhead incurred during production are usually allocated to costs of conversion. That practice is based on the view that they are both incurred in putting inventories in their present location and condition. Fixed production overhead is sometimes excluded in whole or in part from costs of conversion on the grounds that it is not considered to relate directly to putting inventories in their present location and condition.

10. In a period of low production or if there is idle plant, it is customary to restrict the allocation of fixed production overhead to the costs of conversion by relating it to the capacity of the production facilities and not to the actual level of throughput. Capacity of the production facilities is variously interpreted, for example, as the normal production expected to be achieved over a number of periods or seasons or as the maximum production that as a practical matter can be achieved. The interpretation is determined in advance and applied consistently, and is not modified for temporary conditions.

11. Similarly. exceptional amounts of waste — material, labour, or other expenses — which do not relate to bringing the inventories to their present location and condition are excluded from conversion costs.

Other Overheads

12. Overheads other than production overhead are sometimes incurred in bringing inventories to their present location and condition, for example, expenditures incurred in designing products for specific customers. On the other hand, selling expenses, general administrative overheads, research and development costs, and interest are usually considered not to relate to putting the inventories in their present location and condition.

Cost Formula Used

13. Several different formulas with widely different effects are in current use for the purpose of assigning costs, including the following:

(a) First-in, first-out (FIFO)

(b) Weighted average cost

(c) Last-in, first-out (LIFO)

(d) Base stock

(e) Specific identification

(f) Next-in, first-out (NIFO)

(g) Latest purchase price.

14. The FIFO, weighted average cost. LIFO, base stock, and specific identification formulas use costs that have been incurred by the enterprise at one time or another. The NIFO and latest purchase price methods use costs that have not all been incurred and are therefore not based on historical cost.

15. Specific identification is a formula that attributes specific costs to identified items of inventory. This is an appropriate treatment for goods that have been bought or manufactured and are segregated for a specific project. If it is used, however, in respect of items of inventory which are ordinarily interchangeable, the selection of items could be made in such a way as to obtain predetermined effects on profit.

Valuation of Inventories Below Historical Cost

16. The historical cost of inventories may not be realisable if their selling prices have declined, if they are damaged, or if they have become wholly or partially obsolete. The practice of writing inventories down below historical cost to net realisable value accords with the view that current assets should not be carried in excess of amounts expected to be realised. Declines in value are computed separately for individual items, groups of similar items, an entire class of inventory (for example, finished goods), or items relating to a class of business, or they are computed on an overall basis for all the inventories of the enterprise. The practice of writing inventories down based on a class of inventory, on a class of business, or on an overall basis results in offsetting losses incurred against unrealised gains.

17. In some countries, writedowns are made which are not based on the practices described in paragraph 16. For example, writedowns below historical cost are arrived at by applying an arbitrary percentage to the amounts otherwise computed or by undisclosed reductions that result in secret reserves; these produce inappropriate effects on financial statements.

Presentation of Inventories

18. The sub-classification of inventories in financial statements informs readers of the amounts held in different categories and the extent of the changes from period to period. Common sub-classifications are materials, work in progress, finished goods, merchandise, and production supplies.

19. "Inventories" in balance sheets usually consist of items included in the definition of inventories in paragraph 4. Other items are sometimes shown under the heading "Inventories", for example, non-production supplies and research and development supplies.

International Accounting Standard 2
Valuation and Presentation of Inventories in the Context of the Historical Cost System

International Accounting Standard 2 comprises paragraphs 20—36 of this Statement. The Standard should be read in the context of paragraphs 1—19 of this Statement and of the Preface to Statements of International Accounting Standards.

20. Inventories should be valued at the lower of historical cost and net realisable value.

Ascertainment of Historical Cost

21. The historical cost of manufactured inventories should include a systematic allocation of those production overhead costs that relate to putting the inventories in their present location and condition. Allocation of fixed production overhead to the costs of conversion should be based on the capacity of the facilities. If fixed production overhead has been entirely or substantially excluded from the valuation of inventories on the grounds that it does not directly relate to putting the inventories in their present location and condition, that fact should be disclosed.

22. Overheads other than production overhead should be included as part of inventory cost only to the extent that they clearly relate to putting the inventories in their present location and condition.

23. Exceptional amounts of wasted material, labour, or other expenses should not be included as part of inventory cost.

24. Except as set out in paragraphs 25 and 26, the historical cost of inventories should be accounted for using the FIFO formula or a weighted average cost formula.

25. Inventories of items that are not ordinarily interchangeable or goods manufactured and segregated for specific projects should be accounted for by using specific identification of their individual costs.

26. The LIFO or base stock formulas may be used provided that there is disclosure of the difference between the amount of the inventories as shown in the balance sheet and either (a) the lower of the amount arrived at in accordance with paragraph 24 and net realisable value or (b) the lower of current cost at the balance sheet date and net realisable value.

27. Techniques such as the standard cost method of valuing products or the retail method of valuing merchandise may be used for convenience if they approximate consistently the results that would be obtained in accordance with paragraph 20.

Ascertainment of Net Realisable Value

28. Estimates of net realisable value should be based not on temporary fluctuations of price or cost but on the most reliable evidence available at the time the estimates are made as to what the inventories are expected to realise.

29. Inventories should be written down to net realisable value item by item or by groups of similar items; whichever method is used should be consistently applied.

30. The net realisable value of the quantity of inventory held to satisfy firm sales contracts should be based on the contract price. If the sales contracts are for less than the inventory quantities held, net realisable value for the excess should be based on general market prices.[2]

31. Normal quantities of materials and other supplies held for incorporation in the production of goods should not be written down below historical cost if the finished products in which they will be incorporated are expected to be realised at or above historical cost. Nevertheless, a decline in the price of materials may indicate that the historical cost of finished products to be produced will exceed net realisable value in which event a writedown of the materials inventories should be made; in this event, replacement cost may be the best available measure of the net realisable value of those materials.

---

[2] Firm sales contracts beyond inventory quantities held, and firm purchase contracts are beyond the scope of this Statement.

Presentation in the Financial Statements

32. The profit and loss of the period should be charged with the amount of inventories sold or used (unless allocated to other asset accounts) and with the amount of any writedown in the period to net realisable value.

33. Inventories should be sub-classified in balance sheets or in notes to the financial statements in a manner which is appropriate to the business and so as to indicate the amounts held in each of the main categories.

34. The accounting policies adopted for the purpose of valuation of inventories, including the cost formula used, should be disclosed. A change in an accounting policy related to inventories that has a material effect in the current period or may have a material effect in subsequent periods should be disclosed together with the reasons. The effect of the change should, if material, be disclosed and quantified. (See International Accounting Standard 1, Disclosure of Accounting Policies.)

35. If items are shown under the caption "Inventories" other than those comprehended by the definition in paragraph 4, their nature, amounts and basis of valuation should be disclosed.

Effective Date

36. This International Accounting Standard becomes operative for financial statements covering periods beginning on or after 1 January 1976.

International Accounting Standard 3

Consolidated Financial Statements

This Standard has been superseded by IAS 27, Consolidated Financial Statements and Accounting for Investments in Subsidiaries, and IAS 28, Accounting for Investments in Associates, which became operative for financial statements covering periods beginning on or after 1 January, 1990.

International Accounting Standard 4

Depreciation Accounting

Contents

Introduction

1. This Statement deals with depreciation accounting and applies to all depreciable assets except:

   (a) forests and similar regenerative natural resources

   (b) expenditures on the exploration for and extraction of minerals, oil, natural gas and similar non-regenerative resources

   (c) expenditures on research and development

   (d) goodwill.

Definitions

2. In this Statement the following terms are used with the meanings specified.

Depreciation is the allocation of the depreciable amount of an asset over its estimated useful life. Depreciation for the accounting period is charged to income either directly or indirectly.

Depreciable assets are assets which
(a) are expected to be used during more than one accounting period, and
(b) have a limited useful life, and
(c) are held by an enterprise for use in the production or supply of goods and services, for rental to others, or for administrative purposes.

Useful life is either (a) the period over which a depreciable asset is expected to be used by the enterprise; or (b) the number of production or similar units expected to be obtained from the asset by the enterprise.

Depreciable amount of a depreciable asset is its historical cost or other amount substituted for historical cost[1] in the financial statements, less the estimated residual value.

---

[1]This Statement does not deal with the differences which arise when revaluations are substituted for historical cost.

Explanation

3. Depreciable assets comprise a significant portion of the assets of many enterprises. Depreciation can therefore have a significant effect in determining and presenting the financial position and results of operations of those enterprises.

4. The view is sometimes expressed that if the value of an asset has increased over the amount at which it is carried in the financial statements, it is unnecessary to provide for depreciation. It is considered, however, that depreciation should be charged in each accounting period on the basis of the depreciable amount irrespective of an increase in the value of the asset.

Useful Life

5. Estimation of the useful life of a depreciable asset or a group of similar depreciable assets is a matter of judgement ordinarily based on experience with similar types of assets. For an asset using new technology or used in the production of a new product or in the provision of a new service with which there is little experience, estimation of the useful life is more difficult but is nevertheless required.

6. The useful life of a depreciable asset for an enterprise may be shorter than its physical life. In addition to physical wear and tear, which depends on operational factors such as the number of shifts for which the asset is to be used and the repair and maintenance programme of the enterprise, other factors need to be taken into consideration. These include obsolescence arising from technological changes or improvements in production, obsolescence arising from a change in the market demand for the product or service output of the asset, and legal limits such as the expiry dates of related leases.

Residual Value

7. The residual value of an asset is often insignificant and can be ignored in the calculation of the depreciable amount. If the residual value is likely to be significant, it is estimated at the date of acquisition, or the date of any subsequent revaluation of the asset, on the basis of the realisable value prevailing at that date for similar assets which have reached the end of their useful lives and have operated under conditions similar to those in which the asset will be used. The gross residual value in all cases is reduced by the expected costs of disposal at the end of the useful life of the asset.

Depreciation Methods

8. Depreciable amounts are allocated to each accounting period during the useful life of the asset by a variety of systematic methods. Whichever method of depreciation is selected its consistent use is necessary, irrespective of the level of profitability of the enterprise and of taxation considerations, in order to provide comparability of the results of operations of the enterprise from period to period.

Land and Buildings

9. Land normally has an indefinite useful life and is not usually regarded as a depreciable asset. However, land which does have a limited useful life for the enterprise is treated as a depreciable asset.

10. Buildings are depreciable assets because they fall within the definition in paragraph 2.

11. Some enterprises have not treated buildings as depreciable assets for the reason that the aggregate value of the building and the land on which it stands does not decline. As land and buildings are separate assets, recognition for accounting purposes of any increased value of the land is a different issue from the determination of the depreciable amount of the buildings.

Disclosure

12. The selection of an allocation method and the estimation of the useful life of a depreciable asset are matters of judgement. The disclosure of the methods adopted and of the estimated useful lives or depreciation rates used provides users of financial statements with information which allows them to review the policies selected by management and enables comparisons to be made with other enterprises. For similar reasons, it is necessary to disclose the depreciable amount allocated in a period and the accumulated depreciation at the end of that period.

International Accounting Standard 4

Depreciation Accounting

International Accounting Standard 4 comprises paragraphs 13-19 of this Statement. The Standard should be read in the context of paragraphs 1-12 of this Statement and of the Preface to Statements of International Accounting Standards.

13. The depreciable amount of a depreciable asset should be allocated on a systematic basis to each accounting period during the useful life of the asset.

14. The depreciation method selected should be applied consistently from period to period unless altered circumstances justify a change. In an accounting period in which the method is changed, the effect should be quantified and disclosed and the reason for the change should be stated.

15. The useful life of a depreciable asset should be estimated after considering the following factors:
   (a) expected physical wear and tear
   (b) obsolescence
   (c) legal or other limits on the use of the asset.

16. The useful lives of major depreciable assets or classes of depreciable assets should be reviewed periodically and depreciation rates adjusted for the current and future periods if expectations are significantly different from the previous estimates. The effect of the change should be disclosed in the accounting period in which the change takes place.

17. The valuation bases used for determining the amounts at which depreciable assets are stated should be included with the disclosure of other accounting policies — see International Accounting Standard 1, Disclosure of Accounting Policies.

18. The following should be disclosed for each major class of depreciable asset:
   (a) the depreciation methods used
   (b) the useful lives or the depreciation rates used
   (c) total depreciation allocated for the period
   (d) the gross amount of depreciable assets and the related accumulated depreciation.

Effective Date

19. This International Accounting Standard becomes operative for financial statements covering periods beginning on or after 1 January 1977.

International Accounting Standard 5

Information to be Disclosed in Financial Statements

Contents

Introduction

1. This Statement deals with information to be disclosed in financial statements which include a balance sheet, an income statement, notes, and other statements and explanatory material which are identified as part of the financial statements.

2. Financial statements are required, among other purposes, for making evaluations and financial decisions. Users cannot make reliable judgements unless the financial statements are clear and understandable. The information needed for this purpose will often extend beyond the minimum necessary to meet the requirements of local law or regulatory authorities.

3. Certain minimum disclosures are set out in this Standard. These disclosures may be amplified by detailed disclosure requirements included in other International Accounting Standards which deal with specific accounting subjects.

4. This Standard does not propose a particular format for the presentation of financial statements. The layout and groupings used in the Standard are based on the significant items affecting the financial statements of most industrial and commercial enterprises. A different layout and grouping may be appropriate for enterprises such as financial and insurance companies.

5. In this Standard the definitions of parent company, subsidiary company and associated company are the same as those used in International Accounting Standard 3, Consolidated Financial Statements.

International Accounting Standard 5

Information to be Disclosed in Financial Statements

International Accounting Standard 5 comprises paragraphs 6—19 of this Statement. The Standard should be read in the context of paragraphs 1—5 of this Statement and of the Preface to Statements of International Accounting Standards.

General Disclosures

6. All material information should be disclosed that is necessary to make the financial statements clear and understandable.

7. The name of the enterprise, the country of incorporation, the balance sheet date, and the period covered by the financial statements should be stated. A brief description of the nature of the activities of the enterprise, the legal form of the enterprise, and the currency in terms of which the financial statements are expressed should be given if they are not otherwise apparent.

8. The amounts and classifications of items should be supplemented if necessary by additional information to make their meanings clear. Significant items should not be included with, or offset against, other items, without separate identification.

9. Financial statements should show corresponding figures for the preceding period.

Specific Disclosures — Balance Sheet

General

10. The following disclosures should be made:
    (a) Restrictions on the title to assets
    (b) Security given in respect of liabilities
    (c) The methods of providing for pension and retirement plans
    (d) Contingent assets and contingent liabilities, quantified if possible
    (e) Amounts committed for future capital expenditure.

Long-Term Assets

11. *Property, plant and equipment* — The following items should be disclosed:
    (a) Land and buildings
    (b) Plant and equipment
    (c) Other categories of assets, suitably identified
    (d) Accumulated depreciation.

Separate disclosure should be made of leaseholds and of assets being acquired on instalment purchase plans.

12. *Other long-term assets* — The following items should be disclosed separately, including, if applicable, the method and period of depreciation and any unusual write-offs during the period:
    (a) Long-term investments
        Investments in subsidiaries
        Investments in associated companies
        Other investments, stating the market value of listed investments, if different from the carrying amount in the financial statements
    (b) Long-term receivables
        Accounts and notes receivable — trade
        Receivables from directors
        Intercompany[1] receivables
        Associated company receivables
        Other
    (c) Goodwill
    (d) Patents, trademarks, and similar assets
    (e) Expenditures carried forward, for example, preliminary expenses, reorganisation expenses, and deferred taxes.

[1]The term "intercompany" used in this Statement refers to the presentation in the financial statements of balances or transactions between:
(a) A parent company and its subsidiaries
(b) A subsidiary and its parent company or other subsidiaries in the group.

Current Assets

13. The following items should be disclosed separately:
    (a) Cash
        Cash includes cash on hand and current and other accounts
        with banks. Cash which is not immediately available for use,
        for example, balances frozen in foreign banks by exchange
        restrictions, should be disclosed.
    (b) Marketable securities, other than long-term investments
        The market value should be disclosed if different from the
        carrying amount in the financial statements.
    (c) Receivables
        Accounts and notes receivable – trade
        Receivables from directors
        Intercompany receivables
        Associated company receivables
        Other receivables and prepaid expenses
    (d) Inventories

Long-Term Liabilities

14. The following items should be disclosed separately, excluding the
portion repayable within one year:
    (a) Secured loans
    (b) Unsecured loans
    (c) Intercompany loans
    (d) Loans from associated companies.

A summary of the interest rates, repayment terms, covenants, sub-
ordinations, conversion features and amounts of unamortised premium
or discount should be shown.

Current Liabilities

15. The following items should be disclosed separately:
    (a) Bank loans and overdrafts
    (b) Current portions of long-term liabilities
    (c) Payables
        Accounts and notes payable – trade
        Payables to directors
        Intercompany payables
        Associated company payables
        Taxes on income
        Dividends payable
        Other payables and accrued expenses

Other Liabilities and Provisions

16. The significant items included in other liabilities and in provisions and accruals should be separately disclosed. Examples of such items are deferred taxes, deferred income and provisions for pensions.

Shareholders' Interests

17. The following disclosures should be made separately:
   (a) Share capital
       For each class of share capital:
           The number or amount of shares authorised, issued and outstanding[2]
           The capital not yet paid in
           The par or legal value per share
           The movement in share capital accounts during the period
           The rights, preferences, and restrictions with respect to the distribution of dividends and to the repayment of capital
           Cumulative preferred dividends in arrears
           Reacquired shares
           Shares reserved for future issuance under options and sales contracts, including the terms and amounts.

   (b) Other equity, indicating the movement for the period and any restrictions on distribution
           Capital paid-in excess of par value (share premium)
           Revaluation surplus
           Reserves
           Retained earnings.

---

[2]Shares outstanding refers to shares other than those held as "treasury stock." Treasury stock are a company's shares which have been acquired by the issuing company or a consolidated subsidiary company and are legally available for reissue or resale. This practice is not permitted in some countries.

Specific Disclosures — Income Statement

18. The following information should be disclosed:
    (a) Sales or other operating revenues
    (b) Depreciation
    (c) Interest income
    (d) Income from investments
    (e) Interest expense
    (f) Taxes on income
    (g) Unusual charges
    (h) Unusual credits
    (i) Significant intercompany transactions
    (j) Net income.

Effective Date

19. This International Accounting Standard becomes operative for financial statements covering periods beginning on or after 1 January 1977.

International Accounting Standard 7

Statement of Changes in Financial Position

This Standard will be superseded by a revised International Accounting Standard 7, Cash Flow Statements, which becomes operative for financial statements covering periods beginning on or after 1 January, 1994 (see pages 431 to 459).

Contents

Introduction

1. This Statement deals with the presentation of a statement which summarises for the period the resources made available to finance the activities of an enterprise and the uses to which such resources have been put. The title 'Statement of Changes in Financial Position' is descriptive of a statement with that objective.[1]

Explanation

2. A statement of changes in financial position is often presented with the balance sheet and the income statement as an integral part of the financial statements. The inclusion of such a statement is useful to improve the understanding of the operations and activities of an enterprise for the reporting period.

3. The statement of changes in financial position is prepared from financial data generally identifiable in the income statement, balance sheet and related notes. However, the statement of changes in financial position presents information which may not be readily available in a usable form in the other two statements. Sufficient information is generally given to enable the reconciliation of the amounts in the statement of changes in financial position to the related amounts in the other statements.

4. For purposes of this Statement, the term 'funds' generally refers to cash, to cash and cash equivalents, or to working capital. In a statement of changes in financial position the particular use of the term is made clear.

Funds Provided From or Used in Operations

5. Funds provided from or used in the operations of an enterprise are normally shown separately in the statement of changes in financial position. This information indicates the extent to which an enterprise has generated funds from or used funds in its operations.

---

[1]The title 'Statement of Changes in Financial Position' is used throughout this Statement; in some countries 'Statement of Source and Application of Funds', or a similar title, is used.

6. Items which do not relate to the ordinary activities of an enterprise are often presented in the income statement separately from income from the ordinary activities. This practice improves the usefulness of the financial statements. For similar reasons such items are presented separately in the statement of changes in financial position either individually or as a single amount. For the purpose of this Statement these items are referred to as 'unusual items'.

7. Different forms of presentation can be used to present the amount of funds provided from or used in the operations of an enterprise. A method commonly used is to show the net income (or loss) and to make adjustments for those revenues or expenses that do not involve a movement of funds in the current period (for example, depreciation). An alternative method is to begin with revenues that provided funds during the period and deduct the costs and expenses that involve a movement of funds. The resulting amount is described as funds from operations.

8. When unusual items are presented separately in a statement of changes in financial position, they also are adjusted to the extent that they do not involve a movement of funds in the current period.

Other Sources and Uses of Funds

9. Other sources and uses of funds are stated separately from the funds provided from or used in the operations. These include, for example:
  (a) proceeds from the sale of long-term assets
  (b) outlays for the purchase of long-term assets
  (c) dividends in cash or other assets
  (d) issue of long-term debt
  (e) redemption and repayment of long-term debt
  (f) issue of shares for cash or other assets
  (g) redemption or repurchase of shares for cash or other assets.

10. Some financing transactions of an enterprise involve the exchange of one form of security for another. When such exchanges are equivalent to the issue of one security and the redemption of the other, these transactions are part of the financing and investing activities of an enterprise and are disclosed in the statement of changes in financial position. An example of such a transaction is the conversion of long-term debt to common or ordinary shares.

11. To achieve the objective of the statement of changes in financial position, it may be necessary to disclose separately the investment and financing aspects of each type of transaction. For example, the proceeds on disposal of long-term assets are presented separately from the outlay for acquisition of long-term assets and, when an asset is acquired through the issue of long-term debt or equity, the issue of debt or equity and the acquisition of the asset are separately disclosed.

Consolidated Statement of Changes in Financial Position

12. If a consolidated balance sheet and a consolidated income statement are presented, a statement of changes in financial position may be presented only on a consolidated basis. Under some circumstances it may also be appropriate to present a statement of changes in financial position with respect to the financial statements of the parent company.

Investments Accounted for Using the Equity Method

13. In the statement of changes in financial position there are two methods of dealing with income from an investee company accounted for using the equity method of accounting.

14. The amounts included in funds provided from or used in the operations as a result of such an investment may be restricted to the dividends received or currently receivable. This method is based on the view that the unremitted earnings of such an investee company do not represent current resources available to the investor. Under this method the adjustments described in paragraph 7 include the portion of the income from the investee company that does not involve a movement of funds.

15. Alternatively, the investor's entire share of investee earnings can be included in funds provided from or used in operations and no adjustment is required in determining funds provided from or used in the operations. Under this method, the unremitted portion of the income from the investee company is shown separately as a use of funds.

Acquisition or Disposal of Subsidiaries[2]

16. The acquisition or disposal of subsidiaries may be presented in the statement of changes in financial position as a single amount. Alternatively, the amounts of the individual assets and liabilities acquired or disposed of may be included with the separate sources and uses of funds of each asset and liability dealt with in the statement.

17. Under both methods of presenting the acquisition or disposal of subsidiaries the following supplementary information is presented either in the statement of changes in financial position or by way of note:
   (a) the total purchase or disposal price of the subsidiary,
   (b) the portion of the purchase or disposal price discharged by cash and cash equivalents,
   (c) the amount of cash and other working capital items in the subsidiary acquired or disposed of,
   (d) the amounts of the other assets and liabilities in the subsidiary acquired or disposed of, summarised by each major category.

Presentation

18. Several forms of presentation are used for the statement of changes in financial position. For example, the statement may show the sources of funds as equal to the uses of funds. Another form of presentation is to show a difference between the sources and the uses of funds which represents the net increase or decrease either in cash and cash equivalents or in working capital. No particular form of presentation is preferable for all enterprises, but the enterprise selects the form of presentation considered most informative in the circumstances.

19. When a net change in working capital is presented as a single amount in the statement of changes in financial position, additional disclosure regarding changes in individual working capital items is often presented.

---

[2]Not applicable to business combinations described as mergers or poolings of interest.

International Accounting Standard 7

Statement of Changes in Financial Position

International Accounting Standard 7 comprises paragraphs 20-23 of this Statement. The Standard should be read in the context of paragraphs 1-19 of this Statement and of the Preface to Statements of International Accounting Standards.

20. A statement of changes in financial position should be included as an integral part of the financial statements. The statement of changes in financial position should be presented for each period for which the income statement is presented.

21. Funds provided from or used in the operations of an enterprise should be presented in the statement of changes in financial position separately from other sources or uses of funds. Unusual items which are not part of the ordinary activities of the enterprise should be separately disclosed in the statement.

22. Each enterprise or group of enterprises should adopt the form of presentation for the statement of changes in financial position which is most informative in the circumstances.

Effective Date

23. This International Accounting Standard becomes operative for financial statements covering reporting periods beginning on or after 1 January 1979.

International Accounting Standard 8

Unusual and Prior Period Items and Changes in Accounting Policies

Contents

Introduction

1. International Accounting Standard 5, Information to be Disclosed in Financial Statements, requires certain specific information to be disclosed in the income statement, including the identification of an amount described as net income[1] for the period. This Statement deals with the treatment in the income statement[2] of unusual items, prior period items, and changes in accounting policies and estimates.

2. This Statement does not deal with the treatment of revaluations in excess of historical cost or depreciated historical cost, nor does it deal with the treatment of the tax effects of unusual items, prior period items, and changes in accounting policies and estimates.

Definitions

3. For purposes of this Statement, the following terms are used:

Unusual items are gains or losses that derive from events or transactions that are distinct from the ordinary activities of the enterprise and therefore are not expected to recur frequently or regularly.

Prior period items are charges or credits that arise in the current period as a result of errors or omissions in the preparation of the financial statements of one or more prior periods.

Explanation

4. The income statement is the principal financial statement used to present the results of operations of an enterprise for a period. Two views are commonly expressed about which items should be included in the amount described as net income for the period. They are commonly referred to as 'the current operating performance concept' and 'the all inclusive concept'.

---

[1]Terms such as earnings or net profit may also be used; if a loss is incurred the term employed is net loss.

[2]This financial statement may also be known as a profit and loss account.

5. Under *the current operating performance concept*, non-recurring items are excluded from reported net income. These items are shown after the determination of net income or as adjustments to retained earnings. Some consider that this approach facilitates comparisons between the current and prior periods because only items related to the recurring operations of the enterprise are included in the income statement. However, there is a danger that the importance of items excluded from reported net income may not be clearly recognised by users of the financial statements.

6. Under *the all-inclusive concept*, transactions causing a net increase or decrease in shareholders' interests during the period, other than dividends and other transactions between the enterprise and its shareholders, are included in the net income for the period. Non-recurring items, including unusual items arising in the current period, prior period items, or adjustments related to changes in accounting policies, are included in net income but there may be separate disclosure of the individual amounts.

7. Advocates of the all-inclusive concept claim that reporting in the income statement of items affecting the shareholders' interests during the period, other than dividends and other transactions between the enterprise and its shareholders, provides more useful information for the users of financial statements to enable them to evaluate the importance of the items and their effects on operating results. Although the all-inclusive concept is generally supported, there are circumstances in which it may be considered desirable to report certain items outside the income statement for the current period. However, unusual items are generally included in net income.

Income Attributable to Ordinary Activities

8. Under both concepts referred to in paragraph 4, income from the ordinary activities of the enterprise generally is identified separately from unusual items. The fact that an item, otherwise typical of the ordinary activities of the enterprise, is abnormal in amount or infrequent in occurrence does not qualify the item as unusual. It remains a part of income from the ordinary activities although separate disclosure of its nature and amount may be appropriate. An example of such an item would be the write-off of a very large receivable from a regular trade customer.

Unusual Items

9. Items described in some countries as extraordinary or special items are included within the term 'unusual item' as used in this Statement. In those countries the terms extraordinary or special items have a defined meaning and a requirement normally exists for the incorporation of a sub-total within the income statement described as 'income before extraordinary (or special) items'. This Statement does not set forth the specific format of the income statement. Instead it places emphasis on the separate disclosure of unusual items with an explanation of their nature.

10. The gains or losses that may require separate disclosure as unusual items are not determined solely by the nature of the event or transaction but by the nature of the event or transaction in relation to the business ordinarily carried on by the enterprise. For example, in an enterprise which regularly trades in properties, the gains or losses arising on the sale of property would not be an unusual item.

Prior Period Items

11. In rare circumstances, events come to light in the current financial period which show that the financial statements of one or more previous periods were prepared and presented on a wrong or inaccurate basis as a result of an error or an omission. The financial adjustments arising out of such events are referred to in this Statement as prior period items. Prior period items should not be confused with accounting estimates which are, by their nature, approximations that may need correction as additional information becomes known in subsequent periods. The charge or credit arising on the outcome of a contingency, which at the time of occurrence could not be estimated accurately, does not constitute the correction of an error but rather a change in estimate. Such an item is not treated as a prior period item.

12. Prior period items are sometimes reported by adjusting opening retained earnings in the financial statements for the current period and amending the comparative information in respect of prior years which is included in the financial statements. Sometimes prior period items are reported as unusual items in the determination of net income for the current period. Supplementary information may be presented on a pro forma basis to show what the effect on income in prior periods would have been if the items had been reported in the period to which they relate.

13. In order to facilitate comparisons between one period and another, amendment of the comparative information which is included in financial statements in respect of prior periods is useful to correct erroneous financial information presented in the previous financial statements. Whichever method is adopted, there is full disclosure of the amount and nature of the prior period items.

Changes in Accounting Policies

14. A fundamental accounting assumption is that accounting policies are consistently applied—see International Accounting Standard 1, Disclosure of Accounting Policies. A change in an accounting policy used for reporting purposes is made only if the adoption of a new accounting policy is required by statute or by an accounting standard setting body, or if it is considered that the change would result in a more appropriate presentation of the financial statements of an enterprise. In all cases, it is necessary to present an explanation of the reason for a change.

15. A change in an accounting policy can be introduced into the financial statements in different ways. The new policy may be applied:
   (a) to the current and future financial statements. When practicable, supplementary information is presented on a pro forma basis to show what the effect on income in prior periods would have been if the new policy had then been in use;
   (b) retroactively, as though it had always been in use. When a new policy is applied retroactively, the statements of income for all periods presented may be adjusted to reflect the new policy; or
   (c) by presenting as a single item in the income statement for the current period the amount of the cumulative effect on retained earnings at the beginning of the period in which the change is made. Pro forma information is ordinarily presented to show what the effect on income of prior periods would have been if the new policy had then been in use.

Changes in Accounting Estimates

16. The preparation of financial statements involves making estimates which are based on the circumstances existing at the time when the financial statements are prepared. For example, estimates are required of uncollectable receivables, inventory obsolescence, and the useful lives of depreciable assets. It may be necessary to revise an estimate in a subsequent period if there is a change in the circumstances on which the estimate was based. Revision of an estimate does not bring the resulting amount within the definition either of an unusual item or of a prior period item. Revision of an estimate that relates to an item that was treated as an unusual item is itself reported as unusual. A change in an accounting estimate sometimes has so material an effect on the income trend of the enterprise that there is a need to disclose the effects of the change.

17. It is sometimes difficult to distinguish between a change in an accounting policy and a change in an accounting estimate. For example, an enterprise may change from deferring and amortising a cost to reporting it as an expense when incurred because the estimated future benefits have become uncertain. In those cases where it is difficult to draw a clear distinction, it is usual for such changes to be treated as changes in accounting estimates, with appropriate disclosure.

International Accounting Standard 8

Unusual and Prior Period Items and Changes in Accounting Policies

International Accounting Standard 8 comprises paragraphs 18-24 of this Statement. The Standard should be read in the context of paragraphs 1-17 of this Statement and of the Preface to Statements of International Accounting Standards.

18. Income from the ordinary activities of the enterprise during the period should be disclosed in the income statement as part of net income[3]. Unusual items should be included in net income; the nature and amount of each such item should be separately disclosed.

19. Prior period items and the amount of the adjustments, if any, resulting from changes in accounting policies should be either:
   (a) reported by adjusting opening retained earnings in the financial statements for the current period and amending the comparative information in respect of prior years which is included in the financial statements, or
   (b) separately disclosed in the current income statement as part of net income.
In either case the disclosure relating to these items should be adequate to facilitate comparisons of the figures for the periods presented.

---

[3]Terms such as earnings or net profit may also be used; if a loss is incurred, the term employed is net loss.

20. A change in an accounting policy should be made only if the adoption of a different accounting policy is required by statute or by an accounting standard setting body or if it is considered that the change would result in a more appropriate presentation of the financial statements of an enterprise.

21. If there is a change in an accounting policy that has a material effect in the current period, or may have a material effect in subsequent periods, the effect of the change should be disclosed and quantified together with the reasons for the change (see International Accounting Standard 1, Disclosure of Accounting Policies).

22. A change in an accounting estimate should be accounted for as part of income from the ordinary activities of the enterprise in:
   (a) the period of change if the change affects the period only, or
   (b) the period of change and future periods if the change affects both.
Revision of an estimate that relates to an item that was treated as an unusual item should itself be reported as unusual.

23. If there is a change in an accounting estimate that has a material effect in the current period, or may have a material effect in subsequent periods, the effect of the change should be disclosed and quantified.

Effective Date

24. This International Accounting Standard becomes operative for financial statements covering periods beginning on or after 1 January 1979.

International Accounting Standard 9

Accounting for Research and Development Activities

Contents

Introduction

1. This Statement deals with accounting for research and development activities.

2. The Statement does not deal with the following specialised activities:
   (a) research and development activities conducted for others under a contract
   (b) exploration for oil, gas and mineral deposits
   (c) research and development activities of development stage enterprises.

Definitions

3. The following terms are used in this Statement with the meanings specified:

Research is original and planned investigation undertaken with the hope of gaining new scientific or technical knowledge and understanding.

Development is the translation of research findings or other knowledge into a plan or design for the production of new or substantially improved materials, devices, products, processes, systems or services prior to the commencement of commercial production.

Explanation

4. An enterprise undertakes a programme of creative work to increase the stock of its scientific and technical knowledge and to devise new applications which will contribute to the maintenance of its business and its competitive position. The accounting treatment and disclosure of the costs of research and development activities are therefore important for users of financial statements.

The Costs of Research and Development Activities

5. There can be practical difficulties in deciding the amounts of the costs specifically attributable to research and development activities. In order to achieve a reasonable degree of comparability between enterprises, and between accounting periods of the same enterprise, it is necessary to identify the elements comprising research and development costs.

6. The costs incurred for research and development activities include the following:
   (a) salaries, wages and other related costs of personnel
   (b) the costs of materials and services consumed
   (c) the depreciation of equipment and facilities
   (d) a reasonable allocation of overhead costs. This allocation is made on bases similar to those used in allocating overhead costs to inventories (see International Accounting Standard 2, Valuation and Presentation of Inventories in the Context of the Historical Cost System)
   (e) other costs, such as the amortisation of patents and licences.

7. Costs incurred to maintain production or to promote sales of existing products are excluded from the costs of research and development activities. Thus, the costs of routine or periodic minor modifications to existing products, production lines, manufacturing processes and other ongoing operations as well as routine or promotional costs of market research activities are excluded.

8. However, market research activities undertaken prior to the commencement of commercial production to establish the usefulness of a product or the existence of a potential market are similar to development activities. In these cases, the related costs are sometimes treated in the same way as development costs and are written off or deferred based on the same considerations.

The Accounting Treatment of Research and Development Costs

9. The allocation of the costs of research and development activities to accounting periods is determined by their relationship to the expected future benefits to be derived from these activities. In most cases there is little, if any, direct relationship between the amount of current research and development costs and future benefits because the amount of such benefits, and the periods over which they will be received, are usually too uncertain. Research and development costs are therefore usually charged to expense in the period in which they are incurred.

10. If it can be demonstrated, however, that the product or process is technically and commercially feasible and that the enterprise has adequate resources to enable the product or process to be marketed, the uncertainties referred to in paragraph 9 may be significantly reduced. In such circumstances, it may be appropriate to defer the costs of development activities to future periods. Development costs previously written off are not reinstated because they were incurred at a time when the technical and commercial feasibility of the project was too uncertain to establish a relationship with future benefits and they were therefore proper charges to those past periods.

11. Deferred development costs are amortised on a systematic basis, either by reference to the sale or use of the product or process or by reference to a reasonable time period. Technological and economic obsolescence creates uncertainties that restrict the number of units and the time period over which deferred costs are to be amortised.

Disclosure

12. The accounting policy adopted for the costs of research and development activities is included in the statement of accounting policies (see International Accounting Standard 1, Disclosure of Accounting Policies). When applicable, information about amortisation practices is also required (see International Accounting Standard 5, Information to be Disclosed in Financial Statements).

13. The disclosure of (a) research and development costs, including the amortisation of deferred development costs, charged as an expense of each period, and (b) the unamortised balance, if any, of deferred development costs, enables the users of financial statements to consider the significance of such activities in relation to those of other enterprises as well as to the other activities of the enterprise itself.

14. Further information which might usefully be provided could include a general description of the project, the stage which the project has reached, and the estimated future costs to complete it.

International Accounting Standard 9

Accounting for Research and Development Activities

International Accounting Standard 9 comprises paragraphs 15-25 of this Statement. The Standard should be read in the context of paragraphs 1-14 of this Statement and of the Preface to Statements of International Accounting Standards.

15. Research and development costs should include:
    (a) the salaries, wages and other related costs of personnel engaged in research and development activities
    (b) the costs of materials and services consumed in research and development activities
    (c) the depreciation of equipment and facilities to the extent that they are used for research and development activities
    (d) overhead costs related to research and development activities
    (e) other costs related to research and development activities, such as the amortisation of patents and licences.

16. The amount of the research and development costs described in paragraph 15 should be charged as an expense of the period in which they are incurred except to the extent that development costs are deferred in accordance with paragraph 17.

17. Development costs of a project may be deferred to future periods if all the following criteria are satisfied:

   (a) the product or process is clearly defined and the costs attributable to the product or process can be separately identified;

   (b) the technical feasibility of the product or process has been demonstrated;

   (c) the management of the enterprise has indicated its intention to produce and market, or use, the product or process;

   (d) there is a clear indication of a future market for the product or process or, if it is to be used internally rather than sold, its usefulness to the enterprise can be demonstrated; and

   (e) adequate resources exist, or are reasonably expected to be available, to complete the project and market the product or process.

18. The deferral of development costs of a project under the criteria in paragraph 17 should be limited to the amount that, taken together with further development costs, related production costs, and selling and administrative costs directly incurred in marketing the product, can reasonably be expected to be recovered from related future revenues.

19. If an accounting policy of deferral of development costs is adopted, it should be applied to all development projects that meet the criteria in paragraph 17.

20. If development costs of a project are deferred, they should be allocated on a systematic basis to future accounting periods by reference either to the sale or use of the product or process or to the time period over which the product or process is expected to be sold or used.

21. The deferred development costs of a project should be reviewed at the end of each accounting period. When the criteria of paragraph 17, which previously justified the deferral of the costs, no longer apply, the unamortised balance should be charged as an expense immediately. When the criteria for deferral continue to be met but the amount of deferred development costs (and other relevant costs as set out in paragraph 18) that can reasonably be expected to be recovered from related future revenues is exceeded by the unamortised balance of such costs, the excess should be charged as an expense immediately.

22. Development costs once written off should not be reinstated even though the uncertainties which had led to their being written off no longer exist.

Disclosure

23. The total of research and development costs, including amortisation of deferred development costs, charged as expense should be disclosed.

24. The movement in and the balance of unamortised deferred development costs should be disclosed. The basis, proposed or adopted, for the amortisation of the unamortised balance should also be disclosed.

Effective Date

25. This International Accounting Standard becomes operative for financial statements covering periods beginning on or after 1 January 1980.

International Accounting Standard 10

Contingencies and Events Occurring After the Balance Sheet Date

Contents

Introduction

1. This Statement deals with the treatment in financial statements of:
   (a) contingencies, and
   (b) events occurring after the balance sheet date.

2. The following subjects, which may result in contingencies, are excluded from the scope of this Statement:
   (a) liabilities of life assurance companies arising from policies issued
   (b) obligations under retirement benefit plans
   (c) commitments arising from long-term lease contracts
   (d) taxes on income.

Definitions

3. The following terms are used in this Statement with the meanings specified:

A *contingency* is a condition or situation, the ultimate outcome of which, gain or loss, will be confirmed only on the occurrence, or non-occurrence, of one or more uncertain future events.

Events occurring after the balance sheet date are those events, both favourable and unfavourable, that occur between the balance sheet date and the date on which the financial statements are authorised for issue. Two types of events can be identified:
   (1) those that provide further evidence of conditions that existed at the balance sheet date, and
   (2) those that are indicative of conditions that arose subsequent to the balance sheet date.

Explanation

Contingencies

4. The term contingencies used in this Statement is restricted to conditions or situations at the balance sheet date, the financial effect of which is to be determined by future events which may or may not occur. Many such conditions or situations are reflected in accruals in financial statements in following the fundamental accounting concept of accrual.

5. Estimates are required in financial statements for many on-going and recurring activities of an enterprise. However, the fact that an estimate is involved does not of itself create the type of uncertainty which characterises a contingency, although the procedures for determining the amounts stated in the financial statements may be similar. For example, the fact that estimates of useful life are used to determine depreciation does not make depreciation a contingency; the eventual expiry of the useful life of the asset is not uncertain. Also, amounts owed for services received are not contingencies as defined in paragraph 3, even though the amounts may have been estimated; there is nothing uncertain about the fact that these obligations have been incurred.

6. The uncertainty relating to future events can be expressed by a range of outcomes. This range may be presented as quantified probabilities, but in most circumstances this suggests a level of precision that is not supported by the available information. The range of outcomes can also be presented by general description, using terms ranging from probable to remote.

7. The estimates of the outcome and of the financial effect of contingencies are determined by the judgement of the management of the enterprise. This judgement is based on consideration of information available up to the date on which the financial statements are authorised for issue and will include a review of events occurring after the balance sheet date, supplemented by experience of similar transactions and, in some cases, reports from independent experts.

The Accounting Treatment of Contingent Losses

8. The accounting treatment of a contingent loss is determined by the expected outcome of the contingency. If it is probable that a contingency will result in a loss to the enterprise then it is prudent to accrue that loss in the financial statements.

9. The estimation of the amount of a contingent loss to be accrued in the financial statements may be based on information that provides a range of amounts of loss which could result from the contingency. The best estimate of the loss within such a range is accrued. When no amount within the range is indicated as a better estimate than any other amount, at least the minimum amount in the range is accrued. Disclosure of any additional exposure to loss is made if there is a possibility of loss in excess of the amount accrued.

10. If there is conflicting or insufficient evidence on which to estimate the amount of a contingent loss, then disclosure is made of the existence and nature of the contingency.

11. A potential loss to an enterprise may be reduced or avoided because a contingent liability is matched by a related counter-claim or claim against a third party. In such cases the amount of any accrual may be determined after taking into account the probable recovery under the claim.

12. The existence and amount of guarantees, obligations arising from discounted bills of exchange and similar obligations undertaken by an enterprise are generally disclosed in financial statements by way of note, even though it is remote that a loss to the enterprise will occur.

13. Amounts accrued for general or unspecified business risks do not relate to conditions or situations existing at the balance sheet date, and therefore are not justified as provisions for contingencies.

The Accounting Treatment of Contingent Gains

14. Contingent gains are not accrued in financial statements since this may result in the recognition of revenue which may never be realised. However, when the realisation of a gain is virtually certain, then such a gain is not a contingency and accrual of the gain is appropriate.

The Determination of the Amounts at which Contingencies are Included in Financial Statements

15. The amount at which a contingency is stated in the financial statements is based on the information which is available at the date on which the financial statements are authorised for issue. Events occurring after the balance sheet date that indicate that an asset may have been impaired or that a liability may have existed at the balance sheet date are therefore taken into account in identifying contingencies and in determining the amounts at which such contingencies are included in financial statements.

16. In some cases each contingency can be separately identified, and the special circumstances of each situation considered in the determination of the amount of the contingency. A substantial legal claim against the enterprise may represent such a contingency. Among the factors taken into account by management in evaluating the contingency are the progress of the claim at the date on which the financial statements are authorised for issue, the opinions of legal experts or other advisers, the experience of the enterprise in similar cases and the experience of other enterprises in similar situations.

17. If the uncertainties which created a contingency in respect of an individual transaction are common to a large number of similar transactions, then the amount of the contingency need not be individually determined, but may be based on the group of similar transactions. Examples of such contingencies may be warranties for products sold and the estimated uncollectable portion of accounts receivable. These costs are usually incurred frequently and experience provides a means by which the amount of the liability or loss can be estimated with reasonable precision although the particular transactions that may result in a loss are not identified. Accrual of these costs results in their recognition in the same accounting period in which the related transactions took place.

Events Occurring After the Balance Sheet Date

18. Events which occur between the balance sheet date and the date on which the financial statements are authorised for issue may indicate the need for adjustments to assets and liabilities or may require disclosure.

19. The process involved in the authorisation for issue of the financial statements will vary depending upon the management structure and procedures followed in preparing and finalising the financial statements, but the date of authorisation for issue would normally be the date on which the statements are authorised for issue outside the enterprise.

20. Adjustments to assets and liabilities are required for events occurring after the balance sheet date that provide additional information for determining the amounts relating to conditions existing at the balance sheet date. For example, adjustments may be made for a loss on a trade receivable account which is confirmed by the bankruptcy of a customer which occurs after the balance sheet date.

21. Adjustments to assets and liabilities are not appropriate for events occurring after the balance sheet date, if such events do not relate to conditions existing at the balance sheet date. An example is the decline in market value of investments between the balance sheet date and the date on which the financial statements are authorised for issue. The fall in market value does not normally relate to the condition of the investments at the balance sheet date, but reflects circumstances which have occurred in the following period. However, disclosure is generally made of events in subsequent periods that represent unusual changes to the condition of assets or liabilities at the balance sheet date; for example, the destruction of a major production plant by a fire after the balance sheet date.

22. Events occurring after the balance sheet date that are indicative of conditions that arose subsequent to the balance sheet date are disclosed if their non-disclosure would affect the ability of the users of the financial statements to make proper evaluations and decisions. An example of such an event would be a major acquisition of another enterprise.

23. There are events which, although they take place after the balance sheet date, are sometimes reflected in the financial statements because of statutory requirements or because of their special nature. In some countries these special items include the amount of the dividend proposed or declared after the balance sheet date in respect of the period covered by the financial statements.

24. Events occurring after the balance sheet date may indicate that the whole or part of the business of the enterprise ceases to be a going concern. A deterioration in operating results and financial position after the balance sheet date may indicate a need to consider whether it is proper to use the going concern assumption in the preparation of the financial statements.

Disclosure — Contingencies

25. If a contingent loss is not accrued, its nature and an estimate of its financial effect are generally disclosed by way of note unless the possibility of a loss is remote. However, if a reliable estimate of the financial effect cannot be made, this fact is disclosed. Contingencies which are accrued may warrant separate disclosure. The existence and nature of contingent gains are usually disclosed by way of note in financial statements if it is probable that the gain will be realised by the enterprise. It is important that the disclosure avoid giving misleading implications as to the likelihood of realisation.

Disclosure — Events Occurring After the Balance Sheet Date

26. When the effects of events occurring after the balance sheet date are disclosed in the notes to the financial statements, to enable users of financial statements to make proper evaluations and decisions, the information given includes a description of the events and an estimate, if possible, of their financial effects.

International Accounting Standard 10

Contingencies and Events Occurring After the Balance Sheet Date

International Accounting Standard 10 comprises paragraphs 27-35 of this Statement. The Standard should be read in the context of paragraphs 1-26 of this Statement and of the Preface to Statements of International Accounting Standards.

Contingencies

27. The amount of a contingent loss should be accrued by a charge in the income statement if:

(a) **it is probable that future events will confirm that, after taking into account any related probable recovery, an asset has been impaired or a liability incurred at the balance sheet date, and**

(b) **a reasonable estimate of the amount of the resulting loss can be made.**

28. The existence of a contingent loss should be disclosed in the financial statements if either of the conditions in paragraph 27 is not met, unless the possibility of a loss is remote.

29. Contingent gains should not be accrued in financial statements. The existence of contingent gains should be disclosed if it is probable that the gain will be realised.

Events Occurring After the Balance Sheet Date

30. Assets and liabilities should be adjusted for events occurring after the balance sheet date that provide additional evidence to assist with the estimation of amounts relating to conditions existing at the balance sheet date or that indicate that the going concern assumption in relation to the whole or a part of the enterprise is not appropriate.

31. Dividends stated to be in respect of the period covered by the financial statements and that are proposed or declared after the balance sheet date but before approval of the financial statements should be either adjusted for or disclosed.

32. Assets and liabilities should not be adjusted for, but disclosure should be made of, those events occurring after the balance sheet date that do not affect the condition of assets or liabilities at the balance sheet date, but are of such importance that non-disclosure would affect the ability of the users of the financial statements to make proper evaluations and decisions.

Disclosure

33. If disclosure of contingencies is required by paragraphs 28 or 29 of this Statement, the following information should be provided:
- **(a) the nature of the contingency**
- **(b) the uncertain factors that may affect the future outcome**
- **(c) an estimate of the financial effect, or a statement that such an estimate cannot be made.**

34. If disclosure of events occurring after the balance sheet date is required by paragraph 32 of this Statement, the following information should be provided:
- **(a) the nature of the event**
- **(b) an estimate of the financial effect, or a statement that such an estimate cannot be made.**

Effective Date

35. This International Accounting Standard becomes operative for financial statements covering periods beginning on or after 1 January 1980.

International Accounting Standard 11

Accounting for Construction Contracts

Contents

Introduction

1. This Statement deals with accounting for construction contracts in the financial statements of contractors.

2. For the purposes of this Statement a construction contract is a contract for the construction of an asset or of a combination of assets which together constitute a single project. Examples of activity covered by such contracts include the construction of bridges, dams, ships, buildings and complex pieces of equipment.

3. The feature which characterises a construction contract dealt with in this Statement is the fact that the date at which the contract activity is entered into and the date when the contract activity is completed fall into different accounting periods. The specific duration of the contract performance is not used as a distinguishing feature of a construction contract.

4. Contracts for the provision of services come within the scope of this Statement to the extent that they are directly related to a contract for the construction of an asset. Examples of such service contracts are contracts for the services of project managers and architects and for technical engineering services related to the construction of an asset.

Explanation

5. The principal problem relating to accounting for construction contracts is the allocation of revenues and related costs to accounting periods over the duration of the contract.

Types of Construction Contracts

6. Construction contracts are formulated in a variety of ways, but generally fall into two basic types:
   (a) fixed price contracts — the contractor agrees to a fixed contract price, or rate, in some cases subject to cost escalation clauses
   (b) cost plus contracts — the contractor is reimbursed for allowable or otherwise defined costs, plus a percentage of these costs or a fixed fee.
Both types of contract are within the scope of this Statement.

The Accounting Treatment of Construction Contract Costs and Revenues

7. Two methods of accounting for contracts commonly followed by contractors are the 'percentage of completion' method and the 'completed contract' method.

8. Under the percentage of completion method, revenue is recognised as the contract activity progresses. The costs incurred in reaching the stage of completion are matched with this revenue, resulting in the reporting of results which can be attributed to the proportion of work completed.

9. Under the completed contract method, revenue is recognised only when the contract is completed or substantially completed; that is, when only minor work is expected other than warranty work. Costs and progress payments received are accumulated during the course of the contract but revenue is not recognised until the contract activity is substantially completed.

10. Under both methods, provision is made for losses for the stage of completion reached on the contract. In addition, provision is usually made for losses on the remainder of the contract.

11. It may be necessary for accounting purposes to combine contracts made with a single customer or to combine contracts made with several customers if the contracts are negotiated as a package or if the contracts are for a single project. Conversely, if a contract covers a number of projects and if the costs and revenues of such individual projects can be identified within the terms of the overall contract, each such project may be treated as equivalent to a separate contract.

The Costs to be Accumulated for Construction Contracts

12. The total period to be considered for identifying the costs attributable to a contract is the period that commences with the securing of the contract and closes when the contract is completed.

13. Therefore, costs incurred by the contractor before a contract is secured are usually treated as expenses of the period in which they are incurred. However, if costs attributable to securing the contract can be separately identified and there is a clear indication that the contract will be obtained, the costs are often treated as applicable to the contract and are deferred. As a practical matter, costs are sometimes deferred until it is clear whether the contract has been secured or not.

14. Costs attributable to a contract include expected warranty costs. Warranty costs are provided for when such costs can be reasonably estimated (see International Accounting Standard 10, Contingencies and Events Occurring After the Balance Sheet Date).

15. The costs incurred by an enterprise that undertakes construction contracts can be divided into:
  (a) Costs that relate directly to a specific contract
  (b) Costs that can be attributed to the contract activity in general and can be allocated to specific contracts
  (c) Costs that relate to the activities of the enterprise generally, or that relate to contract activity but cannot be related to specific contracts.

16. Examples of costs that relate directly to a specific contract include:
site labour costs, including supervision;
materials used for project construction;
depreciation of plant and equipment used on a contract;
costs of moving plant and equipment to and from a site.

17. Examples of costs that can be attributed to the contract activity in general and can be allocated to specific contracts include:
insurance;
design and technical assistance;
construction overhead.

18. Examples of costs that relate to the activities of the enterprise generally, or that relate to contract activity but cannot be related to specific contracts, include:
general administration and selling costs;
finance costs;
research and development costs;
depreciation of idle plant and equipment that is not used on a particular contract.

19. Costs referred to in paragraph 18 are usually excluded from the accumulated contract costs because they do not relate to reaching the present stage of completion of a specific contract. However, in some circumstances general administrative expenses, development costs and finance costs are specifically attributable to a particular contract and are sometimes included as part of accumulated contract costs.

The Basis for Recognising Revenue on Construction Contracts

The Percentage of Completion Method

20. Under the percentage of completion method, the amount of revenue recognised is determined by reference to the stage of completion of the contract activity at the end of each accounting period. The advantage of this method of accounting for contract revenue is that it reflects revenue in the accounting period during which activity was undertaken to earn such revenue.

21. The stage of completion used to determine revenue to be recognised in the financial statements can be measured in a variety of ways; for example, by calculating the proportion that costs incurred to date bear to the estimated total costs of the contract, by surveys which measure work performed and completion of a physical proportion of the contract work or by a combination of ways.

22. Progress payments and advances received from customers do not necessarily reflect the stage of completion and therefore cannot usually be treated as equivalent to revenue earned.

23. If the percentage of completion method is applied by calculating the proportion that costs to date bear to the latest estimated total costs of the contract, adjustments are made to include only those costs that reflect work performed. Examples of items which may need adjustment include:

    (a) the costs of materials that have been purchased for the contract but have not been installed or used during contract performance, and

    (b) payments to subcontractors to the extent that they do not reflect the amount of work performed under the sub-contract.

24. The application of the percentage of completion method is subject to a risk of error in making estimates. For this reason, profit is not recognised in the financial statements unless the outcome of the contract can be reliably estimated. If the outcome can not be reliably estimated, the percentage of completion method is not used.

25. In the case of fixed price contracts, the conditions which will usually provide this degree of reliability are:
   (a) total contract revenues to be received can be reliably estimated, and
   (b) both the costs to complete the contract and the stage of contract performance completed at the reporting date can be reliably estimated, and
   (c) the costs attributable to the contract can be clearly identified so that actual experienced can be compared with prior estimates.

26. In the case of cost plus contracts, the conditions which will usually provide this degree of reliability are:
   (a) the costs attributable to the contract can be clearly identified, and
   (b) costs other than those that will be specifically reimbursable under the contract can be reliably estimated.

The Completed Contract Method

27. The principal advantage of the completed contract method is that it is based on results as determined when the contract is completed or substantially completed rather than on estimates which may require subsequent adjustment as a result of unforeseen costs and possible losses. The risk of recognising profits that may not have been earned is therefore minimised.

28. The principal disadvantage of the completed contract method is that periodic reported income does not reflect the level of activity on contracts during the period. For example, when a few large contracts are completed in one accounting period but no contracts have been completed in the previous period or will be completed in the subsequent period, the level of reported income can be erratic although the level of activity on contracts may have been relatively constant throughout. Even when numerous contracts are regularly completed in each accounting period, and reported income may appear to reflect the level of activity

on contracts, there is a continuous lag between the time when work is performed and the related revenue is recognised.

Selection of Method

29. The selection of a method of accounting for a construction contract depends on the view taken by the contractor in respect of the uncertainties attached to the estimates of contract costs and revenues. In some cases, the contractor may decide that the level of uncertainty, produced by variations in work which render recoverable costs and revenue subject to further negotiation or by the inherent problem of making estimates, is so significant that the completed contract method is applied. In other cases, the outcome of the contracts can be reliably estimated and some or all of the contracts may be accounted for using the percentage of completion method. The contractor may be using both methods simultaneously for different contracts.

30. When a contractor uses a method for a particular contract, then all other contracts that meet similar criteria ought to be accounted for by the same method.

31. In addition to the consideration of uncertainties, a contractor may use pre-determined criteria for the selection of an accounting method for construction contracts. For example, contracts for which the revenue is less than a stated value, or which have a duration of less than a certain period of time, may be accounted for by the completed contract method even when the outcome of contracts can be reliably estimated.

32. The methods of accounting used by the contractor and the criteria adopted in selecting the methods represent an accounting policy that is consistently applied (see International Accounting Standard 1, Disclosure of Accounting Policies).

Change in Accounting Policy

33. When there is a change in the accounting policy used for construction contracts, there is disclosure of the effect of the change and its amount, together with the reasons for the change (see International Accounting Standard 8, Unusual and Prior Period Items and Changes in Accounting Policies). If the contractor changes from the percentage of completion

method to the completed contract method, it may not be possible to quantify the full effect of the change in the current accounting period. In such cases, there is disclosure in respect of contracts in progress at the beginning of the accounting period of at least the amount of attributable profits reported in prior years.

Provision for Foreseeable Losses

34. When current estimates of total contract costs and revenues indicate a loss, provision is made for the entire loss on the contract irrespective of the amount of work done. In some circumstances, the foreseeable losses may exceed the costs of work done to date. Provision is nevertheless made for the entire loss on the contract.

35. When a contract is of such magnitude that it can be expected to absorb a considerable part of the capacity of the enterprise for a substantial period, indirect costs to be incurred during the period of the completion of the contract are sometimes considered to be directly attributable to the contract and included in the calculation of the provision for loss on the contract.

36. If a provision for loss is required, the amount of such provision is usually determined irrespective of:
   (a) whether or not work has commenced on the contract, and
   (b) the stage of completion of contract activity, and
   (c) the amount of profits expected to arise on other unrelated contracts.

37. The determination of a future loss on a contract may be subject to a high degree of uncertainty. In some cases, it may be possible to accrue the future loss and in other cases only the existence of a contingent loss is disclosed (see International Accounting Standard 10, Contingencies and Events Occurring After the Balance Sheet Date).

Claims and Variations Arising Under Construction Contracts

38. Amounts due in respect of claims made by the contractor and of variations in contract work approved by the customer are recognised as revenue in the financial statements only in circumstances when, and only to the extent that, the contractor has evidence of the acceptability of the amount of the claim or variation.

39. Claims or penalties payable by the contractor arising out of delays in completion or from other causes are provided for in full in the financial statements as costs attributable to the contract. Claims in the nature of contingencies are treated in accordance with International Accounting Standard 10, Contingencies and Events Occurring After the Balance Sheet Date.

Progress Payments, Advances and Retentions

40. Progress payments and advances received from customers in respect of construction contracts are disclosed in financial statements either shown as a deduction from the amount of contract work in progress or as a liability.

41. Progress payments due but not received and amounts retained by customers until the satisfaction of conditions specified in the contract for release of such amounts are either recognised in financial statements as receivables or alternatively indicated by way of a note.

International Accounting Standard 11

Accounting for Construction Contracts

International Accounting Standard 11 comprises paragraphs 42-49 of this Statement. The Standard should be read in the context of paragraphs 1-41 of this Statement and of the Preface to Statements of International Accounting Standards.

42. In accounting for construction contracts in financial statements, either the percentage of completion method or the completed contract method should be used.

43. The percentage of completion method may be used only if the outcome of the contract can be reliably estimated. In the case of fixed price contracts, this degree of reliability would be provided only if all the following conditions are satisfied:

   (a) total contract revenues to be received can be reliably estimated, and

   (b) both the costs to complete the contract and the stage of contract performance completed at the reporting date can be reliably estimated, and

   (c) the costs attributable to the contract can be clearly identified so that actual experience can be compared with prior estimates.

In the case of cost plus contracts, this degree of reliability would be provided only if both the following conditions are satisfied:

   (a) the costs attributable to the contract can be clearly identified, and

   (b) costs other than those that will be specifically reimbursable under the contract can be reliably estimated.

44. The costs included in the amount at which construction contract work is stated should comprise those costs that relate directly to a specific contract and those that are attributable to the contract activity in general and can be allocated to specific contracts.

45. When a contractor uses a method for a particular contract, then all other contracts that meet similar criteria should be accounted for by the same method.

46. A foreseeable loss on a contract should be provided for in the financial statements, both for the stage of completion reached on the contract and for future work on the contract.

Disclosure

47. There should be disclosure in the financial statements of:
    (a) the amount of construction work in progress, and
    (b) cash received and receivable as progress payments, advances and retentions on account of contracts included in construction work in progress, and
    (c) the amount receivable under cost plus contracts not included in construction work in progress.

If both the percentage of completion method and the completed contract method are simultaneously used by the contractor, the amount of contract work described in (a) above should be analysed to disclose separately the amounts attributable to contracts accounted for under each method.

48. Disclosure of changes in an accounting policy used for construction contracts should comply with International Accounting Standard 8, Unusual and Prior Period Items and Changes in Accounting Policies. However, if a contractor changes from the percentage of completion method to the completed contract method for contracts in progress at the beginning of the year, it may not be possible to comply with that standard and quantify the effect of the change. In such cases, disclosure should be made of the amount of attributable profits reported in prior years in respect of contracts in progress at the beginning of the accounting period.

Effective Date

49. This International Accounting Standard becomes operative for financial statements covering periods beginning on or after 1 January 1980.

International Accounting Standard 12

Accounting for Taxes on Income

Contents

Introduction

1. This Statement deals with the accounting for taxes on income in financial statements. This includes the determination of the amount of the expense or saving related to taxes on income in respect of an accounting period and the presentation of such an amount in the financial statements.

2. This Statement does not deal with the methods of accounting for government grants or investment tax credits, and the following taxes are not considered to be within the scope of this Statement:

   (a) taxes based on income that are refundable to the enterprise to the extent that the amount of income upon which the tax was based is distributed in the form of dividends;

   (b) taxes paid by the enterprise at the time a dividend is distributed that the enterprise may offset against taxes due in respect of its income.

Definitions

3. In this Statement the following terms are used with the meanings specified:

Accounting income is the aggregate income or loss for a period, including unusual items[1] as reported in the income statement, before deducting related income tax expense or adding related income tax saving.

The *tax expense* or *tax saving* for the period is the amount of the taxes charged or credited in the income statement, excluding the amount of taxes related and allocated to those items not dealt with in the current income statement.

Taxable income (tax loss) is the amount of the income (loss) for a period, determined in accordance with the rules established by the taxation authorities, upon which the provision for taxes payable (recoverable) is determined.

Provision for taxes payable is the amount of taxes currently payable in respect of taxable income for the period.

Timing differences are the differences between the taxable income and accounting income for a period that arise because the period in which some items of revenue and expense are included in taxable income does not coincide with the period in which they are included in accounting income. Timing differences originate in one period and reverse in one or more subsequent periods.

[1]*Unusual items* is defined in International Accounting Standard 8, Unusual and Prior Period Items and Changes in Accounting Policies.

Permanent differences are the differences between taxable income and accounting income for a period that originate in the current period and do not reverse in subsequent periods.

Explanation

4. The provision for taxes payable is calculated in accordance with rules for determining taxable income established by taxation authorities. In many circumstances these rules differ from the accounting policies applied to determine accounting income. The effect of this difference is that the relationship between the provision for taxes payable and accounting income reported in the financial statements may not be representative of the current level of tax rates.

5. One reason for a difference between taxable income and accounting income is that certain items are considered to be appropriately included in one calculation but are required to be excluded from the other. For example, under many systems of taxation some donations are not an allowable deduction in determining taxable income; however, such amounts would be deducted in determining accounting income. Differences such as these are described as "permanent differences."

6. Another reason for a difference between taxable income and accounting income is that certain items, considered in determining both amounts, are included in the calculation for different periods. For example, accounting policies may specify that certain revenues are included in accounting income at the time goods or services are delivered but tax rules may require or allow their inclusion at the time cash is collected. The total of these revenues included in accounting income and taxable income will ultimately be the same, but the periods of inclusion will differ. Another example is when the depreciation rate used in determining taxable income differs from that used in determining accounting income. These types of difference are described as "timing differences."

7. When gains or losses are credited or charged directly to shareholders' interests, timing differences and permanent differences may also occur.

8. The origination and reversal of timing differences may relate to more than one accounting period. Information on the nature and amount of these timing differences is often considered to be useful to the users of financial statements. However, the method of reflecting the effect of timing differences varies. Sometimes the information is included in notes to the financial statements; sometimes the effect of these differences is reflected by the application of tax effect accounting methods.

9. The revaluation of individual assets in the financial statements or the general application of current value accounting may result in differences between taxable income and accounting income. This matter is dealt with in paragraphs 28-30.

Taxes Payable Method

10. Under the taxes payable method, tax expense in respect of the current period is normally equal to the provision for taxes payable. The extent and potential tax effect of timing differences are sometimes disclosed in notes to the financial statements.

11. Support for this method may be based on the view that taxes are a distribution of income rather than an operating expense of the enterprise. However, there is a broad consensus that taxes on income are expenses. Other support for the taxes payable method may be based on the view that tax effects of timing differences are part of the tax expense of the period in which they are part of taxable income. This view is not in accordance with the accrual assumption, which states that revenues and costs are accrued, that is, recognised as they are earned or incurred (and not as money is received or paid) and recorded in the financial statements of the periods to which they relate — see International Accounting Standard 1, Disclosure of Accounting Policies.

Tax Effect Accounting Methods

12. Under tax effect accounting methods, taxes on income are considered to be an expense incurred by the enterprise in earning income and are accrued in the same periods as the revenue and expenses to which they relate. The resulting tax effects of timing differences are included in the tax expense in the income statement and in the deferred tax balances in the balance sheet. Tax effect accounting methods are used in a number of countries in accounting for taxes on income. Those in common use are described as the deferral method and the liability method.

Deferral Method

13. Under the deferral method, the tax effects of current timing differences are deferred and allocated to future periods when the timing differences reverse. Since deferred tax balances in the balance sheet are not considered to represent rights to receive or obligations to pay money, they are not adjusted to reflect changes in the tax rate or the imposition of new taxes.

14. Under the deferral method, the tax expense for a period comprises:
   (a) the provision for taxes payable, and
   (b) the tax effects of timing differences deferred to or from other periods.

15. The tax effects of timing differences originating in the current period are determined using the current tax rate. The tax effects of individual timing differences originating in previous periods and reversing during the current period are generally determined using the tax rates originally applied. For ease of applying the method, similar timing differences may be grouped.

Liability Method

16. Under the liability method, the expected tax effects of current timing differences are determined and reported either as liabilities for taxes payable in the future or as assets representing advance payment of future taxes. Deferred tax balances are adjusted for changes in the tax rate or for new taxes imposed. The balances may also be adjusted for expected future changes in tax rates.

17. Under the liability method, the tax expense for a period comprises:

    (a) the provision for taxes payable,

    (b) the amount of taxes expected to be payable or considered to be prepaid in respect of timing differences originating or reversing in the current period, and

    (c) the adjustments to deferred tax balances in the balance sheet necessary to reflect either a change in the tax rate or the imposition of new taxes.

18. Under the liability method, the tax effects of timing differences originating or reversing in the current period and adjustments to deferred tax balances are determined using the current tax rate, unless other information indicates that another rate would be more appropriate, for example, where a change in tax rates has been announced as applicable to future years.

Application

19. Normally, tax effect accounting methods are applied to all timing differences. However, under certain circumstances a partial application is used.

20. Under the partial application, tax expense for a period excludes the tax effects of certain timing differences when there is reasonable evidence that those timing differences will not reverse for some considerable period (at least three years) ahead. It is also necessary for there to be no indication that after this period these timing differences are likely to reverse.

Deferred Tax Debits

21. The accounting for timing differences may result in a debit balance or a debit to the deferred tax balance. The consideration of prudence requires that such a debit be carried forward in the balance sheet only if there is a reasonable expectation of realisation, for example, if sufficient future taxable income will be generated in the period in which the timing differences will reverse.

Tax Losses

22. Tax legislation frequently provides that tax losses of the current period may be used either to recover tax paid within a specified carryback period or to reduce or eliminate tax to be paid in future periods. The loss provides a tax saving in the period of the loss or a potential tax saving in some subsequent period. The accounting period in which such a tax saving is included in determining net income in the financial statements varies.

23. A recovery of taxes through the application of a tax loss to the carryback period represents a tax saving that is effectively realised in the period of loss and is included in net income or net loss in the financial statements for that period. In determining the amount of the saving, appropriate adjustment of existing deferred tax balances may be necessary.

24. The realisation of a potential tax saving related to the amount of a tax loss remaining after the carryback described in paragraph 23 requires the existence of taxable income in future periods. For this reason the potential tax saving related to a tax loss carryforward is generally not included in the determination of net income in the period of the loss.

25. However, in rare circumstances, the inclusion of this potential tax saving in the determination of net income for the period of the loss may be considered appropriate. If a potential tax saving is to be dealt with in this manner, the consideration of prudence requires that there is assurance beyond any reasonable doubt that future taxable income will be sufficient to allow the benefit of the loss to be realised. For example, the condition of assurance beyond any reasonable doubt would be satisfied if the following conditions exist:
  (a) the loss results from an identifiable and non-recurring cause, and
  (b) a record of profitability by the enterprise has been established over a long period and is expected to continue.

26. The existence of a credit amount in the deferred tax balance may provide evidence that the tax saving related to a tax loss carryforward can be realised at least in part. The reversal of the timing differences reflected in the deferred tax credit balance will of itself create a corresponding amount of taxable income, against which the tax loss can be offset to realise a tax saving. If the tax rules limit the period during which a tax loss may be carried forward for offset against future taxable income, only those timing differences that will reverse or can be reversed during the limited period are considered in offsetting a tax loss to realise a tax saving. The tax saving as a result of offsetting a tax loss is included in net income for the period of the loss and the debit is carried forward as part of the deferred tax credit balance in the balance sheet. The amount of such a debit may be disclosed.

27. If the tax saving related to a past tax loss was not included in net income in the year of the loss, a tax saving later realised by offsetting such a tax loss against taxable income is included in net income in the period of realisation and disclosed.

Revaluation of Assets

28. In circumstances in which an asset is revalued in the financial statements at an amount in excess of its historical cost or previous revaluation, the substituted amounts do not generally form the basis for the determination of taxes payable. To the extent that revalued assets give rise to charges or credits in accounting income that are not based on historical cost or other bases permitted under the tax rules there will be a difference between taxable income and accounting income. The accounting treatment of this type of difference depends on the accounting treatment accorded the revaluation.

29. One approach is to determine the tax effect related to the increase in the carrying value of the asset and transfer that amount from the revaluation account to the deferred tax balance. Under this approach when a difference such as described in paragraph 28 occurs in a period subsequent to the revaluation the tax effect relating to that difference is charged to the deferred tax balance and consequently is not reflected in the tax expense. In some cases the tax effect is reflected in tax expense and a corresponding amount is transferred from the deferred tax balance to the revaluation account.

30. Another approach is to disclose in the notes to the financial statements the amount of the potential tax effect related to the increase in the carrying value of the asset at the date of the revaluation. In subsequent periods the amount of potential tax effect is revised to reflect the tax effect of the differences described in paragraph 28.

Undistributed Earnings of Subsidiaries and Associated Companies

31. Taxes payable by either the parent company or subsidiaries on distribution to the parent company of the undistributed profits of subsidiaries are accrued unless it is reasonable to assume that those profits will not be distributed or that a distribution will not give rise to a tax liability. A reason for not accruing may be the parent company's intention and power to retain those profits in the subsidiary for long-term reinvestment. If taxes are not accrued in respect of undistributed profits, there is sometimes disclosure of the cumulative amount of those profits.

32. For investments in associated companies accounted for on the equity method, taxes that would be payable on distribution to the investor of the investor's share of the undistributed profits of the investee are sometimes accrued in full when the profits are recognised by the investor. However, since most enterprises do not distribute all of their earnings, these taxes are sometimes accrued only to the extent of expected distributions? If taxes are not accrued in full, there is sometimes disclosure of the cumulative amount of the portion of undistributed profits applicable to the investor on which taxes are not accrued.

Financial Statement Presentation

33. Taxes on income are generally accounted for as tax expense in the determination of net income of the enterprise. However, in some circumstances in which the effect of a transaction is charged or credited directly to shareholders' interests, the related tax effect of the transaction is accounted for and disclosed in the same manner so that the taxes may be directly related to the item to which they apply.

34. The tax expense related to accounting income from the ordinary activities of the enterprise is usually presented as a separate item in the income statement. The tax attributable to an unusual item is included with that item because it directly relates to it. Disclosure is made of this related tax amount.

35. Deferred tax balances are not part of the shareholders' interests and are generally presented as separate items in the balance sheet. Debit and credit balances representing deferred taxes may be offset.

36. In circumstances in which a distinction is made between current and long-term assets and liabilities in the financial statements, the net current and the net long-term portions of the deferred tax balance are sometimes presented separately so as to maintain the appropriate distinction between current and long-term items.

37. Taxes on income which were previously paid and are due to be recovered as a result of the application of a tax loss in accordance with paragraph 23 are shown in the balance sheet as a receivable separate from deferred tax balances.

2This expands on the explanation of this subject given in paragraph 29 of International Accounting Standard 3, Consolidated Financial Statements.

38. Loss carryforward benefits resulting from the application of tax losses in accordance with paragraph 25 are different from other deferred tax balances. The amounts of such carryforward benefits may be disclosed separately in the balance sheet.

39. The relationship between tax expense and accounting income may be affected by such factors as permanent differences, and tax rates in the locations of foreign based operations. Accordingly, an explanation of the relationship is sometimes presented in the financial statements.

International Accounting Standard 12

Accounting for Taxes on Income

*International Accounting Standard 12 comprises
paragraphs 40-56 of this Statement. The Standard
should be read in the context of paragraphs 1-39
of this Statement and of the Preface to Statements of International Accounting Standards.*

40. The tax expense for the period should be included in the determination
of net income of the enterprise.

41. The taxes on income relating to an item that is charged or credited to
shareholders' interests should be accounted for in the same manner as the
relevant item and the amount should be disclosed.

Tax Effect Accounting

42. The tax expense for the period should be determined on the basis of tax
effect accounting, using either the deferral or the liability method. The
method used should be disclosed.

43. The tax effect accounting method used should normally be applied to
all timing differences. However, the tax expense for the period may exclude
the tax effects of certain timing differences when there is reasonable
evidence that these timing differences will not reverse for some considerable
period (at least three years) ahead. There should also be no indication that
after this period these timing differences are likely to reverse. The amount
of timing differences, both current and cumulative, not accounted for should
be disclosed.

44. The tax effect of timing differences that result in a debit balance or a
debit to the deferred tax balance should not be carried forward unless there
is a reasonable expectation of realisation.

45. Deferred tax balances should be presented in the balance sheet of the
enterprise separately from the shareholders' interests.

Tax Losses

46. Taxes relating to a previous period which are recovered as a result of carrying back a tax loss should be included in net income in the period of the loss. Amounts recoverable but not yet received should be included in the balance sheet as receivables.

47. The potential tax saving related to a tax loss that is available to be carried forward for the determination of taxable income in future periods should not be included in net income until the period of realisation, except as described in paragraphs 48 and 49.

48. The potential tax saving relating to a tax loss carryforward may be included in the determination of net income for the period of the loss if there is assurance beyond any reasonable doubt that future taxable income will be sufficient to allow the benefit of the loss to be realised.

49. If the criterion set out in paragraph 48 is not satisfied, the tax saving relating to a tax loss carryforward should be included in the determination of net income for the period of the loss to the extent of the net credits in the deferred tax balance that will reverse or can be reversed within the period during which the loss can be claimed as a tax benefit.

50. The following items in respect of tax losses should be disclosed:
    (a) the amount of the tax saving included in net income in the period of the loss in accordance with the criteria in paragraphs 48 and 49,
    (b) the amount of the tax saving included in net income for the current period as a result of the realisation of a tax loss carryforward that had not been accounted for in the year of the loss, and
    (c) the amount and future availability of tax losses for which the related tax effects have not been included in the net income of any period.

Undistributed Earnings of Subsidiaries and Associated Companies

51. Taxes payable by either the parent company or subsidiaries on distribution to the parent company of the undistributed profits of subsidiaries should be accrued unless it is reasonable to assume that those profits will not be distributed or that a distribution will not give rise to a tax liability.

52. For investments in associated companies accounted for on the equity method, taxes that would be payable on distribution to the investor of the investor's share of the undistributed profits of the investee should be accrued when the profits are recognised by the investor. An exception may be made when it is reasonable to assume that those profits will not be distributed or that a distribution will not give rise to a tax liability.

Other Disclosures

53. The following should be disclosed separately:
   (a) the tax expense related to income from the ordinary activities of the enterprise,
   (b) the tax expense relating to unusual items, to prior period items, and to changes of accounting policy — see International Accounting Standard 8, Unusual and Prior Period Items and Changes in Accounting Policies,
   (c) the tax effects, if any, related to assets that have been revalued to amounts in excess of historical cost or previous revaluation, and
   (d) an explanation of the relationship between tax expense and accounting income if not explained by the tax rates effective in the country of the reporting enterprise.

Tax Contingencies

54. Any contingency related to taxes on income not referred to in paragraphs 40-53 should be dealt with in accordance with International Accounting Standard 10, Contingencies and Events Occurring After the Balance Sheet Date.

Transitional Provisions

55. On the first occasion that the tax expense is presented in the financial statements using a tax effect accounting method, an enterprise that has previously used the taxes payable method should either (a) adjust its financial statements in accordance with International Accounting Standard 8 to record the accumulated deferred tax balance or balances or (b) disclose in the period of change and subsequently any unrecorded amount of deferred taxes that have accumulated prior to the adoption of the tax effect accounting basis. The tax expense deducted in computing reported income should be the same as that which would have resulted if tax effect accounting had been in effect from the beginning. When (b) is adopted, the adjustment to account for the reversal of timing differences not accounted for when they arose should be either charged (credited) to retained earnings or treated in the income statement as an unusual item.

Effective Date

56. This International Accounting Standard becomes operative for financial statements covering periods beginning on or after 1 January 1981.

International Accounting Standard 13

Presentation of Current Assets and Current Liabilities

Contents

Introduction

1. This Statement deals with the meaning and presentation of current assets and current liabilities in financial statements. This Statement does not deal with the basis of valuation of these assets and liabilities.

Explanation

2. The identification of current assets and current liabilities has traditionally been considered useful information to assist users of financial statements in analysing an enterprise's financial position.

3. An excess of current assets over current liabilities is often referred to either as "net current assets" or as "working capital."

Alternative Views of Current Assets and Current Liabilities

4. Some regard the classification of assets and liabilities into "current" and "non-current" as being intended to give an approximate measure of an enterprise's liquidity, that is, its ability to carry on its activities on a day to day basis without encountering financial stringencies. Others regard this classification as providing an identification of those resources and obligations of the enterprise that are continuously circulating.

5. These purposes are to a certain extent incompatible. This is because, in measuring liquidity, the criterion for classifying assets and liabilities as current or non-current is whether the items will be realised or liquidated in the near future. The criterion for identifying assets and liabilities as circulating, however, is whether they are consumed or settled in the production of revenue within the normal operating cycle[1] of an enterprise. For example, construction work in progress would, under the first criterion, be largely excluded from current assets, while under the second criterion it would be included.

[1] The operating cycle of an enterprise normally refers to the average time between the acquisition of materials entering into the process and the final cash realisation.

Present Practice

6. These competing considerations have led to the adoption in many countries of a position whereby items are included in current assets on the basis of whether they are expected to be realised within one year or within the normal operating cycle of the enterprise, whichever is the longer; items are included in current liabilities if they are payable at the demand of the creditor or are expected to be liquidated within one year. Even when this approach is used as the general rule, there are instances of the inclusion or exclusion of individual items based on different criteria. Hence, the classification of items as current or non-current in practice is largely based on convention rather than on any one concept. Paragraphs 7-12 below describe practice as to the classification of certain items.

Items Included in Current Assets

7. Cash and bank balances are included in current assets unless restrictions on their use make them unavailable for current operations.

8. Trade and other receivables are included in current assets to the extent that they are expected to be realised within one year. Sometimes all trade receivables are included in current assets, in which case the amount not expected to be realised within one year may be disclosed.

9. Inventories are usually included in current assets in their entirety, notwithstanding that they may include items not expected to be realised within one year or within the normal operating cycle.

Items Included in Current Liabilities

10. A loan stated to be payable at the demand of the creditor is usually included in current liabilities. However, if the creditor has agreed to a schedule of repayment, the loan is sometimes classified on the basis of scheduled repayment, notwithstanding the creditor's right to demand payment at any time.

11. The portion of a long-term liability payable within one year is usually classified as a current liability. This item is sometimes excluded from current liabilities if the enterprise intends to refinance the obligation on a long-term basis and there is reasonable assurance that the enterprise will be able to do so. Similarly, the portion of a long-term liability payable within one year is sometimes classified as non-current if assets existing

at the balance sheet date, out of which settlement is to be made, have been excluded from current assets.

12. When an enterprise excludes a liability from the current classification in accordance with paragraph 11, the amount and the circumstances are often disclosed.

Presentation in the Financial Statements

13. The usefulness of the current:non-current distinction is improved by grouping and totalling current assets and current liabilities.

14. To permit adequate identification of the separate assets and liabilities of the enterprise, the amount at which a current asset or current liability is stated is generally not reduced by deducting another current liability or current asset. However, such offsetting might be appropriate when a legal right of set-off exists and the offsetting represents the expectation as to the realisation or settlement of the asset or liability.

Limitations of the Current:Non-Current Distinction

15. The current:non-current distinction is generally believed to provide an identification of a relatively liquid portion of an enterprise's total capital that constitutes a margin or buffer for meeting obligations within the ordinary operating cycle of an enterprise. However, as long as a business is a going concern, it must, for example, continuously replace the inventory that it realises with new inventory in order to carry on its operations. Also, current assets may include inventories that are not expected to be realised in the near future. On the other hand, many enterprises finance their operations with bank loans that are stated to be payable on demand and are hence classified as current liabilities. Yet, the demand feature may be primarily a form of protection for the lender and the expectation of both borrower and lender is that the loan will remain outstanding for some considerable period of time.

16. Many regard an excess of current assets over current liabilities as providing some indication of the financial well-being of an enterprise, while an excess of current liabilities over current assets is regarded as an indication of financial problems. It is not appropriate to draw such conclusions without considering the nature of the operations of the enterprise and the individual components of its current assets and current liabilities.

17. The segregation of assets and liabilities between current and non-current is usually not considered appropriate in the financial statements of enterprises with indeterminate or very long operating cycles.

18. Thus, while many believe that the identification of current assets and liabilities is a useful tool in financial analysis, others believe that the limitations of the distinction make it of little use or even misleading in many circumstances. Imposition of a general requirement to identify current assets and liabilities in financial statements might impede further consideration of these questions. Accordingly, this Statement is intended only to harmonise practices followed by enterprises that choose to identify current assets and liabilities in their financial statements.

International Accounting Standard 13

Presentation of Current Assets and Current Liabilities

International Accounting Standard 13 comprises paragraphs 19-28 of this Statement. The Standard should be read in the context of paragraphs 1-18 of the Statement and of the Preface to Statements of International Accounting Standards.

19. Each enterprise should determine whether or not to present current assets and current liabilities as separate classifications in its financial statements. Paragraphs 21-27 of this Standard apply when the current:non-current distinction is made.

20. When the current:non-current distinction is not made in the financial statements of an enterprise, no sub-totals of the amounts of assets and of liabilities should be given that would imply that such distinction is made.

Application of the Current:Non-Current Distinction

Current Assets
21. Among the items included in current assets should be:
   (a) Cash and bank balances available for current operations. Cash or bank balances whose use for current operations is subject to restrictions should be included as a current asset only if the duration of the restrictions is limited to the term of an obligation that has been classified as a current liability or if the restrictions lapse within one year.
   (b) Securities not intended to be retained and capable of being readily realised.
   (c) Trade and other receivables expected to be realised within one year of the balance sheet date. Trade receivables may be included

163

in their entirety in current assets, provided that the amount not expected to be realised within one year is disclosed.

(d) Inventories.

(e) Advance payments on the purchase of current assets.

(f) Expense prepayments expected to be used up within one year of the balance sheet date.

Current Liabilities

22. Among the items included in current liabilities should be obligations payable at the demand of the creditor and those parts of the following obligations whose liquidation is expected within one year of the balance sheet date:

(a) Bank and other loans. If a loan is repayable in accordance with a schedule of repayment agreed with the creditor, the loan may be classified in accordance therewith, notwithstanding a right of the creditor to demand current payment.

(b) The current portion of long-term liabilities, unless excluded under the provisions of paragraph 23.

(c) Trade liabilities and accrued expenses.

(d) Provision for taxes payable (see International Accounting Standard 12, Accounting for Taxes on Income).

(e) Dividends payable.

(f) Deferred revenues and advances from customers.

(g) Accruals for contingencies (see International Accounting Standard 10, Contingencies and Events Occurring After the Balance Sheet Date).

23. The current portion of a long-term liability may be excluded from current liabilities if the enterprise intends to refinance the obligation on a long-term basis and there is reasonable assurance that the enterprise will be able to do so. Demonstration of this ability would require either:

(a) the issue of share capital or a long-term obligation after the date of the balance sheet; or

(b) a non-cancellable financing agreement that does not expire within one year of the balance sheet date and that the lender or investor is financially capable of honouring.

24. When an enterprise excludes a liability from the current classification in accordance with paragraph 23, the amount of the liability and the terms of the refinancing should be disclosed.

Presentation in the Financial Statements

25. The amount at which a current asset or current liability is stated in the financial statements should not be reduced by the deduction of another current liability or current asset unless a legal right of set-off exists and the offsetting represents the expectation as to the realisation of the asset or settlement of the liability.

26. Progress payments and advances may be deducted from the amount of related construction work in progress, provided disclosure is made in accordance with International Accounting Standard 11, Accounting for Construction Contracts.

27. The total amount of current assets and the total amount of current liabilities should be disclosed in the financial statements.

Effective Date

28. This International Accounting Standard becomes operative for financial statements covering periods beginning on or after 1 January 1981.

International Accounting Standard 14

Reporting Financial Information by Segment

Contents

Introduction

1. This Statement deals with reporting financial information by segments of an enterprise — specifically, the different industries and the different geographical areas in which it operates.

2. This Statement applies to enterprises whose securities are publicly traded and to other economically significant entities, including subsidiaries. For purposes of this Statement other economically significant entities including subsidiaries are those whose levels of revenues, profits, assets or employment are significant in the countries in which their major operations are conducted.

3. When both parent company and consolidated financial statements are presented, the information called for by this Statement need only be presented on the basis of consolidated information. If financial statements of subsidiaries are published the segmental information is called for at that level.

Definitions

4. The following terms are used in this Statement with the meanings specified:

Industry segments are the distinguishable components of an enterprise each engaged in providing a different product or service, or a different group of related products or services, primarily to customers outside the enterprise.

Geographical segments are the distinguishable components of an enterprise engaged in operations in individual countries or groups of countries within particular geographical areas as may be determined to be appropriate in an enterprise's particular circumstances.

Segment revenue is revenue that is directly attributable to a segment, or the relevant portion of revenue that can be allocated on a reasonable basis to a segment, and that is derived from transactions with parties outside the enterprise and from other segments of the same enterprise.

Segment expense is expense that is directly attributable to a segment or the relevant portion of an expense that can be allocated on a reasonable basis to the segments.

Explanation

5. Rates of profitability, opportunities for growth, future prospects, and risks to investments may vary greatly among industry and geographical segments. Thus, users of financial statements need segment information to assess the prospects and risks of a diversified enterprise which may not be determinable from the aggregated data. The objective of presenting information by segments is to provide users of financial statements with information on the relative size, profit contribution, and growth trend of the different industries and different geographical areas in which a diversified enterprise operates to enable them to make more informed judgments about the enterprise as a whole.

6. Segmented information is not intended to convey the impression that such segments may be considered as independent businesses or that comparisons between similarly labelled segments of different enterprises would necessarily be valid.

7. Reporting segment information involves decisions that are based in part on judgment. Such decisions include those about the identification of segments and about the allocation of revenues and expenses to those segments. Information about the bases used in the preparation of segmental reporting enhances the user's understanding of the resulting data.

8. Concern is sometimes expressed that disclosing information about segments may weaken an enterprise's competitive position because more detailed information is made available to competitors, customers, suppliers and others. For this reason, some consider it appropriate to allow the withholding of certain segment information where disclosure is deemed to be detrimental to the enterprise. Others believe that this disclosure is no more onerous to the diversified enterprise than is the disclosure of the information required of an enterprise operating in only one industry or geographical area, and that relevant information is often available from other sources. Also, analysis by segment of the aggregated financial information of a diversified enterprise is widely deemed to provide useful data that enables users to make a better assessment of the past performance and future prospects of the enterprise.

Methods of Reporting Segment Information
Identification of Reporting Segments

9. Industry segments and geographical segments are usual bases for presenting information on operations by segment. An enterprise would provide information on both bases if both are applicable to its operations.

10. Industry segment information is usually presented on the basis of general groupings of related products and services, or by types of customer. Geographical segment information is sometimes presented on the basis of the location of operations of the enterprise, sometimes on the basis of markets and sometimes on both. An enterprise's domestic operations are generally considered to be a separate geographical segment. Some countries require separate disclosure of export sales in respect of their domestic operations.

11. Industry and geographical segments may be determined in many ways for reporting purposes. It is the responsibility of management to exercise its judgment in determining how the enterprise activities are to be grouped for reporting as segments. In making such decisions, management normally takes account of many factors. Such factors may include similarities and differences in the enterprise's products and activities; in the profitability, risk and growth of those products and activities; and in the operating and marketing areas and the relative importance of those areas within the enterprise as a whole. The existence of special regulatory requirements and specific industry characteristics such as in the banking and insurance industries may constitute additional factors to be considered in determining segments to be reported.

12. Organisational groupings such as divisions, subsidiaries, or branches, are ordinarily created according to management requirements. Such groupings often correspond with the determinable segments of the enterprise, thus facilitating segment reporting. Where this is not the case, segment reporting may require reclassification of data.

13. It is relevant to consider the interrelationships among the enterprise's activities. For example, it may be potentially misleading to report as separate industry segments parts of an enterprise's activities that are significantly integrated or interdependent. The same considerations would not necessarily apply in determining geographical segments to be reported.

14. Some consider it appropriate to provide guidelines on how material a segment should be before it is reported separately and to limit the segments to a reasonable number so as to avoid unnecessary complexity. Such guidelines may be 10 per cent of consolidated revenue, or operating profit or total assets, although such quantitative guidelines are not the sole factors in identifying segments for reporting.

15. Inter-segment sales and other operating inter-segment revenues cannot always be determined on an arm's length basis. For this reason disclosure of the amount of such revenues and an explanation of the inter-segment pricing basis (such as "fair market value", "cost", or "market price less a discount") is useful.

Segment Result

16. The measure of the profitability of a segment is disclosed as the segment result. The segment result is the difference between segment revenue and segment expense and generally reflects operating profit, although other bases are sometimes found to be more appropriate. Interest earned and interest expense are not normally included in segment result unless the segment's operations are primarily of a financial nature. Also taxes on income, minority interest and unusual items are not usually included in segment result.

17. Where revenues and expenses are not directly attributable to a segment but a reasonable basis for allocation exists, they may be allocated thereto on that basis. In many enterprises, however, common items such as head office expenses are not allocated to individual segments, because they are shared in such a way that any allocation among the segments is not considered useful.

Segment Assets

18. The disclosure of the segment assets gives an indication of the resources employed in generating segment operating results. Such assets include all tangible and intangible assets that can be identified with a particular segment. Assets shared by two or more segments may be allocated between or among those segments if a reasonable basis exists for such allocation. Liabilities are generally not allocated, either because they are considered to relate to the enterprise as a whole, or because they are viewed as giving rise to a financing result rather than an operating result.

Information Reported

19. The following information for each reported segment is generally considered necessary:

(a) a description of the activities of each reported industry segment and an indication of the composition of each reported geographical area,

(b) sales or other operating revenues, distinguishing between revenue derived from customers outside the enterprise and revenue derived from other segments,

(c) segment result, and

(d) segment assets employed, expressed either in money amounts or as percentages of the consolidated totals.

The relationship between the sum of the information on individual segments and the aggregated information in the financial statements is made clear by providing reconciliations. It may also be useful to disclose other information such as the amount of each segment's income from investments accounted for under the equity method, its minority interest or its unusual items. Depreciation, depletion, amortisation, research and development and capital expenditures for the period are sometimes disclosed for each reported segment. Sometimes non-financial information such as the number of employees for each reported segment is also disclosed.

International Accounting Standard 14

Reporting Financial Information by Segment

International Accounting Standard 14 comprises paragraphs 20-26 of this Statement. The Standard should be read in the context of paragraphs 1-19 of this Statement and of the Preface to Statements of International Accounting Standards.

20. Enterprises whose securities are publicly traded and other economically significant entities including subsidiaries should report the financial information described in paragraphs 21-24 for the industry segments and for the geographical segments which are considered to be significant to the enterprise. When both parent company and consolidated financial statements are presented, segment information need be presented only on the basis of consolidated financial statements.

21. The enterprise should describe the activities of each reported industry segment and indicate the composition of each reported geographical area.

22. For each reported industry and geographical segment, the following financial information should be disclosed:
   (a) sales or other operating revenues, distinguishing between revenue derived from customers outside the enterprise and revenue derived from other segments,
   (b) segment result,
   (c) segment assets employed, expressed either in money amounts or as percentages of the consolidated totals, and
   (d) the basis of inter-segment pricing.

23. The enterprise should provide reconciliations between the sum of the information on individual segments and the aggregated information in the financial statements.

24. Changes in identification of segments and changes in accounting practices used in reporting segment information which have a material effect on the segment information should be disclosed. Such disclosure should include a description of the nature of the change, an explanation of the reasons for the change and, where the information is reasonably determinable, the effect of the change.

Transitional Provision

25. No comparative figures need be presented in the first period in respect of which this Standard is introduced if such information is not readily available.

Effective Date

26. This International Accounting Standard becomes operative for financial statements covering periods beginning on or after 1 January 1983 except that, in the interests of uniform application in a particular country, for subsidiaries whose securities are not publicly traded, this Standard becomes operative when the requirements expressed in this Standard become, in all material respects, accepted practice for economically significant domestic entities in that country.

International Accounting Standard 15

Information Reflecting the Effects of Changing Prices

At its meeting in October 1989, the Board of IASC approved the following statement to be added to IAS 15:

"The international consensus on the disclosure of information reflecting the effects of changing prices that was anticipated when IAS 15 was issued has not been reached. As a result, the Board of IASC has decided that enterprises need not disclose the information required by IAS 15 in order that their financial statements conform with International Accounting Standards. However, the Board encourages enterprises to present such information and urges those that do to disclose the items required by IAS 15."

Contents

Introduction

1. This Statement deals with information reflecting the effects of changing prices on the measurements used in the determination of an enterprise's results of operation and financial position. In most countries, such information is supplementary to, but not a part of, the primary financial statements. This Statement does not apply to the accounting and reporting policies required to be used by an enterprise in the preparation of its primary financial statements, unless those financial statements are presented on a basis that reflects the effects of changing prices.

2. This International Accounting Standard supersedes International Accounting Standard 6, Accounting Responses to Changing Prices.

3. This Statement applies to enterprises whose levels of revenues, profit, assets or employment are significant in the economic environment in which they operate. When both parent company and consolidated financial statements are presented, the information called for by this Standard need only be presented on the basis of consolidated information.

4. The information called for by this Standard is not required for a subsidiary operating in the country of domicile of its parent if consolidated information on this basis is presented by the parent. For subsidiaries operating in a country other than the country of domicile of the parent, the information called for by this Standard is only required when it is accepted practice for similar information to be presented by enterprises of economic significance in that country.

5. Presentation of information reflecting the effects of changing prices is encouraged for other entities in the interest of promoting more informative financial reporting.

Explanation

6. Prices change over time as the result of various specific or general economic and social forces. Specific forces such as changes in supply and demand and technological changes may cause individual prices to increase or decrease significantly and independently of each other. In addition, general forces may result in a change in the general level of prices and therefore in the general purchasing power of money.

7. In most countries financial statements are prepared on the historical cost basis of accounting without regard either to changes in the general level of prices or to changes in specific prices of assets held, except to the extent that property, plant and equipment may have been revalued or inventories or other current assets reduced to net realisable value. The information required by this Standard is designed to make users of an enterprise's financial statements aware of the effects of changing prices on the results of its operations. Financial statements, however, whether prepared under the historical cost method or under a method that reflects the effects of changing prices, are not intended to indicate directly the value of the enterprise as a whole.

Responding to Changing Prices

8. Financial information intended as a response to the effects of changing prices is prepared in a number of ways. One way shows financial information in terms of general purchasing power. Another way shows current cost in place of historical cost, recognising changes in specific prices of assets. A third way combines features of both these methods.

9. Underlying these responses are two basic approaches to the determination of income. One recognises income after the general purchasing power of the shareholders' equity in the enterprise has been maintained. The other recognises income after the operating capacity of the enterprise has been maintained, and may or may not include a general price level adjustment.

General Purchasing Power Approach

10. The general purchasing power approach involves the restatement of some or all of the items in the financial statements for changes in the general price level. Proposals on this subject emphasise that general purchasing power restatements change the unit of account but do not change the underlying measurement bases. Under this approach, income normally reflects the effects, using an appropriate index, of general price level changes on depreciation, cost of sales and net monetary items and is reported after the general purchasing power of the shareholders' equity in the enterprise has been maintained.

The Current Cost Approach

11. The current cost approach is found in a number of different methods. In general, these use replacement cost as the primary measurement basis. If, however, replacement cost is higher than both net realisable value and present value, the higher of net realisable value and present value is usually used as the measurement basis.

12. The replacement cost of a specific asset is normally derived from the current acquisition cost of a similar asset, new or used, or of an equivalent productive capacity or service potential. Net realisable value usually represents the net current selling price of the asset. Present value represents a current estimate of future net receipts attributable to the asset, appropriately discounted.

13. Specific price indices are often used as a means to determine current costs for items, particularly if no recent transaction involving those items has occurred, no price lists are available or the use of price lists is not practical.

14. Current cost methods generally require recognition of the effects on depreciation and cost of sales of changes in prices specific to the enterprise. Most such methods also require the application of some form of adjustments which have in common a general recognition of the interaction between changing prices and the financing of an enterprise. As discussed in paragraphs 15-17, opinions differ on the form these adjustments should take.

15. Some current cost methods require an adjustment reflecting the effects of changing prices on all net monetary items, including long-term liabilities, leading to a loss from holding net monetary assets or to a gain from having net monetary labilities when prices are rising, and vice versa. Other methods limit this adjustment to the monetary assets and liabilities included in the working capital of the enterprise. Both types of adjustment recognise that not only non-monetary assets but also monetary items are important elements of the operating capacity of the enterprise. A normal feature of the current cost methods described above is that they recognise income after the operating capacity of the enterprise has been maintained.

16. Another view is that it is unnecessary to recognise in the income statement the additional replacement cost of assets to the extent that they are financed by borrowing. Methods based on this view report income after the portion of the enterprise's operating capacity that is financed by its shareholders has been maintained. This may be achieved, for example, by reducing the total of the adjustment for depreciation, cost of sales, and, where the method requires it, monetary working capital, in the proportion that finance by borrowing bears to finance by the total of borrowing and equity capital.

17. Some current cost methods apply a general price level index to the amount of shareholders' interests. This indicates the extent to which shareholders' equity in the enterprise has been maintained in terms of the general purchasing power when the increase in the replacement cost of the assets arising during the period is less than the decrease in the purchasing power of the shareholders' interests during the same period. Sometimes this calculation is merely noted to enable a comparison to be made between net assets in terms of general purchasing power and net assets in terms of current costs. Under other methods, which recognise income after the general purchasing power of shareholders' equity in the enterprise has been maintained, the difference between the two net assets figures is treated as a gain or loss accruing to the shareholders.

Current Status

18. While financial information is sometimes provided using the various methods for reflecting changing prices described above, either in primary or supplementary financial statements, there is not yet an international consensus on the subject. Consequently, the International Accounting Standards Committee believes that further experimentation is necessary before consideration can be given to requiring enterprises to prepare primary financial statements using a comprehensive and uniform system for reflecting changing prices. Meanwhile, evolution of the subject would be assisted if enterprises that present primary financial statements on the historical cost basis also provide supplementary information reflecting the effects of price changes.

19. There is a variety of proposals as to the items to be included in such information, ranging from a few income statement items to extensive income statement and balance sheet disclosures. It is desirable that there be an internationally established minimum of items to be included in the information.

Minimum Disclosures

20. The minimum disclosures required by this Standard are:
    (a) the adjustments to or the adjusted amounts of depreciation of property, plant and equipment and cost of sales that are necessary to reflect the effects of changing prices;
    (b) adjustments relating to monetary items, the effect of borrowing, or equity interests as described in paragraphs 15-17 when such adjustments are taken into account in determining income under the method adopted; and
    (c) the overall effect on results of adjustments made to reflect the effects of changing prices.

In addition, under a current cost approach, the current cost of property, plant and equipment and of inventories are relevant and are disclosed.

21. A description of the procedures adopted to make the computations, including the nature of any indices used, is necessary for an understanding of the information required by the Standard.

Other Disclosures

22. Enterprises are encouraged to provide additional disclosures, and in particular a discussion of the significance of the information in the circumstances of the enterprise. Disclosure of any adjustments to tax provisions or tax balances is usually helpful.

International Accounting Standard 15

Information Reflecting the Effects of Changing Prices

International Accounting Standard 15 comprises paragraphs 23-28 of this Statement. The Standard should be read in the context of paragraphs 1-22 of this Statement and of the Preface to Statements of International Accounting Standards.

23. Enterprises to which this Standard applies should present information disclosing the items set out in paragraphs 24 to 26 using an accounting method reflecting the effects of changing prices.

24. The items to be presented are:
  (a) the amount of the adjustment to or the adjusted amount of depreciation of property, plant and equipment;
  (b) the amount of the adjustment to or the adjusted amount of cost of sales;
  (c) the adjustments relating to monetary items, the effect of borrowing, or equity interests when such adjustments have been taken into account in determining income under the accounting method adopted; and
  (d) the overall effect on results of the adjustments described in (a) and (b) and, where appropriate, (c), as well as any other items reflecting the effects of changing prices that are reported under the accounting method adopted.

25. When a current cost method is adopted the current cost of property, plant and equipment, and of inventories, should be disclosed.

26. Enterprises should describe the methods adopted to compute the information called for in paragraphs 24 and 25, including the nature of any indices used.

27. The information required by paragraphs 24 to 26 should be provided on a supplementary basis unless such information is presented in the primary financial statements.

Effective Date

28. This International Accounting Standard supersedes International Accounting Standard 6, Accounting Responses to Changing Prices, and becomes operative for financial statements covering periods beginning on or after 1 January 1983.

International Accounting Standard 16

Accounting for Property, Plant and Equipment

Contents

Introduction

1. International Accounting Standard 5, Information to be Disclosed in Financial Statements, requires certain information to be disclosed in the balance sheet, including property, plant and equipment. In many enterprises these assets are grouped into various categories, such as land and buildings, machinery, equipment, fixtures and fittings, and vehicles. This Statement deals with the accounting for such property, plant and equipment, except as described in paragraphs 2-5.

2. This Statement does not deal with the specialised aspects of accounting for property, plant and equipment that arise under a comprehensive system reflecting the effects of changing prices (see International Accounting Standard 15, Information Reflecting the Effects of Changing Prices).

3. This Statement does not deal with accounting for:
   (a) forests and similar regenerative natural resources;
   (b) expenditures on mineral rights, the exploration for and extraction of minerals, oil, natural gas and similar non-regenerative resources; and
   (c) expenditures on real estate development.

Expenditures on individual items of property, plant and equipment used to develop or maintain the activities covered in (a), (b) or (c) above, but separable from those activities, are to be accounted for in accordance with this Statement.

4. This Statement does not cover the allocation of the depreciable amount of property, plant and equipment to future periods since this subject is dealt with in International Accounting Standard 4, Depreciation Accounting.

5. This Statement does not deal with the treatment of Government grants and makes only brief reference to the classification of leasehold rights as property, plant and equipment, to the capitalisation of borrowing costs and to assets acquired in a business combination. These subjects require more extensive consideration than can be given within this Statement.

Definitions

6. The following terms are used in this Statement with the meanings specified:

Property, plant and equipment are tangible assets that:

(a) are held by an enterprise for use in the production or supply of goods and services, for rental to others, or for administrative purposes and may include items held for the maintenance or repair of such assets;

(b) have been acquired or constructed with the intention of being used on a continuing basis; and

(c) are not intended for sale in the ordinary course of business.

Leasehold rights over assets which meet the criteria of (a), (b) and (c) above, may also be treated as property, plant and equipment in certain circumstances.

Fair value is the amount for which an asset could be exchanged between a knowledgeable, willing buyer and a knowledgeable, willing seller in an arm's length transaction.

Recoverable amount is that part of the net carrying amount of an asset that the enterprise can recover from the future use of the asset, including its net realisable value on disposal.

Explanation

7. Property, plant and equipment often comprise a major portion of the total assets of an enterprise, and therefore are significant in the presentation of financial position. Furthermore, the determination of whether an expenditure represents an asset or an expense can have a significant effect on an enterprise's reported results of operations.

Identification of Property, Plant and Equipment

8. The definition in paragraph 6 gives criteria for determining whether items are to be classified as property, plant and equipment. Judgement is required in applying the criteria to specific circumstances or specific types of enterprises. It may be appropriate to aggregate individually insignificant items, such as moulds, tools and dies, and to apply the criteria to the aggregate value. Alternatively, an enterprise may decide to expense an item which could otherwise have been included as property, plant and equipment, because the amount of the expenditure is immaterial.

9. Major spare parts and stand-by equipment are normally capitalised. Other spare parts and servicing equipment are usually carried as inventory and charged to income as consumed. However, if the spare parts and servicing equipment can be used only in connection with an item of property, plant and equipment and their use is expected to be irregular, it may be appropriate to allocate the total cost on a systematic basis to each accounting period over the useful life of the principal item.

10. In certain circumstances, the accounting for property, plant and equipment may be improved if the total expenditure is allocated to its component parts, provided they are in practice separable, and estimates are made of the useful lives of these components. For example, rather than treat an aircraft and its engines as one unit, it may be better to treat the engines as a separate unit if it is likely that their useful life is shorter than that of the aircraft as a whole.

Components of Cost

11. The cost of an item of property, plant and equipment comprises its purchase price, including import duties and non-refundable purchase taxes, and any directly attributable costs of bringing the asset to working condition for its intended use; any trade discounts and rebates are deducted in arriving at the purchase price. Examples of directly attributable costs are:

(a) site preparation;
(b) initial delivery and handling costs;
(c) installation cost, such as special foundations for plant;
(d) professional fees (architects, engineers, etc.).

Financing costs that are attributable to a construction project and that are incurred up to the completion of construction are sometimes also included in the gross carrying amount of the asset to which they relate.

12. When payment for an item of property, plant and equipment in working condition is deferred beyond normal credit terms, it may be appropriate to capitalise the purchase at the cash price equivalent and to charge the difference between this amount and the total payments as interest over the period of deferral.

13. Administration and other general overhead expenses are not a component of the cost of property, plant and equipment, unless they can be specifically related to the acquisition of the asset or bringing it to its working condition.

14. Start-up and related pre-production costs would not form part of the cost of property, plant and equipment unless they are necessary to bring the asset to its working condition.

Self-Constructed Property, Plant and Equipment

15. In arriving at the gross carrying amount of self-constructed property, plant and equipment the same principles apply as those described in paragraphs 11-14. Included in the gross carrying amount are costs of construction that relate directly to the specific asset and costs that are attributable to the construction activity in general and can be allocated to the specific asset. Any internal profits are eliminated in arriving at such costs.[1]

16. Cost inefficiencies in the production of self-constructed assets, whether due to temporarily idle capacity, industrial disputes or other causes, are normally not considered to be suitable for capitalisation. It is usually appropriate to have regard to a comparison with the cost of equivalent purchased assets or, if an enterprise makes similar assets for sale in the normal course of business, the cost of producing the assets for sale.

Non-Monetary Consideration

17. When an asset included in property, plant and equipment is acquired in exchange for another asset, its cost is usually determined by reference to the fair value of the consideration given. It may be appropriate to consider also the fair value of the asset acquired, if this is more clearly evident. An alternative accounting treatment that is sometimes used for an exchange of assets, particularly when the assets exchanged are similar, is to record the asset acquired at the net carrying amount of the asset given up. In each case, an adjustment is made for any balancing receipt or payment of cash or other consideration.

---

[1]In some countries, internal profits of public utilities are not eliminated to the extent that they are recognised in the determination of the rates charged to consumers in accordance with regulations determined by government authorities.

18. When an asset included in property, plant and equipment is acquired in exchange for shares or other securities in the enterprise, it is usually recorded at its fair value, or the fair value of the securities issued, whichever is the more clearly evident.

Improvements and Repairs

19. Frequently it is difficult to determine whether subsequent expenditures related to property, plant and equipment represent improvements that ought to be added to the gross carrying amount or repairs that ought to be charged to income. Only expenditure that increases the future benefits from the existing asset beyond its previously assessed standard of performance is included in the gross carrying amount. Examples of these future benefits include:

(a) an extension in the asset's estimated useful life;
(b) an increase in capacity; or
(c) a substantial improvement in the quality of output or a reduction in previously assessed operating costs.

Recovery of the Carrying Amount

20. The gross carrying amount of depreciable property, plant and equipment is normally recovered on a systematic basis over their useful lives. If the usefulness of an item or a group of items is permanently impaired, for example by damage or technological obsolescence, the recoverable amount may become less than the net carrying amount. In these circumstances, the net carrying amount is reduced to the recoverable amount and the difference is charged to income immediately.

Amount Substituted for Historical Cost

21. Sometimes financial statements that are otherwise prepared on a historical cost basis include part or all of property, plant and equipment at a valuation in substitution for historical cost and depreciation is calculated accordingly. Such financial statements are to be distinguished from financial statements prepared on a basis intended to reflect comprehensively the effects of changing prices. (See International Accounting Standard 15, Information Reflecting the Effects of Changing Prices).

22. A commonly accepted method of restating property, plant and equipment is by appraisal, normally undertaken by professionally qualified valuers. Other methods sometimes used are indexation and reference to current prices.

23. Two methods exist for presenting revalued amounts of property, plant and equipment in financial statements. Under one method, both the gross carrying amount and accumulated depreciation are restated in order to give a net carrying amount equal to the net revalued amount. Under the other method, accumulated depreciation is eliminated and the net revalued amount is treated as the new gross carrying amount. The method used is disclosed. In any event, an upward revaluation does not provide a basis for crediting to income the accumulated depreciation existing at the date of revaluation.

24. Different bases of valuation are sometimes used in the same financial statements to determine the carrying amount of the separate items within each of the categories of property, plant and equipment or for the different categories of property, plant and equipment. In these cases, it is necessary to disclose the gross carrying amounts included on each basis.

25. Selective revaluation of assets can lead to unrepresentative amounts being reported in financial statements. Accordingly, when revaluations do not cover all the assets of a given class, it is appropriate that the selection of assets to be revalued be made on a systematic basis. For example, an enterprise may revalue all its assets on a cyclical basis, or may revalue a whole class of assets within a unit or operating company.

26. It is not appropriate for the revaluation of a class of assets to result in the net carrying amount of that class being greater than the recoverable amount of the assets of that class.

27. An increase in net carrying amount arising on revaluation of property, plant and equipment is normally credited directly to shareholders' interests under the heading of revaluation surplus and is usually regarded as not available for distribution. A decrease in net carrying amount arising on revaluation of property, plant and equipment is charged to income except that, to the extent that such a decrease is considered to be related to a previous increase on revaluation that is included in revaluation surplus, it is sometimes charged against that

earlier increase. It sometimes happens that an increase to be recorded is a reversal of a previous decrease arising on revaluation which has been charged to income, in which case the increase is credited to income to the extent that it offsets the previously recorded decrease.

28. Effects on taxes on income, if any, resulting from the substitution of other amounts for historical cost are dealt with in International Accounting Standard 12, Accounting for Taxes on Income.

Retirements and Disposals

29. An item of property, plant and equipment is eliminated from the financial statements on disposal or when no further benefit to the enterprise is expected from its use and disposal.

30. Items of property, plant and equipment that have been retired from active use and are held for disposal are stated at the lower of their net carrying amount and net realisable value and are shown separately in the financial statements. Any expected loss is recognised immediately in the income statement.

31. In historical cost financial statements gains or losses arising on disposal are generally recognised in the income statement.

32. On disposal of a previously revalued item of property, plant and equipment, the difference between net disposal proceeds and the net carrying amount is normally charged or credited to income. The amount standing in revaluation surplus following the retirement or disposal of an asset which relates to that asset may be transferred to retained earnings.

Disclosure

33. Certain specific disclosures on accounting for property, plant and equipment are already required by International Accounting Standard 4, Depreciation Accounting, and International Accounting Standard 5, Information to be Disclosed in Financial Statements.

34. Further disclosures that are sometimes made in financial statements include:

(a) a reconciliation of the amounts of property, plant and equipment at the beginning and end of an accounting period showing additions, disposals, acquisitions through business combinations and other movements;

(b) the amount of payments on account of property, plant and equipment in the course of construction or acquisition; and

(c) the carrying amount of temporarily idle property, plant and equipment.

International Accounting Standard 16

Accounting for Property, Plant and Equipment

International Accounting Standard 16 comprises paragraphs 35–51 of this Statement. The Standard should be read in the context of paragraphs 1–34 of the Statement and of the Preface to Statements of International Accounting Standards.

35. The items determined in accordance with the definition in paragraph 6 of this Statement should be included under property, plant and equipment in financial statements.

36. The gross carrying amount of an asset included in property, plant and equipment should be either historical cost or a revaluation, computed in accordance with this Standard. The method of accounting for assets included at historical cost is set out in paragraphs 37 to 43; the method of accounting for revalued assets is set out in paragraphs 44 to 49.

Assets carried at Historical Cost

37. The cost of an asset included in property, plant and equipment should comprise its purchase price and any directly attributable costs of bringing the asset to working condition for its intended use.

38. The cost of self-constructed property, plant and equipment should comprise those costs that relate directly to the specific asset and those that are attributable to the construction activity in general and can be allocated to the specific asset. Cost inefficiencies should not be included as part of such cost.

39. When an item of property, plant and equipment is acquired in exchange or in part exchange for another asset, the cost of the asset acquired should be recorded either at fair value or at the net carrying amount of the asset given up, adjusted for any balancing payment or receipt of cash or other consideration. For these purposes fair value may be determined by reference either to the asset given up or to the asset acquired, whichever is the more clearly evident. Property, plant and equipment acquired in exchange for shares or other securities in the enterprise should be recorded at its fair value, or the fair value of the securities issued, whichever is the more clearly evident.

40. Subsequent expenditures related to an item of property, plant and equipment should be added to its carrying amount only if they increase the future benefits from the existing asset beyond its previously assessed standard of performance.

41. If a permanent impairment to an item or a group of items of property, plant and equipment causes the recoverable amount to fall below the net carrying amount, the net carrying amount should be reduced to the recoverable amount and the difference charged to income immediately. Any items retired from active use and held for disposal should be similarly treated and shown separately in the financial statements.

42. Property, plant and equipment should be eliminated from the financial statements on disposal or when no further benefit is expected from its use and disposal.

43. Gains or losses arising from the retirement or disposal of property, plant and equipment which is carried at cost should be recognised in the income statement.

Assets carried at Revalued Amounts

44. When property, plant and equipment is revalued in financial statements, an entire class of assets should be revalued, or the selection of assets for revaluation should be made on a systematic basis. This basis should be disclosed.

45. The revaluation in financial statements of a class of assets should not result in the net carrying amount of that class being greater than the recoverable amount of assets of that class.

46. When property, plant and equipment is revalued upwards, any accumulated depreciation existing at the date of the revaluation should not be credited to income.

47. An increase in net carrying amount arising on revaluation of property, plant and equipment should be credited directly to shareholders' interests under the heading of revaluation surplus, except that, to the extent that such increase is related to and not greater than a decrease arising on revaluation previously recorded as a charge to income, it may be credited to income. A decrease in net carrying amount arising on revaluation of property, plant and equipment should be charged directly to income except that, to the extent that such a decrease is related to an increase which was previously recorded as a credit to revaluation surplus and which has not been subsequently reversed or utilised, it should be charged directly to that account.

48. The provisions of paragraphs 40, 41 and 42 are also applicable to property, plant and equipment included in financial statements at a revaluation.

49. On disposal of a previously revalued item of property, plant and equipment the difference between net disposal proceeds and the net carrrying amount should be charged or credited to income.

Disclosure

50. In addition to the disclosures required by International Accounting Standard 4, Depreciation Accounting, and International Accounting Standard 5, Information to be Disclosed in Financial Statements, the following disclosures should be made:

    (a)   the bases used for determining the gross carrying amounts of property, plant and equipment. When more than one basis has been used, the gross carrying amount for each basis in each category should be given; and

    (b)   in cases where property, plant and equipment are stated at revalued amounts, the method adopted to compute these amounts should be disclosed, including the policy in regard to the frequency of revaluations. The nature of any indices used, the year of any appraisal made, and whether an external valuer was involved should also be disclosed.

Effective Date

51. This International Accounting Standard becomes operative for financial statements covering periods beginning on or after 1 January 1983.

International Accounting Standard 17

Accounting for Leases

Contents

Introduction

1. This Statement deals with accounting for leases. It does not deal with the following specialised types of leases:

   (a) Lease agreements to explore for or use natural resources, such as oil, gas, timber, metals and other mineral rights.

   (b) Licensing agreements for such items as motion picture films, video recordings, plays, manuscripts, patents and copyrights.

Definitions

2. The following terms are used in this Statement with the meanings specified:

Lease: an agreement whereby the lessor conveys to the lessee in return for rent the right to use an asset for an agreed period of time.[1]

Finance lease: a lease that transfers substantially all the risks and rewards incident to ownership of an asset. Title may or may not eventually be transferred.

Operating lease: a lease other than a finance lease.

Non-cancellable lease: a lease that is cancellable only: (a) upon the occurrence of some remote contingency, (b) with the permission of the lessor, (c) if the lessee enters into a new lease for the same or an equivalent asset with the same lessor, or (d) upon payment by the lessee of an additional amount such that, at inception, continuation of the lease is reasonably certain.

Inception of the lease: the earlier of the date of the lease agreement or of a commitment by the parties to the principal provisions of the lease.

Lease term: the non-cancellable period for which the lessee has contracted to lease the asset together with any further terms for which the lessee has the option to continue to lease the asset, with or without further payment, which option at the inception of the lease it is reasonably certain that the lessee will exercise.

---

[1] The definition of a lease includes contracts for the hire of an asset which contain a provision giving the hirer an option to acquire title to the asset upon the fulfilment of agreed conditions. These contracts are described as hire purchase contracts in some countries. In some countries, different names are used for agreements which have the characteristics of a lease (e.g. bare-boat charters).

Minimum lease payments: the payments over the lease term that the lessee is or can be required to make (excluding costs for services and taxes to be paid by and be reimbursable to the lessor) together with:

(a)   in the case of the lessee, any amounts guaranteed by him or by a party related to him; or

(b)   in the case of the lessor, any residual value guaranteed to him by either the lessee or a party related to the lessee or an independent third party financially capable of meeting this guarantee.

However, if the lessee has the option to purchase the asset at a price which is expected to be sufficiently lower than the fair value at the date the option becomes exercisable that, at the inception of the lease, it is reasonably certain that the option will be exercised, the minimum lease payments comprise the minimum rentals payable over the lease term and the payment required to exercise this purchase option.

Fair value: the amount for which an asset could be exchanged between a knowledgeable, willing buyer and a knowledgeable, willing seller in an arm's length transaction.

Useful life: is either (a) the period over which a depreciable asset is expected to be used by the enterprise; or (b) the number of production or similar units expected to be obtained from the asset by the enterprise.

Unguaranteed residual value: that portion of the residual value of the leased asset (estimated at the inception of the lease), the realisation of which by the lessor is not assured or is guaranteed solely by a party related to the lessor.

Gross investment in the lease: the aggregate of the minimum lease payments under a finance lease from the standpoint of the lessor and any unguaranteed residual value accruing to the lessor.

Unearned finance income: the difference between the lessor's gross investment in the lease and its present value.

Net investment in the lease: the gross investment in the lease less unearned finance income.

Net cash investment: the balance of the cash outflows and inflows in respect of the lease excluding flows relating to insurance, maintenance and similar costs rechargeable to the lessee. The cash outflows include payments made to acquire the asset, tax payments, interest and principal on third party financing. Inflows include rental receipts, receipts from residual values, and grants, tax credits and other tax savings or repayments arising from the lease.

Interest rate implicit in the lease: the discount rate that, at the inception of the lease, causes the aggregate present value of (a) the minimum lease payments, from the standpoint of the lessor, and (b) the unguaranteed residual value to be equal to the fair value of the leased asset, net of any grants and tax credits receivable by the lessor.

Lessee's incremental borrowing rate of interest: the rate of interest the lessee would have to pay on a similar lease or, if that is not determinable, the rate that, at the inception of the lease, the lessee would incur to borrow over a similar term and with a similar security the funds necessary to purchase the asset.

Contingent rental: a rental that is not fixed in amount but is based on a factor other than just the passage of time (e.g. percentage of sales, amount of usage, price indices, market rates of interest).

Explanation

Classification of Leases

3. The classification of leases adopted in this Standard is based on the extent to which risks and rewards incident to ownership of a leased asset lie with the lessor or the lessee. Risks include the possibilities of losses from idle capacity or technological obsolescence and of variations in return due to changing economic conditions. Rewards may be represented by the expectation of profitable operation over the asset's economic life and of gain from appreciation in value or realisation of a residual value.

4. Since the transaction between a lessor and a lessee is based on a lease agreement common to both parties, it is appropriate to use consistent definitions. Normally the two parties will classify the lease in the same way. Nevertheless, the application of these definitions to the differing circumstances of the two parties may sometimes result in the same lease being classified differently by lessor and lessee.

5. Whether a lease is a finance lease or not depends on the substance of the transaction rather than the form of the contract. A lease is classified as a finance lease if it transfers substantially all the risks and rewards incident to ownership. Such a lease is normally non-cancellable and secures for the lessor the recovery of his capital outlay plus a return for

the funds invested.[2] A lease is classified as an operating lease if substantially all the risks and rewards incident to ownership are not transferred.

The Accounting Treatment of Leases in the Financial Statements of Lessees

6. Transactions and other events ought to be accounted for and presented in accordance with their substance and financial reality and not merely with legal form. While the legal form of a lease agreement is that the lessee may acquire no legal title to the leased asset, in the case of finance leases the substance and financial reality are that the lessee acquires the economic benefits of the use of the leased asset for the major part of its useful life in return for entering into an obligation to pay for that right an amount approximating to the fair value of the asset and the related finance charge.

7. If such lease transactions are not reflected in the lessee's balance sheet, the economic resources and the level of obligations of an enterprise are understated, thereby distorting financial ratios. It is therefore appropriate that a finance lease be recorded in the lessee's balance sheet both as an asset and as an obligation to pay future rentals.

Finance Leases – Determination of the Amounts of Leased Assets and the Related Liabilities

8. The rights and obligations arising from a finance lease are recorded at the beginning of the lease term at the fair value of the leased property net of grants and tax credits receivable by the lessor, or, if lower, at the present value of the minimum lease payments. At the inception of the lease, the asset and the liability for the future rentals are recorded in the balance sheet at the same amounts.

---

[2] Examples of situations where a lease would normally be classified as a finance lease are:
(a) The lease transfers ownership of the asset to the lessee by the end of the lease term.
(b) The lessee has the option to purchase the asset at a price which is expected to be sufficiently lower than the fair value at the date the option becomes exercisable that, at the inception of the lease, it is reasonably certain that the option will be exercised.
(c) The lease term is for the major part of the useful life of the asset. Title may or may not eventually be transferred.
(d) The present value at the inception of the lease of the minimum lease payments is greater than or equal to substantially all of the fair value of the leased asset net of grants and tax credits to the lessor at that time. Title may or may not eventually be transferred.

9. In calculating the present value of the minimum lease payments the discount factor is the interest rate implicit in the lease, if it is practicable to determine; if not, the lessee's incremental borrowing rate is used.

10. The depreciable amount of a leased asset is allocated to each accounting period during the period of expected use on a systematic basis consistent with the depreciation policy the lessee adopts for depreciable assets that are owned. If there is reasonable certainty that the lessee will obtain ownership by the end of the lease term, the period of expected use is the useful life of the asset; otherwise the asset is depreciated over the shorter of the lease term or its useful life.

11. The difference between the total minimum lease payments over the lease term and the initial recorded liability represents the finance charge. This charge is allocated to periods during the lease term so as to produce a constant periodic rate of interest on the remaining balance of the liability during each period. In practice, some form of approximation is sometimes used to simplify the calculation.

12. A finance lease gives rise to a depreciation charge for the asset and a finance charge for each accounting period. The sum of these amounts is not normally the same as the rentals payable for the period and it is therefore inappropriate simply to charge the rentals payable to income. Accordingly, the asset and the related liability are unlikely to be equal in amount after the inception of the lease.

Operating Leases

13. For operating leases, rental expense (excluding costs for services such as insurance and maintenance) is recognised on a systematic basis that is representative of the time pattern of the user's benefit, even if the payments are not on that basis.

The Accounting Treatment of Leases in the Financial Statements of Lessors

Finance Leases

14. Under a finance lease substantially all the risks and rewards incident to ownership are transferred by the lessor, and thus the lease rentals receivable are treated by the lessor as repayments of principal and finance income to reimburse and reward him for his investment and services.

15. A lessor aims to allocate finance income over the lease term on a systematic and rational basis. This income allocation is usually based on a pattern reflecting a constant periodic return on the lessor's net investment outstanding in respect of the finance lease. Lease rentals relating to the accounting period, excluding costs for services, are applied against the gross investment in the lease to reduce both the principal and the unearned finance income.

16. In spreading income on a systematic basis the lessor recognises uncertainties relating for example to the collectibility of lease rentals or to future levels of interest rates. The longer the term of the lease the greater the risks involved and the consideration of prudence may require modification of the pattern of income recognition to reflect the circumstances.

17. Estimated unguaranteed residual values used in computing the lessor's gross investment in a lease are reviewed regularly. If there has been a permanent reduction in the estimated unguaranteed residual value the income allocation over the lease term is revised and any reduction in respect of amounts already accrued is charged to income immediately.

18. Initial direct costs, such as commissions and legal fees, are often incurred by lessors in negotiating and arranging a lease. For finance leases, these initial direct costs are incurred to produce finance income and are either expensed immediately or allocated against this income over the lease term. The latter may be achieved by charging to income the cost as incurred and recognising as income in the same period a portion of the unearned finance income equal to the initial direct costs.

19. When assessing whether the proposed terms of a lease will produce an acceptable return on the required investment, a lessor would consider the pattern of cash flows associated with the lease transaction. In some cases the pattern of cash flows related to a leased asset will be significantly affected by the reduction or deferral of income taxes, by the receipt of grants and by the provision of finance by third parties as described in paragraph 21.

20. When income tax factors that affect the cash flow are predictable with reasonable certainty, they may be taken into consideration in accounting for income from the lease. In these cases, income recognition in respect of finance leases is sometimes based on a pattern reflecting a constant periodic return, not on the lessor's net investment outstanding

but on the lessor's net cash investment outstanding, subject to the overriding consideration of prudence.

21. Certain finance lease transactions are structured in such a way that they involve at least three parties, the lessee, the lessor and one or more long-term creditors who provide part of the acquisition finance for the leased asset usually without any general recourse to the lessor. These lease transactions are sometimes known as leveraged leases. In such cases, the lessor records his investment in the lease net of the non-recourse debt and the related finance costs to the third-party creditors and recognises finance income on the basis of the lessor's net cash investment outstanding in respect of the finance lease.

22. Since very different results can flow from the use of net investment and the use of net cash investment for allocation of income, the method used needs to be applied consistently to leases of the same financial character and disclosed.

Finance Leasing by Manufacturers or Dealers

23. Manufacturers or dealers often offer to customers the choice of either buying or leasing an asset. A finance lease of an asset by a manufacturer or dealer lessor gives rise to two types of income:

(a) the profit or loss equivalent to the profit or loss resulting from an outright sale of the asset being leased, at normal selling prices, reflecting any applicable volume or trade discounts; and

(b) the finance income over the lease term.

24. The sales revenue recorded at the inception of a finance lease by a manufacturer or dealer lessor is the fair value of the asset, or, if lower, the sum of the present values of the minimum lease payments and the estimated unguaranteed residual value accruing to the lessor, computed at a commercial rate of interest. The cost of sale recognised at the inception of the lease is the cost, or carrying amount if different, of the leased property. The difference between the sales revenue and the cost of sale is the selling profit, which is recognised in accordance with the policy normally followed by the enterprise for sales.

25. Manufacturer or dealer lessors sometimes quote artificially low rates of interest in order to attract customers. The use of such a rate would result in an excessive portion of the total income from the transaction being recognised at the time of sale.

26. Initial direct costs are usually charged to income at the inception of the lease because they are mainly related to earning the manufacturer's or dealer's selling profit.

Operating Leases

27. Under an operating lease, the risks and rewards incident to ownership of an asset remain with the lessor. Therefore, the asset is treated by the lessor as a depreciable asset and rentals receivable are included in income over the lease term. A manufacturer or dealer lessor does not recognise any selling profit on entering into an operating lease because it is not the equivalent of a sale.

28. Costs, including depreciation, incurred in earning the rental income are charged to income. Rental income (excluding receipts for services provided such as insurance and maintenance) is normally recognised on a straight line basis over the lease term even if the receipts are not on such a basis, unless another systematic basis is more representative of the time pattern of the earnings process contained in the lease.

29. A leased asset is depreciated on a basis consistent with the lessor's normal depreciation policy for similar assets: the depreciable amount of the asset being allocated on a systematic basis to each accounting period during its useful life.

30. Initial direct costs incurred specifically to earn revenues from an operating lease are either deferred and allocated to income over the lease term in proportion to the recognition of rental income, or are written off in the period in which they are incurred.

Land and Buildings

31. Leases of land and buildings are classified as operating or finance leases in the same way as leases of other assets. However, a characteristic of land is that it normally has an indefinite useful life and, if title is not expected to pass to the lessee by the end of the lease term, the lessee does not receive substantially all of the risks and rewards incident to ownership. Such a lease is therefore properly classified as an operating lease. A premium paid for such a leasehold represents pre-paid rental charges which are amortised over the lease term.

32. Many buildings that are leased have a useful life that is expected to extend well beyond the end of the lease term. Moreover, long-term leases for buildings often contain provisions whereby rents are regularly

adjusted upwards to market rates. If title is not expected to pass or if rents are regularly adjusted to market rates, the lessor retains a significant part of the risks and rewards incident to ownership and such leases are therefore normally classified as operating leases.

Sale and Leaseback

33. A sale and leaseback transaction involves the sale of an asset by the vendor and the leasing of the same asset back to the vendor. The rentals and the sale price are usually interdependent as they are negotiated as a package and need not represent fair values. The accounting treatment of a sale and leaseback transaction depends upon the type of lease involved.

34. If the leaseback is a finance lease, the transaction is a means whereby the lessor provides finance to the lessee, with the asset as security. For this reason it is not appropriate to regard an excess of sales proceeds over the carrying amount as a realised profit. Such excess, if recognised, is deferred and amortised over the lease term.

35. If the leaseback is an operating lease, and the rentals and the sale price are established at fair value, there has in effect been a normal sale transaction and any profit or loss is normally recognised immediately.

36. If the leaseback is an operating lease and the sale price is below fair value any profit or loss is recognised immediately except that, if the loss is compensated by future rentals at below market price, it is deferred and amortised in proportion to the rental payments over the period for which the asset is expected to be used. If the sale price is above fair value, the excess over fair value is deferred and amortised over the period for which the asset is expected to be used.

37. For operating leases, if the fair value at the time of the transaction is less than the carrying amount, a loss equal to the amount of the difference between the carrying amount and fair value is recognised immediately. For finance leases, no such adjustment is necessary unless there has been a permanent impairment in value in which case the carrying amount is reduced to recoverable amount in accordance with International Accounting Standard 16, Accounting for Property, Plant and Equipment.

Disclosure

Disclosures in the Financial Statements of Lessees

38. It is appropriate that the amount of assets used by the lessee that are the subject of finance leases be separately identified in the financial statements. It is often useful to have this disclosure presented by each major class of asset. The aggregate amount of the related liabilities is shown either as the total of the minimum lease payments, with future finance charges being separately deducted, or as the net present value of the liabilities, disclosing in summary form the interest rates used as the discounting factors. It is not appropriate for the liabilities for leased assets to be presented in the financial statements as a deduction from the leased assets.

39. The rental expense under operating leases is sometimes disclosed for each period for which an income statement is presented. This is intended to indicate the measure of an enterprise's dependence on rented rather than owned assets.

40. International Accounting Standard 5, Information to be Disclosed in Financial Statements, requires disclosure of repayment terms and interest rates for loans falling due in more than one year. For finance leases, it may be more convenient to disclose in summary form the amounts of future payments and the periods in which they will become due (for example, each of the next five years and each succeeding five year period). Similarly, in order to show an enterprise's commitments, it is appropriate to disclose in summary form the future rental payments under non-cancellable operating leases of more than one year and the periods in which they will become due (for example, each of the next five years and each succeeding five year period).

41. Certain other disclosures relevant to both finance and operating leases may also be appropriate. Examples of these are:
   (a) the nature of any renewal options, purchase options or escalation clauses;
   (b) financial restrictions imposed by the lease agreement such as limitations on additional borrowing or further leasing;
   (c) the nature of any contingent rentals such as those based on usage or sales;
   (d) the nature of any contingent liability in respect of costs expected at the end of the lease term.

Disclosures in the Financial Statements of Lessors

42. The lessor's gross investment in finance leases and the amount of unearned finance income is disclosed. As an indicator of growth it is often found useful to disclose also the gross investment less unearned income in new business added during the accounting period after deducting the relevant amounts for cancelled leases. Disclosure is sometimes made of the lessor's general leasing arrangements and of the future minimum lease payments to be received for specified future periods.

43. Assets held for operating leases are usually included as property, plant and equipment in the balance sheet. The amount of these leased assets at each balance sheet date, presented by each major class of asset, is often disclosed. Sometimes information is provided on the lessor's general leasing arrangements, the amount of rental income from operating leases and the minimum future rentals on non-cancellable leases both in the aggregate and in specified future periods.

International Accounting Standard 17
Accounting for Leases

International Accounting Standard 17 comprises paragraphs 44–64 of this Statement. The Standard should be read in the context of paragraphs 1–43 of this Statement and of the Preface to Statements of International Accounting Standards.

Accounting for Leases in the Financial Statements of Lessees

Finance Leases

44. A finance lease should be reflected in the balance sheet of a lessee by recording an asset and a liability at amounts equal at the inception of the lease to the fair value of the leased property net of grants and tax credits receivable by the lessor or, if lower, at the present value of the minimum lease payments. In calculating the present value of the minimum lease payments the discount factor is the interest rate implicit in the lease, if this is practicable to determine; if not, the lessee's incremental borrowing rate is used.

45. Rentals should be apportioned between the finance charge and the reduction of the outstanding liability. The finance charge should be allocated to periods during the lease term so as to produce a constant periodic rate of interest on the remaining balance of the liability for each period. Some form of approximation may be used.

46. A finance lease gives rise to a depreciation charge for the asset as well as a finance charge for each accounting period. The depreciation policy for leased assets should be consistent with that for depreciable assets which are owned, and the depreciation charged should be calculated on the basis set out in International Accounting Standard 4, Depreciation Accounting. If there is no reasonable certainty that the lessee will obtain ownership by the end of the lease term, the asset should be fully depreciated over the shorter of the lease term or its useful life.

Operating Leases

47. The charge to income under an operating lease should be the rental expense for the accounting period, recognised on a systematic basis that is representative of the time pattern of the user's benefit.

Accounting for Leases in the Financial Statements of Lessors

Finance Leases

48. An asset held under a finance lease should be recorded in the balance sheet not as property, plant and equipment but as a receivable, at an amount equal to the net investment in the lease.

49. Subject to the consideration of prudence, the recognition of finance income should be based on a pattern reflecting a constant periodic rate of return on either the lessor's net investment outstanding or the net cash investment outstanding in respect of the finance lease. The method used should be applied consistently to leases of a similar financial character.

50. Manufacturer or dealer lessors should include selling profit or loss in income in accordance with the policy normally followed by the enterprise for outright sales. If artificially low rates of interest are quoted, selling profit should be restricted to that which would apply if a commercial rate of interest were charged. Initial direct costs should be charged to income at the inception of the lease.

Operating Leases

51. Assets held for operating leases should be recorded as property, plant and equipment in the balance sheet of lessors.

52. Rental income should be recognised on a straight line basis over the lease term, unless another systematic basis is more representative of the time pattern of the earnings process contained in the lease.

53. The depreciation of leased assets should be on a basis consistent with the lessor's normal depreciation policy for similar assets, and the depreciation charge should be calculated on the basis set out in International Accounting Standard 4, Depreciation Accounting.

Accounting for Sale and Leaseback Transactions

54. If a sale and leaseback transaction results in a finance lease, any excess of sales proceeds over the carrying amount should not be immediately recognised in income in the financial statements of a seller-lessee. If such an excess is recognised, it should be deferred and amortised over the lease term.

55. If a sale and leaseback transaction results in an operating lease, and it is clear that the transaction is established at fair value, any profit or loss should be recognised immediately. If the sale price is below fair value, any profit or loss should be recognised immediately except that, if the loss is compensated by future rentals at below market price, it should be deferred and amortised in proportion to the rental payments over the period for which the asset is expected to be used. If the sale price is above fair value, the excess over fair value should be deferred and amortised over the period for which the asset is expected to be used.

56. For operating leases, if the fair value at the time of a sale and leaseback transaction is less than the carrying amount of the asset, a loss equal to the amount of the difference between the carrying amount and fair value should be recognised immediately.

Disclosure

Disclosures in the Financial Statements of Lessees

57. Disclosure should be made of the amount of assets that are the subject of finance leases at each balance sheet date. Liabilities related to these leased assets should be shown separately from other liabilities, differentiating between the current and long-term portions.

58. Commitments for minimum lease payments under finance leases and under non-cancellable operating leases with a term of more than one year should be disclosed in summary form giving the amounts and periods in which the payments will become due.

59. Disclosure should be made of significant financing restrictions, renewal or purchase options, contingent rentals and other contingencies arising from leases.

Disclosures in the Financial Statements of Lessors

60. Disclosure should be made at each balance sheet date of the gross investment in leases reported as finance leases, and the related unearned finance income and unguaranteed residual values of leased assets.

61. Disclosure should be made of the basis used for allocating income so as to produce a constant periodic rate of return, indicating whether the return relates to the net investment outstanding or the net cash investment outstanding in the lease. If more than one basis is used, the bases should be disclosed.

62. When a significant part of the lessor's business comprises operating leases, the lessor should disclose the amount of assets by each major class of asset together with the related accumulated depreciation at each balance sheet date.

Effective Date

63. This International Accounting Standard becomes operative for financial statements covering periods beginning on or after 1 January, 1984, subject only to the transitional provisions set out in paragraph 64.

Transitional Provisions for Finance Leases

64. For a period of four years from the effective date of this Standard, transitional arrangements will apply whereby, whilst lessees and lessors are encouraged to apply the full provisions of the Standard, they may opt not to apply it in its entirety provided the following information is disclosed:

by lessees: either (a) (i) the amounts of the assets and liabilities that would have been included in the balance sheet had the finance leases been accounted for in accordance with the requirements of the Standard, and

(ii) the effect on net income which would have resulted;

or (b) (i) the amounts of rentals on such leases charged to income, and

(ii) commitments for rentals on such leases payable in subsequent accounting periods.

by lessors: the methods used to recognise income under finance leases.

Appendix

This appendix has been prepared by the IASC Secretariat for guidance in interpreting Statement of International Accounting Standard 17. It does not form part of that Statement.

Classification of a Lease

A lease is a finance lease if it transfers substantially all the risks and rewards incident to ownership. The following chart represents examples of situations in which a lease would normally be classified as a finance lease. The examples do not necessarily reflect all possible situations in which a lease may be classified as a finance lease, nor should a lease necessarily be classified as a finance lease by virtue of the route followed on this chart. The substance of the transaction determines the classification.

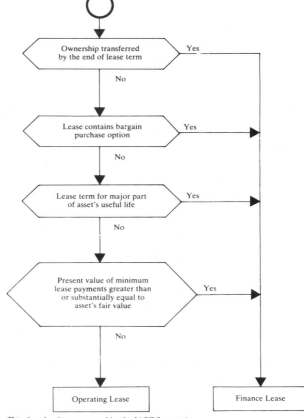

This chart has been prepared by the IASC Secretariat.

220

Accounting for a finance lease by a lessee

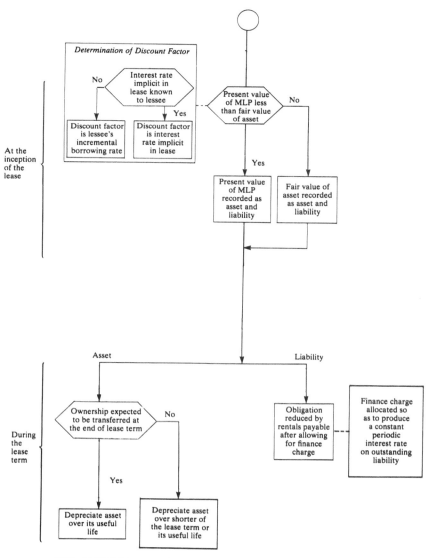

MLP = Minimum lease payments

This chart has been prepared by the IASC Secretariat.

Accounting for a finance lease by a lessor

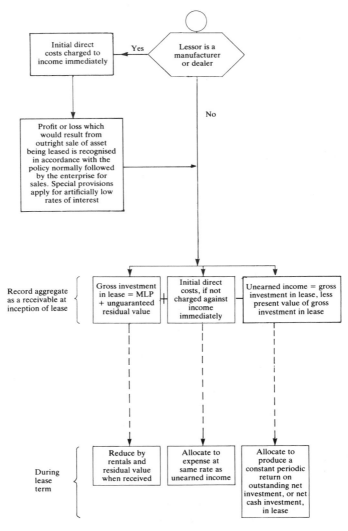

MLP = Minimum lease payments

This chart has been prepared by the IASC Secretariat.

International Accounting Standard 18

Revenue Recognition

Contents

Introduction

1. This Statement deals with the bases for recognition of revenue in the income statements of enterprises. The Statement is concerned with the recognition of revenue arising in the course of the ordinary activities of the enterprise from:

- the sale of goods,
- the rendering of services, and
- the use by others of enterprise resources yielding interest, royalties and dividends.

2. This Statement does not deal with the following specialised aspects of revenue recognition:

(a) Dividends arising from investments which are accounted for under the equity method (see International Accounting Standard 3, Consolidated Financial Statements).

(b) Revenue arising from construction contracts (see International Accounting Standard 11, Accounting for Construction Contracts).

(c) Revenue arising from lease agreements (see International Accounting Standard 17, Accounting for Leases).

(d) Revenue arising from government grants and other similar subsidies.

(e) Revenue of insurance companies arising from insurance contracts.

3. Examples of items not encompassed within the definition of 'revenue' for the purpose of this Statement are:

(a) Realised gains resulting from the disposal of, and unrealised gains resulting from the holding of, non-current assets.

(b) Unrealised holding gains resulting from the change in value of current assets, and the natural increases in herds and agricultural and forest products.

(c) Realised or unrealised gains resulting from changes in foreign exchange rates and adjustments arising on the translation of foreign currency financial statements.

(d) Realised gains resulting from the discharge of an obligation at less than its carrying amount.

(e) Unrealised gains resulting from the restatement of the carrying amount of an obligation.

Definitions

4. The following terms are used in this Statement with the meanings specified:

Revenue is the gross inflow of cash, receivables or other consideration arising in the course of the ordinary activities of an enterprise from the sale of goods, from the rendering of services, and from the use by others of enterprise resources yielding interest, royalties and dividends. Revenue is measured by the charges made to customers or clients for goods supplied and services rendered to them and by the charges and rewards arising from the use of resources by them. It excludes amounts collected on behalf of third parties such as certain taxes. In an agency relationship, the revenue is the amount of commission and not the gross inflow of cash, receivables or other consideration.

Completed contract method [1] is a method of accounting which recognises revenue in the income statement only when the sale of goods or the rendering of services under a contract is completed or substantially completed.

Percentage of completion method [1] is a method of accounting which recognises revenue in the income statement proportionately with the degree of completion of goods or services under a contract.

Fair value is the amount for which an asset could be exchanged between a knowledgeable, willing buyer and a knowledgeable, willing seller in an arm's length transaction.

Explanation

5. Revenue recognition is mainly concerned with when revenue is recognised in the income statement of an enterprise. The amount of revenue arising on a transaction is usually determined by agreement between the parties involved in the transaction. When uncertainties exist regarding the determination of the amount, or its associated costs, these uncertainties may influence the timing of revenue recognition.

---

[1] This term is also used in International Accounting Standard 11, Accounting for Construction Contracts.

Sale of Goods

6. A key criterion for determining when to recognise revenue from a transaction involving the sale of goods is that the seller has transferred to the buyer the significant risks and rewards of ownership of the asset sold. An example of a significant risk of ownership that may be retained by a seller would be liability for unsatisfactory performance not covered by normal warranty provisions. If the seller retains significant risks of ownership, it is normally inappropriate to recognise the transaction as a sale. Where only a non-significant risk of ownership is retained by the seller, this will not normally preclude the recognition of revenue, for example, when title is retained by the seller solely to protect the collectability of the amount due.

7. Assessing when the risks and rewards of ownership are transferred to the buyer with sufficient certainty requires an examination of the circumstances of the transaction. In most cases, transfer of the legal title either results in or coincides with the passing of possession or the transfer of the risks and rewards of ownership to the buyer, such as in the case of most retail sales. In other cases, the passing of legal title may occur at a different time from the passing of possession or of the risks and rewards of ownership.

8. The following considerations are relevant in deciding whether significant risks and rewards of ownership have been transferred to the buyer:

(a) whether any significant acts of performance remain to be completed;

(b) whether the seller retains any continuing managerial involvement in, or effective control of, the goods transferred to a degree usually associated with ownership;

(c) whether the payment of the debt relating to the goods transferred is dependent on the derivation of revenue by the buyer from the goods.

9. At certain stages in specific industries, such as when agricultural crops have been harvested or mineral ores have been extracted, performance may be substantially complete prior to the execution of the transaction generating revenue. In such cases when sale is assured under a forward contract or a government guarantee or where a homogeneous market exists and there is a negligible risk of failure to sell, the goods

involved are often valued at net realisable value. Such amounts, while not revenue as defined in this Statement, are sometimes recognised in the income statement and appropriately described.

Rendering of Services.

10. Revenue from service transactions is usually recognised as the service is performed, either by the percentage of completion method or by the completed contract method.

(a) Percentage of completion method – Performance consists of the execution of more than one act. Revenue is recognised proportionately by reference to the performance of each act. The revenue recognised under this method would be determined on the basis of sales value, associated costs, number of acts or other suitable basis. For practical purposes, when services are provided by an indeterminate number of acts over a specific period of time, revenue is recognised on a straight line basis over the specific period unless there is evidence that some other method better represents the pattern of performance.

(b) Completed contract method – Performance consists of the execution of a single act. Alternatively, services are performed in more than a single act, and the services yet to be performed are so significant in relation to the transaction taken as a whole that performance cannot be deemed to have been completed until the execution of those acts. The completed contract method is relevant to these patterns of performance and accordingly revenue is recognised when the sole or final act takes place.

The Use by Others of Enterprise Resources yielding Interest, Royalties and Dividends

11. The use by others of such enterprise resources gives rise to:
(a) interest – charges for the use of cash resources or amounts due to the enterprise;
(b) royalties – charges for the use of such assets as patents, trademarks and copyrights;
(c) dividends – rewards from the holding of investments not accounted for under the equity method of accounting.

12. Interest accrues, in most circumstances, on a daily basis determined by the principal outstanding and the rate applicable. A discount or premium on debt securities held is treated as though it were interest accruing over the period to maturity.

13. Royalties accrue in accordance with the terms of the relevant agreement and are usually recognised on that basis unless, having regard to the substance of the transaction, it is more appropriate to recognise revenue on some other systematic and rational basis.

14. Dividends from investments not accounted for under the equity method of accounting are not recognised in the income statement until a right to receive payment is established. (See International Accounting Standard 3, Consolidated Financial Statements, for the situation where investments are accounted for under the equity method of accounting).

15. When interest, royalties and dividends from foreign countries require exchange permission and a delay in remittance is anticipated, revenue recognition may need to be postponed.

Effect of Uncertainties on Revenue Recognition

16. Recognition of revenue requires that the revenue is measurable and that at the time of sale or the rendering of the service it would not be unreasonable to expect ultimate collection. A reasonable expectation of ultimate collection does not, of itself, ensure such a collection.

17. Where the ability to assess the ultimate collection with reasonable certainty is lacking at the time of sale or the rendering of the service, revenue recognition is postponed. In such cases, it may be appropriate to recognise revenue only as cash is received. Where there is no uncertainty as to ultimate collection, revenue is recognised at the time of sale even though cash payments are made by instalments.

18. When the uncertainty relates to collectability and arises subsequent to the time of sale or the rendering of the service, it is more appropriate to make a separate provision to reflect the uncertainty rather than to adjust the amount of revenue originally recorded.

19. Uncertainties relating to the measurement of revenue may involve one or more of the following issues:

    (a) *Consideration*

An essential criterion for the recognition of revenue is that the minimum consideration receivable for the sale of goods, the rendering of services or from the use by others of enterprise resources be reasonably determinable. When such consideration is not determinable within reasonable limits, the recognition of revenue is postponed.

    (b) *Costs (including warranties)*

In most situations total costs (including warranties and other associated costs to be incurred after shipment of the product or performance of the service) can reasonably be determined and accrued and, accordingly, revenue recognition is not postponed. When, however, costs to be incurred cannot reasonably be determined, revenue recognition is postponed.

    (c) *Returns*

If an enterprise is exposed to significant and predictable amounts of goods being returned, it may be sufficient to provide therefor. Where, however, an enterprise is exposed to significant and unpredictable amounts of goods being returned, it may be that the criteria for recognition of revenue have not been fully met and, accordingly, revenue recognition is postponed.

20. When the uncertainty relates to the measurability of the amount of revenue arising from a transaction, it is usual not to recognise such revenue until the uncertainty is removed. In such a case, provided there is reasonable assurance that at least the costs clearly identifiable with the transaction will be recovered, it is appropriate to defer such costs for later matching with the revenue.

Non-Monetary Consideration

21. For an exchange of non-monetary assets, the fair value of the assets or services exchanged is normally used to determine the amount of revenue involved. Where the fair value of the assets on one side of the transaction is determinable, that fair value is used in determining the amount of revenue involved in an exchange of dissimilar assets. Exchanges of similar non-monetary assets or services, such as swap transactions, are not regarded as transactions which generate revenue.

International Accounting Standard 18

Revenue Recognition

International Accounting Standard 18 comprises paragraphs 22–27 of this Statement. The Standard should be read in the context of paragraphs 1–21 of this Statement and of the Preface to Statements of International Accounting Standards.

22. Revenue from sales or service transactions should be recognised when the requirements as to performance set out in paragraphs 23 and 24 are satisfied, provided that at the time of performance it is not unreasonable to expect ultimate collection. If at the time of sale or the rendering of the service it is unreasonable to expect ultimate collection, revenue recognition should be postponed.

23. In a transaction involving the sale of goods, performance should be regarded as being achieved when the following conditions have been fulfilled:

   (a) the seller of the goods has transferred to the buyer the significant risks and rewards of ownership, in that all significant acts have been completed and the seller retains no continuing managerial involvement in, or effective control of, the goods transferred to a degree usually associated with ownership; and

   (b) no significant uncertainty exists regarding:

     (i) the consideration that will be derived from the sale of the goods;

     (ii) the associated costs incurred or to be incurred in producing or purchasing the goods;

     (iii) the extent to which goods may be returned.

24. In a transaction involving the rendering of services, performance should be measured either under the completed contract method or under the percentage of completion method, whichever relates the revenue to the work accomplished. In any case, such performance should be regarded as being achieved when no significant uncertainty exists regarding:

(a) the consideration that will be derived from rendering the service, and

(b) the associated costs incurred or to be incurred in rendering the service.

25. Revenues arising from the use by others of enterprise resources yielding interest, royalties and dividends should only be recognised when no significant uncertainty as to measurability or collectability exists. These revenues are recognised on the following bases:

(a) Interest: on a time proportion basis taking account of the principal outstanding and the rate applicable;

(b) Royalties: on an accrual basis in accordance with the terms of the relevant agreement;

(c) Dividends from investments not accounted for under the equity method of accounting: when the shareholder's right to receive payment is established.

Disclosure

26. In addition to the disclosures required by International Accounting Standard 1, Disclosure of Accounting Policies, and International Accounting Standard 5, Information to be Disclosed in Financial Statements, an enterprise should also disclose the circumstances in which revenue recognition has been postponed pending the resolution of significant uncertainties.

Effective Date

27. This International Accounting Standard becomes operative for financial statements covering periods beginning on or after 1 January, 1984.

Appendix

This appendix is illustrative only and does not form part of the accounting standard set forth in this Statement. The purpose of the appendix is to illustrate the application of the Standard to a number of commercial situations in an endeavour to assist in clarifying application of the Standard.

A. Sale of Goods

1. 'Bill and hold' sales, i.e. delivery is delayed at buyer's request but buyer takes title and accepts billing.

   Revenue should be recognised notwithstanding that physical delivery has not been completed so long as there is every expectation that delivery will be made. However, the item must be on hand, identified and ready for delivery to the buyer at the time the sale is recognised rather than there being simply an intention to acquire or manufacture the goods in time for delivery.

2. Shipped subject to conditions
   (a) installation and inspection
   i.e. goods are sold subject to installation, inspection, etc.

   Revenue should normally not be recognised until the customer accepts delivery and installation and inspection are complete. In some cases, however, the installation process may be so simple in nature that it may be appropriate to recognise the sale notwithstanding that installation is not yet completed (e.g. installation of a factory tested television receiver normally only requires unpacking and connection of power and antennae); in other cases, the inspection may only be performed for purposes of final determination of contract prices (e.g. shipments of iron ore, sugar, soya beans, etc.) and it may be appropriate to recognise the estimated amount of the revenue at the date of shipment or other suitable time.

(b) on approval	Revenue should not be recognised until the shipment has been formally accepted by the buyer or the time period for rejection has elapsed.
(c) guaranteed sales i.e. shipment is made giving the buyer an unlimited right of return	Recognition of revenue in such circumstances will depend on the substance of the agreement. In the case of normal retail sales (e.g. chain store offering 'money back if not completely satisfied') it may be appropriate to recognise the sale but to make a suitable provision for returns based on previous experience. In other cases, the substance of the agreement may amount to a sale on consignment, in which case it should be treated as indicated below.
(d) consignment sales i.e. a shipment is made whereby the recipient undertakes to sell the goods on behalf of the shipper.	Revenue should not be recognised until the goods are sold to a third party.
(e) cash on delivery sales	Revenue should not be recognised until cash is received by the seller or his agent.
3. Lay away sales, i.e. those sales where the purchaser makes a series of instalment payments to the seller, and the seller delivers the goods only when the final payment is received.	Revenue from such sales should not be recognised until goods are delivered. However, when experience indicates that most such sales are consummated, revenue may be recognised when a significant deposit is received.

4. Special orders and shipments, i.e. where payment (or partial payment) is received for goods not presently held in stock e.g. the stock is still to be manufactured or is delivered directly to the customer from a third party.

Revenue from such sales should not be recognised until goods are delivered to the buyer.

5. Sale/repurchase agreements (other than swap transactions) i.e. where seller concurrently agrees to repurchase the same goods at a later date.

For such transactions that are in substance a financing arrangement, the resulting cash inflow is not revenue as defined and should not be recognised as revenue.

6. Sales to intermediate parties, i.e. where goods are sold to distributors, dealers or others for resale.

Revenue from such sales can generally be recognised if significant risks of ownership have passed; however, in some situations the buyer may in substance be an agent and in such cases the sale should be treated as a consignment sale.

7. Publication and record subscriptions.

Revenue received or billed should be deferred and recognised either on a straight line basis over time or, where the items shipped vary in value from period to period, revenue should be based on the sales value of the item shipped in relation to the total sales value of all items covered by the subscription.

8. Instalment sales.	When the consideration is receivable in instalments, revenue attributable to the sales price exclusive of interest should be recognised at the date of sale. The interest element should be recognised as revenue, proportionately to the unpaid balance due to the seller. If collection is not reasonably assured, revenue should be recognised as cash instalments are received.
9. Real estate sales.	When property is sold, revenue is usually recognised when the buyer takes possession. However, the buyer's down payment or other commitment may be insufficient to provide assurance of the eventual completion of payment. Although the security of the vendor is usually assured by the ability to foreclose the property or to apply other remedies in the event of default by the buyer, it would be inappropriate to recognise revenue in full at the time of the sale. In these circumstances the transaction should be accounted for as cash instalments are received.
10. Trade discounts and volume rebates.	Trade discounts and volume rebates received are not encompassed within the definition of revenue, since they represent a reduction of cost. Trade discounts and volume rebates given should be deducted in determining revenue.

B. Rendering of Services

1. Installation fees.	In cases where installation fees are other than incidental to the sale of a product, they should be recognised as revenue only when the equipment is installed and accepted by the customer.

2. Servicing fees included in the price of the product.

Where the selling price of a product includes an identifiable amount for subsequent servicing for, say, a warranty period, it will normally be appropriate to defer the relevant portion of the selling price and to recognise it as revenue over the appropriate period.

3. Advertising and insurance agency commissions.

Revenue should be recognised when the service is completed. For advertising agencies, media commissions will normally be recognised when the related advertisement or commercial appears before the public, as opposed to production commission, which will be recognised when the project is completed. Insurance agency commissions should be recognised on the effective commencement or renewal dates of the related policies. In some circumstances the commission may be adjusted depending upon the claims experience in respect of the policies written by the agent. In cases where it is expected that the policy will need servicing during its life, the commission or a relevant part thereof may be recognised over that period.

4. Financial service commissions.

A financial service may be rendered as a single act or may be provided over a period of time. Similarly charges for such services may be made as a single amount or in stages over the period of the service or the life of the transaction to which it relates. Such charges may be settled in full when made or added to a loan or other account and settled in stages. The recognition of such revenue should therefore have regard to:

(a) whether the service has been provided 'once and for all' or is on a 'continuing' basis;

(b) the incidence of the costs relating to the service;

(c) when the payment for the service will be received.

In general, commissions charged for arranging or granting loan or other facilities should be recognised when a binding obligation has been entered into. Commitment, facility or loan management fees which relate to continuing obligations or services should normally be recognised over the life of the loan or facility having regard to the amount of the obligation outstanding, the nature of the services provided and the timing of the costs relating thereto.

5. Admission fees.

Revenue from artistic performances, banquets and other special events should be recognised when the event takes place. When a subscription to a number of events is sold, the fee should be allocated to each event on a systematic and rational basis.

6. Tuition fees.

Revenue should be recognised over the period of instruction.

7. Initiation, entrance and membership fees.

Revenue recognition from these sources will depend on the nature of the services being provided. If the fee permits only membership, and all other services or products are paid for separately, or if there is a separate annual subscription, the fee should be recognised when received. If the fee entitles the member to services or publications to be provided during the year, it should be recognised on a systematic and rational basis having regard to the timing and nature of all services provided.

8. Franchise fees.

Generally, franchise fees may cover the supply of any combination of initial and subsequent services, equipment and other supplies, know-how etc. Frequently, the determination of such matters, and the allocation of the franchise fee thereto, is difficult and requires considerable judgement. As a general guidance, however, the following methods of fee recognition may be appropriate:

– the portion of the initial franchise fee that relates to tangible assets (if any) should be recognised when the items are delivered

– the portion that applies to future services (if any) should be deferred and recognised as revenue when the services are rendered

– if continuing fees receivable under the agreement are inadequate to cover the cost and a reasonable profit level for the continuing services, recognition of some or all of the initial franchise fee should be delayed.

International Accounting Standard 19

Accounting for Retirement Benefits in the Financial Statements of Employers

Contents

Introduction

1. This Statement deals with accounting for retirement benefits in the financial statements of employers. Employment termination indemnities, deferred compensation arrangements, long-service leave benefits, health and welfare plans, and bonus plans are not dealt with by this Statement although, if their predominant characteristics are the same as those of retirement benefits, it would usually be appropriate to account for them in a manner similar to retirement benefit plans.

2. Retirement benefit plans frequently involve separate funds to which contributions are made and from which retirement benefits are paid; this Statement applies whether or not such a fund is created. This Statement does not deal with accounting by such funds.

3. A common investment vehicle for such funds is an insurance contract. The benefits insured by such a contract need have no direct or automatic relationship with the obligations undertaken by the employer. Retirement benefit plans involving insured schemes are subject to the same relationships of accounting and funding as privately invested arrangements and are, accordingly, within the scope of this Statement.

4. Although in some circumstances (e.g. retirement benefit plans covering only a few employees) and under some actuarial valuation methods (such as some projected benefit valuation methods) actuarial calculations are made for each participating employee, the discussion in this Statement, for simplicity, is written in terms of groups of employees rather than in terms of individuals.

Definitions

5. The following terms are used in this Statement with the meanings specified:

Retirement benefit plans are arrangements, formal or informal, whereby an employer provides benefits for employees on or after termination of service (either in the form of an annual income or as a lump sum) when such benefits can be determined or estimated in advance of retirement from the provisions of a document or from the employer's practices.

Defined contribution plans are retirement benefit plans under which amounts to be paid as retirement benefits are determined by contributions to a fund together with investment earnings thereon.

Defined benefit plans are retirement benefit plans under which amounts to be paid as retirement benefits are determinable, usually by reference to employee's earnings and/or years of service.

A final pay plan is a defined benefit plan that promises benefits based on an employee's remuneration at or near retirement. The remuneration considered for this purpose is sometimes that of the final year and sometimes an average of a number of years as specified in the plan.

Funding is the irrevocable transfer of assets to an entity separate from the employer's enterprise to meet future obligations for the payment of retirement benefits.

Actuarial valuation is the process used by an actuary to estimate the present value of benefits to be paid under a retirement benefit plan and the present values of plan assets and sometimes of future contributions.

Accrued benefit valuation methods are actuarial valuation methods that reflect retirement benefits based on service rendered by employees to the date of the valuation. Such methods may incorporate assumptions regarding projected salary levels to date of retirement.[1]

Projected benefit valuation methods are actuarial valuation methods that reflect retirement benefits based on service both rendered and to be rendered by employees as at the date of the actuarial valuation, and may incorporate assumptions regarding projected salary levels to date of retirement.[1]

Current service cost is the cost to an employer under a retirement benefit plan for the services of participating employees exclusive of those elements of cost identified as past service cost, experience adjustments and the effects of a change in an actuarial assumption.

Past service cost is the actuarially-determined cost arising on the introduction of a retirement benefit plan, on the making of improvements to such a plan, or on the completion of minimum service requirements for eligibility in such a plan, all of which give employees credit for benefits for service prior to the occurrence of one or more of those events.

---

[1] Assumptions regarding projected salary levels usually involve factors such as: changes in the general level of productivity in a country or an industry; individual merit increases; and changes in the general level of consumer-prices over the expected remaining working lives of the present employees covered by the plan (the last factor may, to some extent, be offset by changes in the assumptions concerning investment earnings on retirement fund assets).

Experience adjustments are adjustments to retirement benefit costs arising from the differences between the previous actuarial assumptions as to future events and what actually occurred.

Vested benefits are benefits, the rights to which, under the conditions of a retirement benefit plan, are not conditional on continued employment.

Terminal funding is a method of recognising the projected cost of retirement benefits only at the time an employee retires.

Pay-as-you-go is a method of recognising the cost of retirement benefits only at the time that cash payments are made to employees on or after retirement.

Explanation

6. Retirement benefit plans are normally significant elements of an employer's remuneration programme for employees. It is therefore important that retirement benefits are properly accounted for and that appropriate disclosures are made in the financial statements of an employer.

7. While some retirement benefit plans are informal or are evidenced only by an employer's practices, most plans are based on a formal agreement.[2] While some plans permit an employer to terminate the obligation under the plan, it is usually difficult for an employer to cancel a plan if employees are to be retained. In these circumstances, the same basis of accounting is appropriate for such plans as for non-cancellable contractual agreements.

8. A retirement benefit plan often provides for a separate fund to be set up into which contributions are made by the employer and perhaps by employees. Such a fund is usually administered by trustees who may be appointed by the employer and/or the employees and who represent the employer and/or the employees or may be independent of them in regard to investing fund assets.

---

[2] In some countries, employers are required to provide retirement benefits in accordance with a statutorily-determined plan.

9. The plan normally determines the retirement benefits to be provided. When there is a separate fund, it may be the fund trustees who make the commitment to provide the benefits to the employees. In these circumstances, the employer's legal obligation may be limited to an agreed contribution to the fund. The trustees may, or may not, have total discretion as to the use of the funds under such a plan.

10. Defined benefit plans, especially those that promise benefits related to remuneration at or near retirement, present significant difficulties in the estimation of costs. The extent of an employer's obligation under such plans is usually uncertain and likely to remain so over a long period of time. Moreover, in estimating the obligation, assumptions may need to be made regarding future conditions and events which are largely outside the employer's control.

11. As a result of the many factors that frequently enter into the computation of retirement benefits under defined benefit plans and the length of time over which the benefits are earned, allocation problems arise in determining how the costs of the retirement benefits should be recognised in the financial statements of the employer. Furthermore, long-term uncertainties may give rise to adjustments of estimates of earlier years that can be very significant in relation to current service cost.

12. The cost of retirement benefits to an employer results from receiving services from the employees who are entitled to receive such benefits. Consequently, the cost of retirement benefits is accounted for in the period during which these services are rendered. Accounting for retirement benefit costs only when employees retire or receive benefit payments does not allocate those costs to the periods in which the service was rendered.

Accounting and Funding Objectives Distinguished

13. When there is a separate retirement benefit fund, the position is sometimes taken that the amount paid by an employer to the fund during an accounting period provides an appropriate charge to income. While, in many cases, the amount funded may provide a reasonable approximation of the amount to be charged against income, there is a vital distinction between the periodic funding of retirement benefits and the allocation of the cost of providing those benefits.

14. The objective of funding is to make available amounts to meet future obligations for the payment of retirement benefits. Funding is a financing procedure and, in determining the periodic amounts to be funded, the employer may be influenced by such factors as the availability of money and tax considerations.

15. On the other hand, the objective of accounting for the cost of a retirement benefit plan is to ensure that the cost of benefits is allocated to accounting periods on a systematic basis related to the receipt of the employees' services.

16. An indication of the pace of funding of a plan is given by the difference between the amounts funded since the inception of the plan and the amounts charged to income over the same period (together with any adjustment to retained earnings resulting from a change in accounting policy, see International Accounting Standard 8, Unusual and Prior Period Items and Changes in Accounting Policies). For this reason, the amount of any difference is useful disclosure.

Cost Determination

17. Under a defined contribution plan, the employer's cost is determined by a formula stated in the plan and it can normally be calculated with certainty each year.

18. Under a defined benefit plan, the employer's cost can only be estimated since there are many variables that influence the amount of the ultimate benefits and, hence, the cost of those benefits. For example, the amount of future retirement benefits may be determined by employees' earnings and/or by their years of service. The cost to an employer will also be affected by factors such as the investment earnings on retirement fund assets and employee turnover.

19. A retirement benefit plan may stipulate the basis of contributions on which the benefits are determined and, because of this, appear to be a defined contribution plan. However, the provisions of the plan may also result in the employer being responsible for specified benefits or a specified level of benefits. In this case, the plan is, in substance, a defined benefit plan and should be accounted for accordingly.

20. Final pay defined benefit plans involve problems of allocation both in regard to current service cost and in regard to adjustments to estimates of previous years (these are considered in paragraphs 27–32 below). However, it is often the case that career average and flat benefit plans (and also defined contribution plans) are adjusted periodically to offset the erosion in plan benefits caused by inflation. If such adjustments are made regularly, similar considerations may apply to these plans as to final pay plans.

Past Service Cost

21. Views differ as to how to account for past service cost. One view is that the entitlements giving rise to past service cost have been earned by employees through their service in prior periods and, therefore, this cost should be recognised as an expense as soon as it has been determined.

22. Others believe that the entitlements giving rise to past service cost are in return for services to be rendered by employees in the future and that, therefore, the cost ought to be allocated over the periods during which the services are to be rendered. Those who support this view maintain that, regardless of whether these costs are computed by reference to employee service in previous periods, the cost relates to current and future periods.

Actuarial Principles

23. A number of actuarial valuation methods have been developed by the actuarial profession to estimate employer obligations under defined benefit plans. While primarily designed to calculate funding requirements, these methods are frequently used to determine retirement benefit costs for accounting purposes.

24. The actuarial method selected for accounting purposes and the assumptions made can have a significant effect on the expense to be recorded in each accounting period. Therefore, in carrying out a periodic valuation, an actuary chooses an appropriate valuation method and, in consultation with the employer, makes appropriate assumptions about the variable elements affecting the computations.

25. The assumptions are applied to the expected inflow from future contributions and from investments as well as to the expected outgo for

benefits. The uncertainty inherent in projecting future trends in rates of inflation, salary levels and earnings on investments are taken into consideration by the actuary in the actuarial valuations by using a set of compatible assumptions (for example, that the basis of valuing fund assets be compatible with the interest assumption used for determining the actuarial obligation). Usually these projections will be extended until the expected date of death of the last pensioner and are, accordingly, long-term.

26. The present value of future cash flows will be included by the actuary in a statement of plan assets and liabilities and, if this results in a surplus or deficiency, an adjustment in the employer's contribution is usually recommended. An alternative approach is to exclude the employer's future contributions from the statement; in this case, the actuary will assess the appropriate contribution to meet the uncovered obligation.

Suitability of Valuation Methods for Expense Recognition

27. The remuneration paid to employees provides the best available accounting estimate of the benefit received by an enterprise over the working lives of the participating employees. Accordingly, in allocating the cost of retirement benefits over the period in which employees' services are rendered, it is usually appropriate to use an actuarial method that, on the assumptions adopted, will result in annual current service costs that bear a reasonably stable relationship to remuneration.

28. In allocating retirement benefit costs over the working lives of participating employees, significantly different charges to income may result depending on whether an accrued benefit or projected benefit valuation method is used. Thus, disclosure of the method used is necessary for an adequate understanding of the employer's accounting for retirement benefit plans. Accrued benefit methods usually produce an annual cost that increases significantly in proportion to related current salaries as the average age of existing employees rises. This effect may be compounded if retirement benefits are based on final salary and may be further compounded by the impact of inflation on salary levels, though some accrued benefit methods take account of these factors.

Review of Actuarial Assumptions and Valuations

29. The assumptions on which an actuarial valuation is made, such as projected salary levels and turnover of employees, are based on long-term considerations. It may be necessary to modify these assumptions from time to time. For example, salary increases may have exceeded the assumed rate of increase and this trend is expected to continue. On the other hand, the higher salaries may have been due to special circumstances not expected to recur so that the initial assumption about salary increases is expected to be valid in the future. In the latter case, the previous salary assumption would not be changed.

30. If the estimated future cost to the employer is altered as the result of a change in an actuarial assumption, the usual accounting treatment is to spread the new cost over the expected remaining working lives of the participating employees or, alternatively, it can be charged immediately to income.

31. Actuarial valuations may lead to the identification of experience adjustments because the events covered by the assumptions used to make the previous valuation did not coincide with what actually occurred. For example, rates of employee turnover since the prior valuation may have differed from those assumed.

32. Since experience adjustments are necessary to correct past estimates, one view is that they are similar to changes in certain other accounting estimates, such as provisions for doubtful accounts receivable, and are therefore to be accounted for by a charge or credit to income as they arise. A different view is that experience adjustments are merely normal fluctuations in the long-term cost of the plan to be allocated over the expected remaining working lives of participating employees. In view of the difficulty of knowing whether experience adjustments represent fluctuations about the trend of long-term cost or a significant shift in the trend itself, an intermediate course is sometimes adopted and they are allocated over some period shorter than that of the expected remaining working lives of participating employees. Whatever basis of recognition is normally used, if the experience adjustment is the result of an isolated event, such as the closing of a plant, it may be appropriate to charge the adjustment to income in the period in which the event took place.

33. Because of the potentially significant effect of differences between assumptions and experience, it is necessary to obtain actuarial valuations at frequent intervals. At least every three years would be appropriate with additional valuations in intervening years when important changes in the circumstances of the plan are known to have taken place or when events indicate that one or more of the assumptions may have to be modified.

Government and Industry Plans

34. Some payments required to be made by employers pursuant to government legislation or industry plans as contributions to national, state or industry retirement benefits plans are elements of retirement benefit cost that are charged to income as the service is rendered. This accounting treatment is appropriate if such plans, unlike those of the employer, are not the responsibility of the employer and the cost of such plans is assessed on all the enterprises in the country, state or industry concerned. The prospective retirement benefits to be received by employees which arise from such payments are sometimes included in the formula for benefit calculations under the employer's own retirement benefits plan; in this case, they are also taken into account as part of the actuarial valuation of the plan.

Retired Employees

35. When retirement benefits to retired employees are, because of inflation or for other reasons, deemed to be inadequate, the plan may be amended to provide additional benefits to retired employees, benefits which may be extended to present employees as well. Any additional costs would be included in the actuarial valuation of the amended plan.

36. When benefits supplemental to the plan, which constitute a continuing commitment, are promised to retired employees, the present value of the cost of the supplemental benefits is charged to income at the time the promise is made.

Vested Benefits

37. There may be times, for example if benefit rights have been awarded retrospectively, when the total assets set aside to meet the obligations of a plan fall short of the actuarially-determined value of vested benefits under the plan. When this situation arises, there are three principal schools of thought as to the appropriate accounting treatment:

 (a) the shortfall should be charged to income in the period in which it arises or, alternatively, the deficiency should be recorded both as a liability and a deferred charge and charged against income as funding payments are made to eliminate the deficiency;

 (b) the shortfall represents a contingency which should be disclosed in a note;

 (c) provided the plan continues, the shortfall will be made up in future years and, therefore, under the going concern assumption, the information is irrelevant.

38. It is important to recognise that the basis of a calculation comparing vested benefits with total assets available to meet the obligations of the plan is normally different from that underlying the calculation of the ongoing cost of the plan. For instance, the value of vested benefits takes no account of the effect of future salary increases and the valuation of fund assets is based on current net realisable values.

Plan Termination

39. When a plan is to be terminated or when it is probable that it will be terminated, the cost of any unfulfilled obligation is accrued and charged to income immediately unless the remaining obligation is transferred to another plan.

Change in Actuarial Method

40. A change in the actuarial method used to determine retirement benefit costs is a change in accounting policy that is accounted for and disclosed in accordance with International Accounting Standard 8, Unusual and Prior Period Items and Changes in Accounting Policies.

Disclosures

41. In view of the diversity of practices used for accounting for retirement benefit costs, adequate disclosure is essential for an understanding of the significance of such costs to an enterprise.

42. When the financial statements of an enterprise are affected by more than one retirement benefit plan (for example, in consolidated financial statements), the disclosure would summarise the significant and relevant information for all the enterprise's plans. If disclosure of the type of information set out in paragraph 16 is made, the value of the information will be lessened if the amount of a deferred charge in one plan or plans is offset against a liability in another plan or plans.

43. Retirement benefit costs are not always disclosed separately. Since they are considered to be an element of employee remuneration, if the total of such remuneration is not required to be disclosed, it is not usual to disclose retirement benefit costs separately.

44. It is usually considered necessary to disclose the actuarial valuation method(s) used since it is basic to the valuation. Because of their effect on the results of an actuarial valuation, it is sometimes considered desirable to indicate the major assumptions on which the valuation is based.

International Accounting Standard 19

Accounting for Retirement Benefits in the Financial Statements of Employers

International Accounting Standard 19 comprises paragraphs 45–52 of this Statement. The Standard should be read in the context of paragraphs 1 to 44 of this Statement and of the Preface to Statements of International Accounting Standards.

Accounting

45. **In a defined benefit plan:**

   (a) the cost of retirement benefits should be determined, using appropriate and compatible assumptions, by consistently using an accrued benefit valuation method or a projected benefit valuation method. The pay-as-you-go and terminal funding methods should not be used in accounting for the cost of retirement benefits;

   (b) current service costs should be charged to income systematically over the expected remaining working lives of the employees covered by the retirement benefit plan;

   (c) past service costs, experience adjustments, and the effects of changes in actuarial assumptions on retirement benefit costs should be charged or credited to income as they arise or allocated systematically over a period not exceeding the expected remaining working lives of the participating employees; and

   (d) the effect of changes in actuarial method that affect the charge to income in the current period or may affect the charge in subsequent periods should be accounted for and disclosed in accordance with International Accounting Standard 8, Unusual and Prior Period Items and Changes in Accounting Policies.

46. In a defined contribution plan, the employer's contribution applicable to a particular accounting period should be charged against income in that period. If the defined contribution plan includes an element of past service costs, such element should be accounted for in accordance with paragraph 45 of this Standard.

47. When a retirement benefit plan is amended with the result that additional benefits are provided for retired employees, the cost of the additional benefits should be accounted for in accordance with paragraph 45(c).

48. When benefits supplemental to a plan which constitute a continuing commitment are promised to retired employees, the present value of the cost of the supplemental benefits should be charged to income at the time the promise is made.

49. When a plan is to be terminated or when it is probable that it will be terminated, the cost of any unfulfilled obligation should be accrued and charged to income immediately unless the remaining obligation is transferred to another plan.

Disclosures

50. The following information [3] should be disclosed in the financial statements of an employer:

(a) the accounting policies adopted for retirement benefit plan costs, including a general description of the valuation method or methods used (see International Accounting Standard 1, Disclosure of Accounting Policies);

(b) any other significant matters related to retirement benefits that affect comparability with the prior period;

(c) if the amounts funded since the inception of the plan are different from the amounts charged to income (or to retained earnings due to a change in accounting policy) over the same period, the amount of the resulting liability or deferred charge and the funding approach adopted if there is no systematic policy of funding. (When an employer has more than one plan and this

---

[3] When an enterprise has more than one retirement benefit plan, this information may be reported in total for all plans, separately for each plan, or in such groupings as are considered to be the most useful.

results in there being both a liability and a deferred charge, the liability or deferred charge should not be reduced by deducting one from the other);

(d) in the case of a defined benefit plan:

   (i) the amount of the shortfall (if any) of the net realisable value of the fund assets, together with the liability or deferred charge (if any) described in (c) above, from the actuarially-determined value of vested benefits, and

   (ii) a statement of the funding approach adopted. (When an employer has more than one plan, a shortfall of plan assets from the liability for vested benefits of one plan should be disclosed without offsetting an excess of assets over vested benefit liabilities of another plan.);

(e) in the case of a defined benefit plan, the date of the latest actuarial valuation.

Transitional Provisions

51. When the adoption of this Standard constitutes a change in accounting policy, an enterprise should either (a) adjust its financial statements in accordance with International Accounting Standard 8, Unusual and Prior Period Items and Changes in Accounting Policies, to record a liability for the cumulative effect of the change or (b) disclose this amount in the period of change and subsequently disclose the amount still unrecorded. When (b) is adopted, the amount unrecorded at the date of introduction of the Standard should be recorded as a liability over a period not exceeding the expected remaining working lives of participating employees and the resulting debit should be charged in the income statement as an unusual item. The cost of retirement benefits that arises and is charged to income in subsequent years should be charged to income in the same way as it would have been if accrual accounting had been in effect from the beginning.

Effective Date

52. This International Accounting Standard becomes operative for financial statements covering periods beginning on or after 1 January, 1985.

Appendix

Principal Actuarial Valuation Methods

(The titles used in this Appendix are not necessarily those used in all countries)

Actuarial Valuation Methods generally fall into two broad categories: the accrued benefit valuation method and projected benefit valuation methods.

Accrued Benefit Valuation Method

Under this method:

- current service cost is the present value of benefits payable in the future in respect of service in the current period.
- past service cost is the present value on the introduction of a retirement benefit plan, on the making of improvements to such a plan or on the completion of minimum service requirements for eligibility in such a plan, of the units of benefits payable in the future in respect of services rendered prior to the occurrence of one or more of those events.
- accrued actuarial liability is the present value of benefits payable in the future in respect of service to date.

This method, assuming no inflation or deflation, produces a current service cost applicable to an employee that increases each year as the period to retirement shortens, since less investment earnings accumulate on the contributions and the probability of the employee surviving to retirement increases. For a retirement benefit plan as a whole, annual current service cost will tend to be approximately the same each year provided the number and age distribution of participating employees remains relatively unchanged. In a salary-related plan, inflation will add to the rate of increase each year and, accordingly, this method is often modified for final pay plans by introducing salary projections. Under this modification, employees' final earnings are estimated and the benefits based on these final earnings are allocated to years of service in calculating each year's cost.

Projected Benefit Valuation Methods

Projected benefit valuation methods reflect retirement benefits based on service both rendered and to be rendered by employees as at the date of the actuarial valuation. These methods allocate the cost of employees' benefits evenly (either in absolute amounts or as a percentage of salaries) over the full period of employment.

There are four principal forms of the projected benefit valuation method:

(a) The Entry Age Normal Method
Under this method, each employee is assumed to have entered the plan when first employed or as soon as he became eligible. (When a new plan is introduced the assumed date of entry is that on which the employee would have become eligible to join if the plan had been in existence at the time.) The current service cost is a level annual amount or a fixed percentage of salary which, when invested at the rate of interest assumed in the actuarial valuation, is sufficient to provide the required benefit at the employee's retirement. Under this method, past service cost is the present value of the excess of projected retirement benefits over the amount expected to be provided by future contributions based on the current service cost.

While the application of this method conceptually requires calculations to be made for each individual employee, in practice it is often used for groups of employees and the application of the method is often simplified by using one entry date for all employees.

(b) The Individual Level Premium Method
This method, generally used in conjunction with individual annuity insurance policies, allocates the cost of each employee's pension benefit over the period from the date of his entry into the plan to his retirement date by level annual amounts or by a fixed percentage of salary. There is no separate calculation of past service cost since the whole cost of the ultimate benefit is spread between the date the employee enters the plan and his retirement date.

Under this method, annual current service costs are higher than those which would result from the use of the entry age normal method. The reason for this is that, under this method, the costs otherwise identified as past service costs are charged as current service costs.

(c)   The Aggregate Method
This method uses the same basic principles as the individual level premium method but is applied to the plan as a whole rather than to individual employees. The cost of benefits is allocated over the average service lives of active employees. The effect of averaging the cost for all employees or groups of employees under this method is that the relatively high annual cost in the early years of the plan is less pronounced than under the individual level premium method.

Past service cost and experience adjustments are not identified but are spread over future periods through regular computations using this method.

(d)   The Attained Age Normal Method
This method is similar to the aggregate method and the individual level premium method except that, under this method, the past service cost is calculated and identified using the accrued benefit valuation method. Current service costs are determined using the aggregate method but applied only to benefits in respect of service in the future.

International Accounting Standard 20

Accounting for Government Grants and Disclosure of Government Assistance

Contents

Introduction

1.   This Statement deals with accounting for the disclosure of government grants and with disclosure of other forms of government assistance.

2.   This Statement does not deal with:

(a)   the special problems arising in accounting for government grants in financial statements reflecting the effects of changing prices or in supplementary information of a similar nature;

(b)   government assistance that is provided for an enterprise in the form of benefits that are available in determining taxable income or are determined or limited on the basis of income tax liability (such as income tax holidays, investment tax credits, accelerated depreciation allowances and reduced income tax rates);

(c)   government participation in the ownership of the enterprise.

Definitions

3.   The following terms are used in this Statement with the meanings specified:

Government refers to government, government agencies and similar bodies whether local, national or international.

Government assistance is action by government designed to provide an economic benefit specific to an enterprise or range of enterprises qualifying under certain criteria. Government assistance for the purpose of this Statement does not include benefits provided only indirectly through action affecting general trading conditions, such as the provision of infrastructure in development areas or the imposition of trading constraints on competitors.

Government grants [1] are assistance by government in the form of transfers of resources to an enterprise in return for past or future compliance with certain conditions relating to the operating activities of the enterprise. They exclude those forms of government assistance which cannot reasonably have a value placed upon them and transactions with government which cannot be distinguished from the normal trading transactions of the enterprise.

---

[1] Government grants are sometimes called by other names such as subsidies, subventions, or premiums.

Grants related to assets are government grants whose primary condition is that an enterprise qualifying for them should purchase, construct or otherwise acquire long-term assets. Subsidiary conditions may also be attached restricting the type or location of the assets or the periods during which they are to be acquired or held.

Grants related to income are government grants other than those related to assets.

Forgivable loans are loans which the lender undertakes to waive repayment of under certain prescribed conditions.

Fair value is the amount for which an asset could be exchanged between a knowledgeable, willing buyer and a knowledgeable , willing seller in an arm's length transaction.

Explanation

4.   Government assistance takes many forms varying both in the nature of the assistance given and in the conditions which are usually attached to it. The purpose of the assistance may be to encourage an enterprise to embark on a course of action which it would not normally have taken if the assistance was not provided.

5.   The receipt of government assistance by an enterprise may be significant for the preparation of the financial statements for two reasons. Firstly, if resources have been transferred, an appropriate method of accounting for the transfer must be found. Secondly, it is desirable to give an indication of the extent to which the enterprise has benefited from such assistance during the reporting period. This facilitates comparison of an enterprise's financial statements with those of prior periods and with those of other enterprises.

Accounting Treatment of Government Grants
Capital approach versus income approach

6.   Two broad approaches may be found to the accounting treatment of government grants: the capital approach, under which a grant is credited directly to shareholders' interests, and the income approach, under which a grant is taken to income over one or more periods.

7. Those in support of the capital approach argue as follows:

(a) Government grants are a financing device and should be dealt with as such in the balance sheet rather than be passed through the income statement to offset the items of expense which they finance. Since no repayment is expected, they should be credited directly to shareholders' interests.

(b) It is inappropriate to recognise government grants in the income statement, since they are not earned but represent an incentive provided by government without related costs.

8. Arguments in support of the income approach and therefore against the capital approach are as follows:

(a) Since government grants are receipts from a source other than shareholders, they should not be credited directly to shareholders' interests but should be recognised in the income statement in appropriate periods.

(b) Government grants are rarely gratuitous. The enterprise earns them through compliance with their conditions and meeting the envisaged obligations. They should therefore be taken to income and matched with the associated costs which the grant is intended to compensate.

(c) As income and other taxes are charges against income, it is logical to deal also with government grants, which are an extension of fiscal policies, in the income statement.

9. Examination of the above arguments results in the income approach being generally considered the more satisfactory treatment.

Recognition of income

10. It is fundamental to the income approach that government grants be recognised in the income statement on a systematic and rational basis over the periods necessary to match them with the related costs. Income recognition of government grants on a receipts basis is not in accordance with the accrual accounting assumption (see International Accounting Standard 1, Disclosure of Accounting Policies) and would only be acceptable if no basis existed for allocating a grant to periods other than the one in which it was received.

11.   In most cases the periods over which an enterprise recognises the costs or expenses related to a government grant are readily ascertainable and thus grants in recognition of specific expenses are taken to income in the same period as the relevant expense. Similarly, grants related to depreciable assets are usually allocated to income over the periods and in the proportions in which depreciation on those assets is charged.

12.   Grants related to non-depreciable assets may also require the fulfilment of certain obligations and would then be amortised to income over the periods which bear the cost of meeting the obligations. As an example, a grant of land may be conditional upon the erection of a building on the site and it may be appropriate to amortise it to income over the life of the building.

13.   Grants are sometimes received as part of a package of financial or fiscal aids to which a number of conditions are attached. In such cases, care is needed in identifying the conditions giving rise to costs and expenses which determine the periods over which the grant will be earned. It may be appropriate to allocate part of a grant on one basis and part on another.

14.   In certain circumstances, a government grant may be awarded for the purpose of giving immediate financial support to an enterprise rather than as an incentive to undertake specific expenditures. Such grants may be confined to an individual enterprise and may not be available to a whole class of beneficiaries. These circumstances may warrant taking the grant to income in the period in which the enterprise qualifies to receive it, as an unusual item if appropriate, with disclosure to ensure that its effect is clearly understood.

15.   A government grant may become receivable by an enterprise as compensation for expenses or losses incurred in a previous accounting period. Such a grant is recognised in the income statement of the period in which it becomes receivable, as an unusual item if appropriate, with disclosure to ensure that its effect is clearly understood.

16.   A government grant is not recognised in the income statement until there is reasonable assurance that the enterprise will comply with the conditions attaching to it, and that the grant will be received. Receipt of a grant does not of itself provide conclusive evidence that the conditions attaching to the grant have been or will be fulfilled.

17. The manner in which a grant is received does not affect the accounting method to be adopted in regard to the grant. Thus a grant is accounted for in the same manner whether it is received in cash or as a reduction of a liability to the government.

18. A forgivable loan from government is treated as a government grant when there is reasonable assurance that the enterprise will meet the terms for forgiveness of the loan.

19. Once a government grant is recognised, any related contingency would be treated in accordance with International Accounting Standard 10, Contingencies and Events Occurring After the Balance Sheet Date.

Non-monetary government grants

20. A government grant may take the form of a transfer of a non-monetary asset, such as land or other resources, for the use of the enterprise. In these circumstances it is usual to assess the fair value of the non-monetary asset and to account for both grant and asset at that fair value. An alternative course that is sometimes followed is to record both asset and grant at a nominal amount.

Presentation of grants related to assets

21. Two methods of presentation in financial statements of grants (or the appropriate portions of grants) related to assets are regarded as acceptable alternatives.

22. One method sets up the grant as deferred income which is recognised in the income statement on a systematic and rational basis over the useful life of the asset.

23. The other method deducts the grant in arriving at the carrying amount of the asset. The grant is recognised in the income statement over the life of a depreciable asset by way of a reduced depreciation charge.

24. The purchase of assets and the receipt of related grants can cause major movements in the cash flow of an enterprise. For this reason and in order to show the gross investment in assets, such movements are often disclosed as separate items in the statement of changes in financial position regardless of whether or not the grant is deducted from the related asset for the purpose of balance sheet presentation.

Presentation of grants related to income

25. Grants related to income are sometimes presented as a credit in the income statement, either separately or under a general heading such as 'Other income'; alternatively, they are deducted in reporting the related expense.

26. Supporters of the first method claim that it is inappropriate to net income and expense items and that separation of the grant from the expense facilitates comparison with other expenses not affected by a grant. For the second method it is argued that the expenses might well not have been incurred by the enterprise if the grant had not been available and presentation of the expense without offsetting the grant may therefore be misleading.

27. Both methods are regarded as acceptable for the presentation of grants related to income. Disclosure of the grant may be necessary for a proper understanding of the financial statements. Disclosure of the effect of the grants on any item of income or expense which is required to be separately disclosed is usually appropriate.

Repayment of government grants

28. Government grants sometimes become repayable because certain conditions are not fulfilled. A government grant that becomes repayable gives rise to a revision to an accounting estimate and not to a prior period adjustment (see International Accounting Standard 8, Unusual and Prior Period Items and Changes in Accounting Policies).

29. Repayment of a government grant related to income is applied first against any unamortised deferred credit set up in respect of the grant. To the extent that the repayment exceeds any such deferred credit, or where no deferred credit exists, the repayment is charged immediately to income.

30. Repayment of a grant related to an asset is recorded by increasing the carrying amount of the asset or reducing the deferred income balance by the amount repayable. The cumulative additional depreciation that would have been charged to date in the absence of the grant is charged immediately to income. Circumstances giving rise to repayment may require consideration to be given to the possible impairment of the new carrying amount.

Other Forms of Government Assistance

31. Excluded from the definition of government grants in paragraph 3 of this Statement are certain forms of government assistance which cannot reasonably have a value placed upon them and transactions with government which cannot be distinguished from the normal trading transactions of the enterprise.

32. Examples of assistance that cannot reasonably have a value placed upon them are free technical or marketing advice and the provision of guarantees. An example of assistance that cannot be distinguished from the normal trading transactions of the enterprise is a government procurement policy that is responsible for a portion of the enterprise's sales. The existence of the benefit might be unquestioned but any attempt to segregate the trading activities from government assistance could well be arbitrary.

33. The significance of the benefit in the above examples may be such that disclosure of the nature, extent and duration of the assistance is necessary in order that the financial statements may not be misleading.

34. Loans at nil or low interest rates are a form of government assistance, but the benefit is not quantified by the imputation of interest.

35. In this Statement, government assistance does not include the provision of infrastructure by improvement to the general transport and communication network and the supply of improved facilities such as irrigation or water reticulation which is available on an ongoing indeterminate basis for the benefit of an entire local community.

Disclosure

36. The following disclosures are appropriate:

(a) the accounting policy adopted for government grants, including the methods of presentation adopted in the financial statements;

(b) the nature and extent of government grants recognised in the financial statements and an indication of other forms of government assistance from which the enterprise has directly benefited; and

(c) unfulfilled conditions and other contingencies attaching to government assistance that has been recognised.

International Accounting Standard 20
Accounting for Government Grants and Disclosure of Government Assistance

International Accounting Standard 20 comprises paragraphs 37-44 of this Statement. The Standard should be read in the context of paragraphs 1-36 of this Statement and of the Preface to Statements of International Accounting Standards.

Accounting

37.   Government grants, including non-monetary grants at fair value, should not be recognised until there is reasonable assurance that (i) the enterprise will comply with the conditions attaching to them, and (ii) the grants will be received. They should not be credited directly to shareholders' interests.

38.   Government grants should be recognised in the income statement over the periods necessary to match them with the related costs which they are intended to compensate, on a systematic basis.

39.   Government grants related to assets, including non-monetary grants at fair value, should be presented in the balance sheet either by setting up the grant as deferred income or by deducting the grant in arriving at the carrying amount of the asset.

40.   A government grant that becomes receivable as compensation for expenses or losses already incurred or for the purpose of giving immediate financial support to the enterprise with no further related costs should be recognised in the income statement of the period in which it becomes receivable, as an unusual item if appropriate (see International Accounting Standard 8, Unusual and Prior Period Items and Changes in Accounting Policies).

41. A government grant that becomes repayable should be accounted for as a revision to an accounting estimate (see International Accounting Standard 8, Unusual and Prior Period Items and Changes in Accounting Policies). Repayment of a grant related to income should be applied first against any unamortised deferred credit set up in respect of the grant. To the extent that the repayment exceeds any such deferred credit, or where no deferred credit exists, the repayment should be charged immediately to income. Repayment of a grant related to an asset should be recorded by increasing the carrying amount of the asset or reducing the deferred income balance by the amount repayable. The cumulative additional depreciation that would have been charged to date in the absence of the grant should be charged immediately to income.

Disclosure

42. The following matters should be disclosed:

(a) the accounting policy adopted for government grants, including the methods of presentation adopted in the financial statements;

(b) the nature and extent of government grants recognised in the financial statements and an indication of other forms of government assistance from which the enterprise has directly benefited; and

(c) unfulfilled conditions and other contingencies attaching to government assistance that has been recognised.

Transitional Accounting Provisions

43. An enterprise adopting the Standard for the first time should:

(a) comply with the disclosure requirements, where appropriate; and

(b) either (i) adjust its financial statements for the change in accounting policy in accordance with International Accounting Standard 8, Unusual and Prior Period Items and Changes in Accounting Policies;

or (ii) apply the accounting provisions of the Standard only to grants or portions of grants becoming receivable or repayable after the effective date of the Standard.

Effective Date

44. This International Accounting Standard becomes operative for financial statements covering periods beginning on or after 1 January, 1984.

International Accounting Standard 21

Accounting for the Effects of Changes in Foreign Exchange Rates

Contents

Introduction

1.   This Statement deals with accounting for transactions in foreign currencies in the financial statements of an enterprise and with translation of the financial statements of foreign operations into a single reporting currency for the purpose of including them in the financial statements of the reporting enterprise.

2.   This Statement does not deal with the restatement of the financial statements of an enterprise from its reporting currency into another currency for the convenience of readers accustomed to that other currency or for other similar purposes.

Definitions

3.   The following terms are used in this Statement with the meanings specified:

Reporting currency is the currency used in presenting financial statements.

Foreign currency is a currency other than the reporting currency of an enterprise.

Parent (for the purpose of this Statement) is a reporting enterprise that has one or more foreign operations.

Foreign operation is a subsidiary, associated company, joint venture or branch, whose activities are based or conducted in a country other than the country of the parent. Such a foreign operation may or may not constitute a foreign entity as defined below.

Foreign entity is a foreign operation whose activities are not an integral part of those of the parent.

Net investment in a foreign entity is the parent's equity share in the net assets of that entity.

Exchange rate is the ratio at which the currencies of two countries are exchanged at a particular time.

Spot rate is the exchange rate on a particular day for the exchange of foreign currencies on that day.

Forward rate is the exchange rate available by the terms of an agreement for the exchange of two currencies at a future date.

Closing rate is the spot rate that exists at the balance sheet date.

Monetary items are money held and items to be received or paid in money. All other assets and liabilities are non-monetary items.

Foreign currency loan is a loan repayable in a foreign currency, regardless of the currency, or form, in which the loan was received.

Settlement date is the date at which a receivable is collected or a payable is paid.

Long-term items are those assets and liabilities not expected to be realised or settled within one year from the balance sheet date.

Explanation

4.   A reporting enterprise may carry on foreign activity in two ways:

(a)   It may have transactions in foreign currencies. For example, it may purchase or sell goods for which payment is made in a foreign currency, or it may lend or borrow foreign currency. Transactions in foreign currencies must be expressed in the reporting currency of the entity in order to prepare its financial statements.

(b)   It may have foreign operations. In order to prepare the financial statements of the reporting enterprise in its reporting currency, foreign currency financial statements of such operations must be translated.

Accounting for Foreign Currency Transactions

5.   A transaction in a foreign currency is recorded in the financial records of an entity as of the date on which the transaction occurs, normally using the exchange rate on that date. For practical reasons, it is common to use a rate that approximates the actual rate.

6.   When there is a change in the exchange rate between the transaction date and the date of settlement of any monetary items arising from the transaction, an exchange difference will result.

7.   When the transaction is settled within the same accounting period as that in which it occurred, the exchange difference between the amount originally recorded and the settlement amount is a gain or loss except as noted in paragraph 20.

8.   When the transaction is not settled in the same accounting period as that in which it occurred, the resulting foreign monetary item is sometimes included in the financial statements at the end of the accounting period at the rate on the transaction date. Those following this practice claim that in a period of fluctuating exchange rates, the historical rate is as good a guide as the closing rate to the rate at which the transaction will ultimately be settled. However, most believe that, notwithstanding that exchange rates may fluctuate in the future, stating the foreign monetary item at the current equivalent amount in the reporting currency provides a more useful presentation of the financial position of the enterprise at the balance sheet date. Consequently, any difference between the amount presented in the current financial statements and the amount at which the transaction was recorded during the period or at which it was presented in previous financial statements is regarded as a foreign exchange gain or loss.

9.   Current practice varies with regard to the accounting treatment of gains and losses arising from foreign currency transactions that have not been settled at the balance sheet date. Gains and losses on short-term monetary items are usually recognised in income as they are identified. A similar practice is often followed for long-term monetary items. However, some defer gains on the grounds of prudence but recognise losses in income except to the extent of previously deferred gains. Some defer both gains and losses on long-term monetary items and recognise them in income of current and future periods on a systematic basis over the remaining lives of the monetary items to which they relate.

10.   In some circumstances, forward exchange contracts are entered into to establish the amounts of the reporting currency required or available at the settlement dates of foreign currency transactions. The difference between the forward rate and the spot rate at the inception of the contract reflects, among other things, the difference in interest rates existing in the two currency markets and is recognised in income over the life of the contract. For short-term purchase and sale transactions it is common practice to use the exchange rate specified in the related forward contract as the basis for measuring and reporting the transaction. It is also possible for the hedging function of a forward contract to be achieved by other transactions, such as foreign currency loans.

11.   When an exchange difference has occurred as a result of a severe devaluation or of depreciation of a currency against which there is no practical means of hedging and which affects liabilities arising directly on the recent acquisition of assets invoiced in a foreign currency, the

difference is sometimes regarded as an adjustment of cost and included in the carrying amount of the related assets, provided that in each case the adjusted carrying amount does not exceed the lower of replacement cost and the amount recoverable from the use or sale of the asset.

Translation of the Financial Statements of Foreign Operations

12.   Various methods are currently in use for translating the financial statements of foreign operations. A number of methods apply different exchange rates to different assets and liabilities. Chief among these is a method that translates monetary items at the closing rate but other items at the rates in effect when the amounts of the relevant items were determined. When this method is followed, exchange differences arising on the translation of the foreign financial statements are usually regarded as gains or losses and recognised in income. Another method is to translate all the assets and liabilities in the foreign financial statements at the closing rate. When this method is used, exchange differences arising on translation of foreign financial statements are sometimes recognised in income, and are sometimes taken to shareholders' interests.

Approach adopted by the Standard

13.   Under this Standard the method of translating the financial statements of foreign operations is determined by an assessment of the operational and financial characteristics of those operations. For this purpose, foreign operations are regarded as belonging to one of two categories.

14.   In the first category are those foreign operations that accumulate cash and other monetary items, incur expenses and costs, realise revenues and perhaps arrange borrowings, all substantially in the local currency. When there is a change in the exchange rate, there is little or no direct effect on the activities or present and future cash flows from operations of either the parent or the foreign operation because the foreign operation is not an integral part of the operations of the parent. The significance of the exchange rate change to the parent would be based on its net investment in the foreign operation rather than on the particular mix of monetary and non-monetary items held by the foreign operation at the time of the rate change. Foreign operations of this type are referred to in this Statement as 'foreign entities'.

15.   The other category of foreign operations comprises those that are an integral part of the operations of the parent. In these cases, the effect of exchange rate changes is different. In a simple case, a foreign operation might be limited to selling goods imported from the parent and remitting the proceeds to the parent. Should there be a change in the exchange rate, the effect on the parent's cash flow from operations would be almost immediate and would be similar to the one that would occur if the parent had conducted the operation itself. Thus, the effect of an exchange rate change in the case of a foreign operation that is an integral part of the parent's operation is related to the monetary items held by the foreign operation rather than to the parent's net investment in that operation.

16.   There is considerable variation in the operating relationships between parents and their foreign operations. Whether a foreign operation should be regarded as a foreign entity or as an integral part of the parent's operations depends on the particular circumstances. Matters to be considered in making this decision include:

(a)   Are labour, materials and other costs of the foreign operation's products primarily local costs or does the foreign operation depend on products and services obtained primarily from the country in which the parent is located?

(b)   Is there little interrelationship between the day-to-day activities of the foreign operation and those of the parent, or do inter-company transactions with the parent represent a high proportion of the foreign operation's day-to-day activities?

(c)   Are the day-to-day activities of the foreign operation financed mainly from its own operations and local borrowings or are they mainly dependent on finance provided by the parent?

(d)   Is the foreign operation's market mainly outside the parent's country or within it?

(e)   Is there any other factor that would indicate that the cash flows of the parent are insulated from, or, conversely, are directly affected by, the day-to-day activities of the foreign operation?

17.   It is appropriate in translating the financial statements of a foreign entity to preserve as far as possible the results and the interrelationships of amounts appearing in the foreign financial statements. These results and interrelationships are regarded as providing the most meaningful indicator of the performance and financial position of the foreign operation for inclusion in the consolidated or combined financial statements of the enterprise. This is achieved by translating all the assets and liabilities of the

foreign entity at a single rate – the closing rate. The differences arising on translation are excluded from income and taken directly to shareholders' interests because a change in the exchange rate has little or no direct effect on the activities or present and future cash flows from operations of either the parent or the foreign entity and because inclusion of such differences would distort the income statement. The detailed procedures for translating the financial statements of a foreign entity are set out in paragraph 32.

18.   When the foreign operation is an integral part of the operations of the parent, it is appropriate in translating its financial statements to incorporate the individual items of the foreign financial statements into those of the parent in a manner that achieves the same effect as if all transactions of the foreign operation had been entered into by the parent itself. Accordingly, the procedures detailed in paragraph 34 are applied.

Treatment of intercompany monetary items

19.   The incorporation of the financial statements of a foreign entity into those of the reporting enterprise follows normal procedures, such as the elimination of profits on unrealised intercompany transactions (see International Accounting Standard 3, Consolidated Financial Statements). However, an exchange difference arising on an intercompany monetary item, whether short- or long-term, cannot be eliminated. Even though the monetary item reflects intercompany indebtedness, if it represents a commitment to convert one currency into another, it is an exposure to a gain or loss through currency fluctuations. Accordingly, such exchange difference will continue to be recognised in the combined or consolidated financial statements of the enterprise on the same basis as it was recognised in the financial statements of the individual entity. If, however, the intercompany monetary item is in effect an extension to or deduction from the parent's net investment in the foreign entity, exchange gains and losses arising thereon would be taken to shareholders' interests in the combined or consolidated financial statements.

Net investments hedged by foreign loans

20.   Under the provisions of this Standard, exchange gains and losses arising on foreign currency loans taken out by a parent are normally recognised in income of the period, whereas exchange differences arising on a net investment by a parent in a foreign entity are taken to shareholders' interests. If, however, foreign currency loans and other foreign currency transactions are designated as, and provide, an effective hedge

against a net investment in a foreign entity, it is appropriate to offset the exchange differences arising on each.

Translation of financial statements of entities affected by high rates of inflation

21.   Where high rates of inflation exist, it is appropriate to adjust financial statements for the effects of changing prices before the translation process is undertaken (see International Accounting Standard 15, Information Reflecting the Effects of Changing Prices). An alternative is to translate the financial statements of the foreign entity by applying the procedures set out in paragraph 34 (a) - (e).

Tax Effects of Exchange Differences

22.   Gains and losses on foreign currency transactions and exchange differences arising on translation may have associated tax effects which are accounted for in accordance with International Accounting Standard 12, Accounting for Taxes on Income.

Disclosure

23.   Financial statements generally disclose the methods used in translating the financial statements of foreign entities. An understanding of an enterprise's financial statements is assisted by the disclosure of the net exchange difference for the period taken to income as a result of applying the procedures in paragraph 34, and the net exchange difference for the period adjusted against shareholders' interests as a result of applying the procedures in paragraphs 32-33. Disclosure of the procedure selected for translating the income statements of foreign entities is also necessary. Additional disclosures are required if the financial statements include exchange differences which have been deferred or if exchange differences arising on monetary transactions have been included in the carrying amount of assets.

International Accounting Standard 21

Accounting for the Effects of Changes in Foreign Exchange Rates

International Accounting Standard 21 comprises paragraphs 24-39 of this Statement. The Standard should be read in the context of paragraphs 1-23 of this Statement and of the Preface to Statements of International Accounting Standards.

Accounting for Foreign Currency Transactions

24. **A transaction in a foreign currency should, except as provided in paragraph 26, be recorded in the reporting currency of an entity by applying to the foreign currency amount the exchange rate existing at the time of the transaction or a rate that approximates the actual rate.**

25. **At each balance sheet date, foreign currency monetary items that result from transactions of the entity should be reported at the closing rate, except as provided in paragraph 26.**

26. **When a forward exchange contract is entered into to establish the amounts of the reporting currency required or available at the settlement dates of foreign currency transactions, the difference between the forward rate and the spot rate at the inception of the contract should be recognised in income over the life of the contract. For short-term transactions, the forward rates specified in the related foreign exchange contracts may be used as the basis for measuring and reporting the transactions.**

27. **Exchange differences (other than those dealt with in paragraphs 29 and 30) arising on settlement of monetary items or on reporting an entity's short-term foreign currency monetary items at rates different from those at which they were recorded during the period or presented in previous**

financial statements should be recognised in income for the period, except as provided in paragraph 31.

28. Exchange differences (other than those dealt with in paragraphs 29 and 30) arising on reporting an entity's long-term foreign currency monetary items at rates different from those at which they were recorded during the period or presented in previous financial statements should normally be recognised in income for the period (except as provided in paragraph 31). However, such exchange differences may be deferred and recognised in income of current and future periods on a systematic basis, over the remaining lives of the monetary items to which they relate, except that exchange losses on an item should not be deferred for recognition in future periods if it is reasonable to expect that recurring exchange losses will arise on that item in the future.

29. Exchange differences arising on an intercompany monetary item that is in effect an extension to or deduction from a parent's net investment in a foreign entity should be taken to shareholders' interests in the combined or consolidated financial statements.

30. If foreign currency loans and other foreign currency transactions are designated as, and provide, an effective hedge against a net investment in a foreign entity, exchange differences arising on the loans or transactions should be taken to shareholders' interests to the extent that they are covered by exchange differences arising on the net investment.

31. An exchange difference that results from a severe devaluation or from depreciation of a currency against which there is no practical means of hedging and that affects liabilities arising directly on the recent acquisition of assets invoiced in a foreign currency may be included in the carrying amount of the related assets provided that the adjusted carrying amount does not exceed the lower of replacement cost and the amount recoverable from the use or sale of the asset.

Translation of the Financial Statements of a Foreign Entity

32. The following procedures should be applied in translating the financial statements of a foreign entity for the purposes of incorporation in the financial statements of an enterprise (except as provided in paragraph 33):

  (a) assets and liabilities, both monetary and non-monetary, are translated at the closing rate;

(b) the exchange difference resulting from translating the opening net investment in the foreign entity at an exchange rate different from that at which it was previously reported is taken to shareholders' interests;

(c) income statement items are translated either at the closing rate or at the exchange rates at the dates of the transactions (or at a rate that approximates the actual rates). Differences resulting from translating income statement items at exchange rates other than the closing rate but balance sheet items at the closing rate may be taken to shareholders' interests or to income;

(d) any exchange differences arising on other changes to shareholders' interests in the foreign entity are recognised in shareholders' interests.

33. Preferably, the financial statements of a foreign entity that is affected by high rates of inflation should be adjusted for the effects of changing prices before the translation process is undertaken. Alternatively, the procedures set out in paragraph 34 (a) - (e) should be applied.

Translation of the Financial Statements of Foreign Operations that are Integral to the Operations of the Parent

34. The following procedures should be applied in translating the financial statements of a foreign operation that is integral to the operations of the parent:

(a) all monetary items, other than those referred to in (b) below, are translated at the closing rate;

(b) monetary items that are covered by forward exchange contracts in the parent's currency are translated either at:

(i) the closing rate (if gains and losses on forward contracts are separately measured),

(ii) the spot rate existing at the inception of the forward contract, (adjusted by any amortised discount or premium on the contract), or

(iii) for short-term transactions, at the forward rate applicable to the contract;

(c) non-monetary items that are recorded in terms of past events, for example historical cost, are translated at the exchange rates that existed when the relevant transactions occurred;

(d) non-monetary items that are revalued in the foreign financial statements are translated at the exchange rates that existed on the dates of their revaluations;

(e) income statement items are translated at exchange rates that correspond with the dates of the underlying transactions. If transactions are numerous and spread over an extended period of time, an average of the rates that existed during the period may be used to provide an approximation for the actual rates.

Exchange differences arising from the above procedures are taken to income of the period, except that:

(i) exchange differences relating to long-term monetary items may be deferred and recognised in income of current and future periods on a systematic basis over the remaining lives of the monetary items to which they relate, except that exchange losses on an item should not be deferred for recognition in future periods if it is reasonable to expect that recurring exchange losses will arise on that item in the future,

(ii) when differences arise in the circumstances described in paragraph 31, the accounting treatment permitted by that paragraph may be followed.

Disclosure

35. If exchange differences on long-term monetary items resulting from foreign currency transactions or from translating the financial statements of foreign operations that are integral to the operations of the parent are deferred, the cumulative deferred amount still to be credited or charged to income should be disclosed.

36. If exchange differences arising on liabilities associated with the acquisition of assets have been included in the carrying amount of the related assets in accordance with paragraph 31, the amount arising during the period should be disclosed.

37. The following disclosures should be made with regard to the translation of the financial statements of foreign operations for incorporation in the financial statements of a reporting enterprise:

(a) the methods used;

(b) the net exchange difference for the period taken to shareholders' interests as a result of applying the procedures in paragraphs 32-33;

(c) the net exchange difference for the period taken to income as a result of applying the procedures in paragraph 34; and

(d) the procedure selected (closing or average rates) for translating the income statements of foreign entities.

Transitional Provisions

38. On the first occasion that an enterprise applies this Standard, the amount of the adjustments resulting from any change in accounting policy to comply with the Standard should be presented in accordance with International Accounting Standard 8, Unusual and Prior Period Items and Changes in Accounting Policies, except that restatement of comparative information in respect of prior years, though encouraged, is not required.

Effective Date

39. This International Accounting Standard becomes operative for financial statements covering periods beginning on or after 1 January, 1985.

International Accounting Standard 22

Accounting for Business Combinations

Contents

Introduction

1. This Statement deals with accounting for business combinations and the treatment of any resultant goodwill. The Statement is directed principally to consolidated financial statements of incorporated enterprises although certain of its requirements apply to financial statements of individual enterprises.

2. This Statement does not deal with investments that are accounted for under the equity method in accordance with International Accounting Standard 3, Consolidated Financial Statements, nor does it cover transfers or exchanges of assets among enterprises under common control.

Definitions

3. The following terms are used in this Statement with the meanings specified:

A *business combination* is the result of the acquiring of control of one or more enterprises by another enterprise or the uniting of interests of two or more enterprises.

Control is ownership, directly, or indirectly through subsidiaries, of more than one half of the voting power[1] of an enterprise.

Minority interest is that part of the net results of operations and of net assets of a subsidiary which is attributable to shares which are not directly owned by the parent nor indirectly owned by the parent through another subsidiary.

A *subsidiary* is an enterprise that is controlled by another enterprise (known as the parent).

A *parent* is an enterprise that has one or more subsidiaries.

A *uniting of interests* is when the shareholders of two or more enterprises combine in one entity the whole, or effectively the whole, of the net assets and operations of the enterprises in such a way as to achieve a continuing mutual sharing in the risks and benefits of the combined entity.

---

[1] Voting power refers to the rights attaching to voting shares issued and outstanding: that is, shares other than those held as 'treasury stock'. Treasury stock are a company's own shares which have been acquired by the issuing company and are legally available for re-issue. This practice is not permitted in some countries.

An *acquisition* is a business combination that is not a uniting of interests.

Fair value is the amount for which an asset could be exchanged between a knowledgeable, willing buyer and a knowledgeable, willing seller in an arm's length transaction.

Explanation

4.   There is general agreement that most business combinations are in substance acquisitions.

5.   It is also generally accepted that for a business combination to be classified as a uniting of interests, it is essential that, in addition to the criteria specified in the definition in paragraph 3, the basis for the transaction be an exchange of voting common shares of the enterprises involved. The uniting of interests is further demonstrated by continuing participation by management of the combining enterprises in the management of the combined enterprise.

6.   There are, however, differing views regarding the nature of any further conditions that may apply. Some believe that, in addition to an exchange of voting common shares, it is necessary that each party to a uniting of interests obtain a substantial share in the combined enterprise, even to the extent that it should not be possible to identify any one party as dominant therein. This belief is based in part on the view that the exchange of control of one enterprise for an insignificant share in a larger enterprise does not amount to a mutual sharing of risks and benefits.

7.   Others believe that the substance of a uniting of interests is evidenced by meeting certain criteria regarding the relationship of the parties, such as the former independence of the combining enterprises, the manner of their combination and the absence of planned transactions that would undermine the effect of the uniting of interests.

8.   There are two main methods of accounting for business combinations: (a) the purchase method and (b) the pooling of interests method (sometimes called the merger method).

9.   The object of the purchase method is to account for the acquired enterprise by applying the same principles as are applied in the normal purchase of assets. This method is always used in accounting for an acquisition and is sometimes used in accounting for a uniting of interests.

10. The object of the pooling of interests method is to account for the pooled enterprises as though the separate businesses were continuing as before, though now jointly owned and managed. Accordingly only minimal changes are made in aggregating the individual financial statements.

11. The use of the pooling of interests method is confined to circumstances which meet the criteria referred to in paragraph 5 for a uniting of interests.

The Purchase Method

12. Under the purchase method the buyer accounts for the cost of an acquisition by restating identifiable assets and liabilities acquired to their fair value at the date of acquisition. The identifiable assets and liabilities acquired may include assets and liabilities not recorded in the financial statements of the acquired enterprise. However, in attributing fair values to assets and liabilities acquired, it is not appropriate to raise provisions for future operating losses.

13. The determination of fair values may be influenced by the intentions of the buyer. For example, the buyer may have a specialised use for an asset, which is not available to other potential buyers. The buyer may intend to effect changes in the activities of the acquired enterprise which necessitate the creation of specific provisions for the expected costs, e.g. planned employee termination and plant relocation costs.

14. Normally, the results of operations of an acquired business are incorporated into the income statement of the buyer as from the date of acquisition, which is the date on which control of the acquired business is effectively transferred to the buyer. When an acquisition is achieved in stages, as for example when it is achieved by purchases on a stock exchange, the date of acquisition is considered to be the time at which control is obtained. When an acquisition is achieved through share purchases subject to conditions specified by the buyer, control is not deemed to be obtained until all significant conditions have been met.

Cost of acquisition

15. The cost of acquisition in the financial statements of the parent is the purchase consideration plus the expenses incidental thereto.

16. The purchase consideration may consist of cash, securities or other assets. In determining the value of the purchase consideration, an assessment is made of the fair value of its elements. A variety of techniques is applied in arriving at fair value. For example, when the purchase consideration includes quoted securities the market price is normally used in arriving at the fair value of the securities, provided that undue fluctuations or narrowness of the market do not make the market price an unreliable indicator. When the market is unreliable or no quotation exists, the fair value of the securities is estimated by reference to their proportional interest in the fair value of the buyer's business or by reference to the fair value of the business acquired, whichever is the more clearly evident.

17. Many acquisition agreements recognise that adjustments may have to be made to the purchase consideration in the light of one or more future events. When the additional payment is probable, and can reasonably be estimated at the date of the acquisition, it is included in the calculation of the purchase consideration. In all other cases the adjustment is recognised as soon as the amount is determinable (see International Accounting Standard 10, Contingencies and Events Occurring After the Balance Sheet Date).

18. The accounting treatment of any adjustment to the purchase consideration varies according to the nature of the contingency. When, for example, the contingency relates to the level of earnings or confirmation of the value of net assets of the acquired enterprise, the buyer treats the receipt or payment as an adjustment to the cost of acquisition. Effectively, the acquired business is found to have greater, or lesser, value than the provisional estimate made at the date of acquisition. The accounting treatment in the consolidated financial statements is to adjust the relevant assets, or goodwill arising on acquisition, as appropriate.

Treatment of goodwill arising on acquisition

19. Any excess of the cost of acquisition over the fair values of the net identifiable assets acquired is either recognised as an asset in the consolidated financial statements as goodwill arising on acquisition, or immediately adjusted against shareholders' interests.

20. Those who recognise goodwill arising on acquisition as an asset in the consolidated financial statements believe that it represents a payment

made in anticipation of future income, and that it is appropriate to treat it as an asset to be amortised to income on a systematic basis over its useful life.

21.   Factors which may be considered in estimating the useful life of goodwill arising on acquisition include:

- the foreseeable life of the business or industry,
- the effects of product obsolescence, changes in demand and other economic factors,
- the service life expectancies of key individuals or groups of employees,
- expected actions by competitors or potential competitors, and
- legal, regulatory or contractual provisions affecting the useful life.

22.   The view is sometimes held that goodwill arising on an acquisition may be retained as an asset as long as it is regarded as having economic value. This view, however, ignores the fact that with the passage of time the goodwill of a business derives increasingly from the efforts of the continuing business rather than from the amount expended by the buyer at the date of acquisition.

23.   Others believe that any difference (whether positive or negative) between the cost of acquisition and the fair values of the net identifiable assets acquired should be adjusted against shareholders' interests in the period of acquisition. They argue that goodwill is not an independently realisable asset, that it has an indeterminate life for which any amortisation programme is arbitrary, and that, as self-generated goodwill is not recognised, it is inappropriate to recognise goodwill arising on acquisition.

24.   In any case, if it becomes apparent that the excess of the cost of acquisition over the fair values of the net identifiable assets does not represent a payment made in anticipation of future income, a loss has been incurred which is charged to income in the consolidated financial statements. In these circumstances, an adjustment to the carrying amount of the investment in the financial statements of the buyer is normally required.

25.   It sometimes happens that the cost of an acquisition is lower than the aggregate fair value of identifiable assets and liabilities acquired. The difference (sometimes called negative goodwill) may either be treated as

deferred income, and recognised in income over the period similar to that considered in paragraph 21, or allocated over individual depreciable non-monetary assets acquired in proportion to their fair values.

Minority interest

26. Various methods are practised in accounting for a minority interest in a subsidiary following a business combination. The minority interest in the balance sheet immediately following a business combination is variously recorded as the minority's share of:

(a) the post-acquisition values (i.e. the fair values) of the net identifiable assets involved;

(b) the pre-acquisition carrying amounts of the net assets of the subsidiary. In this case the restatement of net assets to fair value is limited to the proportion attributable to the buyer;

(c) the post-acquisition values (i.e. the fair values) of the net identifiable assets acquired adjusted by the goodwill arising on acquisition (or by the shortfall from fair value) that would have arisen if 100 per cent of the subsidiary had been acquired. In this case goodwill arising on acquisition is recorded on an equivalent basis.

27. Supporters of method (a) argue that any restatement of the value of an asset should be for the whole of the asset and that the consolidated financial statements should report the assets controlled by the group at values arrived at in accordance with the group's accounting policies. Support for method (b) is based on the claim that the minority's proportion of the assets has not been acquired and should therefore be retained at pre-acquisition values. For method (c) it is claimed that the amount shown as goodwill arising on acquisition would be more useful if it were calculated by reference to the total net assets of the subsidiary rather than by reference only to the proportion that was acquired by the parent.

28. The first and second methods are acceptable alternatives in accounting for a minority interest but the third method is not acceptable because it cannot be assumed that the purchase consideration for the majority interest can be extrapolated to the hypothetical purchase of all the shares.

The Pooling of Interests Method

29.   The object of the pooling of interests method is to account for the pooled enterprises as though the separate businesses were continuing as before, though now jointly owned. The pooling of interests method does not recognise any goodwill arising on acquisition, and is only used where the purchase consideration is principally an exchange of voting common shares rather than a disbursement of cash or other assets. Under the pooling of interests method the combined assets, liabilities and reserves are recorded at their existing carrying amounts (after having made the adjustments required in paragraph 30). The difference between the amount recorded as share capital issued (plus any additional consideration in the form of cash or other assets) and the amount recorded for the share capital acquired is adjusted against shareholders' interests. The consolidated financial statements include the results of operations and the assets and liabilities of the pooled enterprises as if they had been part of the group for the whole of the current and preceding periods.

30.   If at the time of combination the pooled enterprises have conflicting accounting policies, a uniform set of accounting policies is adopted following the business combination. The effects on the financial statements of any changes in accounting policy are reported in accordance with International Accounting Standard 8, Unusual and Prior Period Items and Changes in Accounting Policies.

Treatment of Taxes on Income

31.   In some countries the method of accounting for business combinations called for by this Statement will differ from that applied under their respective income tax laws. Permanent or timing differences may therefore arise between recognition of income or expenses for financial reporting and for tax purposes. Such differences are recognised in accordance with International Accounting Standard 12, Accounting for Taxes on Income.

32.   An enterprise entering into a business combination may have potential benefits from tax loss carryforwards that have not been recognised in its financial statements because there was no assurance beyond a reasonable doubt that they could be realised. However, this doubt may be removed as a result of the business combination, thus permitting recognition of the assets.

33. Benefits from tax losses not recognised as a separate asset at the date of combination may subsequently be realised. When this occurs, the benefits are normally recognised as income in accordance with International Accounting Standard 12, Accounting for Taxes on Income. A reassessment of the carrying amount of goodwill arising on acquisition is then required to identify any content attributable to those tax benefits, which is charged to income. However, when the difference between the cost of acquisition and the fair values of identifiable assets and liabilities acquired was previously adjusted against shareholders' interests, benefits received subsequently are also adjusted against shareholders' interests.

Disclosure

34. The extent of disclosures that are appropriate in the financial statements immediately following a business combination are set out in paragraphs 50 - 52.

Business Combinations after the Balance Sheet Date

35. When a business combination is effected after the balance sheet date but before the issue of the financial statements of either party to the combination, disclosure is made in accordance with International Accounting Standard 10, Contingencies and Events Occurring After the Balance Sheet Date, but the business combination is not incorporated in the financial statements. In certain circumstances the combination may also provide additional information affecting the financial statements themselves, for instance by allowing the going concern assumption to be maintained.

International Accounting Standard 22
Accounting for Business Combinations

International Accounting Standard 22 comprises paragraphs 36-56 of this Statement. The Standard should be read in the context of paragraphs 1-35 of this Statement and of the Preface to Statements of International Accounting Standards.

36. A business combination should be accounted for under the purchase method detailed in paragraphs 39-45, except in the rare circumstances when it is deemed to be a uniting of interests.

37. A business combination is deemed to be a uniting of interests only if the shareholders of the combining enterprises achieve a continuing mutual sharing in the risks and benefits attaching to the combined enterprise, and

   (a)   the basis of the transaction is principally an exchange of voting common shares of the enterprises involved; and

   (b)   the whole, or effectively the whole, of the net assets and operations of the combining enterprises are combined in one entity.

38. When a business combination is deemed to be a uniting of interests the pooling of interests method detailed in paragraphs 46-47 may be used.

The Purchase Method

39. In preparing consolidated financial statements, the identifiable assets and liabilities of the acquired enterprise should be restated to their fair values at the date of acquisition.

40. An enterprise should adopt one of the following policies for dealing with any difference (whether positive or negative) between the cost of

acquisitions and the fair values of the net identifiable assets acquired:

(a) recognition in income in accordance with the procedures in paragraphs 41-42, or

(b) immediate adjustment against shareholders' interests.

In either case, paragraphs 43-45 apply.

Recognition in income

41. Where the policy in paragraph 40 (a) is adopted, any excess of the cost of acquisition over the fair values of the net identifiable assets acquired should be recognised as an asset in the consolidated financial statements as goodwill arising on acquisition, and amortised to income on a systematic basis over its useful life. If it is found at any time that goodwill arising on acquisition is not supported by future income, it should, to the extent necessary, be charged immediately to income.

42. If the cost of acquisition is lower than the aggregate fair value of net identifiable assets acquired, it should either be treated as deferred income and recognised in income on a systematic basis, or allocated over individual depreciable non-monetary assets acquired in proportion to their fair values.

Other procedures

43. The cost of acquisition should include any non-cash element at fair value.

44. When the acquisition agreement provides for an adjustment to the purchase consideration contingent on one or more future events, the amount should be included in the cost of acquisition if payment is probable and a reasonable estimate of the amount can be made. In all other cases the adjustment should be recognised as soon as the amount is determinable, in accordance with the provisions of International Accounting Standard 10, Contingencies and Events Occurring After the Balance Sheet Date.

45. A minority interest that arises on a business combination should preferably be stated at the appropriate proportion of the post-acquisition fair values of the net identifiable assets of the subsidiary. Alternatively it may be stated at the appropriate proportion of the pre-acquisition carrying amounts of the net assets of the subsidiary.

The Pooling of Interests Method

46.   In applying the pooling of interests method, the assets and liabilities of the combining enterprises and their revenues and expenses for the period in which the combination occurs and for any comparative periods disclosed should be included in the financial statements of the combined enterprises as if they had been combined from the start of those periods.

47.   The difference between the amount recorded as share capital issued (plus any additional consideration in the form of cash or other assets) and the amount recorded for the share capital acquired should be adjusted against shareholders' interests.

Treatment of Taxes on Income

48.   Permanent and timing differences between the recognition of income and expenses for financial reporting and for tax purposes should be dealt with in accordance with International Accounting Standard 12, Accounting for Taxes on Income.

49.   Unless paragraph 40 (b) was applied, benefits received from tax loss carryforwards of an acquired enterprise that existed but were not recognised as an asset at the date of acquisition should be recognised as income in accordance with International Accounting Standard 12, Accounting for Taxes on Income. The carrying amount of goodwill arising on acquisition should be re-assessed to identify any content attributable to the benefits received, which should be charged to income. If paragraph 40 (b) was applied, such benefits should be adjusted against shareholders' interests.

Disclosure

50.   For all business combinations the following disclosures should be made in the financial statements immediately following the combination:

(a)   names and descriptions of the combining enterprises;

(b)   effective date of the combination for accounting purposes; and

(c)   the method of accounting used to reflect the combination.

Other disclosures are required by International Accounting Standard 3, Consolidated Financial Statements, and International Accounting Standard 5, Information to be Disclosed in Financial Statements.

51. For business combinations accounted for under the purchase method, the following additional disclosures should be made in the first financial statements following the combination:

(a)   the percentage of voting shares acquired;

(b)   cost of acquisition and a description of the purchase consideration paid or contingently payable; and

(c)   the amount of any difference between cost of acquisition and the aggregate fair value of net identifiable assets acquired, and the treatment thereof, including the period of amortisation of any goodwill arising on acquisition.

52. For business combinations accounted for under the pooling of interests method, the following additional disclosures should be made in the first financial statements following the combination:

(a)   description and number of shares issued, together with the percentage of each enterprise's voting shares exchanged to effect the combination;

(b)   amounts of assets and liabilities contributed by each enterprise; and

(c)   details of the results of operations of the enterprises prior to the date of the combination that are included in the net income shown by the combined financial statements. Details should include sales, other operating revenues, unusual items and net income.

Business Combinations after the Balance Sheet Date

53. The financial statements of an enterprise should not incorporate a business combination to which the enterprise is a party if the date of the combination is after the date of the balance sheet included in the financial statements.

54. Business combinations which have been effected after the balance sheet date and before the date on which the financial statements of one of the combining enterprises are authorised for issue should be disclosed if they are of such importance that non-disclosure would affect the ability of the users of the financial statements to make proper evaluations and decisions (see International Accounting Standard 10, Contingencies and Events Occurring After the Balance Sheet Date). Disclosure should comprise such of the applicable details in paragraphs 50-52 of this Standard as can be estimated or, alternatively, a statement that no such estimate can be made.

Effective Date

55. This International Accounting Standard becomes operative for business combinations effected on or after 1 January, 1985.

Transitional Provisions

56. Retrospective application of this Standard is encouraged but not required. If the Standard is not applied retrospectively, enterprises are encouraged to deal with pre-existing goodwill arising on acquisition either by:

(a) recognition in income in accordance with the procedures in paragraphs 41-42, or

(b) immediate adjustment against shareholders' interests.

International Accounting Standard 23

Capitalisation of Borrowing Costs

Contents

Introduction

1.   This Statement deals with the capitalisation of borrowing costs in the financial statements of enterprises as a part of the historical cost of acquiring certain assets. It does not deal with the capitalisation of actual or imputed costs of equity or preferred capital.

Definition

2.   The following term is used in this Statement with the meaning specified:

> *Borrowing costs* are interest costs incurred by an enterprise in connection with the borrowing of funds. This includes amortisation of discount or premium arising on the issue of debt securities, amortisation of ancillary costs incurred in connection with the arrangement of borrowing and foreign currency differences relating to borrowed funds to the extent that they are regarded as an adjustment to interest costs.

Scope

3.   This Statement does not insist on capitalisation of borrowing costs. Rather this Statement:

(a)   requires each enterprise that has incurred borrowing costs to adopt, and consistently apply, a policy of capitalisation or non-capitalisation of borrowing costs for assets that require a substantial period of time to get them ready for their intended use or sale;

(b)   sets out the requirements to be followed in the event that the enterprise elects to follow the capitalisation approach; and

(c)   sets out disclosure requirements.

Explanation

4.   Views differ on the appropriate accounting treatment for borrowing costs. Some regard such costs as forming part of the cost of the asset with which they can be identified either directly or indirectly. Others regard them as costs which are charged to income regardless of how the borrowing is applied. The significant amounts of borrowing costs incurred by enterprises make the accounting treatment of borrowing costs an important consideration in the preparation of financial statements.

5.   For many years public utilities in various countries and companies in the construction industry have capitalised borrowing costs. This practice has been increasing in other industries.

For and Against Capitalisation

6.   Proponents of the view that borrowing costs be capitalised, under prescribed conditions, as part of the cost of acquiring assets, advance the following points in support of their view:

(a)   Borrowing costs incurred as a consequence of a decision to acquire an asset are not intrinsically different from other costs that are commonly capitalised. If an asset requires a period of time to bring it to the condition and location necessary for its intended use, the borrowing costs incurred during that period as a result of expenditures on the asset are a part of the cost of acquiring the asset.

(b)   Failure to capitalise the borrowing costs associated with the acquisition of assets reduces current earnings as a consequence of the acquisition of assets.

(c)   Capitalisation results in a greater degree of comparability between the costs of those assets paid for in stages during construction and those paid for on completion (the price of which usually takes borrowing costs into account).

7.   Proponents of the view that borrowing costs always be treated as a charge to income, regardless of how the borrowing is applied, advance the following points in support of their view:

(a)   Borrowing costs are incurred in support of the whole of the activities of the enterprise. Any attempt to associate borrowing costs with a particular asset is necessarily arbitrary.

(b)   Capitalisation of borrowing costs results in the same type of asset having a different carrying amount, depending on the method of financing adopted by the enterprise.

(c)   Treating borrowing costs as a charge against income results in financial statements giving more comparable results from period to period thus providing a better indication of the future cash flows of an enterprise. Interest costs fluctuate with the borrowing levels and rates which give rise to them, not with asset acquisition.

Methods of Capitalising Borrowing Costs

8. For those enterprises which have adopted a policy of capitalisation, borrowing costs are capitalised when such costs are significant to the enterprise and there have been expenditures on assets that require a substantial period of time to get them ready for their intended use or sale. Borrowing costs are capitalised by applying a capitalisation rate to these expenditures.

9. Capitalisation of borrowing costs usually begins when:

   (a) expenditures for the asset are being incurred;

   (b) activities that are necessary to prepare the asset for its intended use or sale are in progress or, for investments in enterprises, activities preparatory to the commencement of the investee's planned principal operations are in progress; and

   (c) borrowing costs are being incurred.

10. Capitalisation of borrowing costs usually ceases:

   (a) for property, plant and equipment, when the asset is ready for use;

   (b) for investments in enterprises, when the investee begins its operations;

   (c) for inventory that requires a significant period of time to bring to a saleable condition, and real estate and other long-term development projects, when those assets are ready for their intended use or sale.

11. Borrowing costs are not usually capitalised for inventories that are routinely manufactured or otherwise produced in large quantites on a repetitive basis.

12. Where the construction of an asset is completed in parts and each part is capable of being used whilst construction continues on the other parts, it is usual to cease capitalisation of borrowing costs for each part as it is completed. Where all of the components need to be completed in their entirety before any part of the asset can be used, it is usual for capitalisation of borrowing costs to continue until the entire asset is completed.

13. When active development of assets is interrupted the capitalisation of borrowing costs is usually suspended until active development resumes.

14. Capitalisation of borrowing costs normally continues even where this results in the total capitalised cost of the asset exceeding recoverable amount or net realisable value. In this situation an adjustment is made in accordance with International Accounting Standard 2, Valuation and Presentation of Inventories in the Context of the Historical Cost System, International Accounting Standard 3, Consolidated Financial Statements, or International Accounting Standard 16, Accounting for Property, Plant and Equipment.

Determination of Amount and Rate

15. The amount of borrowing costs to be capitalised is in principle that part of the total borrowing costs incurred by an enterprise that would have been avoided if expenditure for an asset had not been made. The amount capitalised is usually calculated by applying a capitalisation rate to the expenditure on the asset. In practice the capitalisation rate is generally determined by comparing the total borrowing costs with borrowings outstanding during the period. However, the rate on new borrowings associated with expenditures on the acquisition, construction or production of specific assets is also used. The use of the relevant market rate for borrowings available to the enterprise is generally not considered appropriate because it may not represent that part of total borrowing costs that could have been avoided if expenditure for an asset had not been made.

16. Sometimes the financing arrangements for specific projects may result in an enterprise incurring a borrowing cost from the commencement date of the agreement on the full amount of the obligation. Under such arrangements, funds are often temporarily invested pending their requirement. Occasionally, interest-bearing compensating balances are required. It is appropriate to offset such investment income against the associated borrowing costs in determining the capitalisation rate.

17. In a group of companies various problems may exist in identifying the borrowings from which the capitalisation rate is determined. Such problems can arise from the complexities of borrowing money in different countries at varying rates of interest and lending that money on various bases throughout the group. Other complications arise through loans denominated in or linked to foreign currencies, by group operations in highly inflationary economies or by fluctuating exchange rates. Thus, in some circumstances, it may be appropriate to include all borrowings of the

parent company and its consolidated subsidiaries; in other circumstances it may be appropriate for each foreign subsidiary to use an average of the rates applicable to its own borrowings. Selection of a capitalisation rate requires judgement to determine a reasonable measure of the cost of borrowing in terms of costs incurred that could otherwise have been avoided.

Limit to Capitalisation

18.   An overall restriction on the total amount of borrowing costs that may be capitalised in an accounting period is that they should not exceed the total amount of borrowing costs incurred by an enterprise in that period. In consolidated financial statements, the limitation is applied by reference to the consolidated amount of borrowing costs.

Effect on Taxes on Income

19.   The effect on income tax expense of a difference between the treatment of borrowing costs for tax accounting and financial reporting is dealt with in accordance with International Accounting Standard 12, Accounting for Taxes on Income.

Disclosure

20.   It is appropriate to disclose the amount of borrowing costs capitalised during the period in financial statements of enterprises that adopt a policy of capitalising borrowing costs.

International Accounting Standard 23
Capitalisation of Borrowing Costs

International Accounting Standard 23 comprises paragraphs 21-30 of this Statement. The Standard should be read in the context of paragraphs 1-20 of this Statement and of the Preface to Statements of International Accounting Standards*.

21. An enterprise that has incurred borrowing costs and incurred expenditures on assets that take a substantial period of time to get them ready for their intended use or sale should adopt a policy of either capitalising borrowing costs or not capitalising borrowing costs for those assets. The policy should be applied consistently in accordance with International Accounting Standard 8, Unusual and Prior Period Items and Changes in Accounting Policy. Paragraphs 22 to 29 of this Standard apply when a policy of capitalising borrowing costs is adopted.

Capitalisation of Borrowing Costs

22. Borrowing costs should be capitalised as part of the cost of an asset by applying a capitalisation rate to expenditures on the acquisition, construction or production of assets that require a substantial period of time to get them ready for their use or sale.

23. The capitalisation rate should be determined by relating the borrowing costs incurred during a period to the borrowings outstanding during that period. When a new borrowing is associated with expenditures on the acquisition, construction or production of specific assets, the capitalisation rate may be determined on the basis of the actual borrowing costs incurred on that borrowing.

---

* International Accounting Standards are not intended to apply to immaterial items (see paragraph 12 of the Preface).

24.   Capitalisation of borrowing costs, for assets other than investments, should commence when:

  (a)   expenditures for the asset are being incurred;

  (b)   activities that are necessary to prepare the asset for its intended use or sale are in progress; and

  (c)   borrowing costs are being incurred.

Capitalisation of borrowing costs for investments should commence when conditions (a) and (c) above are satisfied and the investee has activities in progress necessary to commence its planned principal operations.

25.   Capitalisation of borrowing costs should cease when the asset is ready for its intended use or sale or, in the case of investments, when the investee has commenced its planned principal operations. Capitalisation should be suspended during extended periods in which active development is interrupted.

26.   Where the construction of an asset is completed in parts and each part is capable of being used whilst construction continues on other parts, capitalisation of borrowing costs should cease on each part as it is complete.

27.   The amount of borrowing costs capitalised during a period should not exceed the total amount of borrowing costs incurred by the enterprise in that period. In consolidated financial statements, the limitation applied is the consolidated amount of borrowing costs.

Disclosure

28.   The financial statements should disclose the amount of borrowing costs that have been capitalised during the period.

Transitional Provisions

29.   A change in accounting policy to comply with this Standard should be applied to borrowing costs incurred in current and future periods and should be disclosed in accordance with the provisions of International Accounting Standard 8, Unusual and Prior Period Items and Changes in Accounting Policies.

Effective Date

30.   This International Accounting Standard becomes operative for financial statements covering periods beginning on or after 1 January, 1986.

International Accounting Standard 24

Related Party Disclosures

Contents

Introduction

1.   This statement deals with the disclosure of related parties and transactions between a reporting enterprise and its related parties.

2.   The requirements of this Statement apply to the financial statements of each reporting enterprise.

3.   No disclosure of transactions is required:

   (a)   in consolidated financial statements in respect of intra-group transactions,

   (b)   in parent financial statements when they are made available or published with the consolidated financial statements,

   (c)   in financial statements of a wholly-owned subsidiary if its parent is incorporated in the same country and provides consolidated financial statements in that country, and

   (d)   in financial statements of state-controlled enterprises of transactions with other state-controlled enterprises.

Definitions

4.   The following terms are used in this Statement with the meanings specified:

Related party – parties are considered to be related if one party has the ability to control the other party or exercise significant influence over the other party in making financial and operating decisions.

Related party transaction – a transfer of resources or obligations between related parties, regardless of whether a price is charged.

Control – ownership, directly, or indirectly through subsidiaries, of more than one half of the voting power of an enterprise, or a substantial interest in voting power and the power to direct, by statute or agreement, the financial and operating policies of the management of the enterprise.

Significant influence (for the purpose of this Statement) – participation in the financial and operating policy decisions of an enterprise, but not control of those policies. Significant influence may be exercised in several ways, usually by representation on the board of directors but also by, for example, participation in the policy making process, material intercompany transactions, interchange of managerial personnel or dependence on technical information. Significant influence may be gained by share ownership, statute or agreement. With share ownership, significant influence is presumed in accordance with the definition contained in International Accounting Standard 3, Consolidated Financial Statements.

Explanation

5.   This Statement deals only with those related party relationships described in (a) to (e) below:

(a)   enterprises that directly, or indirectly through one or more intermediaries, control, or are controlled by, or are under common control with, the reporting enterprise. (This includes holding companies, subsidiaries and fellow subsidiaries);

(b)   associated enterprises (see International Accounting Standard 3, Consolidated Financial Statements);

(c)   individuals owning, directly or indirectly, an interest in the voting power of the reporting enterprise that gives them significant influence over the enterprise, and close members ofthe family[1] of any such individual;

(d)   key management personnel, that is, those persons having authority and responsibility for planning, directing and controlling the activities of the reporting enterprise, including directors and officers of companies and close members of the families of such individuals; and

(e)   enterprises in which a substantial interest in the voting power is owned, directly or indirectly, by any person described in (c) or (d) or over which such a person is able to exercise significant influence, this includes enterprises owned by directors or major shareholders of the reporting enterprise and enterprises that have a member of key management in common with the reporting enterprise.

In considering each possible related party relationship, attention is directed to the substance of the relationship, and not merely the legal form.

---

[1] Close members of the family of an individual are those that may be expected to influence, or be influenced by, that person in their dealings with the enterprise.

6. In the context of this Statement, the following are deemed not to be related parties:

    (a) two companies simply because they have a director in common, notwithstanding paragraphs 5 (d) and (e) above, (but it is necessary to consider the possibility, and to assess the likelihood, that the director would be able to affect the policies of both companies in their mutual dealings);

    (b) (i)   providers of finance,
        (ii)   trade unions,
        (iii) public utilities, and
        (iv) government departments and agencies,
in the course of their normal dealings with an enterprise by virtue only of those dealings (although they may circumscribe the freedom of action of an enterprise or participate in its decision-making process); and

    (c) a single customer, supplier, franchisor, distributor or general agent with whom an enterprise transacts a significant volume of business merely by virtue of the resulting economic dependence.

The Related Party Issue

7. Related party relationships are a normal feature of commerce and business. For example, enterprises frequently carry on separate parts of their activities through subsidiary or associated enterprises and acquire interests in other enterprises – for investment purposes or for trading reasons – that are of sufficient proportions that the investing company can control or exercise significant influence on the financial and operating decisions of its investee.

8. A related party relationship could have an effect on the financial position and operating results of the reporting enterprise. Related parties may enter into transactions which unrelated parties would not enter into. Also, transactions between related parties may not be effected at the same amounts as between unrelated parties.

9. The operating results and financial position of an enterprise may be affected by a related party relationship even if related party transactions do not occur. The mere existence of the relationship may be sufficient to affect the transactions of the reporting enterprise with other parties. For

example, a subsidiary may terminate relations with a trading partner on acquisition by the parent of a fellow subsidiary engaged in the same trade as the former partner. Alternatively, one party may refrain from acting because of the significant influence of another – for example, a subsidiary may be instructed by its parent not to engage in research and development.

10.　　Because there is an inherent difficulty for management to determine the effect of infuences which do not lead to transactions, disclosure of such effects is not required by this Statement.

11.　　Accounting recognition of a transfer of resources is normally based on the price agreed between the parties. Between unrelated parties the price is an arm's length price. Related parties may have a degree of flexibility in the price-setting process that is not present in transactions between unrelated parties.

12.　　A variety of methods is used to price transactions between related parties.

13.　　One way of determining a price for a transaction between related parties is by the comparable uncontrolled price method, which sets the price by reference to comparable goods sold in an economically comparable market to a buyer unrelated to the seller. Where the goods or services supplied in a related party transaction, and the conditions relating thereto, are similar to those in normal trading transactions, this method is often used. It is also often used for determining the cost of finance.

14.　　Where goods are transferred between related parties before sale to an independent party, the resale price method is often used. This reduces the resale price by a margin, representing an amount from which the re-seller would seek to cover his costs and make an appropriate profit, to arrive at a transfer price to the re-seller. There are problems of judgement in determining a compensation appropriate to the re-seller's contribution to the process. This method is also used for transfers of other resources, such as rights and services.

15.　　Another approach is the cost-plus method, which seeks to add an appropriate mark-up to the supplier's cost. Difficulties may be experienced in determining both the elements of cost attributable and the mark-up. Among the yardsticks that may assist in determining transfer prices are comparable returns in similar industries on turnover or capital employed.

16.   Sometimes prices of related party transactions are not determined under one of the methods described in paragraphs 13 to 15 above. Sometimes, no price is charged – as in the examples of the free provision of management services and the extension of free credit on a debt.

17.   Sometimes, transactions would not have taken place if the relationship had not existed. For example, a company that sold a large proportion of its production to its parent company at cost might not have found an alternative customer if the parent company had not purchased the goods.

Disclosure

18.   In many countries the laws require financial statements to give disclosures about certain categories of related parties. In particular, attention is focussed on transactions with the directors of an enterprise, especially their remuneration and borrowings, because of the fiduciary nature of their relationship with the enterprise. In addition, International Accounting Standard 5, Information to be Disclosed in Financial Statements, calls for disclosures of significant intercompany transactions and investments in and balances with group and associated companies and with directors. International Accounting Standard 3, Consolidated Financial Statements, requires in such statements a list of significant subsidiaries and associated companies, and, for unconsolidated subsidiaries, intra-group balances and the nature of transactions with the remainder of the group. International Accounting Standard 8, Unusual and Prior Period Items and Changes in Accounting Policies, requires disclosure of unusual items.

19   The following are examples of situations where related party transactions may lead to disclosures by a reporting enterprise in the period which they affect:

- purchases or sales of goods (finished or unfinished)
- purchases or sales of property and other assets
- rendering or receiving of services
- agency arrangements
- leasing arrangements
- transfer of research and development
- licence agreements
- finance (incuding loans and equity contributions in cash or in kind)
- guarantees and collaterals
- management contracts.

20.   In order for a reader of financial statements to form a view about the effects of related party relationships on a reporting enterprise, it is appropriate to disclose the related party relationship where control exists, irrespective of whether there have been transactions between the related parties.

21.   If there have been transactions between the related parties, it is appropriate to disclose the types of transactions and the elements of transactions necessary for an understanding of the financial statements. These elements would normally include:

   (a)   an indication of the volume of the transactions, either as an amount or as an appropriate proportion,
   (b)   amounts or appropriate proportions of outstanding items, and
   (c)   pricing policies.

22.   Similar items are usually aggregated unless separate disclosure is necessary for an understanding of the effects of related party transactions on the financial statements of the reporting enterprise.

23.   Disclosure of transactions between members of a group is unnecessary in consolidated financial statements because consolidated financial statements present information about the parent and subsidiaries as a single reporting enterprise. Transactions with associated enterprises accounted for under the equity method are not eliminated and therefore require separate disclosure as related party transactions.

International Accounting Standard 24
Related Party Disclosures

International Accounting Standard 24 comprises paragraphs 24-28 of this Statement. The Standard should be read in the context of paragraphs 1-23 of this Statement and of the Preface to Statements of International Accounting Standards [2].

24.   This Standard applies only to those related party relationships described in paragraph 5, as modified by paragraph 6.

25.   Related party relationships where control exists should be disclosed irrespective of whether there have been transactions between the related parties.

26.   If there have been transactions between related parties, the reporting enterprise should disclose the nature of the related party relationships as well as the types of transactions and the elements of the transactions necessary for an understanding of the financial statements.

27.   Items of similar nature may be disclosed in aggregate except when separate disclosure is necessary for an understanding of the effects of related party transactions on the financial statements of the reporting enterprise.

Effective Date

28.   This International Accounting Standard becomes operative for financial statements covering the periods beginning on or after 1 January, 1986.

---

[2] International Accounting Standards are not intended to apply to immaterial items (see paragraph 12 of the Preface).

International Accounting Standard 25

Accounting for Investments

Contents

Introduction

1.   This Statement deals with accounting for investments in the financial statements of enterprises and with related disclosure requirements.

2.   This Statement does not deal with :

(a)   the bases for recognition of interest, royalties, dividends and rentals earned on investments, which are covered by International Accounting Standard 18, Revenue Recognition, and International Accounting Standard 17, Accounting for Leases;

(b)   investments in subsidiaries;

(c)   investments in associates and joint ventures;

(d)   goodwill, patents, trademarks and similar assets;

(e)   finance leases as defined in International Accounting Standard 17, Accounting for Leases; and

(f)   investments of retirement benefit plans and life insurance enterprises.

Definitions

3.   The following terms are used in this Statement with the meanings specified:

An *investment* is an asset held by an enterprise for the accretion of wealth through distribution (such as interest, royalties, dividends and rentals), for capital appreciation or for other benefits to the investing enterprise such as those obtained through trading relationships. Inventories as defined in International Accounting Standard 2, Valuation and Presentation of Inventories in the Context of the Historical Cost System, are not investments. Property, plant and equipment as defined in International Accounting Standard 16, Accounting for Property, Plant and Equipment, (other than investment properties) are not investments.

A *current investment* is an investment that is by its nature readily realisable and is intended to be held for not more than one year.

A *long-term investment* is an investment other than a current investment.

An *investment property* is an investment in land or buildings that are not occupied substantially for use by, or in the operations of, the investing enterprise or another enterprise in the same group as the investing enterprise.

Fair value is the amount for which an asset could be exchanged between a knowledgeable, willing buyer and a knowledgeable, willing seller in an arm's length transaction.

Market value is the amount obtainable from the sale of an investment in an active market.

Marketable means that there is an active market from which a market value (or some indicator that enables a market value to be calculated) is available.

Explanation

Forms of Investments

4.   Enterprises hold investments for diverse reasons. For some enterprises, investment activity is a significant element of operations, [1] and assessment of the performance of the enterprise may largely, or solely, depend on the reported results of this activity. Some hold investments as a store of surplus funds and some hold trade investments in order to cement a trading relationship or establish a trading advantage.

5.   Some investments are represented by certificates or similar documents; others are not. The nature of an investment may be that of a debt, other than a short or long-term trade debt, representing a monetary amount owing to the holder and usually bearing interest; alternatively it may be a stake in an enterprise's results, such as an equity share. Most investments represent financial rights, but some are tangible — such as certain investments in land or buildings and direct investments in gold, diamonds or other marketable commodities.

6.   For some investments, an active market exists from which a market value can be established. For such investments, market value is an indicator of fair value. For other investments, an active market does not exist and other means are used to determine fair value.

Classification of Investments

7.   Most enterprises present balance sheets that distinguish current assets from long-term assets in accordance with International Accounting Standard

---

[1] Enterprises for which investment activity is a significant element of operations, such as insurance companies and some banks, are often subject to regulatory control. The Preface to Statements of International Accounting Standards provides that International Accounting Standards do not override local regulations governing the issue of financial statements.

13, Presentation of Current Assets and Current Liabilities. Current investments are included in current assets. The fact that a marketable investment has been retained for a considerable period does not necessarily preclude its classification as current.

8.   Investments held primarily to protect, facilitate or further existing business or trading relations, often called trade investments, are not made with the intention that they will be available as additional cash resources and are thus classified as long-term. Other investments, such as investment properties, are intended to be held for a number of years to generate income and capital gain. They are therefore classified as long-term assets even though they may be marketable.

9.   Some enterprises choose not to distinguish between current and long-term assets, and others may be required by regulations to adopt a balance sheet format that makes no distinction. Many such enterprises operate in the financial field, such as banks and insurance companies. Although such enterprises do not intend to realise their assets in current operations, they usually regard many of their investments as being available for the purposes of their current operations if required.

10.   However, such enterprises may have investments properly regarded as long-term assets, for example a bank may hold shares in a leasing company.

11.   Many such enterprises therefore analyse their investments and attribute carrying amounts to them according to whether their characteristics are those of current investments or long-term investments.

Cost of Investments

12.   The cost of an investment includes acquisition charges such as brokerages, fees, duties and bank fees.

13.   If an investment is acquired, or partly acquired, by the issue of shares or other securities, the acquisition cost is the fair value of the securities issued and not their nominal or par value. If an investment is acquired in exchange, or part exchange, for another asset, the acquisition cost of the investment is determined by reference to the fair value of the asset given up. It may be appropriate to consider the fair value of the investment acquired if it is more clearly evident.

14.   Interest, royalties, dividends and rentals receivable in connection with an investment are generally regarded as income, being the return on the investment. However, in some circumstances, such inflows represent a recovery of cost and do not form part of income. For example, when unpaid interest has accrued before the acquisition of an interest-bearing investment and is therefore included in the price paid for the investment, the subsequent receipt of interest is allocated between pre-acquisition and post-acquisition periods; the pre-acquisition portion is deducted from cost. When dividends on equity securities are declared from pre-acquisition profits a similar treatment applies. If it is difficult to make such an allocation except on an arbitrary basis, the cost of an investment is normally reduced by dividends receivable only if they clearly represent a recovery of part of cost.

15.   The difference between the acquisition cost and redemption value of an investment in debt securities (the discount or premium on acquisition) is usually amortised by the investor over the period from acquisition to its maturity so that a constant yield is earned on the investment. The amortised discount or premium is credited or charged to income as though it were interest and added to or subtracted from the carrying amount of the security. The resulting carrying amount is then regarded as cost.

Carrying Amount of Investments
Current investments

16.   Opinions differ on the appropriate carrying amount for current investments. Some maintain that, for financial statements prepared under the historical cost convention, the general rule of lower of cost and net realisable value is applicable to investments; and since most current investments are marketable, the carrying amount is the lower of cost and market value. Supporters of this method of determining carrying amount claim that it provides a prudent balance sheet amount and does not result in recognising unrealised gains in income. They also claim that fortuitous swings in stock market prices, which may reverse, are not brought to account merely as the result of the choice of a particular balance sheet date.

17.   Others argue that, since current investments are a readily realisable store of wealth, or a cash substitute, it is appropriate to value them at fair value, usually market value. The enterprise is not concerned with the cost of such items but with the cash it could raise by disposing of them. Investments are distinguished from inventories because they can generally be sold without effort, whereas it would normally be inappropriate to recognise profit on sale of inventories before the sale was assured. Each investment is dispensable by

the business — for example an equity investment could be sold and the proceeds re-invested in a bank deposit account without detriment to the business — and therefore it is appropriate to report it at market value. Supporters of market value also argue that reporting investments at historical cost allows management to recognise income at its discretion, since selected investments can be sold and immediately repurchased and the resulting profit reported in income, although such transactions have not changed the enterprise's economic position.

18.   In general, the concern of an enterprise is with the overall value of its current investment portfolios, and not with each individual investment, since the investments are held collectively as a store of wealth. Consistent with this view, investments carried at the lower of cost and market value are valued on an aggregate portfolio basis, in total or by category of investment, and not on an individual investment basis. However, some argue that the use of the portfolio basis results in losses being offset against unrealised gains.

Long-term investments

19.   Long-term investments are usually carried at cost. However, when there is a decline, other than temporary, in the value of a long-term investment, the carrying amount is reduced to recognise the decline. Indicators of the value of an investment may be obtained by reference to its market value, the investee's assets and results and the expected cash flows from the investment. Risk and the type and extent of the investor's stake in the investee are also taken into account. Restrictions on distributions by the investee or on disposal by the investor may affect the value attributed to the investment.

20.   Many long-term investments are of individual importance to the investing enterprise. The carrying amount of long-term investments is therefore normally determined on an item-by-item basis. However, in some countries, marketable equity securities classified as long-term investments may be carried at the lower of cost and market value determined on a portfolio basis. In these cases, temporary reductions and reversals of such reductions are included in equity.

21.   Reductions for other than a temporary decline in the carrying amounts of long-term investments are charged in the income statement unless they offset a previous revaluation (see paragraph 23). Reductions in carrying amount may be reversed when there is a rise in the value of the investment, or if the reasons for the reduction no longer exist. However, in some countries reductions in the carrying amount are not reversed.

Revaluations

22.   Sometimes long-term investments are revalued to fair value. In the interests of consistency, a policy for the frequency of revaluation is adopted and all long-term investments are revalued at the same time or, at the minimum, an entire category is revalued.

23.   An increase in carrying amount arising from revaluation of long-term investments is credited directly to owners' equity as a revaluation surplus. To the extent that a decrease in carrying amount offsets a previous increase, for the same investment, that has been credited to revaluation surplus and not subsequently reversed or utilised, it is charged against that revaluation surplus. In all other cases, a decrease in carrying amount is charged to income. An increase on revaluation which is directly related to a previous decrease in carrying amount for the same investment that was charged to income, is credited to income to the extent that it offsets the previously recorded decrease.

Investment properties

24.   Some enterprises elect to account for investment properties as long-term investments. Other enterprises prefer to account for investment properties under their accounting policy for property, plant and equipment, in accordance with International Accounting Standard 16, Accounting for Property, Plant and Equipment, and charge depreciation in accordance with International Accounting Standard 4, Depreciation Accounting.

25.   Enterprises that account for investment properties as long-term investments consider that changes in their fair value, usually market value, are more significant than their depreciation. The properties are therefore revalued periodically on a systematic basis. Where fair values are recognised in the carrying amount, any changes in carrying amount are accounted for in accordance with paragraph 23. Where such fair values are not recognised in the carrying amount, they are disclosed.

Disposals of Investments

26.   On the sale of an investment, the difference between the carrying amount and the proceeds of sale, net of expenses, is recognised in the income statement as the profit or loss on sale. If the investment has previously been revalued, or was carried at market value, and the increase in carrying amount has been credited to, and still remains in, a revaluation surplus within owners' equity, the amount of the increase is transferred either to income or to retained earnings. The former treatment has the advantage of including all accretions of wealth arising from investments in the income statement.

27.   Any reduction to market value of current investments carried at the lower of cost and market value on a portfolio basis is made against the cost of the portfolio in aggregate; individual investments continue to be recorded at cost. Accordingly the profit or loss on sale of an individual investment is based on cost; however the aggregate reduction to market value of the portfolio needs to be assessed.

28.   When disposing of part of an enterprise's holding of a particular investment, a carrying amount must be allocated to the part sold. This carrying amount is usually determined from the average carrying amount of the total holding of the investment.

Transfers of Investments

29.   Sometimes long-term investments are re-classified as current investments. Transfers are made at:

(a)   the lower of cost and carrying amount if current investments are carried at the lower of cost and market value. If the investment was previously revalued, any remaining related revaluation surplus is reversed on the transfer; and

(b)   carrying amount if current investments are carried at fair value. If changes in fair value of current investments are included in income, any remaining related revaluation surplus is transferred to income and presented in accordance with International Accounting Standard 8, Unusual and Prior Period Items and Changes in Accounting Policies.

30.   Investments re-classified from current to long-term are each transferred at the lower of cost and market value, or at market value if they were previously stated at that value.

Switches of Investments in a Portfolio

31.   An enterprise with significant investment activity typically maintains a portfolio of investments in which it trades constantly. In doing so, the enterprise seeks to improve the quality and yield of its portfolio of investments. On disposing of a particular investment, funds released are available for reinvestment or may remain as the cash element of the investment portfolio.

32.   In view of the constant changes in investments in such a portfolio, different opinions are held as to the appropriate accounting treatment on disposal of a particular investment:

(a)   some maintain that an excess or deficiency of net sale proceeds over carrying amount represents a realised profit or loss, which should be recognised in income immediately;

(b)   others argue that the disposal merely reflects an adjustment of the constituents of the portfolio, representing no value increase or decrease since it is only a substitution of one investment for another, and that therefore no profit or loss should be reflected in income; and

(c)   a few advocate a middle course, whereby the difference between net sale proceeds and cost is amortised to income over a given period.

33.   Alternative (a) is the preferred method. Alternative (b) is appropriate only when the market value basis is used and changes in market value are included in income, since the adjustments to market value will already have been accounted for. Alternative (c) is inappropriate because it fails to recognise the whole of the profit or loss in the period in which it arises.

Income Statement

34.   Some enterprises that carry current investments at market value on the grounds that they are a store of freely disposable wealth recognise any gains or losses in market value as an element of income to be accounted for in the income statement along with profits and losses on disposals. However, in some countries such gains are not permitted to be included in income and are credited direct to owners' equity and accounted for in the same way as revaluation surplus on long-term investments.

35.   If current investments are carried at the lower of cost and market value, any reductions to market value and any reversals of such reductions are included in the income statement along with profits and losses on disposals.

36.   Any reductions in carrying amount for other than a temporary decline in value of long-term investments, and reversals of such reductions, and profits and losses on disposal of long-term investments, are included in income and presented in accordance with International Accounting Standard 8, Unusual and Prior Period Items and Changes in Accounting Policies.

Specialised Investment Enterprises

37.   In certain countries, there are specialised investment enterprises whose main business is the holding of a portfolio of marketable securities as an investment vehicle for their individual shareholders. These enterprises carry

their investments at fair value, usually market value, because this is the most appropriate basis in the circumstances. They regard realised profits and losses on their investments as being the same in substance as unrealised gains and losses and therefore account for them in the same way. They disclose a summary of all the movements in the value of their investments for the period.

38.   The constitutions of these enterprises prohibit the distribution as dividends of profits on disposal of investments and require a distinction to be drawn between income arising from interest and dividends and the gains or losses arising on the disposal of the investments. Hence these enterprises exclude from income all changes in value of investments whether or not they are realised.

Taxes

39.   Accounting for tax consequences resulting from the application of this Statement is dealt with in accordance with International Accounting Standard 12, Accounting for Taxes on Income.

Disclosure

40.   The following disclosures are appropriate:

(a)   the accounting policies for:

(i)   the determination of carrying amount of investments,

(ii)   the treatment of changes in market value of current investments carried at market value, and

(iii)   the treatment of the revaluation surplus on the sale of a revalued investment;

(b)   the significant amounts included in investment income for:

(i)   interest, royalties, dividends and rentals on long-term and current investments, and

(ii)   profits and losses on disposal of current investments and changes in value of such investments;

(c)   the market value of marketable investments if they are not carried at market value;

(d)   the fair value of investment properties if they are accounted for as long-term investments and not carried at fair value;

(e)   significant restrictions on the realisability of investments or the remittance of income and proceeds of disposal;

(f)   for long-term investments stated at revalued amounts:

(i)   the policy for the frequency of revaluations,

      (ii)   the date of the latest revaluation, and

      (iii) the basis of revaluation and whether an external valuer was involved;

(g)   the movements for the period in revaluation surplus and the nature of such movements; and

(h)   for enterprises whose main business is the holding of investments an analysis of the portfolio of investments.

41.   The following disclosures may be provided to assist a reader's understanding of the financial statements:

(a)   an analysis of long-term investments by category;

(b)   the directors' assessment of the fair value of investments that are not marketable;

(c)   where investments are not marketable, the method of assessing value used for comparison with cost, where applicable;

(d)   the amount of any previous revaluation surplus which related to the investments disposed of during the year and which has been previously distributed or converted into share capital; and

(e)   details of any single investment which represents a significant proportion of the reporting enterprise's assets.

International Accounting Standard 25
Accounting for Investments

International Accounting Standard 25 comprises paragraphs 42-56 of this Statement. The Standard should be read in the context of paragraphs 1-41 of this Statement and of the Preface to Statements of International Accounting Standards. [2]

42.   Enterprises should account for investments in accordance with paragraphs 43 to 53, unless they are specialised investment enterprises in which case they may account for investments in accordance with paragraph 54.

Classification of Investments

43.   An enterprise that distinguishes between current and long-term assets in its financial statements should present current investments as current assets and long-term investments as long-term assets.

44.   Enterprises that do not distinguish between current and long-term investments in their balance sheets should nevertheless make a distinction for measurement purposes and determine the carrying amount for investments in accordance with paragraphs 46-47.

Investment Properties

45.   An enterprise holding investment properties should either:

(a)   treat them as property in accordance with International Accounting Standard 16, Accounting for Property, Plant and Equipment, and depreciate them in accordance with International Accounting Standard 4, Depreciation Accounting; or

(b)   account for them as long-term investments.

---

[2]International Accounting Standards are not intended to apply to immaterial items (see paragraph 12 of the Preface.

Carrying Amount of Investments

46.   Investments classified as current assets should be carried in the balance sheet at either:

    (a)   market value, or

    (b)   the lower of cost and market value.

If current investments are carried at the lower of cost and market value, the carrying amount should be determined either on an aggregate portfolio basis, in total or by category of investment, or on an individual investment basis.

47.   Investments classified as long-term assets should be carried in the balance sheet at either:

    (a)   cost, or

    (b)   revalued amounts, or

    (c)   in the case of marketable equity securities, the lower of cost and market value determined on a portfolio basis.

If revalued amounts are used, a policy for the frequency of revaluations should be adopted and an entire category of long-term investments should be revalued at the same time.

The carrying amount of all long-term investments should be reduced to recognise a decline other than temporary in the value of the investments, such reduction being determined and made for each investment individually.

Changes in Carrying Amount of Investments

48.   An increase in carrying amount arising from the revaluation of long-term investments should be credited to owners' equity as a revaluation surplus. To the extent that a decrease in carrying amount offsets a previous increase, for the same investment, that has been credited to revaluation surplus and not subsequently reversed or utilised, it should be charged against that revaluation surplus. In all other cases, a decrease in carrying amount should be charged to income. An increase on revaluation directly related to a previous decrease in carrying amount for the same investment that was charged to income, should be credited to income to the extent that it offsets the previously recorded decrease.

49.   An enterprise that carries current investments at market value should adopt, and consistently apply, a policy for accounting for increases or decreases in carrying amount which should either:

    (a)   be included in income, or

    (b)   be accounted for in accordance with paragraph 48.

Disposals of Investments

50.   On disposal of an investment the difference between net disposal proceeds and the carrying amount should be charged or credited to income. If the investment was a current asset carried on a portfolio basis at the lower of cost and market value, the profit or loss on sale should be based on cost. If the investment was previously revalued, or was carried at market value and an increase in carrying amount transferred to revaluation surplus, the enterprise should adopt a policy either of crediting the amount of any remaining related revaluation surplus to income or of transferring it to retained earnings. This policy should be applied consistently in accordance with International Accounting Standard 8, Unusual and Prior Period Items and Changes in Accounting Policies.

Transfers of Investments

51.   For long-term investments re-classified as current investments, transfers should be made at:

(a)   the lower of cost and carrying amount, if current investments are carried at the lower of cost and market value. If the investment was previously revalued, any remaining related revaluation surplus should be reversed on the transfer; and

(b)   carrying amount if current investments are carried at market value. If changes in market value of current investments are included in income any remaining related revaluation surplus should be transferred to income.

52.   Investments re-classified from current to long-term should each be transferred at the lower of cost and market value, or at market value if they were previously stated at that value.

Income Statement

53.   The following should be included in income:

(a)   investment income arising from:

(i)   interest, royalties, dividends and rentals on long-term and current investments,

(ii)   profits and losses on disposal of current investments,

(iii)   unrealised gains and losses on current investments carried at market value, where that policy is adopted under paragraph 49, and

(iv)   reductions to market value and reversals of such reductions required to state current investments at the lower of cost and market value;

(b)   reductions of the carrying amount for other than a temporary decline in value of long-term investments, and reversals of such reductions; and

(c)   profits and losses on disposal of long-term investments, calculated in accordance with paragraph 50.

Specialised Investment Enterprises

54.   Specialised investment enterprises which are prohibited from distributing profits on the disposal of investments may exclude from income changes in value of investments, whether realised or not, provided they carry their investments at fair value. Such enterprises should include in the financial statements a summary of all the movements in value of their investments for the period.

Disclosure

55.   The following should be disclosed:

(a)   the accounting policies for:

   (i)   the determination of carrying amount of investments,

   (ii)   the treatment of changes in market value of current investments carried at market value, and

   (iii)   the treatment of a revaluation surplus on the sale of a revalued investment;

(b)   the significant amounts included in income for:

   (i)   interest, royalties, dividends and rentals on long-term and current investments, and

   (ii)   profits and losses on disposal of current investments, and changes in value of such investments;

(c)   the market value of marketable investments if they are not carried at market value;

(d)   the fair value of investment properties if they are accounted for as long-term investments and not carried at fair value;

(e)   significant restrictions on the realisability of investments or the remittance of income and proceeds of disposal;

(f)   for long-term investments stated at revalued amounts:

   (i)   the policy for the frequency of revaluations,

   (ii)   the date of the latest revaluation, and

   (iii)   the basis of revaluation and whether an external valuer was involved;

(g)   the movements for the period in revaluation surplus and the nature of such movements; and

(h)   for enterprises whose main business is the holding of investments an analysis of the portfolio of investments.

Effective Date

56.   This International Accounting Standard becomes operative for financial statements covering periods beginning on or after 1 January, 1987.

International Accounting Standard 26

Accounting and Reporting by Retirement Benefit Plans

Contents

Introduction

1.   This Statement deals with the contents of reports by retirement benefit plans[1] where such reports are prepared. It regards a retirement benefit plan as a reporting entity separate from the employers of the participants in the plan. All other International Accounting Standards apply to the reports of retirement benefit plans to the extent that they are not superseded by this Statement.

2.   This Statement deals with accounting and reporting by the plan to all participants as a group. It does not deal with reports to individual participants about their retirement benefit rights.

3.   International Accounting Standard 19, Accounting for Retirement Benefits in the Financial Statements of Employers, is concerned with the determination of the cost of retirement benefits in the financial statements of employers having plans. Hence this Statement complements IAS 19.

4.   Retirement benefit plans may be defined contribution plans or defined benefit plans. Many require the creation of separate funds, which may or may not have separate legal identity and may or may not have trustees, to which contributions are made and from which retirement benefits are paid. This Statement applies regardless of whether such a fund is created and regardless of whether there are trustees.

5.   Retirement benefit plans with assets invested with insurance companies are subject to the same accounting and funding requirements as privately invested arrangements. Accordingly, they are within the scope of this Statement unless the contract with the insurance company is in the name of a specified participant or a group of participants and the retirement benefit obligation is solely the responsibility of the insurance company.

6.   This Statement does not deal with other forms of employment benefits such as employment termination indemnities, deferred compensation arrangements, long-service leave benefits, special early retirement or redundancy plans, health and welfare plans or bonus plans. Government social security type arrangements are also excluded from the scope of this Statement.

---

[1] Retirement benefit plans are sometimes referred to by various other names, such as 'pension schemes', 'superannuation schemes' or 'retirement benefit schemes'.

Definitions

7.   The following terms are used in this Statement with the same meanings as specified in International Accounting Standard 19, Accounting for Retirement Benefits in the Financial Statements of Employers:

Retirement benefit plans are arrangements, formal or informal, whereby an employer[2] provides benefits for employees on or after termination of service (either in the form of an annual income or as a lump sum) when such benefits can be determined or estimated in advance of retirement from the provisions of a document or from the employer's practices.

Defined contribution plans are retirement benefit plans under which amounts to be paid as retirement benefits are determined by contributions to a fund together with investment earnings thereon.

Defined benefit plans are retirement benefit plans under which amounts to be paid as retirement benefits are determinable usually by reference to employee's earnings and/or years of service.

Vested benefits are benefits the rights to which, under the conditions of a retirement benefit plan, are not conditional on continued employment.

For the purposes of this Statement the following terms are also used:

Actuarial present value of promised retirement benefits is the present value of the expected payments by a retirement benefit plan to existing and past employees, attributable to the service already rendered.

Funding is the transfer of assets to an entity separate from the employer's enterprise to meet future obligations for the payment of retirement benefits.

Net assets available for benefits are the assets of a plan less liabilities other than the actuarial present value of promised retirement benefits.

Participants are the members of a retirement benefit plan and others who are entitled to benefits under the plan.

---

[2] Some retirement benefit plans have sponsors other than employers; this Statement also applies to the reports of such plans.

Explanation

Retirement Benefit Plan Accounting and Reporting

8.   Most retirement benefit plans are based on formal agreements. Some plans are informal but have acquired a degree of obligation as a result of employers' established practices. While some plans permit employers to limit their obligations under the plans, it is usually difficult for an employer to cancel a plan if employees are to be retained. The same basis of accounting and reporting applies to an informal plan as to a formal plan.

9.   Many retirement benefit plans provide for the establishment of separate funds into which contributions are made and out of which benefits are paid. Such funds may be administered by parties who act independently in managing fund assets. Those parties are called trustees in some countries. The term trustee is used in this Statement to describe such parties regardless of whether a trust has been formed.

10.   Retirement benefit plans are normally described as either defined contribution plans or defined benefit plans, each having their own distinctive characteristics. Occasionally plans exist that contain characteristics of both. Such hybrid plans are considered to be defined benefit plans for the purposes of this Statement.

Defined contribution plans

11.   Under a defined contribution plan, the amount of a participant's future benefits is determined by the contributions paid by the employer, the participant, or both, and the operating efficiency and investment earnings of the fund. An employer's obligation is usually discharged by contributions to the fund. An actuary's advice is not normally required although such advice is sometimes used to estimate future benefits that may be achievable based on present contributions and varying levels of future contributions and investment earnings.

12.   The participants are interested in the activities of the plan because they directly affect the level of their future benefits. Participants are interested in knowing whether contributions have been received and proper control has been exercised to protect the rights of beneficiaries. An employer is interested in the efficient and fair operation of the plan.

13.   The objective of reporting by a defined contribution plan is periodically to provide information about the plan and the performance of its investments. That objective is usually achieved by providing a report including the following:

(a)   a description of significant activities for the period and the effect of any changes relating to the plan, and its membership and terms and conditions;

(b)   statements reporting on the transactions and investment performance for the period and the financial position of the plan at the end of the period; and

(c)   a description of the investment policies.

Defined benefit plans

14.   Under a defined benefit plan, the payment of promised retirement benefits depends on the financial position of the plan and the ability of contributors to make future contributions to the plan as well as the investment performance and operating efficiency of the plan.

15.   A defined benefit plan needs the periodic advice of an actuary to assess the financial condition of the plan, review the assumptions and recommend future contribution levels.

16.   The objective of reporting by a defined benefit plan is periodically to provide information about the financial resources and activities of the plan that is useful in assessing the relationships between the accumulation of resources and plan benefits over time. This objective is usually achieved by providing a report including the following:

(a)   a description of significant activities for the period and the effect of any changes relating to the plan, and its membership and terms and conditions;

(b)   statements reporting on the transactions and investment performance for the period and the financial position of the plan at the end of the period;

(c)   actuarial information either as part of the statements or by way of a separate report; and

(d)   a description of the investment policies.

Actuarial present value of promised retirement benefits

17.   The present value of the expected payments by a retirement benefit plan may be calculated and reported using current salary levels or projected salary levels up to the time of retirement of participants.

18.   The reasons given for adopting a current salary approach include:

    (a)   the actuarial present value of promised retirement benefits, being the sum of the amounts presently attributable to each participant in the plan, can be calculated more objectively than with projected salary levels because it involves fewer assumptions;

    (b)   increases in benefits attributable to a salary increase become an obligation of the plan at the time of the salary increase; and

    (c)   the amount of the actuarial present value of promised retirement benefits using current salary levels is generally more closely related to the amount payable in the event of termination or discontinuance of the plan.

19.   Reasons given for adopting a projected salary approach include:

    (a)   financial information should be prepared on a going concern basis, irrespective of the assumptions and estimates that must be made;

    (b)   under final pay plans, benefits are determined by reference to salaries at or near retirement date; hence salaries, contribution levels and rates of return must be projected; and

    (c)   failure to incorporate salary projections, when most funding is based on salary projections, may result in the reporting of an apparent overfunding when the plan is not overfunded, or in reporting adequate funding when the plan is underfunded.

20.   The actuarial present value of promised retirement benefits based on current salaries is disclosed in the report of a plan to indicate the obligation for benefits earned to the date of the report. The actuarial present value of promised retirement benefits based on projected salaries is disclosed to indicate the magnitude of the potential obligation on a going concern basis which is generally the basis for funding. In addition to disclosure of the actuarial present value of promised retirement benefits, sufficient explanation may need to be given so as to indicate clearly the

context in which the actuarial present value of promised retirement benefits should be read. Such explanation may be in the form of information about the adequacy of the planned future funding and of the funding policy based on salary projections. This may be included in the financial information or in the actuary's report.

Frequency of actuarial valuations

21.   In many countries, actuarial valuations are not obtained more frequently than every three years. If an actuarial valuation has not been prepared at the date of the report, the most recent valuation is used as a base and the date of the valuation disclosed.

Report content for defined benefit plans

22.   For defined benefit plans, information is presented in one of the following formats which reflect different practices in the disclosure and presentation of actuarial information:

(a)   a statement is included in the report that shows the net assets available for benefits, the actuarial present value of promised retirement benefits, and the resulting excess or deficit. The report of the plan also contains statements of changes in net assets available for benefits and changes in the actuarial present value of promised retirement benefits. The report may include a separate actuary's report supporting the actuarial present value of promised retirement benefits.

(b)   a report that includes a statement of net assets available for benefits and a statement of changes in net assets available for benefits. The actuarial present value of promised retirement benefits is disclosed in a note to the statements. The report may also include a report from an actuary supporting the actuarial present value of promised retirement benefits.

(c)   a report that includes a statement of net assets available for benefits and a statement of changes in net assets available for benefits with the actuarial present value of promised retirement benefits contained in a separate actuarial report.

(d)   a report that contains a statement of net assets available for benefits and a statement of changes in net assets available for benefits. The actuarial present value of promised retirement benefits (based on current salary levels) is disclosed when it is greater than net assets available for benefits. Where the net assets available for benefits exceed the actuarial present value of promised retirement benefits, it is not disclosed; the fact that there is an excess is stated and the report includes a statement on the adequacy of future funding policy. The actuarial present value of promised retirement benefits and the statement on the adequacy of future funding policy may be contained in a separate actuarial report.

(e)   a statement that reflects only the activities of the fund. Information about the actuarial present value of promised retirement benefits is not given.

In each format a trustees' report in the nature of a management or directors' report and an investment report may also accompany the statements.

23.   The formats described in paragraphs 22 (d) and 22 (e) are considered inadequate because they are incomplete. The other formats discussed in paragraph 22 have varying degrees of acceptance.

24.   Those in favour of the formats described in paragraphs 22 (a) and 22 (b) believe that the quantification of promised retirement benefits and other information provided under those approaches help users to assess the current status of the plan and the likelihood of the plan's obligations being met. They also believe that financial reports should be complete in themselves and not rely on accompanying statements. However, some believe that the format described in paragraph 22 (a) could give the impression that a liability exists, whereas the actuarial present value of promised retirement benefits does not in their opinion have all the characteristics of a liability.

25.   Those who favour the format described in paragraph 22 (c) believe that the actuarial present value of promised retirement benefits should not be included in a statement of net assets available for benefits as in the format described in paragraph 22 (a) or even be disclosed in a note as in 22 (b), because it will be compared directly with plan assets and such a comparison may not be valid. They contend that actuaries do not necessarily compare actuarial present value of promised retirement benefits with market values of investments but may instead assess the present value of cash flows expected from the investments. Therefore, those in favour of this format believe that such a comparison is unlikely to reflect the actuary's overall assessment of the plan and that it may be misunderstood.

Also, some believe that, regardless of whether quantified, the information about promised retirement benefits should be contained solely in the separate actuarial report where a proper explanation can be provided.

26.   This Statement accepts the views in favour of permitting disclosure of the information concerning promised retirement benefits in a separate actuarial report. It rejects arguments against the quantification of the actuarial present value of promised retirement benefits. Accordingly, the formats described in paragraphs 22 (a) and 22 (b) are considered acceptable under this Statement, as is the format described in paragraph 22 (c) so long as the financial information contains a reference to, and is accompanied by, an actuarial report that includes the actuarial present value of promised retirement benefits.

Valuation of Plan Assets

27.   Retirement benefit plan investments are usually carried at fair value. In the case of marketable securities fair value is usually market value because this is considered the most useful measure of the securities at the report date and of the investment performance for the period. Those securities that have a fixed redemption value and that have been acquired to match the obligations of the plan, or specific parts thereof, may be carried at amounts based on their ultimate redemption value assuming a constant rate of return to maturity. Where plan investments are held for which an estimate of fair value is not possible, such as total ownership of an enterprise, disclosure is made of the reason why fair value is not used. To the extent that investments are carried at amounts other than market value or fair value, fair value is generally also disclosed. Assets used in the operations of the fund are accounted for in accordance with the applicable International Accounting Standards.

Disclosure

28.   Reports provided by retirement benefit plans may include the following, if applicable:

     (a)   a statement of net assets available for benefits disclosing:
          (i)   assets at the end of the period suitably classified,
          (ii)   the basis of valuation of assets,
          (iii)   details of any single investment exceeding either 5% of the net assets available for benefits or 5% of any class or type of security,

      (iv)   details of any investment in the employer, and

      (v)   liabilities other than the actuarial present value of promised retirement benefits;

(b)   a statement of changes in net assets available for benefits showing the following:

      (i)   employer contributions,

      (ii)   employee contributions,

      (iii)   investment income such as interest and dividends,

      (iv)   other income,

      (v)   benefits paid or payable (analysed, for example, as retirement, death and disability benefits, and lump sum payments),

      (vi)   administrative expenses,

      (vii)   other expenses,

      (viii)   taxes on income,

      (ix)   profits and losses on disposal of investments and changes in value of investments, and

      (x)   transfers from and to other plans;

(c)   a description of the funding policy;

(d)   a summary of significant accounting policies;

(e)   for defined benefit plans, the actuarial present value of promised retirement benefits (which may distinguish between vested benefits and non-vested benefits) based on the benefits promised under the terms of the plan, on service rendered to date and using either current salary levels or projected salary levels; this information may be included in an accompanying actuarial report to be read in conjunction with the related financial information; and

(f)   for defined benefit plans, a description of the significant actuarial assumptions made and the method used to calculate the actuarial present value of promised retirement benefits.

29.   The report of a retirement benefit plan contains a description of the plan, either as part of the financial information or in a separate report. It may contain the following:

(a)   the names of the employers and the employee groups covered;

(b)   the number of participants receiving benefits and the number of other participants, classified as appropriate;

(c)   the type of plan – defined contribution or defined benefit;

(d)   a note as to whether participants contribute to the plan;

(e)   a description of the retirement benefits promised to participants;

(f)   a description of any plan termination terms; and

(g)   changes in items (a) to (f) during the period covered by the report.

It is not uncommon to refer to other documents that are readily available to users and in which the plan is described, and to include only information on subsequent changes in the report.

International Accounting Standard 26

Accounting and Reporting by Retirement Benefit Plans

International Accounting Standard 26 comprises paragraphs 30-36 of this Statement. The Standard should be read in the context of paragraphs 1-29 of this Statement and of the Preface to Statements of International Accounting Standards.[3]

30. The report of a defined benefit plan should contain either:

(a) a statement that shows the net assets available for benefits, the actuarial present value of promised retirement benefits, distinguishing between vested benefits and non-vested benefits, and the resulting excess or deficit; or

(b) a statement of net assets available for benefits including either a note disclosing the actuarial present value of promised retirement benefits, distinguishing between vested benefits and non-vested benefits, or a reference to this information in an accompanying actuarial report.

If an actuarial valuation has not been prepared at the date of the report, the most recent valuation should be used as a base and the date of the valuation disclosed.

31. For the purposes of paragraph 30, the actuarial present value of promised retirement benefits should be based on the benefits promised under the terms of the plan on service rendered to date using either current salary levels or projected salary levels with disclosure of the basis used. The effect of any changes in actuarial assumptions that have had a significant effect on the actuarial present value of promised retirement benefits should also be disclosed.

---

[3] International Accounting Standards are not intended to apply to immaterial items (see paragraph 12 of the Preface).

32.   The report should explain the relationship between the actuarial present value of promised retirement benefits and the net assets available for benefits and the policy for the funding of promised benefits.

33.   The report of a defined contribution plan should contain a statement of net assets available for benefits and a description of the funding policy.

34.   The report of a retirement benefit plan, whether defined benefit or defined contribution, should also contain the following information:

(a)   a statement of changes in net assets available for benefits;

(b)   a summary of significant accounting policies; and

(c)   a description of the plan and the effect of any changes in the plan during the period.

35.   Retirement benefit plan investments should be carried at fair value. In the case of marketable securities fair value is market value. Where plan investments are held for which an estimate of fair value is not possible disclosure should be made of the reason why fair value is not used.

Effective Date

36.   This International Accounting Standard becomes operative for financial statements of retirement benefit plans covering periods beginning on or after 1 January, 1988.

International Accounting Standard 27

Consolidated Financial Statements and Accounting for Investments in Subsidiaries

Contents

International Accounting Standard 27

Consolidated Financial Statements and Accounting for Investments in Subsidiaries

Introduction

1.   This Statement deals with the preparation and presentation of consolidated financial statements for a group of enterprises under the control of a parent. Consolidated financial statements have been developed to meet the need for information concerning the financial position, results of operations and changes in financial position of a group of enterprises.

2.   This Statement also deals with accounting for investments in subsidiaries in a parent's separate financial statements.

3.   This Statement supersedes International Accounting Standard 3, Consolidated Financial Statements, except in so far as that Statement deals with accounting for investments in associates.

4.   Consolidated financial statements are encompassed by the term "financial statements" included in the Preface to Statements of International Accounting Standards. Therefore, consolidated financial statements are prepared in accordance with International Accounting Standards.

5.   This Statement does not deal with:

(a) methods of accounting for business combinations and their effects on consolidation, including goodwill arising on a business combination (see International Accounting Standard 22, Accounting for Business Combinations);

(b) accounting for investments in associates (see International Accounting Standard 28, Accounting for Investments in Associates); and

(c) accounting for investments in joint ventures.

Definitions

6.   The following terms are used in this Statement with the meanings specified:

Control (for the purpose of this Statement) is the power to govern the financial and operating policies of an enterprise so as to obtain benefits from its activities.

A *subsidiary* is an enterprise that is controlled by another enterprise (known as the parent).

A *parent* is an enterprise that has one or more subsidiaries.

A *group* is a parent and all its subsidiaries.

Consolidated financial statements are the financial statements of a group presented as those of a single enterprise.

Minority interest is that part of the net results of operations and of net assets of a subsidiary attributable to interests which are not owned, directly or indirectly through subsidiaries, by the parent.

Explanation

Need for Consolidated Financial Statements

7.   Users of the financial statements of a parent are usually concerned with, and need to be informed about, the financial position, results of operations and changes in financial position of the group as a whole. This need is served by consolidated financial statements, which present financial information about the group as that of a single enterprise without regard for the legal boundaries of the separate legal entities.

8.   A parent that is itself wholly owned by another enterprise may not always present consolidated financial statements since such statements may not be required by its parent and the needs of other users may be best served by the consolidated financial statements of its parent. In some countries, a parent is also exempted from presenting consolidated financial statements if it is virtually wholly owned by another enterprise and the parent obtains the approval of the owners of the minority interest. Virtually wholly owned is often taken to mean that the parent owns 90% or more of the voting power.

9.   A parent that does not present consolidated financial statements because it is itself a subsidiary discloses in its separate financial statements:

(a)   the reason why consolidated financial statements are not presented; and

(b)   the bases used to account for subsidiaries.

It also usually discloses the name and registered office of its parent which presents consolidated financial statements.

Scope of Consolidated Financial Statements

10.   The consolidated financial statements include all enterprises that are controlled by the parent, other than those subsidiaries excluded for the reasons set out in paragraph 11. Control is presumed to exist when the

parent owns, directly or indirectly through subsidiaries, more than one half of the voting power of an enterprise unless, in exceptional circumstances, it can be clearly demonstrated that such ownership does not constitute control. Control also exists even when the parent owns one half or less of the voting power of an enterprise when there is:

(a) power over more than one half of the voting rights by virtue of an agreement with other investors;

(b) power to govern the financial and operating policies of the enterprise under a statute or an agreement;

(c) power to appoint or remove the majority of the members of the board of directors or equivalent governing body; or

(d) power to cast the majority of votes at meetings of the board of directors or equivalent governing body.

11.   A subsidiary is commonly excluded from consolidation when:

(a) control is intended to be temporary because the subsidiary is acquired and held exclusively with a view to its subsequent disposal in the near future; or

(b) it operates under severe long term restrictions which significantly impair its ability to transfer funds to the parent.

Such subsidiaries are accounted for as if they are investments in accordance with International Accounting Standard 25, Accounting for Investments.

12.   Sometimes a subsidiary is excluded from consolidation when its business activities are dissimilar from those of the other enterprises within the group. Exclusion on these grounds is not justified because better information is provided by consolidating such subsidiaries and disclosing additional information in the consolidated financial statements about the different business activities of subsidiaries. For example, the disclosures required by International Accounting Standard 14, Reporting Financial Information by Segment, help to explain the significance of different business activities within the group.

Consolidation Procedures

13.   In preparing consolidated financial statements, the financial statements of the parent and its subsidiaries are combined on a line by line basis by adding together like items of assets, liabilities, equity, income and expenses. In order that the consolidated financial statements present

financial information about the group as that of a single enterprise, the following steps are then taken:

(a) the carrying amount of the parent's investment in each subsidiary and the parent's portion of equity of each subsidiary are eliminated (see International Accounting Standard 22, Accounting for Business Combinations, which also describes the treatment of any resultant goodwill);

(b) intragroup balances and intragroup transactions, including sales, expenses and dividends, are eliminated in full;

(c) unrealised profits resulting from intragroup transactions that are included in the carrying amount of assets, such as inventory and fixed assets, are eliminated in full;

(d) unrealised losses resulting from intragroup transactions that are deducted in arriving at the carrying amount of assets are also eliminated unless cost cannot be recovered;

(e) timing differences that arise from the elimination of unrealised profits and losses resulting from intragroup transactions are dealt with in accordance with International Accounting Standard 12, Accounting for Taxes on Income;

(f) minority interests in the net income of consolidated subsidiaries for the reporting period are identified and adjusted against the income of the group in order to arrive at the net income attributable to the owners of the parent; and

(g) minority interests in the net assets of consolidated subsidiaries are identified and presented in the consolidated balance sheet separately from liabilities and the parent shareholders' equity. Minority interests in the net assets consist of:

   (i) the amount at the date of the original combination, calculated in accordance with International Accounting Standard 22, Accounting for Business Combinations; and

   (ii) the minority's share of movements in equity since the date of the combination.

14.   Taxes payable by either the parent or its subsidiaries on distribution to the parent of the profits retained in subsidiaries are accounted for in

accordance with International Accounting Standard 12, Accounting for Taxes on Income.

15.   The financial statements of the parent and its subsidiaries used in the preparation of the consolidated financial statements are usually drawn up to the same date. When the reporting dates are different, the subsidiary often prepares, for consolidation purposes, statements as at the same date as the group. When it is impracticable to do this, financial statements drawn up to different reporting dates may be used provided the difference is no greater than three months. The consistency principle dictates that the length of the reporting periods and any difference in the reporting dates should be the same from period to period.

16.   When financial statements with different reporting dates are consolidated, adjustments are made for the effects of any significant events or intragroup transactions that occur between those dates and the date of the group's financial statements.

17.   Consolidated financial statements are usually prepared using uniform accounting policies for like transactions and events in similar circumstances. In many cases, if a member of the group uses accounting policies other than those adopted in the consolidated financial statements for like transactions and events in similar circumstances, appropriate adjustments are made to its financial statements when they are used in preparing the consolidated financial statements. If it is not practicable for such adjustments to be calculated, that fact is disclosed, together with the proportions of the items in the consolidated financial statements to which the different accounting policies have been applied.

18.   The results of operations of a subsidiary are included in the consolidated financial statements as from the date of acquisition, which is the date on which control of the acquired subsidiary is effectively transferred to the buyer, in accordance with International Accounting Standard 22, Accounting for Business Combinations. The results of operations of a subsidiary disposed of are included in the consolidated income statement until the date of disposal which is the date on which the parent ceases to have control of the subsidiary. The difference between the proceeds from the disposal of the subsidiary and the carrying amount of its assets less liabilities as of the date of disposal is recognised in the consolidated income statement as the profit or loss on the disposal of the subsidiary. In order to ensure the comparability of the financial statements from one accounting period to the next, supplementary information is often provided about the effect of the acquisition and disposal of subsidiaries on the financial position at the reporting date and the results for the reporting period and on the corresponding amounts for the preceding period.

19.   As from the date that it ceases to fall within the definition of a subsidiary and does not become an associate as defined in International Accounting Standard 28, Accounting for Investments in Associates, an investment in an enterprise is accounted for in accordance with International Accounting Standard 25, Accounting for Investments, because it is no longer part of the group. The carrying amount of the investment at the date that it ceases to be a subsidiary is regarded as cost thereafter.

20.   The losses applicable to the minority in a consolidated subsidiary may exceed the minority interest in the equity of the subsidiary. The excess, and any further losses applicable to the minority, are charged against the majority interest except to the extent that the minority has a binding obligation to, and is able to, make good the losses. If the subsidiary subsequently reports profits, the majority interest is allocated all such profits until the minority's share of losses previously absorbed by the majority has been recovered.

21.   If a subsidiary has outstanding cumulative preferred shares which are held outside the group, the parent computes its share of profits or losses after adjusting for the subsidiary's preferred dividends, whether or not dividends have been declared.

Accounting for Investments in Subsidiaries in a Parent's Separate Financial Statements

22.   In many countries separate financial statements are presented by a parent in order to meet legal or other requirements. Where such separate financial statements are presented, investments in subsidiaries that are included in the consolidated financial statements are either:

(a)   accounted for using the equity method as described in International Accounting Standard 28, Accounting for Investments in Associates; or

(b)   carried at cost or revalued amounts under the parent's accounting policy for long-term investments (see International Accounting Standard 25, Accounting for Investments).

23.   Investments in subsidiaries that are excluded from consolidation are accounted for in the parent's separate financial statements as if they are investments in accordance with International Accounting Standard 25, Accounting for Investments.

Disclosure

24.   In order that the users of the consolidated financial statements may understand the relationships between members of the group, the following disclosures are made:

(a)   a listing of significant subsidiaries including the name, country of incorporation or residence, proportion of ownership interest and, if different, proportion of voting power;

(b)   the reasons for not consolidating a subsidiary;

(c)   the nature of the relationship between the parent and a subsidiary of which the parent does not own, directly or indirectly through subsidiaries, more than one half of the voting power; and

(d)   the name of an enterprise in which more than one half of the voting power is owned, directly or indirectly through subsidiaries, but which, because of the absence of control, is not a subsidiary.

25.   In order that the users of the separate financial statements of the parent are aware of the method used to account for subsidiaries, a description of the method is disclosed.

International Accounting Standard 27

Consolidated Financial Statements and Accounting for Investments in Subsidiaries

International Accounting Standard 27 comprises paragraphs 26-38 of this Statement. The Standard should be read in the context of paragraphs 1-25 of this Statement and of the Preface to Statements of International Accounting Standards.[1]

Presentation of Consolidated Financial Statements

26.   A parent, other than a parent mentioned in paragraph 27, should present consolidated financial statements.

27.   A parent that is a wholly owned subsidiary, or is virtually wholly owned need not present consolidated financial statements provided, in the case of one that is virtually wholly owned, the parent obtains the approval of the owners of the minority interest. Such a parent should disclose the reasons why consolidated financial statements have not been presented together with the bases on which subsidiaries are accounted for in its separate financial statements. The name and registered office of its parent that publishes consolidated financial statements should also be disclosed.

Scope of Consolidated Financial Statements

28.   A parent which issues consolidated financial statements should consolidate all subsidiaries, foreign and domestic, other than those referred to in paragraph 29.

29.   A subsidiary should be excluded from consolidation when:

   (a)   control is intended to be temporary because the subsidiary is acquired and held exclusively with a view to its subsequent disposal in the near future; or

---

[1]International Accounting Standards are not intended to apply to immaterial items (see paragraph 12 of the Preface).

(b) it operates under severe long-term restrictions which significantly impair its ability to transfer funds to the parent.

Such subsidiaries should be accounted for as if they are investments in accordance with International Accounting Standard 25, Accounting for Investments.

Consolidation Procedures

30. Intragroup balances and intragroup transactions and resulting unrealised profits should be eliminated in full. Unrealised losses resulting from intragroup transactions should also be eliminated unless cost cannot be recovered.

31. When the financial statements used in the consolidation are drawn up to different reporting dates, adjustments should be made for the effects of significant transactions or other events that occur between those dates and the date of the parent's financial statements. In any case, the difference between reporting dates should be no more than three months.

32. Consolidated financial statements should be prepared using uniform accounting policies for like transactions and other events in similar circumstances. If it is not practicable to use uniform accounting policies in preparing the consolidated financial statements, that fact should be disclosed together with the proportions of the items in the consolidated financial statements to which the different accounting policies have been applied.

33. Minority interests should be presented in the consolidated balance sheet separately from liabilities and the parent shareholders' equity. Minority interests in the income of the group should also be separately presented.

34. An investment in an enterprise should be accounted for in accordance with International Accounting Standard 25, Accounting for Investments from the date that it ceases to fall within the definition of a subsidiary and does not become an associate as defined in International Accounting Standard 28, Accounting for Investments in Associates.

Accounting for Investments in Subsidiaries in a Parent's Separate Financial Statements

35. In a parent's separate financial statements investments in subsidiaries that are included in the consolidated financial statements should be either:

(a) accounted for using the equity method as described in International Accounting Standard 28, Accounting for Investments in Associates; or

(b) carried at cost or revalued amounts under the parent's accounting policy for long-term investments (see International Accounting Standard 25, Accounting for Investments).

36. Investments in subsidiaries that are excluded from consolidation should be accounted for in the parent's separate financial statements as if they are investments in accordance with International Accounting Standard 25, Accounting for Investments.

Disclosure

37. In addition to those disclosures required by paragraphs 27 and 32, the following disclosures should be made:

(a) in consolidated financial statements a listing of significant subsidiaries including the name, country of incorporation or residence, proportion of ownership interest and, if different, proportion of voting power held;

(b) in consolidated financial statements, where applicable:

(i) the reasons for not consolidating a subsidiary;

(ii) the nature of the relationship between the parent and a subsidiary of which the parent does not own, directly or indirectly through subsidiaries, more than one half of the voting power;

(iii) the name of an enterprise in which more than one half of the voting power is owned, directly or indirectly through subsidiaries, but which, because of the absence of control, is not a subsidiary;

(iv) the effect of the acquisition and disposal of subsidiaries on the financial position at the reporting date, the results for the reporting period and on the corresponding amounts for the preceding period; and

(c) in the parent's separate financial statements, a description of the method used to account for subsidiaries.

Effective Date

38.   This International Accounting Standard becomes operative for financial statements covering periods beginning on or after 1 January, 1990.

International Accounting Standard 28

Accounting for Investments in Associates

Contents

International Accounting Standard 28

Accounting for Investments in Associates

Introduction

1.   This Statement deals with accounting by an investor for investments in associates.   It supersedes International Accounting Standard 3, Consolidated Financial Statements, in so far as that Statement deals with accounting for investments in associates.

Definitions

2.   The following terms are used in this Statement with the meanings specified:

An *associate* is an enterprise in which the investor has significant influence and which is neither a subsidiary nor a joint venture of the investor.

Significant influence is the power to participate in the financial and operating policy decisions of the investee but is not control over those policies.

Control (for the purpose of this Statement) is the power to govern the financial and operating policies of an enterprise so as to obtain benefits from its activities.

A *subsidiary* is an enterprise that is controlled by another enterprise (known as the parent).

The *equity method* is a method of accounting whereby the investment is initially recorded at cost and adjusted thereafter for the post acquisition change in the investor's share of net assets of the investee. The income statement reflects the investor's share of the results of operations of the investee.

The *cost method* is a method of accounting whereby the investment is recorded at cost. The income statement reflects income from the investment only to the extent that the investor receives distributions from accumulated net profits of the investee arising subsequent to the date of acquisition.

Explanation

Significant Influence

3.   The term "associate" is used to describe an enterprise in which an investor has significant influence.

4.   If an investor holds, directly or indirectly through subsidiaries, 20% or more of the voting power of the investee, it is presumed that the investor does have significant influence, unless it can be clearly demonstrated that this is not the case. Conversely, if the investor holds, directly or indirectly

through subsidiaries, less than 20% of the voting power of the investee, it is presumed that the investor does not have significant influence, unless such influence can be clearly demonstrated. A substantial or majority ownership by another investor does not necessarily preclude an investor from having significant influence.

5.   The existence of significant influence by an investor is usually evidenced in one or more of the following ways:

(a)   representation on the board of directors or equivalent governing body of the investee;

(b)   participation in policy making processes;

(c)   material transactions between the investor and the investee;

(d)   interchange of managerial personnel; or

(e)   provision of essential technical information.

Accounting Methods

Equity method

6.   Under the equity method, the investment is initially recorded at cost and the carrying amount is increased or decreased to recognise the investor's share of the profits or losses of the investee after the date of acquisition. Distributions received from an investee reduce the carrying amount of the investment. Adjustments to the carrying amount may also be necessary for alterations in the investor's proportionate interest in the investee arising from changes in the investee's equity that have not been included in the income statement. Such changes include those arising from the revaluation of property, plant, equipment and investments, from foreign exchange translation differences and from the adjustment of differences arising on business combinations.

Cost method

7.   Under the cost method, an investor records its investment in the investee at cost. The investor recognises income only to the extent that it receives distributions from the accumulated net profits of the investee arising subsequent to the date of acquisition by the investor. Distributions received in excess of such profits are considered a recovery of investment and are recorded as a reduction of the cost of the investment in accordance with International Accounting Standard 25, Accounting for Investments.

Choice of Accounting Method in Consolidated Financial Statements

8.   The recognition of income on the basis of distributions received may not be an adequate measure of the income earned by an investor on an investment in an associate because the distributions received may bear little relationship to the performance of the associate. As the investor has significant influence over the associate, the investor has a measure of responsibility for the associate's performance and, as a result, the return on its investment. The investor accounts for this stewardship by extending the scope of its consolidated financial statements to include its share of results of such an associate and so provides an analysis of earnings and investment from which more useful ratios can be calculated. As a result, the application of the equity method provides more informative reporting of the net assets and net income of the investor.

9.   An investment in an associate is accounted for using the cost method when it operates under severe long-term restrictions that significantly impair its ability to transfer funds to the investor. Investments in associates are also accounted for using the cost method when the investment is acquired and held exclusively with a view to its disposal in the near future.

10.   The investor discontinues the use of the equity method from the date that:

(a)   it ceases to have significant influence in an associate but retains, either in whole or in part, its investment; or

(b)   the use of the equity method is no longer appropriate for the reasons described in paragraph 9.

The carrying amount of the investment at that date is regarded as cost thereafter.

Choice of Accounting Method in the Separate Financial Statements of the Investor

11.   The preparation of consolidated financial statements does not, in itself, obviate the need for separate financial statements for an investor. When such statements are presented by an investor that issues consolidated financial statements, an investment in an associate is either:

(a)   accounted for using the equity method or the cost method whichever is used for the associate in the investor's consolidated financial statements; or

(b) carried at cost or revalued amounts under the investor's accounting policy for long-term investments (see International Accounting Standard 25, Accounting for Investments).

12. An investor that has investments in associates may not issue consolidated financial statements because it does not have subsidiaries. It is appropriate that such an investor provides the same information about its investments in associates as those enterprises that issue consolidated financial statements. In order to give this information, an investment in an associate is either;

(a) accounted for using the equity method or the cost method whichever would be appropriate for the associate if the investor issued consolidated financial statements; or

(b) carried at cost or revalued amounts under the investor's accounting policy for long-term investments (see International Accounting Standard 25, Accounting for Investments). Where the equity method would be the appropriate accounting method for the associate if the investor issued consolidated financial statements, the investor discloses what would have been the effect had the equity method been applied.

Application of the Equity Method

13. Many of the procedures appropriate for the application of the equity method are similar to the consolidation procedures set out in International Accounting Standard 27, Consolidated Financial Statements and Accounting for Investments in Subsidiaries. Furthermore, the broad concepts underlying the consolidation procedures used in the acquisition of a subsidiary are adopted on the acquisition of an investment in an associate.

14. An investment in an associate is accounted for under the equity method from the date on which it falls within the definition of an associate. On acquisition of the investment any difference (whether positive or negative) between the cost of acquisition and the investor's share of the fair values of the net identifiable assets of the associate is accounted for in accordance with International Accounting Standard 22, Accounting for Business Combinations. Appropriate adjustments to the investor's share of the profits or losses after acquisition are made to account for:

(a) depreciation of the depreciable assets, based on their fair values; and

(b) amortisation of the difference between the cost of the investment and the investor's share of the fair values of the net identifiable assets.

15. The most recent available financial statements of the associate are used by the investor in applying the equity method; they are usually drawn up to the same date as the financial statements of the investor. When the reporting dates of the investor and the associate are different, the associate often prepares, for the use of the investor, statements as at the same date as the financial statements of the investor. When it is impracticable to do this, financial statements drawn up to a different reporting date may be used. The consistency principle dictates that the length of the reporting periods, and any difference in the reporting dates, are consistent from period to period.

16. When financial statements with a different reporting date are used, adjustments are made for the effects of any significant events or transactions between the investor and the associate that occur between the date of the associate's financial statements and the date of the investor's financial statements.

17. The investor's financial statements are usually prepared using uniform accounting policies for like transactions and events in similar circumstances. In many cases, if an associate uses accounting policies other than those adopted by the investor for like transactions and events in similar circumstances, appropriate adjustments are made to the associate's financial statements when they are used by the investor in applying the equity method. If it is not practicable for such adjustments to be calculated, that fact is generally disclosed.

18. If an associate has outstanding cumulative preferred shares, held by outside interests, the investor computes its share of profits or losses after adjusting for the preferred dividends, whether or not the dividends have been declared.

19. If, under the equity method, an investor's share of losses of an associate equals or exceeds the carrying amount of an investment, the investor ordinarily discontinues including its share of further losses. The investment is reported at nil value. Additional losses are provided for to the extent that the investor has incurred obligations or made payments on behalf of the associate to satisfy obligations of the associate that the investor has guaranteed or otherwise committed. If the associate subsequently reports profits, the investor resumes including its share of those profits only after its share of the profits equals the share of net losses not recognised.

20.   When there is a decline, other than temporary, in the value of an investment in an associate, the carrying amount is reduced to recognise the decline. As many investments in associates are of individual importance to the investor, the carrying amount is determined for each associate individually

Income Taxes

21.   Income taxes arising from investments in associates are accounted for in accordance with International Accounting Standard 12, Accounting for Taxes on Income.

Contingencies

22.   In accordance with International Accounting Standard 10, Contingencies and Events Occurring after the Balance Sheet Date, the investor discloses:

     (a)   its share of the contingencies and capital commitments of an associate for which it is also contingently liable; and

     (b)   those contingencies that arise because the investor is severally liable for all the liabilities of the associate.

Disclosure

23.   In order that the users of financial statements may obtain a clear understanding of its affairs, the investor discloses a listing and description of significant associates including the proportion of ownership interests and, if different, the proportion of voting power held. Users also wish to distinguish those items included in the investor's financial statements as a result of the existence of significant influence from those that are included as a result of the existence of control. Hence the amounts relating to investments in associates accounted for under the equity method are classified as long-term assets in the balance sheet and are disclosed separately in the balance sheet and the income statement.

International Accounting Standard 28

Accounting for Investments in Associates

International Accounting Standard 28 comprises paragraphs 24-31 of this Statement. The Standard should be read in the context of paragraphs 1-23 of this Statement and of the Preface to Statements of International Accounting Standards.[1]

Consolidated Financial Statements

24.   An investment in an associate should be accounted for in consolidated financial statements under the equity method except when the investment is acquired and held exclusively with a view to its disposal in the near future in which case it should be accounted for under the cost method.

25.   An investor should discontinue the use of the equity method from the date that:

(a)   it ceases to have significant influence in an associate but retains, either in whole or in part, its investment; or

(b)   the use of the equity method is no longer appropriate because the associate operates under severe long-term restrictions that significantly impair its ability to transfer funds to the investor.

The carrying amount of the investment at that date should be regarded as cost thereafter.

Separate Financial Statements

26.   An investment in an associate that is included in the separate financial statements of an investor that issues consolidated financial statements should be either:

---

[1] International Accounting Standards are not intended to apply to immaterial items (see paragraph 12 of the Preface).

(a) accounted for using the equity method or the cost method whichever is used for the associate in the investor's consolidated financial statements; or

(b) carried at cost or revalued amounts under the accounting policy for long-term investments (see International Accounting Standard 25, Accounting for Investments).

27. An investment in an associate that is included in the financial statements of an investor that does not issue consolidated financial statements should be either:

(a) accounted for using the equity method or the cost method whichever would be appropriate for the associate if the investor issued consolidated financial statements; or

(b) carried at cost or revalued amounts under the accounting policy for long-term investments (see International Accounting Standard 25, Accounting for Investments). If the equity method would be the appropriate accounting method for the associate if the investor issued consolidated financial statements, the investor should disclose what would have been the effect had the equity method been applied.

Application of the Equity Method

28. The carrying amount of an investment in an associate should be reduced to recognise a decline, other than temporary, in the value of the investment, such reduction being determined and made for each investment individually.

Disclosure

29. In addition to the disclosure required by paragraph 27, the following disclosures should be made:

(a) an appropriate listing and description of significant associates including the proportion of ownership interest and, if different, the proportion of voting power held; and

(b) the methods used to account for such investments.

30.   Investments in associates accounted for using the equity method should be classified as long-term assets and disclosed as a separate item in the balance sheet. The investor's share of the profits or losses of such investments should be disclosed as a separate item in the income statement. The investor's share of any unusual or prior period items should also be separately disclosed.

Effective Date

31.   This International Accounting Standard becomes operative for financial statements covering periods beginning on or after 1 January, 1990.

International Accounting Standard 29

Financial Reporting in Hyperinflationary Economies

Contents

Introduction

1.   This Statement applies to the primary financial statements, including the consolidated financial statements, of any enterprise that reports in the currency of a hyperinflationary economy.

2.   In a hyperinflationary economy, reporting of operating results and financial position in the local currency without restatement is not useful. Money loses purchasing power at such a rate that comparison of amounts from transactions and other events that have occurred at different times, even within the same accounting period, is misleading.

3.   This Statement does not establish an absolute rate at which hyperinflation is deemed to arise. It is a matter of judgement when restatement of financial statements in accordance with this Statement becomes necessary. Hyperinflation is indicated by characteristics of the economic environment of a country which include, but are not limited to, the following:

(a)   the general population prefers to keep its wealth in nonmonetary assets or in a relatively stable foreign currency. Amounts of local currency held are immediately invested to maintain purchasing power;

(b)   the general population regards monetary amounts not in terms of the local currency but in terms of a relatively stable foreign currency. Prices may be quoted in that currency;

(c)   sales and purchases on credit take place at prices that compensate for the expected loss of purchasing power during the credit period, even if the period is short;

(d)   interest rates, wages and prices are linked to a price index; and

(e)   the cumulative inflation rate over three years is approaching, or exceeds, 100%.

4.   It is preferable that all enterprises that report in the currency of the same hyperinflationary economy apply this Statement from the same date. Nevertheless, this Statement applies to the financial statements of any enterprise from the beginning of the reporting period in which it identifies the existence of hyperinflation in the country in whose currency it reports.

Explanation

5.   Prices change over time as the result of various specific or general political, economic and social forces. Specific forces such as changes in supply and demand and technological changes may cause individual prices to increase or decrease significantly and independently of each other. In addition, general forces may result in changes in the general level of prices and therefore in the general purchasing power of money.

6.   In most countries, primary financial statements are prepared on the historical cost basis of accounting without regard either to changes in the general level of prices or to increases in specific prices of assets held, except to the extent that property, plant and equipment and investments may be revalued. Some enterprises, however, present primary financial statements that are based on a current cost approach that reflects the effects of changes in the specific prices of assets held.

7.   In a hyperinflationary economy, financial statements, whether they are based on a historical cost approach or a current cost approach, are useful only if they are expressed in terms of the measuring unit current at the balance sheet date. As a result, this Statement applies to the primary financial statements of enterprises reporting in the currency of a hyperinflationary economy. Presentation of the information required by this Statement as a supplement to unrestated financial statements is not permitted. Furthermore, separate presentation of the financial statements before restatement is discouraged.

8.   The restatement of financial statements in accordance with this Statement requires the application of certain procedures as well as judgement. The consistent application of these procedures and judgements from period to period is more important than the precise accuracy of the resulting amounts included in the restated financial statements.

The Restatement of Historical Cost Financial Statements

Balance Sheet

9.   Balance sheet amounts not already expressed in terms of the measuring unit current at the balance sheet date are restated by applying a general price index.

10.   Monetary items are not restated because they are already expressed in terms of the monetary unit current at the balance sheet date. Monetary items are money held and items to be received or paid in money.

11. Assets and liabilities linked by agreement to changes in prices, such as index linked bonds and loans, are adjusted in accordance with the agreement in order to ascertain the amount outstanding at the balance sheet date. These items are carried at this adjusted amount in the restated balance sheet.

12. All other assets and liabilities are nonmonetary. Some nonmonetary items are carried at amounts current at the balance sheet date, such as net realisable value and market value, so they are not restated. All other nonmonetary assets and liabilities are restated.

13. Most nonmonetary items are carried at cost or cost less depreciation; hence they are expressed at amounts current at their date of acquisition. The restated cost, or cost less depreciation, of each item is determined by applying to its historical cost and accumulated depreciation the change in a general price index from the date of acquisition to the balance sheet date. Hence, property, plant and equipment, investments, inventories of raw materials and merchandise, goodwill, patents, trademarks and similar assets are restated from the dates of their purchase. Inventories of partly-finished and finished goods are restated from the dates on which the costs of purchase and of conversion were incurred.

14. Detailed records of the acquisition dates of items of property, plant and equipment may not be available or capable of estimation. In these rare circumstances, it may be necessary, in the first period of application of this Statement, to use an independent professional assessment of the value of the items as the basis for their restatement.

15. A general price index may not be available for the periods for which the restatement of property, plant and equipment is required by this Statement. In these rare circumstances, it may be necessary to use an estimate based, for example, on the movements in the exchange rate between the reporting currency and a relatively stable foreign currency.

16. Some nonmonetary items are carried at amounts current at dates other than that of acquisition or that of the balance sheet, for example property, plant and equipment that has been revalued at some earlier date. In these cases, the carrying amounts are restated from the date of the revaluation.

17. The restated amount of a nonmonetary item is reduced, in accordance with appropriate International Accounting Standards, when it exceeds the amount recoverable from the item's future use (including sale or other disposal). Hence, in such cases, restated amounts of property, plant and equipment, goodwill, patents and trademarks are reduced to

recoverable amount, restated amounts of inventories are reduced to net realisable value and restated amounts of current investments are reduced to market value.

18.   An investee that is accounted for under the equity method may report in the currency of a hyperinflationary economy. The balance sheet and income statement of such an investee are restated in accordance with this Statement in order to calculate the investor's share of its net assets and results of operations. Where the restated financial statements of the investee are expressed in a foreign currency they are translated at closing rates.

19.   The impact of inflation is usually recognised in borrowing costs. It is not appropriate both to restate the capital expenditure financed by borrowing and to capitalise that part of the borrowing costs that compensates for the inflation during the same period. This part of the borrowing costs is recognised as an expense in the period in which the costs are incurred.

20.   An enterprise may acquire assets under an arrangement that permits it to defer payment without incurring an explicit interest charge. Where it is impracticable to impute the amount of interest, such assets are restated from the payment date and not the date of purchase.

21.   International Accounting Standard 21, Accounting for the Effects of Changes in Foreign Exchange Rates, permits an enterprise to include foreign exchange differences on borrowings in the carrying amount of assets following a severe and recent devaluation. Such a practice is not appropriate for an enterprise reporting in the currency of a hyperinflationary economy when the carrying amount of the asset is restated from the date of its acquisition.

22.   At the beginning of the first period of application of this Statement, the components of owners' equity, except retained earnings and any revaluation surplus, are restated by applying a general price index from the dates the components were contributed or otherwise arose. Any revaluation surplus that arose in previous periods is eliminated. Restated retained earnings are derived from all the other amounts in the restated balance sheet.

23.   At the end of the first period and in subsequent periods, all components of owners' equity are restated by applying a general price index from the beginning of the period or the date of contribution, if later. The movements for the period in owners' equity are disclosed in accordance with International Accounting Standard 5, Information to be Disclosed in Financial Statements.

Income Statement

24. This Statement requires that all items in the income statement are expressed in terms of the measuring unit current at the balance sheet date. Therefore all amounts need to be restated by applying the change in the general price index from the dates when the items of income and expenses were initially recorded in the financial statements.

Gain or Loss on Net Monetary Position

25. In a period of inflation, an enterprise holding an excess of monetary assets over monetary liabilities loses purchasing power and an enterprise with an excess of monetary liabilities over monetary assets gains purchasing power to the extent the assets and liabilities are not linked to a price level. This gain or loss on the net monetary position may be derived as the difference resulting from the restatement of non-monetary assets, owners equity and income statement items and the adjustment of index linked assets and liabilities. The gain or loss may be estimated by applying the change in a general price index to the weighted average for the period of the difference between monetary assets and monetary liabilities.

26. The gain or loss on the net monetary position is included in net income. The adjustment to those assets and liabilities linked by agreement to changes in prices made in accordance with paragraph 11 is offset against the gain or loss on net monetary position. Other income statement items, such as interest income and expense, and foreign exchange differences related to invested or borrowed funds, are also associated with the net monetary position. Although such items are separately disclosed, it may be helpful if they are presented together with the gain or loss on net monetary position in the income statement.

The Restatement of Current Cost Financial Statements

Balance Sheet

27. Items stated at current cost are not restated because they are already expressed in terms of the measuring unit current at the balance sheet date. Other items in the balance sheet are restated in accordance with paragraphs 9 to 23.

Income Statement

28. The current cost income statement, before restatement, generally reports costs current at the time at which the underlying transactions or events occurred. Cost of sales and depreciation are recorded at current costs at the time of consumption; sales and other expenses are recorded at

their money amounts when they occurred. Therefore all amounts need to be restated into the measuring unit current at the balance sheet date by applying a general price index.

Gain or Loss on Net Monetary Position

29. The gain or loss on the net monetary position is accounted for in accordance with paragraphs 25 and 26. The current cost income statement may, however, already include an adjustment reflecting the effects of changing prices on monetary items in accordance with paragraph 15 of IAS 15, Information Reflecting the Effects of Changing Prices. Such an adjustment is part of the gain or loss on net monetary position.

Taxes

30. The restatement of financial statements in accordance with this Statement may give rise to differences between taxable income and accounting income. These differences are accounted for in accordance with International Accounting Standard 12, Accounting for Taxes on Income.

Statement of Changes in Financial Position

31. This Statement requires that all items in the statement of changes in financial position are expressed in terms of the measuring unit current at the balance sheet date. Therefore, the statement of changes in financial position may be prepared using the opening and closing balance sheets and the income statement expressed in terms of the measuring unit current at the balance sheet date. This Statement requires that the statement of changes in financial position of an enterprise that reports in the currency of a hyperinflationary currency is presented in terms of cash or cash equivalents rather than in terms of working capital.

Corresponding Figures

32. Corresponding figures for the previous reporting period, whether they were based on a historical cost approach or a current cost approach, are restated by applying a general price index so that the comparative financial statements are presented in terms of the measuring unit current at the end of the reporting period. Information that is disclosed in respect of earlier periods is also expressed in terms of the measuring unit current at the end of the reporting period.

Consolidated Financial Statements

33. A parent that reports in the currency of a hyperinflationary economy may have subsidiaries that also report in the currencies of hyperinflationary economies. The financial statements of any such subsidiary need to be restated by applying a general price index of the

country in whose currency it reports before they are included in the consolidated financial statements issued by its parent. Where such a subsidiary is a foreign subsidiary, its restated financial statements are translated at closing rates. The financial statements of subsidiaries that do not report in the currencies of hyperinflationary economies are dealt with in accordance with IAS 21, Accounting for the Effects of Changes in Foreign Exchange Rates.

34.   If financial statements with different reporting dates are consolidated, all items, whether nonmonetary or monetary, need to be restated into the measuring unit current at the date of the consolidated financial statements.

Selection and Use of the General Price Index

35.   The restatement of financial statements in accordance with this Statement requires the use of a general price index that reflects changes in general purchasing power. It is preferable that all enterprises that report in the currency of the same economy use the same index.

Economies Ceasing to be Hyperinflationary

36.   When an economy ceases to be hyperinflationary, an enterprise may discontinue the presentation of financial statements prepared in accordance with this Statement. In such circumstances, the enterprise treats the amounts expressed in the measuring unit current at the end of the previous reporting period as the basis for the carrying amounts in its subsequent financial statements.

Disclosures

37.   The disclosures required by this Statement are needed to make clear the basis of dealing with the effects of inflation in the financial statements. They are also intended to provide other information necessary to understand that basis and the resulting amounts.

International Accounting Standard 29

Financial Reporting in Hyperinflationary Economies

International Accounting Standard 29 comprises paragraphs 38-43 of this Statement. The Standard should be read in the context of paragraphs 1-37 of this Statement and of the Preface to Statements of International Accounting Standards.[1]

38.   The financial statements of an enterprise that reports in the currency of a hyperinflationary economy, whether they are based on a historical cost approach or a current cost approach, should be stated in terms of the measuring unit current at the balance sheet date. The corresponding figures for the previous period required by International Accounting Standard 5, Information to be Disclosed in Financial Statements, and any information in respect of earlier periods should also be stated in terms of the measuring unit current at the balance sheet date.

39.   The gain or loss on the net monetary position should be included in net income and separately disclosed.

40.   The statement of changes in financial position of an enterprise that reports in the currency of a hyperinflationary economy should be presented in terms of cash and cash equivalents.

41.   The following disclosures should be made:

   (a)   the fact that the financial statements and the corresponding figures for previous periods have been restated for the changes in the general purchasing power of the reporting currency and, as a result, are stated in terms of the measuring unit current at the balance sheet date;

   (b)   whether the financial statements are based on a historical cost approach or a current cost approach; and

---

[1]International Accounting Standards are not intended to apply to immaterial items (see paragraph 12 of the Preface).

(c)   the identity and level of the price index at the balance sheet date and the movement in the index during the current and the previous reporting period.

42.   When an economy ceases to be hyperinflationary and an enterprise discontinues the preparation and presentation of financial statements prepared in accordance with this Statement, it should treat the amounts expressed in the measuring unit current at the end of the previous reporting period as the basis for the carrying amounts in its subsequent financial statements.

Effective Date

43.   This International Accounting Standard becomes operative for financial statements covering periods beginning on or after 1 January, 1990.

International Accounting Standard 30

Disclosures in the Financial Statements of Banks and Similar Financial Institutions

Contents

Introduction

1.   This Statement deals with disclosures in the financial statements of banks and similar financial institutions (subsequently referred to as banks). It also encourages the presentation of a commentary on the financial statements which deals with such matters as the management and control of liquidity and risk.

2.   For the purposes of this Statement, the term "bank" includes all financial institutions one of whose principal activities is to take deposits and borrow with the objective of lending and investing and which are within the scope of banking or similar legislation.   The Statement is relevant to such enterprises whether or not they have the word "bank" in their name.

3.   Banks represent a significant and influential sector of business worldwide. Most individuals and organisations make use of banks, either as depositors or borrowers. Banks play a major role in maintaining confidence in the monetary system through their close relationship with regulatory authorities and governments and the regulations imposed on them by those governments. Hence there is considerable and widespread interest in the well-being of banks, and in particular their solvency and liquidity and the relative degree of risk that attaches to the different types of their business. The operations, and thus the accounting and reporting requirements, of banks are different from those of other commercial enterprises.   This Statement recognises their special needs.

4.   This Statement supplements other International Accounting Standards which also apply to banks unless they are specifically exempted in a Statement.

5.   This Statement applies to the separate financial statements and the consolidated financial statements of a bank.   Where a group undertakes banking operations, this Statement is applicable in respect of those operations on a consolidated basis.

Explanation

6.   The users of the financial statements of a bank need relevant, reliable and comparable information which assists them in evaluating the financial position and performance of the bank and which is useful to them in making economic decisions. They also need information which gives them a better understanding of the special characteristics of the operations of a

bank. Users need such information even though a bank is subject to supervision and provides the regulatory authorities with information that is not always available to the public. Therefore disclosures in the financial statements of a bank need to be sufficiently comprehensive to meet the needs of users, within the constraint of what it is reasonable to require of management.

7.   The users of the financial statements of a bank are interested in its liquidity and solvency and the risks related to the assets and liabilities recognised on its balance sheet and to its off balance sheet items. Liquidity refers to the availability of sufficient funds to meet deposit withdrawals and other financial commitments as they fall due. Solvency refers to the excess of assets over liabilities and, hence, to the adequacy of the bank's capital. A bank is exposed to liquidity risk and to risks arising from currency fluctuations, interest rate movements, changes in market prices and from counterparty failure. These risks may be reflected in the financial statements, but users obtain a better understanding if management provides a commentary on the financial statements which describes the way it manages and controls the risks associated with the operations of the bank.

Accounting Policies

8.   Banks use differing methods for the recognition and measurement of items in their financial statements. While harmonisation of these methods is desirable it is beyond the scope of this Statement. In order to comply with International Accounting Standard 1, Disclosure of Accounting Policies, and thereby enable users to understand the basis on which the financial statements of a bank are prepared, accounting policies dealing with the following items may need to be disclosed:

(a)   the recognition of the principal types of income (see paragraph 9);

(b)   the valuation of investment and dealing securities (see paragraph 19);

(c)   the distinction between those transactions and other events that result in the recognition of assets and liabilities on the balance sheet and those transactions and other events that only give rise to contingencies and commitments (see paragraphs 20 to 23);

(d)   the basis for the determination of losses on loans and advances and for writing off uncollectable loans and advances (see paragraphs 35 to 39); and

(e) the basis for the determination of charges for general banking risks and the accounting treatment of such charges (see paragraphs 40 and 41).

Some of these topics are the subject of existing International Accounting Standards while others may be dealt with at a later date.

Income Statement

9. The principal types of income arising from the operations of a bank include interest, fees for services, commissions and dealing results. Each type of income is separately disclosed in order that users can assess the performance of a bank. Such disclosures are in addition to those of the source of income required by International Accounting Standard 14, Reporting Financial Information by Segment.

10. The principal types of expenses arising from the operations of a bank include interest, commissions, losses on loans and advances, charges relating to the reduction in the carrying amount of investments and general administrative expenses. Each type of expenses is separately disclosed in order that users can assess the performance of a bank.

11. Income and expense items are not offset in the income statement except for those relating to hedges and to assets and liabilities which have been offset as described in paragraph 16. Offsetting in other cases prevents users from assessing the performance of the separate activities of a bank and the return that it obtains on particular classes of assets.

12. Gains and losses arising from each of the following are normally reported on a net basis:

(a) disposals and changes in the carrying amount of dealing securities;

(b) disposals of investment securities; and

(c) dealings in foreign currencies.

13. Interest income and interest expense are disclosed separately in order to give a better understanding of the composition of, and reasons for changes in, net interest.

14. Net interest is a product of both interest rates and the amounts of borrowing and lending. It is desirable for management to provide a commentary about average interest rates, average interest earning assets and average interest bearing liabilities for the period. In some countries,

governments provide assistance to banks by making deposits and other credit facilities available at interest rates which are substantially below market rates. In these cases, management's commentary often discloses the extent of these deposits and facilities and their effect on net income.

Balance Sheet

15.   The most useful approach to the classification of the assets and liabilities of a bank is to group them by their nature and list them in the approximate order of their liquidity; this may equate broadly to their maturities. Current and non-current items are not presented separately because most assets and liabilities of a bank can be realised or settled in the near future.

16.   The amount at which any asset or liability is stated in the balance sheet is not offset by the deduction of another liability or asset unless a legal right of set-off exists and the offsetting represents the expectation as to the realisation or settlement of the asset or liability. Offsetting in other cases reduces the usefulness of balance sheet disclosures.

17.   The distinction between balances with other banks and those with other parts of the money market and from other depositors is relevant information because it gives an understanding of a bank's relations with, and dependence on, other banks and the money market. Hence, a bank discloses separately:

(a)   balances with the central bank;

(b)   placements with other banks;

(c)   other money market placements;

(d)   deposits from other banks;

(e)   other money market deposits; and

(f)   other deposits.

18.   A bank generally does not know the holders of its certificates of deposit because they are usually traded on an open market. Hence, a bank discloses separately deposits that have been obtained through the issue of its own certificates of deposit or other negotiable paper.

19.   It is important to distinguish dealing securities from investment securities and from other investments. Dealing securities are marketable securities that are acquired and held with the intention of reselling them in the short term. Investment securities are acquired and held for yield or capital growth purposes and are usually held to maturity. The market values of dealing securities and marketable investment securities are disclosed, in accordance with International Accounting Standard 25, Accounting for Investments, if these values are different from the carrying amounts in the financial statements. It is not appropriate in the financial statements of a bank to account for loans, advances and similar transactions as investments.

Contingencies and Commitments including Off Balance Sheet Items

20.   International Accounting Standard 10, Contingencies and Events Occurring After the Balance Sheet Date, deals generally with accounting for, and disclosure of, contingencies. The Statement is of particular relevance to banks because banks often become engaged in many types of contingencies and commitments, some revocable and others irrevocable, which are frequently significant in amount and substantially larger than those of other commercial enterprises.

21.   Many banks also enter into transactions that are presently not recognised as assets or liabilities in the balance sheet but which give rise to contingencies and commitments. Such off balance sheet items often represent an important part of the business of a bank and may have a significant bearing on the level of risk to which the bank is exposed. These items may add to, or reduce, other risks, for example by hedging assets or liabilities on the balance sheet. Off balance sheet items may arise from transactions carried out on behalf of customers or from the bank's own trading position.

22.   Off balance sheet items may take a number of different forms including the following:

(a)   direct credit substitutes including general guarantees of indebtedness, bank acceptance guarantees and standby letters of credit serving as financial guarantees for loans and securities;

(b)   certain transaction-related contingencies including performance bonds, bid bonds, warranties and standby letters of credit related to particular transactions;

(c)   short-term self-liquidating trade-related contingencies arising from the movement of goods, such as documentary credits where the underlying shipment is used as security;

(d)   those sale and repurchase agreements not recognised in the balance sheet;

(e)   interest and foreign exchange rate related items including swaps, options and futures; and

(f)   other commitments, note issuance facilities and revolving underwriting facilities.

23.   The users of the financial statements need to know about the contingencies and irrevocable commitments of a bank because of the demands they may put on its liquidity and solvency and the inherent possibility of potential losses.   Users also require adequate information about the nature and amount of off balance sheet transactions undertaken by a bank. Thus a bank discloses, in addition to any other contingencies required by International Accounting Standard 10, Contingencies and Events Occurring After the Balance Sheet Date:

(a)   the nature and amount of commitments to extend credit that are irrevocable because they cannot be withdrawn at the discretion of the bank without the risk of incurring significant penalty or expense; and

(b)   the nature and amount of contingencies and commitments arising from off balance sheet items. For the purposes of this disclosure, off balance sheet items are grouped according to their nature.

Maturities of Assets and Liabilities

24.   The matching and controlled mismatching of the maturities and interest rates of assets and liabilities is fundamental to the management of a bank. It is unusual for banks ever to be completely matched since business transacted is often of uncertain term and of different types. An unmatched position potentially enhances profitability but can also increase the risk of losses.

25.   The maturities of assets and liabilities and the ability to replace, at an acceptable cost, interest-bearing liabilities as they mature, are important factors in assessing the liquidity of a bank and its exposure to changes in interest rates and exchange rates. In order to provide information that is

relevant for the assessment of its liquidity, a bank discloses, as a minimum, an analysis of assets and liabilities into relevant maturity groupings.

26.   The maturity groupings applied to individual assets and liabilities differ between banks and in their appropriateness to particular assets and liabilities. Examples of periods used include the following:

> Up to 1 month
>
> From 1 month to 3 months
>
> From 3 months to 1 year
>
> From 1 year to 5 years
>
> From 5 years and over.

Frequently the periods are combined, for example, in the case of loans and advances, by grouping those under one year and those over one year. When repayment is spread over a period of time, each instalment is allocated to the period in which it is contractually agreed or expected to be paid or received.

27.   It is essential that the maturity periods adopted by a bank are the same for assets and liabilities. This makes clear the extent to which the maturities are matched and the consequent dependence of the bank on other sources of liquidity.

28.   Maturities may be expressed in terms of:

(a)   the remaining period to the repayment date;

(b)   the original period to the repayment date; or

(c)   the remaining period to the next date at which interest rates may be changed.

The analysis of assets and liabilities by their remaining periods to the repayment dates provides the best basis to evaluate the liquidity of a bank. A bank may also disclose repayment maturities based on the original period to the repayment date in order to provide information about its funding and business strategy. In addition, a bank may disclose maturity groupings based on the remaining period to the next date at which interest rates may be changed in order to demonstrate its exposure to interest rate risks. Management may also provide, in its commentary on the financial statements, information about interest rate exposure and about the way it manages and controls such exposures.

29.   Repayment maturities may be expressed in terms of the remaining period to either the contractual maturity date or the effective maturity date. In many countries, deposits made with a bank may be withdrawn on demand and advances given by a bank may be repayable on demand. However, in practice, these deposits and advances are often maintained for long periods without withdrawal or repayment; hence, the effective date of repayment is later than the contractual date. Nevertheless, a bank discloses an analysis expressed in terms of contractual maturities even though the contractual repayment period is often not the effective period because contractual dates reflect the liquidity risks attaching to the bank's assets and liabilities.

30.   Some assets of a bank do not have a contractual maturity date. The period in which these assets are assumed to mature is usually taken as the expected date on which the assets will be realised.

31.   The users' evaluation of the liquidity of a bank from its disclosure of maturity groupings is made in the context of local banking practices, including the availability of funds to banks. In some countries, short-term funds are available, in the normal course of business, from the money market or, in an emergency, from the central bank. In other countries, this is not the case.

32.   In order to provide users with a full understanding of the maturity groupings, the disclosures in the financial statements may need to be supplemented by information as to the likelihood of repayment within the remaining period. Hence, management may provide, in its commentary on the financial statements, information about the effective periods and about the way it manages and controls the risks and exposures associated with different maturity and interest rate profiles.

Concentrations of Assets, Liabilities and Off Balance Sheet Items

33.   A bank discloses significant concentrations in the distribution of its assets and in the source of its liabilities because it is a useful indication of the potential risks inherent in the realisation of the assets and the funds available to the bank. Such disclosures are made in terms of geographical areas, customer or industry groups or other concentrations of risk which are appropriate in the circumstances of the bank. A similar analysis and explanation of off balance sheet items is also important. Geographical areas may comprise individual countries, groups of countries or regions within a country; customer disclosures may deal with sectors such as governments, public authorities, and commercial and business enterprises. Such disclosures are made in addition to any segment information required by

International Accounting Standard 14, Reporting Financial Information by Segment.

34.   The disclosure of significant net foreign currency exposures is also a useful indication of the risk of losses arising from changes in exchange rates.

Losses on Loans and Advances

35.   It is inevitable that in the ordinary course of business, banks suffer losses on loans, advances and other credit facilities as a result of their becoming partly or wholly uncollectable. The amount of losses which have been specifically identified is recognised as an expense and charged against income and deducted from the carrying amount of the appropriate category of loans and advances as a provision for losses on loans and advances. The amount of potential losses not specifically identified but which experience indicates are present in the portfolio of loans and advances is also recognised as an expense and charged against income and deducted from the total carrying amount of loans and advances as a provision for losses on loans and advances. The assessment of these losses depends on the judgement of management; it is essential, however, that management applies its assessments in a consistent manner from period to period.

36.   Local circumstances or legislation may require or allow a bank to make charges against income for losses on loans and advances in addition to those losses which have been specifically identified and those potential losses which experience indicates are present in the portfolio of loans and advances. Any such charges represent appropriations of retained earnings and not expenses in determining net income for the period. Similarly, any credits resulting from the reduction of such charges result in an increase in retained earnings and are not included in the determination of net income.

37.   Users of the financial statements of a bank need to know the impact that losses on loans and advances have had on the financial position and performance of the bank; this helps them judge the effectiveness with which the bank has employed its resources. Therefore a bank discloses the aggregate amount of the provision for losses on loans and advances at the balance sheet date and the movements in the provision during the period. The movements in the provision, including the amounts previously written off that have been recovered during the period, are shown separately.

38.   A bank may decide not to accrue interest on a loan or advance, for example when the borrower is more than a particular period in arrears with respect to the payment of interest or principal. A bank discloses the aggregate amount of loans and advances at the balance sheet date on which interest is not being accrued and the basis used to determine the carrying

amount of such loans and advances. It is also desirable that a bank discloses whether it recognises interest income on such loans and advances and the impact which the non accrual of interest has on its income statement.

39.   When loans and advances cannot be recovered, they are written off and charged against the provision for losses. In some cases, they are not written off until all the necessary legal procedures have been completed and the amount of the loss is finally determined. In other cases, they are written off earlier, for example when the borrower has not paid any interest or repaid any principal that was due in a specified period. As the time at which uncollectable loans and advances are written off differs, the gross amount of loans and advances and of the provisions for losses may vary considerably in similar circumstances. As a result, a bank discloses its policy for writing off uncollectable loans and advances.

General Banking Risks

40.   Local circumstances or legislation may require or allow a bank to make charges against income for general banking risks, including future losses or other unforeseeable risks, in addition to the charges for losses on loans and advances determined in accordance with paragraph 35. A bank may also be required or allowed to make charges against income for contingencies in addition to those for which accrual is required by International Accounting Standard 10, Contingencies and Events Occurring After the Balance Sheet Date. These charges may result in the overstatement of liabilities, understatement of assets or undisclosed accruals and provisions. They present the opportunity to distort net income and equity. '

41.   The income statement cannot present relevant and reliable information about the performance of a bank if net income includes the effects of undisclosed charges for general banking risks or additional contingencies, or undisclosed credits resulting from the reversal of such charges. Similarly, the balance sheet cannot provide relevant and reliable information about the financial position of a bank if the balance sheet includes overstated liabilities, understated assets or undisclosed accruals and provisions. Hence, any charges for general banking risks or additional contingencies are separately disclosed as appropriations of retained earnings. Any credits resulting from the reduction of such charges result in an increase in retained earnings and are not included in the determination of net income.

Assets Pledged as Security

42.   In some countries, banks are required, either by law or national custom, to pledge assets as security to support certain deposits and other liabilities. The amounts involved are often substantial and so may have a

significant impact on the assessment of the financial position of a bank. In these circumstances, a bank discloses the aggregate amount of secured liabilities and the nature and carrying amount of the assets pledged as security.

Trust Activities

43.   Banks commonly act as trustees and in other fiduciary capacities that result in the holding or placing of assets on behalf of individuals, trusts, retirement benefit plans and other institutions. Provided the trustee or similar relationship is legally supported, these assets are not assets of the bank and, therefore, are not included in its balance sheet. If the bank is engaged in significant trust activities, disclosure of that fact and an indication of the extent of those activities is made in its financial statements because of the potential liability if it fails in its fiduciary duties. For this purpose, trust activities do not encompass safe custody functions.

Related Party Transactions

44.   International Accounting Standard 24, Related Party Disclosures, deals generally with the disclosures of related party relationships and transactions between a reporting enterprise and its related parties. In some countries, the law or regulatory authorities prevent or restrict banks entering into transactions with related parties whereas in others such transactions are permitted. International Accounting Standard 24, Related Party Disclosures, is of particular relevance in the presentation of the financial statements of a bank in a country that permits such transactions.

45.   Certain transactions between related parties may be effected on different terms from those with unrelated parties. For example, a bank may advance a larger sum or charge lower interest rates to a related party than it would in otherwise identical circumstances to an unrelated party; advances or deposits may be moved between related parties more quickly and with less formality than is possible when unrelated parties are involved. Even when related party transactions arise in the ordinary course of a bank's business, information about such transactions is relevant to the needs of users and its disclosure is required by International Accounting Standard 24, Related Party Disclosures.

46.   When a bank has entered into transactions with related parties, it is appropriate to disclose the nature of the related party relationship, the types of transactions, and the elements of transactions necessary for an understanding of the financial statements of the bank. The elements that would normally be disclosed to conform with International Accounting Standard 24, Related Party Disclosures, include a bank's lending policy to related parties and, in respect of related party transactions, the amount included in or the proportion of:

(a) each of loans and advances, deposits and acceptances and promissory notes; disclosures may include the aggregate amounts outstanding at the beginning and end of the period, as well as advances, deposits, repayments and other changes during the period;

(b) each of the principal types of income, interest expense and commissions paid;

(c) the amount charged against income in the period for losses on loans and advances and the amount of the provision at the balance sheet date; and

(d) irrevocable commitments and contingencies and commitments arising from off balance sheet items.

International Accounting Standard 30

Disclosures in the Financial Statements of Banks and Similar Financial Institutions

International Accounting Standard 30 comprises paragraphs 47-61 of this Statement. The Standard should be read in the context of paragraphs 1-46 of this Statement and of the Preface to Statements of International Accounting Standards[1].

Income Statement

47.   A bank should present an income statement which groups income and expenses by nature and discloses the amounts of the principal types of income and expenses.

48.   In addition to the requirements of other International Accounting Standards, the disclosures in the income statement or the notes to the financial statements should include, but are not limited to, the following items of income and expenses:

Interest and similar income

Interest expense and similar charges

Dividend income

Fee and commission income

Fee and commission expense

Gains less losses arising from dealing securities

Gains less losses arising from investment securities

Gains less losses arising from dealing in foreign currencies

Other operating income

Losses on loans and advances

General administrative expenses

Other operating expenses

---

[1]International Accounting Standards are not intended to apply to immaterial items (see paragraph 12 of the Preface).

49.   Income and expense items should not be offset except for those relating to hedges and to assets and liabilities which have been offset in accordance with paragraph 52.

Balance Sheet

50.   A bank should present a balance sheet that groups assets and liabilities by nature and lists them in an order that reflects their relative liquidity.

51.   In addition to the requirements of other International Accounting Standards, the disclosures in the balance sheet or the notes to the financial statements should include, but are not limited to, the following assets and liabilities:

Assets

Cash and balances with the central bank

Treasury bills and other bills eligible for rediscounting with the central bank

Government and other securities held for dealing purposes

Placements with, and loans and advances to, other banks

Other money market placements

Loans and advances to customers

Investment securities

Liabilities

Deposits from other banks

Other money market deposits

Amounts owed to other depositors

Certificates of deposits

Promissory notes and other liabilities evidenced by paper

Other borrowed funds

52.   The amount at which any asset or liability is stated in the balance sheet should not be offset by the deduction of another liability or asset unless a legal right of set-off exists and the offsetting represents the expectation as to the realisation or settlement of the asset or liability.

53.   A bank should disclose the market value of dealing securities and marketable investment securities if these values are different from the carrying amounts in the financial statements.

Contingencies and Commitments including Off Balance Sheet Items

54. A bank should disclose the following contingencies and commitments required by International Accounting Standard 10, Contingencies and Events Occurring After the Balance Sheet Date;

(a) the nature and amount of commitments to extend credit that are irrevocable because they cannot be withdrawn at the discretion of the bank without the risk of incurring significant penalty or expense; and

(b) the nature and amount of contingencies and commitments arising from off balance sheet items including those relating to:

(i) direct credit substitutes including general guarantees of indebtedness, bank acceptance guarantees and standby letters of credit serving as financial guarantees for loans and securities;

(ii) certain transaction-related contingencies including performance bonds, bid bonds, warranties and standby letters of credit related to particular transactions;

(iii) short-term self-liquidating trade-related contingencies arising from the movement of goods, such as documentary credits where the underlying shipment is used as security;

(iv) those sale and repurchase agreements not recognised in the balance sheet;

(v) interest and foreign exchange rate related items including swaps, options and futures; and

(vi) other commitments, note issuance facilities and revolving underwriting facilities.

Maturities of Assets and Liabilities

55. A bank should disclose an analysis of assets and liabilities into relevant maturity groupings based on the remaining period at the balance sheet date to the contractual maturity date.

Concentrations of Assets and Liabilities

56.   A bank should disclose any significant concentrations of its assets, liabilities and off balance sheet items. Such disclosures should be made in terms of geographical areas, customer or industry groups or other concentrations of risk. A bank should also disclose the amount of significant net foreign currency exposures.

Losses on Loans and Advances

57.   A bank should disclose the following:

(a)   the accounting policy which describes the basis on which uncollectable loans and advances are recognised as an expense and written off;

(b)   details of the movements in the provision for losses on loans and advances during the period. It should disclose separately the amount charged to income in the period for losses on uncollectable loans and advances, the amount charged in the period for loans and advances written off and the amount credited in the period for loans and advances previously written off that have been recovered;

(c)   the aggregate amount of the provision for losses on loans and advances at the balance sheet date; and

(d)   the aggregate amount included in the balance sheet for loans and advances on which interest is not being accrued and the basis used to determine the carrying amount of such loans and advances.

58.   Any amounts set aside in respect of losses on loans and advances in addition to those losses that have been specifically identified or potential losses which experience indicates are present in the portfolio of loans and advances should be accounted for as appropriations of retained earnings. Any credits resulting from the reduction of such amounts result in an increase in retained earnings and are not included in the determination of net income.

General Banking Risks

59.   Any amounts set aside in respect of general banking risks, including future losses and other unforeseeable risks or contingencies in addition to those for which accrual must be made in accordance with International Accounting Standard 10, Contingencies and Events

Occurring After the Balance Sheet Date, should be separately disclosed as appropriations of retained earnings. Any credits resulting from the reduction of such amounts result in an increase in retained earnings and are not included in the determination of net income.

Assets Pledged as Security

60.   A bank should disclose the aggregate amount of secured liabilities and the nature and carrying amount of the assets pledged as security.

Effective Date

61.   This International Accounting Standard becomes operative for the financial statements of banks covering periods beginning on or after 1 January, 1991.

International Accounting Standard 31

Financial Reporting of Interests in Joint Ventures

Contents

International Accounting Standard 31

Financial Reporting of Interests
in Joint Ventures   40 - 54

Introduction

1.   This Statement deals with accounting for interests in joint ventures and the reporting of joint venture assets, liabilities, income and expenses in the financial statements of venturers and investors, regardless of the structures or forms under which the joint venture activities take place.

Definitions

2.   The following terms are used in this Statement with the meanings specified:

A *joint venture* is a contractual arrangement whereby two or more parties undertake an economic activity which is subject to joint control.

Control is the power to govern the financial and operating policies of an economic activity so as to obtain benefits from it.

Joint control is the contractually agreed sharing of control over an economic activity.

Significant influence is the power to participate in the financial and operating policy decisions of an economic activity but is not control or joint control over those policies.

A *venturer* is a party to a joint venture and has joint control over that joint venture.

An *investor in a joint venture* is a party to a joint venture and does not have joint control over that joint venture.

Proportionate consolidation is a method of accounting and reporting whereby a venturer's share of each of the assets, liabilities, income and expenses of a jointly controlled entity is combined on a line-by-line basis with similar items in the venturer's financial statements or reported as separate line items in the venturer's financial statements.

The *equity method* is a method of accounting and reporting whereby an interest in a jointly controlled entity is initially recorded at cost and adjusted thereafter for the post acquisition change in the venturer's share of net assets of the jointly controlled entity. The income statement reflects the venturer's share of the results of operations of the jointly controlled entity.

Explanation

3.   Joint ventures take many different forms and structures. This Statement identifies three broad types - jointly controlled operations, jointly controlled assets and jointly controlled entities - which are commonly described as, and meet the definition of, joint ventures. The following characteristics are common to all joint ventures:

(a)   two or more venturers are bound by a contractual arrangement; and

(b)   the contractual arrangement establishes joint control.

Contractual Arrangement

4.   The existence of a contractual arrangement distinguishes interests which involve joint control from investments in associates in which the investor has significant influence (see International Accounting Standard 28, Accounting for Investments in Associates). Activities which have no contractual arrangement to establish joint control are not joint ventures for the purposes of this Statement.

5.   The contractual arrangement may be evidenced in a number of ways, for example by a contract between the venturers or minutes of discussions between the venturers. In some cases, the arrangement is incorporated in the articles or other by-laws of the joint venture. Whatever its form, the contractual arrangement is usually in writing and deals with such matters as:

(a)   the activity, duration and reporting obligations of the joint venture;

(b)   the appointment of the board of directors or equivalent governing body of the joint venture and the voting rights of the venturers;

(c)   capital contributions by the venturers; and

(d)   the sharing by the venturers of the output, income, expenses or results of the joint venture.

6.   The contractual arrangement establishes joint control over the joint venture. Such a requirement ensures that no single venturer is in a position to control unilaterally the activity. The arrangement identifies those

decisions in areas essential to the goals of the joint venture which require the consent of all the venturers and those decisions which may require the consent of a specified majority of the venturers.

7.   The contractual arrangement may identify one venturer as the operator or manager of the joint venture. The operator does not control the joint venture but acts within the financial and operating policies which have been agreed by the venturers in accordance with the contractual arrangement and delegated to the operator. If the operator has the power to govern the financial and operating policies of the economic activity, it controls the venture and the venture is a subsidiary of the operator and not a joint venture.

Jointly Controlled Operations

8.   The operation of some joint ventures involves the use of the assets and other resources of the venturers rather than the establishment of a corporation, partnership or other entity, or a financial structure that is separate from the venturers themselves. Each venturer uses its own property, plant and equipment and carries its own inventories. It also incurs its own expenses and liabilities and raises its own finance, which represent its own obligations. The joint venture activities may be carried out by the venturer's employees alongside the venturer's similar activities. The joint venture agreement usually provides a means by which the revenue from the sale of the joint product and any expenses incurred in common are shared among the venturers.

9.   An example of a jointly controlled operation is when two or more venturers combine their operations, resources and expertise in order to manufacture, market and distribute jointly a particular product, such as an aircraft. Different parts of the manufacturing process are carried out by each of the venturers. Each venturer bears its own costs and takes a share of the revenue from the sale of the aircraft, such share being determined in accordance with the contractual arrangement.

10.   In respect of its interests in jointly controlled operations, each venturer includes in its accounting records and recognises in its separate financial statements and consequently in its consolidated financial statements:

(a)   the assets that it controls and the liabilities that it incurs; and

(b)   the expenses that it incurs and its share of the income that it earns from the sale of goods or services by the joint venture.

Because the assets, liabilities, income and expenses are already recognised in the separate financial statements of the venturer, and consequently in its consolidated financial statements, no adjustments or other consolidation procedures are required in respect of these items when the venturer presents consolidated financial statements.

11.   Separate accounting records may not be required for the joint venture itself and financial statements may not be prepared for the joint venture. However, the venturers may prepare management accounts so that they may assess the performance of the joint venture.

Jointly Controlled Assets

12.   Some joint ventures involve the joint control, and often the joint ownership, by the venturers of one or more assets contributed to, or acquired for the purpose of, the joint venture and dedicated to the purposes of the joint venture. The assets are used to obtain benefits for the venturers. Each venturer may take a share of the output from the assets and each bears an agreed share of the expenses incurred.

13.   These joint ventures do not involve the establishment of a corporation, partnership or other entity, or a financial structure that is separate from the venturers themselves. Each venturer has control over its share of future economic benefits through its share in the jointly controlled asset.

14.   Many activities in the oil, gas and mineral extraction industries involve jointly controlled assets; for example, a number of oil production companies may jointly control and operate an oil pipeline. Each venturer uses the pipeline to transport its own product in return for which it bears an agreed proportion of the expenses of operating the pipeline. Another example of a jointly controlled asset is when two enterprises jointly control a property, each taking a share of the rents received and bearing a share of the expenses.

15.   In respect of its interest in jointly controlled assets, each venturer includes in its accounting records and recognises in its separate financial statements and consequently in its consolidated financial statements:

(a)   its share of the jointly controlled assets, classified according to the nature of the assets rather than as an investment. For example, a share of a jointly controlled oil pipeline is classified as property, plant and equipment;

(b) any liabilities which it has incurred, for example those incurred in financing its share of the assets;

(c) its share of any liabilities incurred jointly with other venturers in relation to the joint venture;

(d) any income from the sale or use of its share of the output of the joint venture, together with its share of any expenses incurred by the joint venture; and

(e) any expenses which it has incurred in respect of its interest in the joint venture, for example those related to financing the venturer's interest in the assets and selling its share of the output.

Because the assets, liabilities, income and expenses are already recognised in the separate financial statements of the venturer, and consequently in its consolidated financial statements, no adjustments or other consolidation procedures are required in respect of these items when the venturer presents consolidated financial statements.

16. The treatment of jointly controlled assets reflects the substance and economic reality and, usually, the legal form of the joint venture. Separate accounting records for the joint venture itself may be limited to those expenses incurred in common by the venturers and ultimately borne by the venturers according to their agreed shares. Financial statements may not be prepared for the joint venture, although the venturers may prepare management accounts so that they may assess the performance of the joint venture.

Jointly Controlled Entities

17. A jointly controlled entity is a joint venture which involves the establishment of a corporation, partnership or other entity in which each venturer has an interest. The entity operates in the same way as other enterprises, except that a contractual arrangement between the venturers establishes joint control over the economic activity of the entity.

18. A jointly controlled entity controls the assets of the joint venture, incurs liabilities and expenses and earns income. It may enter into contracts in its own name and raise finance for the purposes of the joint venture activity. Each venturer is entitled to a share of the results of the jointly controlled entity, although some jointly controlled entities also involve a sharing of the output of the joint venture.

19.   A common example of a jointly controlled entity is when two enterprises combine their activities in a particular line of business by transferring the relevant assets and liabilities into a jointly controlled entity. Another example arises when an enterprise commences a business in a foreign country in conjunction with the government or other agency in that country, by establishing a separate entity which is jointly controlled by the enterprise and the government or agency.

20.   Many jointly controlled entities are similar in substance to those joint ventures referred to as jointly controlled operations or jointly controlled assets. For example, the venturers may transfer a jointly controlled asset, such as an oil pipeline, into a jointly controlled entity, for tax or other reasons. Similarly, the venturers may contribute into a jointly controlled entity assets which will be operated jointly. Some jointly controlled operations also involve the establishment of a jointly controlled entity to deal with particular aspects of the activity, for example, the design, marketing, distribution or after-sales service of the product.

21.   A jointly controlled entity maintains its own accounting records and prepares and presents financial statements in the same way as other enterprises in conformity with the appropriate national requirements and International Accounting Standards.

22.   Each venturer usually contributes cash or other resources to the jointly controlled entity. These contributions are included in the accounting records of the venturer and recognised in its separate financial statements as an investment in the jointly controlled entity.

Reporting Interests in Jointly Controlled Entities in the Consolidated Financial Statements of a Venturer

23.   When reporting an interest in a jointly controlled entity in consolidated financial statements, it is essential that a venturer reflects the substance and economic reality of the arrangement, rather than the joint venture's particular structure or form. In a jointly controlled entity, a venturer has control over its share of future economic benefits through its share of the assets and liabilities of the venture. This substance and economic reality is reflected in the consolidated financial statements of the venturer when the venturer reports its interests in the assets, liabilities, income and expenses of the jointly controlled entity by using one of the two reporting formats for proportionate consolidation described in paragraph 29.

24.   Some venturers report their interests in jointly controlled entities using the equity method, as described in International Accounting Standard 28, Accounting for Investments in Associates. The use of the equity method is supported by those who argue that it is inappropriate to combine controlled items with jointly controlled items and by those who believe that venturers have significant influence, rather than joint control, in a jointly controlled entity. This Statement does not recommend the use of the equity method because proportionate consolidation better reflects the substance and economic reality of a venturer's interest in a jointly controlled entity, that is control over the venturer's share of the future economic benefits. Nevertheless, this Statement permits the use of the equity method, as an allowed alternative treatment, when reporting interests in jointly controlled entities.

25.   The use of either proportionate consolidation or the equity method is inappropriate when the interest in a jointly controlled entity is acquired and held exclusively with a view to its subsequent disposal in the near future. It is also inappropriate when the jointly controlled entity operates under severe long-term restrictions which significantly impair its ability to transfer funds to the venturer. Such interests are accounted for as if they are investments in accordance with International Accounting Standard 25, Accounting for Investments.

26.   A venturer discontinues the use of proportionate consolidation from the date on which it ceases to share in the control of a jointly controlled entity. This may happen, for example, when the venturer disposes of its interest or when external restrictions are placed on the jointly controlled entity such that it can no longer achieve its goals. When a venturer uses the equity method to report its interests in a jointly controlled entity, it discontinues the use of the equity method from the date on which it ceases to share in the control of, or have significant influence in, the jointly controlled entity.

27.   When a jointly controlled entity becomes a subsidiary of a venturer, because the venturer has acquired control of the entity, the venturer accounts for its interest in accordance with International Accounting Standard 27, Consolidated Financial Statements and Accounting for Investments in Subsidiaries.

Application of Proportionate Consolidation in the Consolidated Financial Statements of a Venturer

28.   The application of proportionate consolidation means that the consolidated balance sheet of the venturer includes its share of the assets that it controls jointly and its share of the liabilities for which it is jointly

responsible. The consolidated income statement of the venturer includes its share of the income and expenses of the jointly controlled entity. Many of the procedures appropriate for the application of proportionate consolidation are similar to the procedures for the consolidation of investments in subsidiaries, which are set out in International Accounting Standard 27, Consolidated Financial Statements and Accounting for Investments in Subsidiaries.

29.   Different reporting formats may be used to give effect to proportionate consolidation. The venturer may combine its share of each of the assets, liabilities, income and expenses of the jointly controlled entity with the similar items in its consolidated financial statements on a line-by-line basis. For example, it may combine its share of the jointly controlled entity's inventory with the inventory of the consolidated group and its share of the jointly controlled entity's property, plant and equipment with the same items of the consolidated group. Alternatively, the venturer may include separate line items for its share of the assets, liabilities, income and expenses of the jointly controlled entity in its consolidated financial statements. For example, it may show its share of the current assets of the jointly controlled entity separately as part of the current assets of the consolidated group; it may show its share of the property, plant and equipment of the jointly controlled entity separately as part of the property, plant and equipment of the consolidated group. Both these reporting formats result in the reporting of identical amounts of net income and of each major classification of assets, liabilities, income and expenses; both formats are acceptable for the purposes of this Statement.

30.   Whatever format is used to give effect to proportionate consolidation, it is inappropriate to offset any assets or liabilities by the deduction of other liabilities or assets or any income or expenses by the deduction of other expenses or income, unless a legal right of set-off exists and the offsetting represents the expectation as to the realisation of the asset or the settlement of the liability.

Reporting Interests in Jointly Controlled Entities in the Separate Financial Statements of a Venturer

31.   In many countries separate financial statements are presented by a venturer in order to meet legal or other requirements. Such separate financial statements are prepared in order to meet a variety of needs with the result that different reporting practices are in use in different countries. Accordingly, this Statement does not indicate a preference for any particular treatment.

Transactions between a Venturer and a Joint Venture

32.   When a venturer contributes or sells assets to a joint venture, a question arises as to whether the venturer may recognise any gain or loss arising upon the contribution or sale and, if so, at what amount. Recognition of any portion of such a gain or loss depends on the substance of the transaction, in particular whether a transaction has taken place. While the assets are retained by the joint venture, and provided the venturer has transferred the significant risks and rewards of ownership, the venturer recognises only that portion of the gain attributable to the interests of the other venturers. The venturer recognises the full amount of any loss when the contribution or sale provides evidence of a reduction in the net realisable value of current assets or a decline, other than temporary, in the carrying amount of long-term assets.

33.   When a venturer purchases assets from a joint venture, the venturer does not recognise its share of the profits of the joint venture from the transaction until it resells the assets to an independent party. A venturer recognises its share of the losses resulting from these transactions in the same way as profits except that losses are recognised immediately when they represent a reduction in the net realisable value of current assets or a decline, other than temporary, in the carrying amount of long-term assets.

Reporting Interests in Joint Ventures in the Financial Statements of an Investor

34.   The interest of an investor in a joint venture, which does not have joint control, is reported in accordance with International Accounting Standard 25, Accounting for Investments, or, if the investor has significant influence in the joint venture, in accordance with International Accounting Standard 28, Accounting for Investments in Associates.

Operators of Joint Ventures

35.   One or more venturers may act as the operator or manager of a joint venture. Operators are usually paid a management fee for such duties. The fees are accounted for by the joint venture as an expense and are recognised in the operator's income statement in accordance with International Accounting Standard 18, Revenue Recognition.

Disclosure

36.   In accordance with International Accounting Standard 10, Contingencies and Events Occurring after the Balance Sheet Date, a venturer discloses the aggregate amount of the following contingencies, unless the probability of loss is remote, separately from the amount of other contingencies:

(a)   any contingencies that the venturer has incurred in relation to its interests in joint ventures and its share of the contingencies which have been incurred jointly with other venturers;

(b)   its share of the contingencies of the joint ventures themselves for which it is contingently liable; and

(c)   those contingencies that arise because the venturer is contingently liable for the liabilities of the other venturers of a joint venture.

37.   In accordance with International Accounting Standard 5, Information to be Disclosed in Financial Statements, a venturer discloses the aggregate amount of the following commitments, separately from the amount of other commitments:

(a)   any capital commitments of the venturer in relation to its interests in joint ventures and its share of the capital commitments that have been incurred jointly with other venturers; and

(b)   its share of the capital commitments of the joint ventures themselves.

38.   In order that the users of the financial statements of the venturer may obtain a clear understanding of its affairs, a venturer discloses a listing and description of interests in significant joint ventures and the proportion of ownership interest held in jointly controlled entities. A venturer which reports its interests in jointly controlled entities using either the line-by-line reporting format for proportionate consolidation or the equity method also discloses the aggregate amounts of each of current assets, long-term assets, current liabilities, long-term liabilities, income and expenses related to its interests in joint ventures.

39.   It is appropriate that a venturer which does not prepare consolidated financial statements because it does not have subsidiaries provides the same information about its interests in joint ventures as those venturers that issue consolidated financial statements. In order to give this information, such a venturer discloses the information set out in paragraphs 36, 37 and 38.

International Accounting Standard 31

Financial Reporting of Interests in Joint Ventures

International Accounting Standard 31 comprises paragraphs 40-54 of this Statement. The Standard should be read in the context of paragraphs 1-39 of this Statement and of the Preface to Statements of International Accounting Standards[1].

Reporting Interests in Jointly Controlled Operations

40.   In respect of its interests in jointly controlled operations, a venturer should recognise in its separate financial statements and consequently in its consolidated financial statements:

   (a)   the assets that it controls and the liabilities that it incurs; and

   (b)   the expenses that it incurs and its share of the income that it earns from the sale of goods or services by the joint venture.

Reporting Interests in Jointly Controlled Assets

41.   In respect of its interest in jointly controlled assets, a venturer should recognise in its separate financial statements and consequently in its consolidated financial statements:

   (a)   its share of the jointly controlled assets, classified according to the nature of the assets;

   (b)   any liabilities which it has incurred;

   (c)   its share of any liabilities incurred jointly with the other venturers in relation to the joint venture;

---

[1]International Accounting Standards are not intended to apply to immaterial items (see paragraph 12 of the Preface).

(d)   any income from the sale or use of its share of the output of the joint venture, together with its share of any expenses incurred by the joint venture; and

(e)   any expenses which it has incurred in respect of its interest in the joint venture.

Reporting Interests in Jointly Controlled Entities in the Consolidated Financial Statements of a Venturer

42.   *Benchmark Treatment* - in its consolidated financial statements, a venturer should report its interest in a jointly controlled entity using one of the two reporting formats for proportionate consolidation.

Allowed Alternative Treatment - in its consolidated financial statements, a venturer should report its interest in a jointly controlled entity using the equity method.

43.   A venturer should account for the following interests as if they are investments in accordance with International Accounting Standard 25, Accounting for Investments:

(a)   an interest in a jointly controlled entity which is acquired and held exclusively with a view to its subsequent disposal in the near future; and

(b)   an interest in a jointly controlled entity which operates under severe long-term restrictions that significantly impair its ability to transfer funds to the venturer.

44.   A venturer should discontinue the use of proportionate consolidation from the date on which it ceases to have joint control over a jointly controlled entity.   A venturer should discontinue the use of the equity method from the date on which it ceases to have joint control over, or have significant influence in, a jointly controlled entity.

45.   From the date on which a jointly controlled entity becomes a subsidiary of a venturer, the venturer accounts for its interest in accordance with International Accounting Standard 27, Consolidated Financial Statements and Accounting for Investments in Subsidiaries.

Transactions between a Venturer and a Joint Venture

46.   When a venturer contributes or sells assets to a joint venture, recognition of any portion of a gain or loss from the transaction should reflect the substance of the transaction. While the assets are retained by the joint venture, and provided the venturer has transferred the significant risks and rewards of ownership, the venturer should recognise only that portion of the gain which is attributable to the interests of the other venturers. The venturer should recognise the full amount of any loss when the contribution or sale provides evidence of a reduction in the net realisable value of current assets or a decline, other than temporary, in the carrying amount of a long term asset.

47.   When a venturer purchases assets from a joint venture, the venturer should not recognise its share of the profits of the joint venture from the transaction until it resells the assets to an independent party. A venturer should recognise its share of the losses resulting from these transactions in the same way as profits except that losses should be recognised immediately when they represent a reduction in the net realisable value of current assets or a decline, other than temporary, in the carrying amount of long term assets.

Reporting Interests in Joint Ventures in the Financial Statements of an Investor

48.   An investor in a joint venture, which does not have joint control, should report its interest in a joint venture in accordance with International Accounting Standard 25, Accounting for Investments, or, if it has significant influence in the joint venture, in accordance with International Accounting Standard 28, Accounting for Investments in Associates.

Operators of Joint Ventures

49.   Operators or managers of a joint venture should account for any fees in accordance with International Accounting Standard 18, Revenue Recognition.

Disclosure

50.   In accordance with International Accounting Standard 10, Contingencies and Events Occurring after the Balance Sheet Date, a venturer should disclose the aggregate amount of the following contingencies, unless the probability of loss is remote, separately from the amount of other contingencies:

    (a)   any contingencies that the venturer has incurred in relation to its interests in joint ventures and its share in each of the contingencies which have been incurred jointly with other venturers;

    (b)   its share of the contingencies of the joint ventures themselves for which it is contingently liable; and

    (c)   those contingencies that arise because the venturer is contingently liable for the liabilities of the other venturers of a joint venture.

51.   In accordance with International Accounting Standard 5, Information to be Disclosed in Financial Statements, a venturer should disclose the aggregate amount of the following commitments in respect of its interests in joint ventures separately from other commitments:

    (a)   any capital commitments of the venturer in relation to its interests in joint ventures and its share in the capital commitments that have been incurred jointly with other venturers; and

    (b)   its share of the capital commitments of the joint ventures themselves.

52.   A venturer should disclose a listing and description of interests in significant joint ventures and the proportion of ownership interest held in jointly controlled entities. A venturer which reports its interests in jointly controlled entities using the line-by-line reporting format for proportionate consolidation or the equity method should disclose the aggregate amounts of each of current assets, long-term assets, current liabilities, long-term liabilities, income and expenses related to its interests in joint ventures.

53.   A venturer which does not issue consolidated financial statements, because it does not have subsidiaries, should disclose the information required in paragraphs 50, 51 and 52.

Effective Date

54.   This International Accounting Standard becomes operative for financial statements covering periods beginning on or after 1st January 1992.

International Accounting Standard 7 (revised 1992)

Cash Flow Statements

This revised International Accounting Standard becomes operative for financial statements covering periods beginning on or after 1 January 1994, and will supersede International Accounting Standard 7, Statement of Changes in Financial Position (see pages 95 to 101).

Revised International Accounting Standard

Contents

International Accounting Standard 7 (revised 1992)

Cash Flow Statements

Objective

Continued../..

Appendices

International Accounting Standard 7
(revised 1992)

Cash Flow Statements

The standards, which have been set in bold italic type should be read in the context of the background material and implementation guidance in this Standard, and in the context of the Preface to International Accounting Standards. International Accounting Standards are not intended to apply to immaterial items (see paragraph 12 of the Preface).

Objective

Information about the cash flows of an enterprise is useful in providing users of financial statements with a basis to assess the ability of the enterprise to generate cash and cash equivalents and the needs of the enterprise to utilise those cash flows. The economic decisions that are taken by users require an evaluation of the ability of an enterprise to generate cash and cash equivalents and the timing and certainty of their generation.

The objective of this Standard is to require the provision of information about the historical changes in cash and cash equivalents of an enterprise by means of a cash flow statement which classifies cash flows during the period from operating, investing and financing activities.

Scope

1.   An enterprise should prepare a cash flow statement in accordance with the requirements of this Standard and should present it as an integral part of its financial statements for each period for which financial statements are presented.

2.   This Standard supersedes International Accounting Standard IAS 7, Statement of Changes in Financial Position, approved in July 1977.

3.   Users of an enterprise's financial statements are interested in how the enterprise generates and uses cash and cash equivalents. This is the case regardless of the nature of the enterprise's activities and irrespective of

whether cash can be viewed as the product of the enterprise, as may be the case with a financial institution. Enterprises need cash for essentially the same reasons however different their principal revenue-producing activities might be. They need cash to conduct their operations, to pay their obligations, and to provide returns to their investors. Accordingly, this Standard requires all enterprises to present a cash flow statement.

Benefits of Cash Flow Information

4.   A cash flow statement, when used in conjunction with the rest of the financial statements, provides information that enables users to evaluate the changes in net assets of an enterprise, its financial structure (including its liquidity and solvency) and its ability to affect the amounts and timing of cash flows in order to adapt to changing circumstances and opportunities. Cash flow information is useful in assessing the ability of the enterprise to generate cash and cash equivalents and enables users to develop models to assess and compare the present value of the future cash flows of different enterprises. It also enhances the comparability of the reporting of operating performance by different enterprises because it eliminates the effects of using different accounting treatments for the same transactions and events.

5.   Historical cash flow information is often used as an indicator of the amount, timing and certainty of future cash flows. It is also useful in checking the accuracy of past assessments of future cash flows and in examining the relationship between profitability and net cash flow and the impact of changing prices.

Definitions

6.   *The following terms are used in this Standard with the meanings specified:*

Cash comprises cash on hand and demand deposits.

Cash equivalents are short-term, highly liquid investments that are readily convertible to known amounts of cash and which are subject to an insignificant risk of changes in value.

Cash flows are inflows and outflows of cash and cash equivalents.

Operating activities are the principal revenue-producing activities of the enterprise and other activities that are not investing or financing activities.

Investing activities are the acquisition and disposal of long-term assets and other investments not included in cash equivalents.

Financing activities are activities that result in changes in the size and composition of the equity capital and borrowings of the enterprise.

Cash and Cash Equivalents

7.   Cash equivalents are held for the purpose of meeting short-term cash commitments rather than for investment or other purposes. For an investment to qualify as a cash equivalent it must be readily convertible to a known amount of cash and be subject to an insignificant risk of changes in value. Therefore, an investment normally qualifies as a cash equivalent only when it has a short maturity of, say, three months or less from the date of acquisition. Equity investments are excluded from cash equivalents unless they are, in substance, cash equivalents, for example in the case of preferred shares acquired within a short period of their maturity and with a specified redemption date.

8.   Bank borrowings are generally considered to be financing activities. However, in some countries, bank overdrafts which are repayable on demand form an integral part of an enterprise's cash management. In these circumstances, bank overdrafts are included as a component of cash

and cash equivalents. A characteristic of such banking arrangements is that the bank balance often fluctuates from being positive to overdrawn.

9.   Cash flows exclude movements between items that constitute cash or cash equivalents because these components are part of the cash management of an enterprise rather than part of its operating, investing and financing activities. Cash management includes the investment of excess cash in cash equivalents.

Presentation of a Cash Flow Statement

10.   The cash flow statement should report cash flows during the period classified by operating, investing and financing activities.

11.   An enterprise presents its cash flows from operating, investing and financing activities in a manner which is most appropriate to its business. Classification by activity provides information that allows users to assess the impact of those activities on the financial position of the enterprise and the amount of its cash and cash equivalents. This information may also be used to evaluate the relationships among those activities.

12.   A single transaction may include cash flows that are classified differently. For example, when the cash repayment of a loan includes both interest and capital, the interest element may be classified as an operating activity and the capital element is classified as a financing activity.

Operating Activities

13.   The amount of cash flows arising from operating activities is a key indicator of the extent to which the operations of the enterprise have generated sufficient cash flows to repay loans, maintain the operating capability of the enterprise, pay dividends and make new investments without recourse to external sources of financing. Information about the specific components of historical operating cash flows is useful, in conjunction with other information, in forecasting future operating cash flows.

14.   Cash flows from operating activities are primarily derived from the principal revenue-producing activities of the enterprise. Therefore, they generally result from the transactions and other events that enter into the

determination of net profit or loss. Examples of cash flows from operating activities are:

(a)   cash receipts from the sale of goods and the rendering of services;

(b)   cash receipts from royalties, fees, commissions and other revenue;

(c)   cash payments to suppliers for goods and services;

(d)   cash payments to and on behalf of employees;

(e)   cash receipts and cash payments of an insurance enterprise for premiums and claims, annuities and other policy benefits;

(f)   cash payments or refunds of income taxes unless they can be specifically identified with financing and investing activities; and

(g)   cash receipts and payments from contracts held for dealing or trading purposes.

Some transactions, such as the sale of an item of plant, may give rise to a gain or loss which is included in the determination of net profit or loss. However, the cash flows relating to such transactions are cash flows from investing activities.

15.   An enterprise may hold securities and loans for dealing or trading purposes, in which case they are similar to inventory acquired specifically for resale. Therefore, cash flows arising from the purchase and sale of dealing or trading securities are classified as operating activities. Similarly, cash advances and loans made by financial institutions are usually classified as operating activities since they relate to the main revenue-producing activity of that enterprise.

Investing Activities

16.   The separate disclosure of cash flows arising from investing activities is important because the cash flows represent the extent to which expenditures have been made for resources intended to generate future income and cash flows. Examples of cash flows arising from investing activities are:

(a)   cash payments to acquire property, plant and equipment, intangibles and other long-term assets. These payments include those relating to capitalised development costs and self-constructed property, plant and equipment;

(b)   cash receipts from sales of property, plant and equipment, intangibles and other long-term assets;

(c)   cash payments to acquire equity or debt instruments of other enterprises and interests in joint ventures (other than payments for those instruments considered to be cash equivalents or those held for dealing or trading purposes);

(d)   cash receipts from sales of equity or debt instruments of other enterprises and interests in joint ventures (other than receipts for those instruments considered to be cash equivalents and those held for dealing or trading purposes);

(e)   cash advances and loans made to other parties (other than advances and loans made by a financial institution);

(f)   cash receipts from the repayment of advances and loans made to other parties (other than advances and loans of a financial institution);

(g)   cash payments for futures contracts, forward contracts, option contracts and swap contracts except when the contracts are held for dealing or trading purposes, or the payments are classified as financing activities; and

(h)   cash receipts from futures contracts, forward contracts, option contracts and swap contracts except when the contracts are held for dealing or trading purposes, or the receipts are classified as financing activities.

When a contract is accounted for as a hedge of an identifiable position, the cash flows of the contract are classified in the same manner as the cash flows of the position being hedged.

Financing Activities

17.   The separate disclosure of cash flows arising from financing activities is important because it is useful in predicting claims on future cash flows by providers of capital to the enterprise.   Examples of cash flows arising from financing activities are:

(a)   cash proceeds from issuing shares or other equity instruments;

(b)   cash payments to owners to acquire or redeem the enterprise's shares;

(c)   cash proceeds from issuing debentures, loans, notes, bonds, mortgages and other short or long-term borrowings;

(d)   cash repayments of amounts borrowed; and

(e)   cash payments by a lessee for the reduction of the outstanding liability relating to a finance lease.

Reporting Cash Flows from Operating Activities

18.   An enterprise should report cash flows from operating activities using either:

(a)   the direct method, whereby major classes of gross cash receipts and gross cash payments are disclosed; or

(b)   the indirect method, whereby net profit or loss is adjusted for the effects of transactions of a non-cash nature, any deferrals or accruals of past or future operating cash receipts or payments, and items of income or expense associated with investing or financing cash flows.

19.   Enterprises are encouraged to report cash flows from operating activities using the direct method. The direct method provides information which may be useful in estimating future cash flows and which is not available under the indirect method.   Under the direct method, information about major classes of gross cash receipts and gross cash payments may be obtained either:

(a)   from the accounting records of the enterprise; or

(b)   by adjusting sales, cost of sales (interest and similar income and interest expense and similar charges for a financial institution) and other items in the income statement for:

   (i)   changes during the period in inventories and operating receivables and payables;

   (ii)   other non-cash items; and

   (iii)   other items for which the cash effects are investing or financing cash flows.

20.   Under the indirect method, the net cash flow from operating activities is determined by adjusting net profit or loss for the effects of:

(a)   changes during the period in inventories and operating receivables and payables;

(b)   non-cash items such as depreciation, provisions, deferred taxes, unrealised foreign currency gains and losses, undistributed profits of associates, and minority interests; and

(c)   all other items for which the cash effects are investing or financing cash flows.

Alternatively, the net cash flow from operating activities may be presented under the indirect method by showing the revenues and expenses disclosed in the income statement and the changes during the period in inventories and operating receivables and payables.

Reporting Cash Flows from Investing and Financing Activities

21.   An enterprise should report separately major classes of gross cash receipts and gross cash payments arising from investing and financing activities, except to the extent that cash flows described in paragraphs 22 and 24 are reported on a net basis.

Reporting Cash Flows on a Net Basis

22.   *Cash flows arising from the following operating, investing or financing activities may be reported on a net basis:*

(a)   *cash receipts and payments on behalf of customers when the cash flows reflect the activities of the customer rather than those of the enterprise; and*

(b)   *cash receipts and payments for items in which the turnover is quick, the amounts are large, and the maturities are short.*

23.   Examples of cash receipts and payments referred to in paragraph 22(a) are:

(a)   the acceptance and repayment of demand deposits of a bank;

(b)   funds held for customers by an investment enterprise; and

(c)   rents collected on behalf of, and paid over to, the owners of properties.

Examples of cash receipts and payments referred to in paragraph 22(b) are advances made for, and the repayment of:

(a)   principal amounts relating to credit card customers;

(b)   the purchase and sale of investments; and

(c)   other short-term borrowings, for example, those which have a maturity period of three months or less.

24.   *Cash flows arising from each of the following activities of a financial institution may be reported on a net basis:*

(a)   *cash receipts and payments for the acceptance and repayment of deposits with a fixed maturity date;*

(b)   *the placement of deposits with and withdrawal of deposits from other financial institutions; and*

(c)   cash advances and loans made to customers and the repayment of those advances and loans.

Foreign Currency Cash Flows

25.   Cash flows arising from transactions in a foreign currency should be recorded in an enterprise's reporting currency by applying to the foreign currency amount the exchange rate between the reporting currency and the foreign currency at the date of the cash flow.

26.   The cash flows of a foreign subsidiary should be translated at the exchange rates between the reporting currency and the foreign currency at the dates of the cash flows.

27.   Cash flows denominated in a foreign currency are reported in a manner consistent with International Accounting Standard IAS 21, Accounting for the Effects of Changes in Foreign Exchange Rates. This permits the use of an exchange rate that approximates the actual rate. For example, a weighted average exchange rate for a period may be used for recording foreign currency transactions or the translation of the cash flows of a foreign subsidiary. However, IAS 21 does not permit use of the exchange rate at the balance sheet date when translating the cash flows of a foreign subsidiary.

28.   Unrealised gains and losses arising from changes in foreign currency exchange rates are not cash flows. However, the effect of exchange rate changes on cash and cash equivalents held or due in a foreign currency is reported in the cash flow statement in order to reconcile cash and cash equivalents at the beginning and the end of the period. This amount is presented separately from cash flows from operating, investing and financing activities and includes the differences, if any, had those cash flows been reported at end of period exchange rates.

Extraordinary Items

29.   The cash flows associated with extraordinary items should be classified as arising from operating, investing or financing activities as appropriate and separately disclosed.

30.   The cash flows associated with extraordinary items are disclosed separately as arising from operating, investing or financing activities in the cash flow statement, to enable users to understand their nature and effect on the present and future cash flows of the enterprise. These disclosures are in addition to the separate disclosures of the nature and amount of extraordinary items required by International Accounting Standard IAS 8, Extraordinary Items, Fundamental Errors and Changes in Accounting Policies.

Interest and Dividends

31.   Cash flows from interest and dividends received and paid should each be disclosed separately. Each should be classified in a consistent manner from period to period as either operating, investing or financing activities.

32.   The total amount of interest paid during a period is disclosed in the cash flow statement whether it has been recognised as an expense in the income statement or capitalised in accordance with the allowed alternative treatment in International Accounting Standard IAS 23, Borrowing Costs.

33.   Interest paid and interest and dividends received are usually classified as operating cash flows for a financial institution. However, there is no consensus on the classification of these cash flows for other enterprises. Interest paid and interest and dividends received may be classified as operating cash flows because they enter into the determination of net profit or loss. Alternatively, interest paid and interest and dividends received may be classified as financing cash flows and investing cash flows respectively, because they are costs of obtaining financial resources or returns on investments.

34.   Dividends paid may be classified as a financing cash flow because they are a cost of obtaining financial resources. Alternatively, dividends paid may be classified as a component of cash flows from operating activities in order to assist users to determine the ability of an enterprise to pay dividends out of operating cash flows.

Taxes on Income

35.   Cash flows arising from taxes on income should be separately disclosed and should be classified as cash flows from operating activities unless they can be specifically identified with financing and investing activities.

36.   Taxes on income arise on transactions that give rise to cash flows that are classified as operating, investing or financing activities in a cash flow statement.   While tax expense may be readily identifiable with investing or financing activities, the related tax cash flows are often impracticable to identify and may arise in a different period from the cash flows of the underlying transaction.   Therefore, taxes paid are usually classified as cash flows from operating activities.   However, when it is practicable to identify the tax cash flow with an individual transaction that gives rise to cash flows that are classified as investing or financing activities the tax cash flow is classified as an investing or financing activity as appropriate.   When tax cash flows are allocated over more than one class of activity, the total amount of taxes paid is disclosed.

Investments in Subsidiaries, Associates and Joint Ventures

37.   When accounting for an investment in an associate or a subsidiary accounted for by use of the equity or cost method, an investor restricts its reporting in the cash flow statement to the cash flows between itself and the investee, for example, to dividends and advances.

38.   An enterprise which reports its interest in a jointly controlled entity (see International Accounting Standard IAS 31, Financial Reporting of Interests in Joint Ventures) using proportionate consolidation, includes in its consolidated cash flow statement its proportionate share of the jointly controlled entity's cash flows.   An enterprise which reports such an interest using the equity method includes in its cash flow statement the cash flows in respect of its investments in the jointly controlled entity, and distributions and other payments or receipts between it and the jointly controlled entity.

Acquisitions and Disposals of Subsidiaries and Other Business Units

39.   The aggregate cash flows arising from acquisitions and from disposals of subsidiaries or other business units should be presented separately and classified as investing activities.

40.   An enterprise should disclose, in aggregate, in respect of both acquisitions and disposals of subsidiaries or other business units during the period each of the following:

(a)   the total purchase or disposal consideration;

(b)   the portion of the purchase or disposal consideration discharged by means of cash and cash equivalents;

(c)   the amount of cash and cash equivalents in the subsidiary or business unit acquired or disposed of; and

(d)   the amount of the assets and liabilities other than cash or cash equivalents in the subsidiary or business unit acquired or disposed of, summarised by each major category.

41.   The separate presentation of the cash flow effects of acquisitions and disposals of subsidiaries and other business units as single line items, together the with separate disclosure of the amounts of assets and liabilities acquired or disposed of, helps to distinguish those cash flows from the cash flows arising from the other operating, investing and financing activities. The cash flow effects of disposals are not deducted from those of acquisitions.

42.   The aggregate amount of the cash paid or received as purchase or sale consideration is reported in the cash flow statement net of cash and cash equivalents acquired or disposed of.

Non-cash Transactions

43. Investing and financing transactions that do not require the use of cash or cash equivalents should be excluded from a cash flow statement. Such transactions should be disclosed elsewhere in the financial statements in a way that provides all the relevant information about these investing and financing activities.

44. Many investing and financing activities do not have a direct impact on current cash flows although they do affect the capital and asset structure of an enterprise. The exclusion of non-cash transactions from the cash flow statement is consistent with the objective of a cash flow statement as these items do not involve cash flows in the current period. Examples of non-cash transactions are:

(a) the acquisition of assets either by assuming directly related liabilities or by means of a finance lease;

(b) the acquisition of an enterprise by means of an equity issue; and

(c) the conversion of debt to equity.

Components of Cash and Cash Equivalents

45. An enterprise should disclose the components of cash and cash equivalents and should present a reconciliation of the amounts in its cash flow statement with the equivalent items reported in the balance sheet.

46. In view of the variety of cash management practices and banking arrangements around the world and in order to comply with International Accounting Standard IAS 1, Disclosure of Accounting Policies, an enterprise discloses the policy which it adopts in determining the composition of cash and cash equivalents.

47. The effect of any change in the policy for determining components of cash and cash equivalents, for example, a change in the classification of financial instruments previously considered to be part of an enterprise's investment portfolio, is reported in accordance with International Accounting Standard IAS 8, Extraordinary Items, Fundamental Errors and Changes in Accounting Policies.

Other Disclosures

48. *An enterprise should disclose, together with a commentary by management, the amount of significant cash and cash equivalent balances held by the enterprise that are not available for use by the group.*

49.   There are various circumstances in which cash and cash equivalent balances held by an enterprise are not available for use by the group. Examples include cash and cash equivalent balances held by a subsidiary that operates in a country where exchange controls or other legal restrictions apply when the balances are not available for general use by the parent or other subsidiaries.

50.   Additional information may be relevant to users in understanding the financial position and liquidity of an enterprise. Disclosure of this information, together with a commentary by management, is encouraged and may include:

(a)   the amount of undrawn borrowing facilities that may be available for future operating activities and to settle capital commitments, indicating any restrictions on the use of these facilities;

(b)   the aggregate amounts of the cash flows from each of operating, investing and financing activities related to interests in joint ventures reported using proportionate consolidation;

(c)   the aggregate amount of cash flows that represent increases in operating capacity separately from those cash flows that are required to maintain operating capacity; and

(d)   the amount of the cash flows arising from the operating, investing and financing activities of each reported industry and geographical segment (see International Accounting Standard IAS 14, Reporting Financial Information by Segment).

51.   The separate disclosure of cash flows that represent increases in operating capacity and cash flows that are required to maintain operating capacity is useful in enabling the user to determine whether the enterprise is investing adequately in the maintenance of its operating capacity. An enterprise that does not invest adequately in the maintenance of its operating capacity may be prejudicing future profitability for the sake of current liquidity and distributions to owners.

52.   The disclosure of segmental cash flows enables users to obtain a better understanding of the relationship between the cash flows of the business as a whole and those of its component parts and the availability and variability of segmental cash flows.

Effective Date

53.   This International Accounting Standard becomes operative for financial statements covering periods beginning on or after 1 January, 1994.

Appendix 1

Cash Flow Statement for an Enterprise other than a Financial Institution

The appendix is illustrative only and does not form part of the standards. The purpose of the appendix is to illustrate the application of the standards to assist in clarifying their meaning.

1.   The examples show only current period amounts. Corresponding amounts for the preceding period are required to be presented in accordance with International Accounting Standard IAS 5, Information to be Disclosed in Financial Statements.

2.   Information from the income statement and balance sheet is provided to show how the statements of cash flows under the direct method and indirect method have been derived. Neither the income statement nor the balance sheet are presented in conformity with the disclosure and presentation requirements of International Accounting Standards.

3.   The following additional information is also relevant for the preparation of the statements of cash flows:

•   all of the shares of a subsidiary were acquired for 590. The fair values of assets acquired and liabilities assumed were as follows:

inventories	100
accounts receivable	100
cash	40
property, plant and equipment	650
trade payables	100
long-term debt	200

•   250 was raised from the issue of share capital and a further 250 was raised from long-term borrowings.

- interest expense was 400 of which 170 was paid during the period. 100 relating to interest expense of the prior period was also paid during the period.

- dividends paid were 1,200.

- the liability for tax at the beginning and end of the period was 1000 and 400 respectively. During the period, a further 200 tax was provided for. Withholding tax on dividends received amounted to 100.

- during the period, the group acquired property, plant and equipment with an aggregate cost of 1,250 of which 900 was acquired by means of finance leases. Cash payments of 350 were made to purchase property, plant and equipment.

- plant with original cost of 80 and accumulated depreciation of 60 was sold for 20.

- accounts receivable as at end of 19-2 include 100 of interest receivable.

Consolidated Income Statement for the period ended 19-2

Sales	30,650
Cost of sales	(26,000)
Gross profit	4,650
Depreciation	(450)
Administrative and selling expenses	(910)
Interest expense	(400)
Investment income	500
Foreign exchange loss	(40)
Net profit before taxation and extraordinary item	3,350
Extraordinary item - Insurance proceeds from earthquake disaster settlement	180
Net profit after extraordinary item	3,530
Taxes on income	(300)
Net profit	3,230

Consolidated Balance Sheet as at end of 19-2

	19-2		19-1	
Assets				
Cash and cash equivalents		410		160
Accounts receivable		1,900		1,200
Inventory		1,000		1,950
Portfolio investments		2,500		2,500
Property, plant and equipment at cost	3,730		1,910	
Accumulated depreciation	(1,450)		(1,060)	
Property, plant and equipment net		2,280		850
Total assets		8,090		6,660
Liabilities				
Trade payables		250		1,890
Interest payable		230		100
Income taxes payable		400		1,000
Long term debt		2,300		1,040
Total liabilities		3,180		4,030
Shareholders Equity				
Share capital		1,500		1,250
Retained earnings		3,410		1,380
Total shareholders equity		4,910		2,630
Total liabilities and shareholders equity		8,090		6,660

Direct Method Cash Flow Statement (paragraph 18a)

		19-2
Cash flows from operating activities		
Cash receipts from customers	30,150	
Cash paid to suppliers and employees	(27,600)	
Cash generated from operations	2,550	
Interest paid	(270)	
Income taxes paid	(900)	
Cash flow before extraordinary item	1,380	
Proceeds from earthquake disaster settlement	180	
Net cash from operating activities		1,560
Cash flows from investing activities		
Acquisition of subsidiary X, net of cash acquired (Note A)	(550)	
Purchase of property, plant and equipment (Note B)	(350)	
Proceeds from sale of equipment	20	
Interest received	200	
Dividends received	200	
Net cash used in investing activities		(480)
Cash flows from financing activities		
Proceeds from issuance of share capital	250	
Proceeds from long-term borrowings	250	
Payment of finance lease liabilities	(90)	
Dividends paid*	(1,200)	
Net cash used in financing activities		(790)
Net increase in cash and cash equivalents		290
Cash and cash equivalents at beginning of period (note C)		120
Cash and cash equivalents at end of period (note C)		410

*This could also be shown as an operating cash flow.
See notes on pages 26 and 27.

Indirect Method Cash Flow Statement (paragraph 18b)

19-2

Cash flows from operating activities

Net profit before taxation, and extraordinary item.	3,350	
Adjustments for:		
Depreciation	450	
Foreign exchange loss	40	
Investment income	(500)	
Interest expense	400	
Operating profit before working capital changes	3,740	
Increase in trade and other receivables	(500)	
Decrease in inventories	1,050	
Decrease in trade payables	(1,740)	
Cash generated from operations	2,550	
Interest paid	(270)	
Income taxes paid	(900)	
Cash flow before extraordinary item	1,380	
Proceeds from earthquake disaster settlement	180	
Net cash from operating activities		1,560

Cash flows from investing activities

Acquisition of subsidiary X net of cash acquired (Note A)	(550)	
Purchase of property, plant and equipment (Note B)	(350)	
Proceeds from sale of equipment	20	
Interest received	200	
Dividends received	200	
Net cash used in investing activities		(480)

Cash flows from financing activities

Proceeds from issuance of share capital	250	
Proceeds from long-term borrowings	250	
Payment of finance lease liabilities	(90)	
Dividends paid*	(1,200)	
Net cash used in financing activities		(790)
Net increase in cash and cash equivalents		290
Cash and cash equivalents at beginning of period (Note C)		120
Cash and cash equivalents at end of period (Note C)		410

*This could also be shown as an operating cash flow.
See notes on pages 26 and 27.

Notes to the Cash Flow Statement
(direct method and indirect method)

A.   Acquisition of Subsidiary

During the period the group acquired subsidiary X. The fair value of assets acquired and liabilities assumed were as follows:

Cash	40
Inventories	100
Accounts receivable	100
Property, plant and equipment	650
Trade payables	(100)
Long-term debt	(200)
Total purchase price	590
Less: Cash of X	(40)
Cash flow on acquisition net of cash acquired	550

B.   Property, Plant and Equipment

During the period, the Group acquired property, plant and equipment with an aggregate cost of 1,250 of which 900 was acquired by means of finance leases. Cash payments of 350 were made to purchase property, plant and equipment.

C.   Cash and Cash Equivalents

Cash and cash equivalents consist of cash on hand and balances with banks, and investments in money market instruments. Cash and cash equivalents included in the cash flow statement comprise the following balance sheet amounts:

	19-2	19-1
Cash on hand and balances with banks	40	25
Short-term investments	370	135
Cash and cash equivalents as previously reported	410	160
Effect of exchange rate changes	-	(40)
Cash and cash equivalents as restated	410	120

Cash and cash equivalents at the end of the period include deposits with banks of 100 held by a subsidiary which are not freely remissible to the holding company because of currency exchange restrictions.

The Group has undrawn borrowing facilities of 2,000 of which 700 may be used only for future expansion.

D.   Segment Information

	Segment A	Segment B	Total
Cash flows from:			
Operating activities	1,700	(140)	1,560
Investing activities	(640)	160	(480)
Financing activities	(570)	(220)	(790)
	490	(200)	290

Alternative Presentation (indirect method)

As an alternative, in an indirect method cash flow statement, operating profit before working capital changes is sometimes presented as follows:

Revenues excluding investment income	30,650
Operating expense excluding depreciation	(26,910)
Operating profit before working capital changes	3,740

Appendix 2

Cash Flow Statement for a Financial Institution

The appendix is illustrative only and does not form part of the standards. The purpose of the appendix is to illustrate the application of the standards to assist in clarifying their meaning.

1.   The example shows only current period amounts. Corresponding amounts for the preceding period are required to be presented in accordance with International Accounting Standard IAS 5, Information to be Disclosed in Financial Statements.

2.   The example is presented using the direct method.

Cash flows from operating activities

Interest and commission receipts	28,447
Interest payments	(23,463)
Recoveries on loans previously written off	237
Cash payments to employees and suppliers	(997)
Operating profit before changes in operating assets	4,224
(Increase) decrease in operating assets:	
Short-term funds	(650)
Deposits held for regulatory or monetary control purposes	234
Funds advanced to customers	(288)
Net increase in credit card receivables	(360)
Other short-term negotiable securities	(120)
Increase (decrease) in operating liabilities:	
Deposits from customers	600
Negotiable certificates of deposit	(200)
Net cash from operating activities before income tax	3,440
Income taxes paid	(100)

Net cash from operating activities   3,340

Cash flows from investing activities

Disposal of subsidiary Y	50
Dividends received	200
Interest received	300
Proceeds from sales of non-dealing securities	1,200
Purchase of non-dealing securities	(600)
Purchase of property, plant and equipment	(500)

Net cash from investing activities   650

Cash flows from financing activities

Issue of loan capital	1,000
Issue of preference shares by subsidiary undertaking	800
Repayment of long-term borrowings	(200)
Net decrease in other borrowings	(1,000)
Dividends paid	(400)

Net cash from financing activities   200

Effects of exchange rate changes on cash and cash equivalents   600

Net increase in cash and cash equivalents	4,790
Cash and cash equivalents at beginning of period	4,050
Cash and cash equivalents at end of period	8,840

Proposed New
International
Accounting Standard

Financial Instruments

Exposure Draft

Introductory Note

1.   The purpose of this Introductory Note is to provide an overview of the main features of this proposed Statement and to highlight a number of significant matters on which the IASC Board particularly invites comments.

2.   This proposed Statement is the product of a joint project with the Accounting Standards Committee of The Canadian Institute of Chartered Accountants (CICA) to develop recognition, measurement and disclosure standards for financial instruments. A similar Exposure Draft, which proposes standards for inclusion in the CICA Handbook, is being issued in Canada concurrently with this Exposure Draft. The main features of the Canadian Exposure Draft are substantially the same as this proposed Statement with the significant exception that an allowed alternative of measuring all financial assets and financial liabilities at fair value is not provided.

The main features of the proposals

3.   The main features of the proposed standards are:

- The terms financial instrument, financial asset, financial liability and equity instrument are defined to include a wide range of items from cash and trade receivables to interest rate and currency options and swaps. Commodity contracts are excluded. For many of the more straightforward instruments falling within the scope of the definitions, such as cash and trade receivables, the proposed standards are not expected to require any significant change from current practice.

- A financial asset or financial liability should be recognised in the balance sheet when the risks and rewards associated with the asset or liability have been assumed and it can be measured reliably. Recognition ceases when the risks and rewards have been transferred to others or the underlying right or obligation has been exercised, discharged or cancelled, or has expired.

- When a financial instrument includes both a maturity date and a right to convert into an equity instrument of the issuer, the component parts of such an instrument should be identified on initial recognition and accounted for separately according to their particular characteristics. For example, the proceeds of a bond that provides the holder with the right to convert into common equity of the issuer would be allocated between the element that represents a financial liability and the element that represents an equity instrument, i.e., the right to convert into common equity.

- When the substance of a financial instrument is such that it commits the issuer to deliver cash or other financial assets to the holder, the instrument should be classified as a liability regardless of whether its legal form is that of equity or a liability.

• Criteria are provided that define the circumstances in which a financial asset and a financial liability should be offset and the net amount reported.

• A set of benchmark measurement standards for financial assets and financial liabilities is supplemented by allowed alternative measurement standards for investing and financing financial assets and financial liabilities.

• For purposes of determining the appropriate basis of measurement in accordance with the benchmark standards, financial assets and financial liabilities are classified as between investing and financing, operating and hedging. Investing and financing items, those held for the long term or until maturity, are measured on a historical cost basis. Operating items are measured at fair value and changes in fair value are recognised in income as they arise. Hedging items are measured on the same basis as the positions that they hedge and changes in fair value are recognised in income at the same time as changes in the fair value of the hedged position. The allowed alternative measurement standards require measurement of all financial assets and financial liabilities at fair value, changes in fair value being recognised in income as they arise.

• A decline in the value of a financial asset that is measured on a historical cost basis is required to be recognised immediately unless there is persuasive evidence that the historical cost carrying amount will be recoverable in the foreseeable future. A write-down to reflect a decline in value should be reversed to the extent there is persuasive evidence of a recovery in value that is likely to persist for the foreseeable future.

• Standards are established for dealing with matters such as the discontinuance of hedge accounting, reclassification of instruments between categories, and recognition and measurement of interest income and expense.

• To assist users of financial statements in understanding the effects of transactions in financial instruments on the amount, timing and certainty of future cash flows, the proposals require disclosure of information about the terms and conditions of the instruments, the exposure to interest rate and credit risk to which they give rise, and the fair value of financial assets and financial liabilities carried on a historical cost basis.

4. An appendix to the proposed Statement provides examples of application of the definitions and the recognition and measurement standards in a number of common situations.

Invitation to comment

5.   The IASC Board requests comments on all aspects of the proposals but particularly invites comments on the matters identified below. Comments are most helpful if they are related to a specific paragraph or group of paragraphs, clearly explain the problem and provide a suggestion for alternative wording with supporting reasoning.

The existence of benchmark and allowed alternative measurement standards

6.   The proposal to introduce benchmark and allowed alternative measurement standards raises the question of whether it is appropriate to permit a choice of measurement standards for financial instruments and, if so, whether the choice of standards to be identified as the benchmark is appropriate.

The use of fair value in measurement and disclosure standards

7.   The extent to which fair value measurements of assets and liabilities are recognised or disclosed currently in financial statements varies from country to country. A fundamental issue raised by this proposed Statement is the extent to which fair value measurements should be required in the case of financial assets and financial liabilities. The Board recognises that issues associated with the determination of fair value measurements for use in external financial reports may not be well understood. Specific comments from enterprises with practical experience in addressing these issues, such as financial institutions that carry financial instrument portfolios at fair value, would therefore be particularly helpful. Comments should address matters such as factors that may influence whether fair value measurements are sufficiently reliable for recognition or disclosure in financial statements.

8.   With respect to the use of fair value, particularly in the context of the allowed alternative measurement standards, other issues that commentators may wish to address include:

*   the desirability of permitting the use of fair value measurements for selected classes of financial assets or liabilities rather than requiring their use for all financial assets and financial liabilities; and

*   the relevance and practicability of implementing disclosure requirements in existing International Accounting Standards, such as International Accounting Standard 5, Information to be Disclosed in Financial Statements. For example, is it practicable and relevant to analyse changes in fair values of financial assets and financial liabilities and to disclose components such as

interest income or expense, loan losses, foreign exchange gains or losses and effects of changes in prevailing market interest rates? Also, is it practicable and relevant to segregate each of these components into their realised and unrealised portions?

The role of management intent in determining an appropriate measurement basis

9. The measurement basis applied to a financial asset or a financial liability under the benchmark measurement standards is governed by management's intent with respect to dealing with that asset or liability. This raises fundamental questions as to the extent to which management's intent is an essential element of the substance of a transaction and should therefore play a role in determining the appropriate measurement basis to be applied.

10. In accordance with the benchmark measurement standards, when a substantive event occurs that causes management to change its intent with respect to a particular financial instrument, reclassification from one class to another (e.g., from investing to operating) may be required, sometimes resulting in a change in measurement basis. Commentators are encouraged to comment on the acceptability of this practice, particularly with respect to income recognition of unrealised gains arising on reclassification.

Level of detail

11. The objective of the proposed Statement is to establish standards that will provide a sound basis from which to resolve practical issues arising in accounting for many different types of financial instruments. Consistent with this approach, application of the proposed standards in certain commonly encountered situations is illustrated in the Appendix but detailed guidance on application to the multitude of specific instruments that exist is not provided. This raises the issue of whether the IASC and perhaps national standard-setting bodies should, in the future, develop more specific standards on some issues by building on the basis established by this proposed Statement.

12. Commentators are also invited to indicate whether the Appendix is sufficiently helpful in understanding how the definitions and standards are intended to be applied that it should be retained in the final Statement.

Scope of application

13. With few exceptions, the proposed Statement applies to all types of financial

instruments and no exceptions are made for particular types of enterprises. Commentators should consider whether there are specific circumstances, types of instruments or types of enterprises for which application of the proposed standards may present particular difficulties.

Relationships with other International Accounting Standards

14.   The proposed Statement is generally compatible with existing International Accounting Standards, taking into account revisions to be made in accordance with the Statement of Intent on Comparability of Financial Statements. However, particular attention is drawn to the fact that a large part of the subject matter of International Accounting Standard 25, Accounting for Investments, is encompassed within the scope of this proposed Statement. This is recognised in the Statement of Intent on Comparability of Financial Statements which indicates that consideration of the following issues relating to IAS 25 has been deferred pending further work on the financial instruments project:

•   measurement of long-term investments;

•   measurement of marketable equity securities held as long-term investments;

•   measurement of current investments; and

•   recognition of increases and decreases in market values of current investments.

Each of these issues is addressed in this draft and the positions taken differ significantly from those taken in IAS 25. Prior to publication of an International Accounting Standard on financial instruments, the Board will consider modification of IAS 25 or its withdrawal and replacement with a new standard to deal with investments other than those that are financial instruments.

Extent of change from existing practices

15.   The proposed Statement incorporates standards that differ significantly from existing practices for various aspects of accounting for financial instruments in certain countries. Examples of potentially significant changes include:

•   separate recognition and measurement of the component parts of compound instruments;

•   application of a stringent test for removal of assets and liabilities from the balance sheet consequent upon a transaction such as a securitisation of receivables or an "in substance" defeasance of debt;

•   limiting the circumstances in which financial assets and financial liabilities should be offset for purposes of balance sheet presentation;

- permitting reversal of write-downs of assets carried on a cost basis when there is a recovery in value; and

- requiring disclosure of the fair value of the financial liabilities of all types of enterprises.

Format of the exposure draft

16.   The format of this exposure draft differs from that of International Accounting Standards and exposure drafts published before 1991. The format in this draft is proposed for all International Accounting Standards to enhance their clarity and comprehensibility.

Contents

International Accounting Standard – Financial Instruments

**Measurement of Financial Assets and
Financial Liabilities** (continued)

Appendix

Examples of the application of the definitions
and the recognition and measurement standards

International Accounting Standard – Financial Instruments

The standards, which have been set in bold type, should be read in the context of the background material and implementation guidance and in the context of the Preface to International Accounting Standards. International Accounting Standards are not intended to apply to immaterial items (see paragraph 12 of the Preface).

Introduction

The dynamic nature of international financial markets has resulted in a great variety of financial instruments, ranging from the simple bond to options, futures, swaps and many others that combine the features of two or more types of instruments. Innovation will continue as users of financial instruments seek new ways to hedge exposures in volatile markets and traders seek new ways to exploit opportunities to profit from that volatility. The continuing process of innovation emphasises the need for sound general principles of accounting for financial instruments.

The objective of this Statement is to assist enterprises in providing useful information about their financial position and performance as a result of being a party to a financial instrument. The Statement provides guidance to enterprises in developing appropriate accounting policies for recognising, presenting, measuring and disclosing existing types of financial instruments and variations that may emerge in the future.

Scope

1.   This Statement deals with the accounting for and disclosure of all types of financial instruments.

2.   Other Statements of International Accounting Standards specific to certain types of financial instruments may contain additional requirements that are more extensive and explicit or more restrictive than the requirements of this Statement. For example, International Accounting Standard 17, Accounting for Leases, incorporates specific requirements relating to finance leases and International Accounting Standard 26, Accounting and Reporting by Retirement Benefit Plans, requires measurement of retirement benefit plan investments at fair value rather than allowing the choice of measurement standards permitted in this Statement.

3.   This Statement does not apply to:

(a)   interests in subsidiaries, as defined in International Accounting Standard 27, Consolidated Financial Statements and Accounting for Investments in Subsidiaries;

(b)   interests in associates, as defined in International Accounting Standard 28, Accounting for Investments in Associates;

(c)   interests in joint ventures, as defined in International Accounting Standard 31, Financial Reporting of Interests in Joint Ventures;

(d)   employers' and plans' obligations for retirement benefits as described in International Accounting Standard 19, Accounting for Retirement Benefits in the Financial Statements of Employers, and International Accounting Standard 26, Accounting and Reporting by Retirement Benefit Plans, respectively; and

(e)   employers' obligations under employee stock option and stock purchase plans.

Definitions

4.   **The following terms are used in this Statement with the meanings specified:**

A *financial instrument* is any contract that gives rise to both a (recognised or unrecognised) financial asset of one enterprise[1] and a (recognised or unrecognised) financial liability or equity instrument of another enterprise.

A *financial asset* is any asset that is:

(a)   cash;

(b)   a contractual right to receive cash or another financial asset from another enterprise;

(c)   a contractual right to exchange financial instruments with another enterprise under conditions that are potentially favourable; or

(d)   an equity instrument of another enterprise.

A *financial liability* is any liability that is a contractual obligation:

(a)   to deliver cash or another financial asset to another enterprise; or

(b)   to exchange financial instruments with another enterprise under conditions that are potentially unfavourable.

---

[1]   For purposes of these definitions, the term "enterprise" should be read to include individuals, partnerships, incorporated bodies and government agencies.

An *equity instrument* is any contract that evidences a residual interest in the assets of an enterprise after deducting all of its liabilities.

Fair value is the amount for which an asset could be exchanged, or a liability settled, between knowledgeable, willing parties in an arm's length transaction.

Market value is the amount obtainable from the sale, or payable on the acquisition, of a financial instrument in an active market. In the case of assets that are traded in an active market and for which there is a quoted market price, that price generally provides the best evidence of fair value.

Investing activities are transactions that result in the acquisition of financial assets that are intended to be held for the long term or until maturity.

Financing activities are transactions that result in the assumption of financial liabilities that are intended to be held for the long term or until maturity.

Hedging activities are transactions that result in the acquisition of financial assets or the assumption of financial liabilities that are intended to eliminate or reduce substantially the risk of loss from a specifically identified position exposed to risk of loss from price changes.

Operating activities are transactions that result in the acquisition of financial assets or the assumption of financial liabilities that are not identified as hedges and that do not meet the definitions of investing activities or financing activities.

5.   It should be noted that the definitions of the terms investing activities, financing activities and operating activities differ from the definitions of those terms adopted for purposes of classifying cash flows in accordance with Exposure Draft 36, Cash Flow Statements.   Further discussion and explanation of the definitions is provided in paragraphs 6 to 14, as well as in those parts of the Statement in which the definitions are particularly relevant.   The Appendix to this Statement provides examples of the application of the definitions, illustrating how each component of the definitions can be applied in identifying financial assets, financial liabilities and equity instruments in a range of circumstances.

6.   Parts of the definitions of a financial asset and a financial liability are recursive, because the terms financial asset and financial instrument are included in them, but they are not circular. There must be a contractual right or obligation to exchange instruments, and instruments to be exchanged must be financial assets, financial liabilities, or equity instruments.

7.   A financial instrument gives rise to a financial asset of one enterprise and a financial liability, an equity instrument or both a financial liability and an equity instrument of another enterprise. It does not necessarily follow, however, that these assets, liabilities and equity instruments qualify for recognition in financial statements either at inception of the contract or at some later date.

8.   Financial instruments include both primary instruments, such as cash, receivables, payables and equity securities, and secondary or derivative instruments, such as options, futures and forward contracts relating to financial instruments and interest rate and currency swaps. Secondary or derivative instruments create rights and obligations that have the effect of transferring one or more of the financial risks inherent in an underlying primary financial instrument and the value of the contract normally reflects changes in the value of the underlying financial instrument. Derivative instruments do not result in a transfer of the underlying primary financial instrument on inception of the contract, nor does a transfer necessarily take place on maturity of the derivative instrument.

9.   Financial instruments may also be characterised as simple instruments or compound instruments. Simple instruments comprise a single financial asset, financial liability or equity instrument, such as a receivable, payable or common share. Compound instruments comprise a combination of financial assets, financial liabilities and equity instruments, such as a bond receivable with an option to convert into common or preferred share of the issuer, or a bond receivable with an option to exchange for other financial instruments held by the issuer.

10.   Physical assets such as inventories, property, plant and equipment, leased assets and intangible assets such as patents, trademarks, and goodwill are not financial assets. These assets may eventually be converted to cash but, because ownership of physical or intangible assets does not create a present obligation on the part of another enterprise to deliver cash or another financial asset, an enterprise owning physical or intangible assets has no present right to receive cash or another financial asset.

11.   Other assets, such as prepaid expenses, for which the future economic benefit is the receipt of goods or services instead of the right to receive cash or another financial asset are not financial assets. Similarly, many liabilities such as deferred revenue and most warranty obligations are not financial liabilities because the probable outflow of economic benefits associated with them is the delivery of goods and services rather than cash or another financial asset.

12.   Contractual rights (obligations) that can be settled only by receipt (delivery) of non-financial assets, such as commodities (e.g., a silver option, futures or forward contract), or the provision of services (e.g., an operating lease for use of a physical asset) do not fall within the scope of the definition of a financial instrument since they do not involve a transfer of a financial asset[2]. A contractual right of one party to

---

[2]   The standards in this Statement were not developed for application to assets or liabilities involving rights to receive or obligations to deliver a commodity. Such non-financial assets and liabilities are accounted for in accordance with other International Accounting Standards and an enterprise's accounting policies for other similar items. It may be appropriate, however, for an enterprise to adapt some of the standards in this Statement when formulating an accounting policy for non-financial assets and liabilities arising under commodity contracts.

receive a non-financial asset or service and the corresponding obligation of the other party do not establish a present right or obligation of either party to receive, deliver or exchange a financial asset. However, delivery of the non-financial asset or provision of the service in the future in accordance with the contract may give rise at that time to a right to receive (and an obligation of the other party to deliver) cash or another financial asset, which right (obligation) would fall within the scope of the definition of a financial instrument.

13. The definition of a financial instrument includes within its scope a commodity-linked instrument that provides for the holder to receive either a financial asset, including cash, or a specified amount of a commodity. For example, a bond that allows the holder the option of receiving on maturity either the face amount of the bond in cash or a specified quantity of oil comprises two elements, a financial asset (a receivable) and a non-financial asset (an option to exchange that receivable for oil). The intentions of the holder concerning exercise of the option do not affect the substance or the accounting treatment of the component assets.

14. The ability to exercise contractual rights or the requirement to satisfy contractual obligations may be absolute, or it may be contingent on the occurrence of a future event. A financial guarantee, for example, is a financial liability of the guarantor (the contractual obligation to pay the lender if the borrower defaults) and a financial asset of the lender (the contractual right to receive cash from the guarantor if the borrower defaults). The contractual rights and obligations exist because of a past transaction or event (acceptance of the guarantee), even though the lender's ability to exercise its right and the requirement for the guarantor to perform under its obligation are both contingent on an act of default by the borrower. Contingent items meet the definitions of a financial asset and a financial liability but are not recognised in the balance sheet when they fail to satisfy the recognition criteria in this Statement or in other International Accounting Standards.

Recognition of Financial Assets and Financial Liabilities

Initial recognition of a financial asset or financial liability

15. **A financial asset or financial liability should be recognised on an enterprise's balance sheet when:**

(a) **the risks and rewards associated with the asset or liability have been transferred to the enterprise; and**

(b) **the cost or value of the asset to the enterprise or the amount of the obligation assumed can be measured reliably.**

16. The International Accounting Standards Committee's Framework for the Preparation and Presentation of Financial Statements (the Framework) describes recognition as "the process of incorporating in the balance sheet or income statement an item that meets the definition of an element and satisfies the criteria for recognition..." and sets out the criteria in general terms[3]. The recognition standard in paragraph 15 applies the general recognition criteria in the Framework to financial assets and financial liabilities. The Framework also indicates that an item possessing the essential characteristics of an element but failing to meet the criteria for recognition may nonetheless warrant disclosure in the notes, explanatory material or supplementary schedules.

17. Assumption by an enterprise of the risks and rewards associated with a financial asset is the key indicator that it is probable the future economic benefits from the asset will flow to the enterprise. Similarly, assumption of the risks and rewards associated with a financial liability is the key indicator that it is probable there will be an outflow from the enterprise of resources embodying economic benefits. Assumption of risks and rewards exposes an enterprise to the potential for gain or loss inherent in a financial asset or financial liability.

18. Contractual rights and obligations arising from a financial instrument may create exposure to risks and rewards regardless of the extent of performance or whether an unconditional right to receive or obligation to pay any consideration exists. Accordingly, financial assets and financial liabilities arising from financial instruments under which obligations are partially or completely unperformed are recognised when they satisfy the criteria in paragraph 15.

19. Financial instruments result in an enterprise assuming or transferring to another party one or more of the financial risks described below.

---

[3]   Paragraphs 82 to 91 of the Framework.

Price risk

There are three types of price risk: currency risk, interest rate risk and market risk. Currency risk is the risk that the value of a financial instrument will fluctuate due to changes in foreign exchange rates. Interest rate risk is the risk that the value of a financial instrument will fluctuate due to changes in market interest rates. Market risk is the risk that the value of a financial instrument will fluctuate as a result of changes in market prices whether those changes are caused by factors specific to the individual security or its issuer or factors affecting all securities traded in the market. The term "price risk" embodies not only the potential for loss but also the potential for gain.

Credit risk

Credit risk is the risk that one party to a financial instrument will fail to discharge an obligation and cause the other party to incur a financial loss.

Liquidity risk

Liquidity risk is the risk that an enterprise will encounter difficulty in raising funds at short notice to meet commitments associated with financial instruments (also referred to as funding risk). Liquidity risk may result from an inability to sell a financial asset quickly at close to its fair value.

Changes in the market's perception of these risks give rise to fluctuations in the market price of a financial instrument. For example, the market price of a debt security is affected by changes in the market's perception of credit risk, as well as by changes in market interest rates and, in some cases, currency risk.

20.   The rewards associated with a financial asset may include not only potential gains as a result of having assumed price risk, but also rights to receive interest and payments of principal, to pledge the instrument as security for obligations, to dispose of the instrument for consideration and to use the instrument to settle an obligation. Financial liabilities usually arise from transactions in which the enterprise has received some past benefit, such as a receipt of cash, and may also have the potential for future benefits as a result of exposure to price risk.

21.   To determine whether it has assumed the risks and rewards of a particular financial instrument, an enterprise first identifies and assesses the various benefits and exposures to gain or loss associated with the instrument. For example, a fixed rate loan receivable in a foreign currency exposes the lender to credit risk, interest rate risk and currency risk, each of which may cause the fair value of the loan to fluctuate. The lender is also normally entitled to collect the principal amount of the loan on maturity, to pledge the loan as security or to sell it. Assumption of these risks and rewards indicates that the lender has acquired a financial asset that satisfies the

first of the two recognition criteria in paragraph 15. From the perspective of the issuer of a fixed rate bond, the benefits include the initial receipt of cash from the bondholders and the exposure to possible future gain or loss as a result of changes in fair value caused by changes in market interest rates or the market's perception of credit risk to the holders.

22.   Determining whether an estimate of the cost or value of a financial asset or the amount of a financial liability is sufficiently reliable to justify recognition is a matter for the exercise of judgment in each situation. In an arm's length transaction for cash consideration, the amount to be recognised may be readily and reliably measurable. Measurement of non-monetary transactions, such as an exchange of holdings of investments or the issuance of shares to acquire an investment, requires reference to market values or estimation techniques.

23.   When a financial instrument is traded in an active and highly liquid market, its fair value is often determined by reference to the quoted market price for transactions in substantially the same instrument. However, when there is infrequent activity in a market, the market is not well established (for example, some "over the counter" markets) or small volumes are traded relative to the number of trading units of an instrument to be valued, quoted market prices may not be indicative of fair value. Fair value of an instrument based on market value is derived from the appropriate quoted market price (for example, last bid price for an asset held or liability to be issued and last offer, or asking, price for an asset to be acquired or liability held) and takes into account any transaction costs that would be incurred in an actual transaction.

24.   When a quoted market value is not available, estimation techniques may be used to determine fair value with sufficient reliability to satisfy the recognition criterion in paragraph 15 or certain of the measurement and disclosure standards. Techniques that are well established in financial markets include reference to the current market value of another instrument that is substantially the same, discounted cash flow analysis and option pricing models. In applying discounted cash flow analysis, an enterprise uses a discount rate equal to the rate of interest prevailing in the market at the time the estimate is made for financial instruments having substantially the same principal terms and characteristics, such as creditworthiness of the debtor, the remaining term over which the contractual interest rate is fixed, the remaining term to repayment of the principal and the currency in which payments are made. In unusual circumstances, when estimation techniques cannot be applied or do not result in a sufficiently reliable estimate of the cost or fair value of a financial asset or the amount of a financial liability, an enterprise does not recognise the asset or liability on its balance sheet but discloses information about it in accordance with the disclosure standards in this Statement.

Recognition of separate components of a compound financial instrument

25.   When a financial instrument has both a maturity date and either a right of exchange for an asset other than cash or a right to convert into an equity instrument of the issuer, on initial recognition the holder and the issuer should identify the instrument's component parts and account for them separately according to their particular characteristics.

26.   Financial instruments for which it is necessary to identify and take into account the component parts in determining the appropriate accounting normally include those that incorporate:

(a)   a primary financial asset together with an option to convert that primary asset into, or exchange it for, another financial asset (for example, a bond convertible into common shares of the issuer of the bond or a bond exchangeable for common shares of a third party that will be delivered by the issuer of the bond), in which case the financial assets of one party to the financial instrument are matched by corresponding financial liabilities or a financial liability and an equity instrument of the other party; or

(b)   a financial asset together with an option to exchange that financial asset for a non-financial asset (for example, a bond for which the holder may elect to receive either cash or a fixed quantity of a specified commodity on maturity), in which case the financial asset and non-financial asset of one party to the financial instrument are matched by a corresponding financial liability and non-financial liability of the other party.

27.   A bond or similar instrument convertible into common shares is properly viewed by the issuer as comprising two components: a financial liability (a contractual arrangement to deliver cash or other financial assets) and an equity instrument (a call option granting the holder the right, for a specified period of time, to convert into common equity of the issuer). The issuer accounts for the two components separately, each being recognised initially in the balance sheet at its fair value. The economic effect of issuing a debt instrument that is convertible into common shares is substantially the same as issuing debt accompanied by warrants to purchase common shares, the differences being primarily a matter of legal form. The holder of such a compound financial instrument similarly accounts separately for the component parts.

28.   The sum of the carrying amounts assigned to the components of a compound financial instrument on initial recognition is always equal to the value of the instrument as a whole. No gain or loss arises from separation of the compound instrument into its components. There are several approaches to measurement of the individual components, including:

(a)   assigning the residual amount to the least easily measurable component (often an equity instrument), after deducting from the value of the compound instrument as a whole the amounts separately determined for each of the other components; and

(b)   measuring each component separately and then adjusting the amounts so determined on a pro rata basis so that the sum of the components equals the value of the instrument as a whole.

In the case of a bond convertible into common shares, the financial liability recognised initially reflects the present value of the contractual arrangement to settle the obligation at maturity and to make the scheduled periodic interest payments prior to maturity. The interest rate used in determining the present value of the financial liability is the prevailing market rate for a similar liability that does not have an associated equity instrument. The value of the option to convert into common shares may be determined separately by reference to the value of a similar option, if one exists, or by using an option pricing model. Alternatively, the value of the option may be determined as the residual amount after deducting from the value of the financial instrument as a whole the value of the financial liability component.

Discontinuing recognition of a financial asset or financial liability

29.   A recognised financial asset or financial liability should be removed from an enterprise's balance sheet when:

(a)   the risks and rewards associated with the asset or liability have been transferred to others; or

(b)   the underlying right or obligation has been exercised, discharged or cancelled, or has expired.

30.   Many transactions or circumstances that cause an enterprise to discontinue recognition of a financial asset or financial liability are readily identifiable. Removal of a recognised financial asset or financial liability from an enterprise's balance sheet is appropriate when, for example, a financial asset is sold or settled (as in the case of collection in full of an account receivable), a financial liability is discharged, or a contract time period has expired (as in the case of expiry of an option or warrant). All of these circumstances are characterised by the expiration or substantive transfer of the risks and rewards that provided the basis for the initial recognition of the financial asset or financial liability. In other cases, a financial asset or financial liability may be transferred to others in a manner that involves the retention of some of the original risks and rewards. In such cases, it is inappropriate for the enterprise to recognise a sale or settlement and to discontinue recognition of the asset or liability.

31.   Determination of whether the risks and rewards associated with a financial asset or financial liability have been transferred to another party is a matter for the exercise of judgment by the management of an enterprise, taking into account the characteristics of the particular financial asset or financial liability and the circumstances in which the transfer takes place. An enterprise removes a financial asset or financial liability from its balance sheet only when it is no longer exposed to risks and no longer has the potential for rewards associated with the underlying financial instrument. The discussion of risks and rewards in paragraphs 17 to 21 is relevant to an assessment of whether a transfer has occurred.

32.   As a matter of business policy, enterprises may use various risk management techniques, such as hedging, risk diversification, risk pooling, guarantees and various types of insurance (including sureties and "hold harmless" agreements), to minimise exposures to financial risks. These techniques generally reduce the exposure to loss from only one of several different financial risks associated with a financial instrument and may involve the assumption of additional but partially offsetting risks and rewards. A currency swap, for example, may lessen the potential for losses from a currency price risk but does not eliminate that risk, and also results in the assumption of a credit risk. An enterprise continues to recognise a financial asset or financial liability when it remains exposed to the associated risks and rewards assumed at the inception of the underlying financial instrument, whether or not it has offset any of the risks by using risk management techniques.

33.   Transfers of accounts receivable through transactions such as factoring or securitisation provide examples of the practical difficulties an enterprise may encounter in determining whether to remove a financial asset from its balance sheet. If the transferee has the right to receive compensation from the transferor for part or all of the economic loss arising from failure of debtors to pay when due, the transferor remains exposed to the primary risk, credit risk, associated with the receivables. In such circumstances, the transaction is not considered to be a disposition and it is not appropriate to remove the accounts receivable from the transferor's balance sheet. When the risks and rewards have been transferred, leaving the transferor with no obligation to compensate the buyer for credit risk or price risk, the transfer is treated as a disposition. When a transaction such as a securitisation or factoring does not meet the criteria for removing a financial asset from the balance sheet, the transaction is treated as a financing transaction and the financial asset remains in the balance sheet of the transferor, together with a corresponding financial liability for amounts received from the transferee.

34.   Disposition of part of a financial asset or settlement of part of a financial liability can be distinguished from a transaction such as a transfer of receivables with recourse. A partial disposition or settlement involves transferring all risks and rewards relating to a part of a financial asset or financial liability, rather than

transferring a part of the risks and rewards relating to an entire financial asset or financial liability. A partial disposition arises, for example, when half of the principal amount of an investment in an issue of bonds is sold. All of the risks and rewards associated with half of the original investment have been transferred. On the other hand, in the case of a transfer of half of an enterprise's portfolio of receivables with full recourse, the transfer of risks and rewards is not proportionate to the risks and rewards associated with the entire portfolio of accounts receivable because more than half of the original risk has been retained. In the former case, it is appropriate to remove from the balance sheet the part of the financial asset or financial liability for which all of the risks and rewards have been transferred; in the latter case, it is not appropriate to remove from the balance sheet any part of the financial asset or financial liability.

35. Certain debt agreements provide for the legal procedure known as defeasance. When that procedure is undertaken, a debtor's obligation under a debt agreement may be discharged by depositing cash or other assets with a third party that agrees to assume the debtor's obligations. The creditor likewise agrees to look to the third party for repayment of the receivable. In these circumstances, it is appropriate for the debtor to remove the liability from its balance sheet since it has fully discharged its contractual obligation and the creditor has not retained any right of recourse against the debtor.

36. On occasion, a similar procedure is undertaken in connection with a debt agreement that does not contain a defeasance provision. In such a transaction, sometimes called an "in substance defeasance", cash or other assets are deposited in a trust to be used solely to satisfy scheduled payments under the debt agreement but the creditor is not a party to the arrangement and often is unaware that it exists. Although the transaction is called an "in substance defeasance", the debtor is not released from the primary obligation under the debt agreement to repay to the creditor the principal amount of the debt plus interest; the risks associated with the obligation have not been transferred. As a result, both the assets deposited in trust and the debt obligation intended to be serviced are reported separately as an asset and a liability in the balance sheet of the debtor.

37. The inability to remeasure a financial asset or financial liability reliably from time to time is not a basis for ceasing to recognise the asset or liability. Such circumstances may, however, have implications for the measurement of the asset or liability (see the discussion in paragraphs 59 to 144).

Presentation

Classification between liabilities and equity

38.   The classification of a financial instrument, or its component parts, as between liabilities and equity should reflect the substance of the contractual arrangement on initial recognition. That classification should be consistent with the definitions of a financial liability and an equity instrument.

39.   In the majority of cases, the legal form of a financial instrument is consistent with its substance. Innovations in corporate financing activities sometimes result, however, in financial instruments that combine features associated with equity instruments and features associated with financial liabilities. Also, some financial instruments take the legal form of equity but are liabilities in substance and, conversely, some instruments having the legal form of liabilities contain provisions that make them, in substance, equity. The recognition, measurement and disclosure standards in this Statement are based on the definitions of financial assets, financial liabilities and equity instruments and, consequently, it is important to be able to distinguish among the types of balance sheet elements, particularly between liabilities and equity.

40.   A financial instrument may contain many features that are common to both liabilities and equity, such as voting rights, rights to a return on capital in the form of interest or dividends, and liquidation priorities.   One feature is critical in differentiating a financial liability from an equity instrument - the contractual obligation of one party to the underlying financial instrument (the issuer) to deliver cash or another financial asset to the other party (the holder) or to exchange another financial instrument with the holder under conditions that are potentially unfavourable to the issuer. When such a contractual obligation is a feature of a financial instrument, that instrument meets the definition of a financial liability regardless of the form in which the contractual obligation is settled. When such a contractual obligation is not a feature of a financial instrument, that instrument is an equity instrument. The holder of an equity instrument may be entitled to receive a pro rata share of any dividends or other distributions out of equity, but the issuer has no contractual obligation to make such distributions.

41.   An obligation of an enterprise to issue or deliver its own equity instruments is not a financial liability; the enterprise is not obliged to deliver cash or another financial asset and an obligation to exchange its own equity instruments for financial assets of another party is not potentially unfavourable because it cannot result in any loss to the enterprise.

42.   The substance of a financial instrument, rather than its form, governs its balance sheet classification. For example, certain forms of preferred shares not only

have preferential rights in relation to dividends and repayment of capital upon liquidation but also provide for mandatory redemption by the issuer at a fixed or determinable future date. Other forms of preferred shares do not have a specified mandatory redemption date but the holder of the preferred shares may have the right to require the issuer to redeem the shares at or after a particular date. When a financial instrument such as a preferred share specifies a scheduled settlement or redemption date, or provides the holder with the ability to require settlement or redemption, it meets the definition of a financial liability.

43.   Certain types of preferred shares receive priority in a liquidation over common shares but do not provide the holder with the right to require redemption in normal circumstances. In such situations, the attribute of a liability is missing. However, that attribute may exist even when no specified redemption date exists. A preferred share may, for example, have a contractually provided accelerating dividend such that, within the foreseeable future, the dividend yield is scheduled to be so high that the issuer will be economically compelled to redeem the instrument. In this situation, the substance on initial recognition indicates a contractual obligation to settle the instrument and classification as a financial liability is appropriate. A financial instrument labelled as a share may also entitle the holder to require redemption upon the occurrence of some possible future event. On initial recognition, consideration of the circumstances may lead to a judgment that occurrence of the future event is probable and classification as a financial liability best reflects the substance of the instrument.

44.   On initial recognition of a compound financial instrument, an enterprise segregates the component parts of the instrument according to their principal characteristics and classifies them as liabilities and equity. For example, the liability component of a bond convertible into common shares is normally grouped with the liability components of other similar convertible financial instruments and presented within the liabilities section of the balance sheet. The value attributed to the option to convert the bond into common shares is presented within the shareholders' equity section of the balance sheet but separately from common shares. Other disclosures about the bond in accordance with the disclosure standards in this Statement provide sufficient information to permit financial statement users to associate the liability and equity components.

45.   An enterprise removes a financial liability from its balance sheet when the criteria for doing so are met, but may concurrently give initial recognition to an equity instrument. For example, the liability component of a debt instrument convertible into common shares is removed from the issuer's balance sheet when the holder exercises the right to convert into shares and the shares resulting from conversion are accorded initial recognition. The option to convert the instrument, recognised on its inception, is also removed from the balance sheet when the option

is exercised. In other circumstances, an enterprise may remove an equity instrument from its balance sheet and concurrently accord initial recognition to a financial liability (for example, upon the acquisition by an enterprise of its own shares in exchange for a note).

46.   The financial liability component of a compound financial instrument continues to be recognised and classified as a liability on an enterprise's balance sheet until the criteria in paragraph 29 for its removal are met. Changes in the likelihood of conversion do not result in any change in presentation of the financial liability or equity instrument components, even when conversion may appear to have become economically advantageous to some holders. Holders may not always act in the manner that might be expected because, for example, the acquisition cost of the instrument and the tax consequences resulting from conversion may differ among holders. Furthermore, the likelihood of conversion will change from time to time.

Classification of interest, dividends, gains and losses

47.   The classification of interest, dividends, gains and losses as between the income statement and the disclosure of changes in shareholders' equity should be consistent with the balance sheet classification of related financial liabilities and equity instruments.

48.   Just as the substance of a financial instrument determines its classification in the balance sheet, so that substance determines the classification of related items in the income statement and in the disclosure of changes in shareholders' equity. The cost of debt, or liability, financing is recognised as an expense in the income statement and the cost of equity financing is recognised as a reduction in shareholders' equity. Similarly, gains and losses associated with redemptions or refinancings of instruments accounted for as liabilities are presented in the income statement, while redemptions or refinancings of instruments accounted for as equity are presented in the disclosure of changes in shareholders' equity.

49.   When the components of a financial instrument are separately recognised and classified, that classification determines the basis of recognition and classification of the stream of future dividends, interest or other periodic cash flows associated with the instrument. Amounts paid or payable by the parties to a financial instrument, other than on account of principal, are recognised as they accrue by a charge to income or as an element of the changes in shareholders' equity, according to their substance. Similarly, amounts received or receivable are recognised in accordance with their substance.

50.   In some circumstances, because of significant differences between interest and dividends with respect to matters such as tax deductibility, it is desirable to

disclose each separately within the income statement and the disclosure of changes in shareholders' equity. Disclosures of the amounts of tax effects are made in accordance with International Accounting Standard 12, Accounting for Taxes on Income.

Offsetting of a financial asset and a financial liability

51.   A financial asset and a financial liability should be offset and the net amount reported in the balance sheet when an enterprise has a legally enforceable right to set off the recognised amounts and realisation or settlement is intended to take place through exercise of that right.

52.   For purposes of balance sheet presentation, a financial liability recognised in the balance sheet is not presented net of a financial asset and, similarly, a financial asset is not presented net of a financial liability, unless a right of set-off exists. A right of set-off is a debtor's legal right, by contract or otherwise, to settle or otherwise eliminate all or a portion of an obligation due to a creditor by applying against that obligation an amount due to the debtor. The offsetting amount owed to the debtor is not necessarily owed by the creditor; the offsetting amount may be owed to the debtor by a third party, as long as there is an agreement amongst all of the parties that clearly establishes the debtor's right to set-off. The nature of an "in substance defeasance" arrangement is such that it does not qualify for offsetting because the creditor has not accepted the assets placed in trust in settlement of the liability and the debtor therefore has no right of set-off against that liability.

53.   Since the right of set-off is a legal right, the conditions supporting the right may vary from one legal jurisdiction to another and care must be taken to establish which set of laws applies to the relationships between the parties involved. When there is a legal right of set-off, the exposure to risks and rewards in respect of financial assets and financial liabilities is substantively different than when there is no such right. The existence of an intention by one or both parties to settle on a net basis in the absence of a legal right to do so is not sufficient to justify offsetting in the balance sheet since the exposure to the risks and rewards inherent in the individual financial assets and financial liabilities remains.

54.   The conditions set out in paragraph 51 are not usually satisfied, and offsetting is therefore inappropriate, when:

(a)   several different financial instruments are used to emulate the features of a single financial instrument (i.e., a "synthetic" instrument);

(b)   financial assets and financial liabilities arise from financial instruments having the same primary risk exposure (for example, assets and liabilities within a portfolio of foreign exchange forward contracts) but involve different parties; or

(c)   financial or other assets are pledged as security for non-recourse financial liabilities.

55.   Offsetting a financial asset and a financial liability differs from not recognising or ceasing to recognise an asset and a liability. Satisfaction of the conditions in paragraph 51 requires an enterprise to present on its balance sheet only the net amount of a recognised financial asset and financial liability. In contrast, ceasing to recognise a financial asset or a financial liability involves removal from the balance sheet of a previously recognised item and may result in recognition of a gain or a loss. Some derivative financial instruments are characterised as "off balance sheet" because they involve offsetting of financial assets and financial liabilities that happen to have equal carrying amounts, with the result that there is no net carrying amount presented in the balance sheet. Although the "off balance sheet" characterisation implies non-recognition, the financial asset and financial liability have been recognised and, in accordance with paragraph 51, subsequently offset in the balance sheet. This is the case, for example, on inception of a forward foreign exchange contract under which an enterprise has both a right and an obligation to exchange a fixed amount of foreign currency for a fixed amount of cash, and also a right to set-off the two amounts. At inception, the value of the rights (asset) equals the value of the obligations (liability) and the two amounts are offset.

56.   Income and expense items normally presented on a gross basis are offset and reported on a net basis to the extent that the conditions in paragraph 51 for offsetting are satisfied in respect of the related cash flows. This presentation will, in many cases, result in offsetting of items in the income statement and disclosure of changes in shareholders' equity on a basis that is consistent with offsetting of the related financial asset and financial liability in the balance sheet. When the terms of financial instruments are such that the basis of presentation of income and expense differs from the basis of presentation of the related financial asset and financial liability and the effect of the inconsistency in presentation is significant, it is desirable for an enterprise to explain the circumstances.

Measurement of Financial Assets and Financial Liabilities

Measurement on initial recognition

57. **When a financial asset or a financial liability is recognised initially, it should be measured at the amount of cash or the fair value of other assets exchanged.**

58.   Measurement is described in the Framework[4] as "the process of determining the monetary amounts at which the elements of the financial statements are to be recognised and carried in the balance sheet and income statement". In either a historical cost transaction based accounting model or a fair value model, assets are generally recorded initially at "the amount of cash or cash equivalents paid or the fair value of the consideration given to acquire them". Similarly, liabilities are recorded at "the amount of proceeds received in exchange for the obligation, or in some circumstances ..., at the amounts of cash or cash equivalents expected to be paid to satisfy the liability in the normal course of business". In the case of a non-monetary exchange transaction, fair value of the consideration exchanged may be determined by reference either to the asset given up or to the asset acquired, whichever is more clearly evident. In either type of accounting model, the initial carrying amount so determined is commonly referred to as the historical cost of the asset or proceeds of the liability.

Measurement subsequent to initial recognition

BENCHMARK MEASUREMENT STANDARDS

59.   Paragraphs 62 to 130 set out the benchmark standards for measurement of financial assets and financial liabilities subsequent to their initial recognition and for recognition of interest income and interest expense. Under these standards, management's intent in entering into a transaction involving a financial instrument, as well as the nature of the financial instrument, is considered to be a primary factor in determining the substance of the transaction. Intent is the criterion for selecting a measurement basis to apply to the resulting financial asset or financial liability. For purposes of the benchmark measurement standards, financial instruments are classified into three broad categories: investing and financing; operating; and hedging.

60.   In general, financial instruments are classified as investing or financing when they are held for the long term or until maturity (which may be for a relatively short

---

period), hedging when they are held to offset an exposure to financial risk (regardless of the expected holding period), and operating when they do not fall into one of the other categories. This basis of classification is discussed further in relation to the measurement standards for each category.

61.   The appropriate classification for a financial instrument under the benchmark standards is based on management's primary purpose in respect of the instrument. For example, if an enterprise purchases a long term bond primarily with a view to holding it for the long term, that purpose is the basis for classification of the transaction. In this case, the classification is not affected by the fact that the bond may be readily marketable in the short term. In unusual circumstances, as a result of a change in management's original intentions with respect to a particular financial instrument, a change in classification for accounting purposes may be justified with a consequent change in the measurement basis. Such changes take place as a result of changes in business policy and not merely because of fluctuations in market prices or decisions to change accounting policies.

Investing and financing

Measurement of a financial asset or financial liability

62.   Subsequent to initial recognition, a financial asset or a financial liability resulting from investing or financing activities should continue to be measured and reported in the balance sheet at the amount initially recognised, except as provided otherwise by paragraphs 63, 72 and 73.

63.   A financial asset or a financial liability resulting from investing or financing activities that is to be settled through scheduled payments of fixed or determinable amounts should be remeasured at each balance sheet date. Such an asset or liability should be remeasured and reported at the amount of the scheduled future payments discounted at the rate of interest inherent in the initially recognised carrying amount of the asset or liability, except as provided otherwise by paragraphs 72 and 73.

64.   Financial assets and financial liabilities are considered to be investing or financing in nature when they are intended to be held for the long term or when their nature is such that they are held for continuing use in the business and will be held until maturity, which may be a relatively short period. An investing asset may be readily realisable through sale or other form of transfer but is not intended to be realised currently. Similarly, an enterprise usually assumes financial liabilities categorised as financing primarily as capital to support ongoing business activities. A financing liability may be readily capable of settlement before maturity but is not intended for settlement currently. Even an item with a relatively short life, such as

a trade account receivable or payable due for payment within one year, is considered to be investing or financing in nature if it is not intended to be transferred prior to realisation or settlement on maturity.

65. When determining whether it intends to hold a financial asset or financial liability for the long term, an enterprise's management exercises judgment in light of the particular circumstances. In the case of fixed term financial assets such as bonds and mortgage loans, for example, factors to be considered include an intention to hold the instrument to maturity and the ability to do so. An enterprise's intention to hold a financial asset primarily to yield a return over time in the form of a stream of interest, dividends or similar periodic cash flows or through appreciation in value over time usually indicates an intention to hold for the long term.

66. Transactions in derivative financial instruments do not normally qualify for classification as investing or financing activities. It is characteristic of derivative instruments that their primary purpose is to transfer risk and they are usually used for hedging or operating purposes.

67. The extent of activity within a portfolio intended to be held for the long term, rather than the purpose of the portfolio itself, is significant in determining whether individual financial instruments in the portfolio are investing items. For example, when active management of the portfolio results in frequent replacement of individual instruments held, perhaps with a view to enhancing the overall yield or quality of the portfolio, the individual instruments are not classified as investing. The classification of an individual financial asset reflects management's intentions with respect to that particular asset rather than the overall intentions with respect to the portfolio of which the item is a part. Experience over time will either confirm management's intention to hold certain financial instruments for the long term and their classification as investing items, or indicate a need to reconsider the accounting classification of such items.

68. Paragraphs 62 and 63 require measurement of financial assets resulting from investing activities at their historical cost and financial liabilities resulting from financing activities at their historical proceeds (subject to adjustments required by paragraphs 72 and 73), unless they are to be settled through fixed or determinable future payments. The amount of a determinable payment is established by reference to a source other than the financial instrument and may involve a calculation. For example, financial instruments are often settled in cash but the amount may be determined by reference to the fair value of another financial asset or the result of a calculation that takes into account a price index. In some circumstances, payment may be made by delivery of a non-cash financial asset that has a determinable value. When the amount of a scheduled payment is determinable rather than fixed, it is estimated at each reporting date based on current information.

69.   A financial asset acquired or a financial liability assumed that has a fixed or determinable maturity amount and periodic payments of interest or principal may be initially recognised at an amount that differs from its maturity amount (i.e., at a discount or premium). For example, in the case of a compound financial instrument such as a bond convertible into common shares, the issuer normally reports an initial discount on the liability component after assigning a portion of the cash proceeds to the equity component. To amortise an initial discount or premium, a financial asset or financial liability is remeasured periodically at the amount of scheduled future payments discounted at the rate of interest inherent in the carrying amount at which the asset or liability was initially recognised. The use of a present value method to amortise discounts and premiums is consistent with a cost based approach to measurement because the discount rate inherent in the transaction on initial recognition of the asset is a historical discount rate rather than a market rate at the reporting date.

70.   Historical cost in respect of a financial asset and historical proceeds in respect of a financial liability take into account any transaction costs, such as brokerage commissions or debt issue costs, incurred on initial acquisition or assumption of the asset or liability. Such costs affect the determination of premium or discount on initial recognition and are, therefore, amortised over the period to maturity of the financial asset or financial liability in accordance with paragraph 63.

71.   In the case of a commodity-linked instrument such as a bond repayable in either cash or a specified quantity of a commodity, paragraphs 62 and 63 apply only to the financial asset of the holder and the financial liability of the issuer. The option to convert the cash amount of the bond on maturity into the commodity is a non-financial asset and liability. However, in the case of an option to convert an entitlement to receive a fixed cash amount of principal or interest on a bond into an entitlement to receive a cash amount determinable by reference to a commodity price and a fixed quantity of the commodity, the option does qualify as a financial asset of the holder and financial liability of the issuer.

Decline in the fair value of a financial asset below its carrying amount

72.   When the fair value of a financial asset resulting from investing activities has declined below its carrying amount, the carrying amount should be reviewed. In the absence of persuasive evidence that the carrying amount of the asset will be recoverable in the foreseeable future, the carrying amount should be reduced to the estimated recoverable amount. The amount of the reduction should be charged to income in the period in which it is recognised.

73.   When the carrying amount of a financial asset has been written down to estimated recoverable amount at a previous balance sheet date, the estimated

recoverable amount may subsequently have increased. **If there is persuasive evidence that the increase will persist for the foreseeable future, the write-down should be reversed to the extent of the increase in estimated recoverable amount. The amount of the reversal should be credited to income in the period in which it is recognised.**

74. When a financial asset is classified as an investing asset, that classification results from a decision by management that it intends to hold the asset for the long term or until maturity. In the event the fair value of such an investing asset declines below its carrying amount, the asset is written down to management's best estimate of the amount that will be recovered in the foreseeable future ("estimated recoverable amount") unless management's examination of the circumstances giving rise to the decline provides persuasive evidence that those circumstances are likely to change within a clearly foreseeable period of time, with the result that the value will recover. The amount of any write-down is recognised as a loss and the estimated recoverable amount becomes the new carrying amount of the asset.

75. A reduction in fair value that persists for the long term usually results from pervasive changes in economic and other factors that are fundamental to the value of a financial asset. While such changes are not necessarily permanent, their effect is recognised unless there is persuasive evidence that the decline in fair value will reverse in the foreseeable future. In reaching a conclusion as to whether a write-down is required, management takes into account not only available evidence as to the likelihood of recovery, but also the enterprise's intent and ability to hold the asset for the period within which circumstances are expected to change.

76. The existence of active markets for many financial assets results in the ready availability of reliable market prices to provide a basis for determining whether the fair value of an investing asset has declined below its carrying amount. The lack of a readily available and reliable market price may make it more difficult to establish that the fair value of a financial asset has declined below its carrying amount, but it is still necessary to review the carrying amount of the asset in relation to its fair value. Fair value can be estimated by accepted valuation techniques such as those noted in paragraph 24.

77. A decline in the fair value of a financial asset below its carrying amount results from a change in circumstances that affects one or more of the financial risks associated with that asset. In the case of debt instruments, the primary risks are credit and interest rate risk. In the case of equity instruments, the primary risk is market risk. In the case of a debt or equity instrument for which the price is established in a currency other than the reporting currency of the enterprise, currency risk is also a factor. Management's assessment of the nature of the change in the financial risks that have caused an instrument to decline in value affect the decision as to whether a write-down is required.

78.   In the case of a loan or a debt security that has declined in value below its carrying amount, management examines the underlying causes of the decline to determine whether they relate to an increase in the prevailing level of interest rates for instruments with a similar term and a similar credit risk or whether they relate to a decline in the credit status of the borrower. If a contributory factor to the decline in value is a deterioration in the credit status of the borrower, giving rise to an increased probability of default, a write-down is usually required. On the other hand, if there is persuasive evidence that the decline in value relates solely to an increase in the general level of interest rates and the enterprise has the intent and ability to hold the asset to maturity, a write-down may not be required.

79.   A decline in the fair value of an investment in an equity instrument of another enterprise results from exposure to market price risk and is generally affected by factors more complex than those affecting the value of debt securities. It is, therefore, often more difficult to determine the underlying causes of a decline in the fair value of an equity instrument and to establish persuasive evidence that there will be a change in circumstances leading to a recovery in value in the foreseeable future. In the absence of such evidence, a write-down to estimated recoverable amount is taken immediately.

80.   When the fair value of an equity investment has declined below its carrying amount but a write-down has not been recognised because management has adduced persuasive evidence that the carrying amount will be recoverable in the foreseeable future, management monitors the situation at subsequent reporting dates to confirm that the recovery in value has occurred or that the evidence remains persuasive. Examples of circumstances that call into question the persuasiveness of any evidence that a recovery in value can be expected and therefore confirm the need for a write-down to be recognised include:

(a)   the market value of the asset remaining below its carrying amount for a period of three years;

(b)   suspension of trading in the asset;

(c)   severe losses by the investee in the current year or current and prior years;

(d)   continued losses by the investee for a period of three years;

(e)   liquidity or going concern problems of the investee; or

(f)   appraisal of the fair value of the asset at less than its carrying amount.

In the event the amount of the initial decline in fair value below carrying amount has not reversed within three years and the circumstances giving rise to the decline persist, any evidence that there will be a recovery in value is presumed to be no longer persuasive.

81.   A write-down of an investing financial asset to reflect a reduction in value is not the same as a mark-to-market adjustment of an asset carried at fair value. Depending on the circumstances, current market value, the present value of expected future cash flows or a value determined by another accepted valuation technique may be used to estimate the recoverable amount. The estimated recoverable amount may be either more or less than market value at the time of the write-down. When management of an enterprise reasonably foresees recovery of an amount having a present value greater than market value, the carrying amount of a financial asset is written down to the present value of the recoverable amount rather than to market value. On the other hand, existing conditions may lead management to expect future declines in market value of the asset before it can be disposed of, resulting in a write-down below market value.

82.   In the case of a restructured loan receivable, for example, the amount of any write-down is determined by comparing the carrying amount of the loan before the restructuring with the present value of the expected future cash flows after the restructuring, either from selling the loan or continuing to hold it, depending on management's intentions. The present value of the loan is determined using an appropriate current interest rate (i.e., the market rate applicable to a new loan having substantially the same amount, terms and credit risk).

83.   An enterprise assesses its financial assets individually, rather than on a portfolio basis, when determining whether a reduction in their carrying amount is required. A decline in the estimated recoverable amount of one asset below its carrying amount is not offset against an unrecognised increase in the value of another asset in determining the amount of any necessary write-down.

84.   Subsequent to a write-down in the carrying amount of a financial asset, the write-down is reversed to the extent that the estimated recoverable amount has increased to an amount greater than the written down carrying amount and there is persuasive evidence that the increase will persist for the foreseeable future. For example, an equity investment in a petrochemical company might have been written down to reflect a decline in fair value arising from persistent losses caused by the lack of a stable source of supply of raw materials for the plant and low product prices. In the event there is a recovery in the fair value of the investment, reflecting a return to profitable operation resulting from the acquisition of a stable source of supply of raw materials and an increase in product prices that is expected to persist for several years, the original write-down would be reversed to the extent of the recovery in fair value. Reversal of a write-down does not result in increasing the carrying amount of a financial asset above its historical cost. When an asset was carried at amortised cost prior to having been written down, reversal of the write-down results in a carrying amount immediately after the reversal that is no greater than the amortised cost would have been if there had been no write-down.

85.   The carrying amount of a financial liability classified as financing is not adjusted to reflect a change in its fair value, whether due to a deterioration in the financial condition of the debtor or to changes in the financial markets. In the event of a debt restructuring, the enterprise removes the old financial liability from its balance sheet and recognises the new liability, based on currently prevailing market interest rates and the rescheduled future cash flows. A restructuring results in a gain or loss equal to the difference between the carrying amounts of the old and new liabilities. In practice, a debt restructuring often involves a reduction in the liabilities of a financially troubled enterprise, giving rise to a gain. The gain or loss is separately classified in the income statement and the nature of the restructuring is disclosed when the amount of gain or loss is material.

Gain and loss recognition

86.   **Except as otherwise provided by paragraphs 72 and 73, a gain or loss on a financial asset or financial liability resulting from investing or financing activities should be recognised in income only upon realisation when the asset or liability is removed from the balance sheet.**

87.   Recognition of gains and losses in income only when realised is consistent with the measurement of transactions undertaken for investing or financing purposes at historical cost. Realisation of a gain or loss coincides with the removal of an asset or liability from the balance sheet as a result of a transaction or event that transfers cash or other consideration and settles the rights and obligations associated with the asset or liability.

88.   In cases of partial disposition or settlement, it is appropriate to remove a portion of a financial asset or financial liability from the balance sheet as described in paragraph 34. The carrying amount of the asset or liability is allocated between the portion disposed of or settled and the remaining portion on the basis of relative fair values at the date of the partial disposition or settlement.

Operating

89.   **Subsequent to initial recognition and measurement, a financial asset or financial liability resulting from operating activities should be remeasured at each balance sheet date and reported at its fair value.**

90.   **A gain or loss from a change in the fair value of a financial asset or financial liability resulting from operating activities should be recognised in income as it arises.**

91.   Transactions that do not qualify as investing or financing activities are, in the absence of designation as a hedge, considered to be operating activities. Operating

activities include transactions undertaken as part of an active programme of buying and selling financial instruments with a view to short term gain. Traders seek to profit from short term movements in the financial markets by buying and selling both primary and derivative instruments, creating positions that are, by their nature, readily realisable and normally intended to be held for less than one year. Operating transactions in financial instruments may be ancillary to other business activities or they may constitute a significant, separate business on which an assessment of an enterprise's performance is largely dependent.

Hedging

Identification of a hedge

92. **A financial instrument should be accounted for as a hedge when:**

(a) **the position to be hedged is specifically identified and exposes the enterprise to risk of loss from price changes; and**

(b) **it is highly probable that changes in the fair value of the instrument and opposite changes in the fair value of the position being hedged will have a high degree of correlation so that the hedging instrument will be effective as a hedge, i.e., it eliminates or reduces substantially the risk of loss from the position being hedged.**

When a financial instrument is accounted for as a hedge, it should be designated as such.

93. Hedging in an economic sense concerns the reduction or elimination of the effects of market risk, interest rate risk or currency risk, each of which may be present to some extent in a financial instrument. It involves entering into a transaction in the expectation that it will reduce an enterprise's exposure to loss from price risk, normally with the additional consequence of reducing the potential for profit. Paragraph 92 sets out the conditions under which a financial instrument is considered a hedge for accounting measurement purposes.

94. A financial instrument is generally viewed as a hedge when an enterprise has a specifically identified position that is exposed to the risk of loss as a result of adverse price changes in financial markets and the effect of holding the instrument is to offset that risk of loss. A hedge is achieved by taking a position exposed to effects of price changes that are equal and opposite to the effects of price changes on an existing or expected position. In practice, hedges are seldom perfect because the relationship between the value of the position being hedged and the value of the hedging instrument is seldom constant. Identified positions that may be exposed to a risk of loss are not confined to financial assets; they may also pertain to specific

financial liabilities, both recognised and unrecognised and to assets and liabilities expected to arise from future transactions as a result of current commitments. In the latter case, the objective is to enter into a transaction currently that will offset changes in the economic value of a position that will not be recognised until the future.

95.   Many different financial instruments can be used for hedging purposes. The more commonly used, however, are derivative instruments, such as interest rate and currency swaps, that are designed to transfer one element of the risks inherent in a particular primary instrument. Some instruments, such as forward rate agreements, caps, collars and floors, are designed specifically for use by enterprises that wish to reduce their exposure to interest rate movements that may affect their borrowing costs. As is the case with most instruments, however, they may also be used for other purposes. Financial instruments that are accounted for as hedges are not distinguishable on their face from similar or identical instruments that are not hedges.

96.   The substance of a hedging instrument is not evident from or determined by its form, but is based partly on management's intent. For that reason, one of the requirements of paragraph 92 is that management designate a hedge as such, identifying the specific exposed position intended to be hedged and the period over which the hedge is intended to be effective. Designation of an asset or liability as a hedge subsequent to its initial recognition by an enterprise is possible, but does not result in any retroactive recognition of the hedge relationship such as an adjustment to defer any previously recognised income or expense associated with the hedging instrument.

97.   A financial instrument is not properly designated as a hedge unless the enterprise is subject to a risk of loss from an existing or expected price exposure. To determine whether the enterprise has a price exposure that can be hedged effectively, management must consider whether the specific exposed position is already offset, in whole or in part, by other financial assets, financial liabilities or commitments, even though they are not accounted for as hedges. If a position exposed to price risk is already matched by an equal and opposite position elsewhere in the enterprise, entering into a transaction that might appear to result in a hedge when viewed on a transaction by transaction basis actually increases the price exposure of the enterprise. That transaction does not, therefore, qualify as a hedging transaction.

98.   A position to be hedged is defined broadly. A financial instrument may be accounted for as a hedge when it has an exposure to price risk that is equal but opposite to that of a group of financial instruments or a portion of one instrument. There is no requirement for a specific one-to-one identification of hedges and individual financial instruments to be hedged. However, because different assets and liabilities have substantially different exposures to potential gain or loss, a position may not be construed so broadly as to allow an enterprise to consider that all of its assets and liabilities collectively hedge each other. The items constituting the

position must be homogeneous at least to the extent of the common price risk being hedged.

99. A financial instrument may be accounted for as a hedge if it offsets a specific risk for part of a position or a part of the life of a position. For example, as long as both of the criteria in paragraph 92 are satisfied, it is appropriate to account for a currency swap as a hedge even though it is equal to 50% of the total amount of an associated foreign currency liability and the swap will last for half of the life of the liability. In that case, 50% of the currency risk of the liability is considered fully hedged for the life of the hedging instrument. In the absence of any other hedge, 50% of the liability is considered fully exposed to currency risk during the life of the hedging instrument and the entire liability is fully exposed after the swap arrangement has matured.

100. An exposed position to be hedged may result from an unrecognised or expected financial asset or financial liability. Such a hedge requires that the position hedged be clearly identifiable and likely to materialise, so that there is a true price risk exposure. These conditions are satisfied only when an enterprise has contractual commitments for future transactions. For example, an enterprise may hedge a fixed rate loan commitment that exposes it to risk of loss from future interest rate fluctuations, or a right to receive a stream of foreign currency lease payments that exposes it to risk of loss from future fluctuations in exchange rates. On the other hand, economic hedging of possible future purchases of financial instruments or of budgeted future foreign currency net income do not create situations in which it is appropriate to account for a financial instrument as a hedge because the possible future exposure does not relate to specific firm commitments.

101. For a financial instrument to qualify as a hedge, paragraph 92 requires a high degree of probability that the hedge will be effective. Effectiveness means that, throughout the hedge period, there will be a high degree of correlation between changes in the fair value of the hedging instrument and opposite changes in the fair value of the position being hedged. Thus, the effects of price changes in the hedging instrument will fully offset, but not more than offset, the effects of price changes in the exposed position. A high degree of correlation exists when the economic relationship between the prices of the two items is clear and a high correlation in the price movements throughout the hedge period is highly probable, even though the hedge instrument is not identical to the position at risk. An assessment of the likelihood of this price correlation is necessary at the time management designates a financial instrument as a hedge, requiring the exercise of judgment.

102. In assessing the degree of correlation between changes in the fair values of a hedged position and a hedging instrument, an enterprise normally takes into consideration only intrinsic values of derivative financial instruments. The intrinsic

value of a derivative financial instrument is the excess, if any, of the fair value of the underlying financial instrument over the contractual exercise price at which the underlying instrument is to be exchanged. Time value[5] is total fair value less intrinsic value, and reflects the value associated with the remaining term to maturity of the derivative instrument and volatility of the fair value of the underlying instrument (i.e., the value placed on the possibility that intrinsic value will increase in future prior to maturity of the derivative instrument) and also the interest cost or benefit of holding the underlying instrument.

103.   If an enterprise cannot determine periodic changes in fair value of a position to be hedged or a financial instrument intended as a hedge, the high degree of correlation required for designation of a hedging instrument cannot be demonstrated. An enterprise may be unable to establish fair values reliably from time to time without quoted market values or a dependable surrogate.

Income recognition of gain or loss on a hedging instrument

104.   A gain or loss from a change in the fair value of a financial asset or a financial liability accounted for as a hedge should be recognised when the corresponding loss or gain from a change in the fair value of the hedged position is recognised. In the case of a hedge of an unrecognised contractual commitment, however, a gain or loss from a change in the fair value of the hedging instrument should be recognised in income as it arises to the extent it is not offset by a change in the fair value of the financial instrument position expected to result from the identified future position being hedged.

105.   An enterprise's primary purpose in accounting for a financial instrument as a hedge is to match the timing of income statement recognition of changes in the value of that instrument with recognition of equal but opposite changes in the value of a particular exposed position. This process of matching is referred to as "hedge accounting". Some exposed positions comprise financial instruments classified as operating and are carried at fair value, with the result that value changes are reflected in income in the period in which they occur. Other positions comprise financial instruments classified as investing or financing and are reported on the cost basis, with the result that value changes are reflected in income only when the exposed position is settled, except for changes in carrying amount from application of paragraphs 63, 72 and 73. The measurement basis used for a hedging instrument is

---

[5]   International Accounting Standard 21, Accounting for the Effects of Changes in Foreign Exchange Rates, requires separate accounting for the time value of a forward exchange contract that hedges an anticipated future transaction.

the same as that used for the related hedged position, regardless of how that instrument would be measured if it were not designated as a hedge.

106.   The consequences of entering into a hedge are reflected in the timing of income statement recognition of changes in the fair value of a hedging instrument. If the hedge has been perfect, the gain (loss) on the hedging instrument exactly offsets the loss (gain) on the exposed position. If the hedge has been imperfect, the extent of the imperfection is recognised in income in the period in which the gain or loss on the exposed position is recognised, other than in the case of a hedge of a contractual commitment for which imperfections are recognised in income as they arise.

107.   Changes in the fair value of the hedging instrument subsequent to inception of the hedge are matched against changes in the carrying amount of the exposed position. In the case of a hedge of a recognised operating asset or liability, changes in the fair value of both the hedged position and the hedging instrument are recognised in income as they occur. In the case of a hedge of an investing asset or a financing liability, changes in the fair value of the hedging instrument are recognised in income prior to disposal or settlement of the hedged position only to the extent of any changes in the carrying amount of the hedged position recognised in accordance with paragraphs 63, 72 and 73. Income recognition of a gain (loss) on a hedging instrument is deferred until the matching loss (gain) on the hedged position is recognised in income which, in some circumstances, may mean deferring recognition of a gain (loss) on a hedging instrument beyond its maturity.

108.   In the case of a hedge of a contractual commitment, an enterprise has not yet recognised in its financial statements the expected future position being hedged and, consequently, has not yet recognised the effect of changes in the fair value of financial instruments constituting that position. Changes in the fair value of that position during a period are normally recognised by the enterprise in financial statements of a later period. The enterprise measures and reports the hedging instrument on the basis that will be applied to the hedged position when it is subsequently recognised. When the hedging instrument is measured at fair value, to the extent changes in its fair value correlate with opposite changes in the fair value of the unrecognised hedged position, those changes in value of the hedging instrument are not included in income for the period but are carried forward to be matched against the changes in value of the hedged future position. To the extent changes in the value of a hedging instrument do not correlate with unrecognised changes in value of the future position, the hedging relationship is imperfect. Gains and losses from changes in value of the hedging instrument that do not correlate with changes in value of the future position being hedged are included in income of the enterprise as they arise.

109.   In the case of a hedge of a contractual commitment in which the hedging instrument is accounted for on the cost basis because the hedged future position will

be accounted for on the cost basis, changes in fair value of the hedging instrument that are correlated with unrecognised changes in the fair value of the hedged position are not recognised prior to initial recognition of the hedged position. The effects of imperfections in the hedge are recognised in income as they arise, however.

Discontinuance of hedge accounting

110.   If the expected high degree of correlation between changes in the fair value of a financial asset or a financial liability accounted for as a hedge and opposite changes in the fair value of the hedged position is not achieved, hedge accounting should be discontinued.   At the date of discontinuance of hedge accounting, the hedging instrument should be reclassified as an operating, investing or financing instrument.   To the extent that changes in the fair value of the hedging instrument have been correlated with opposite changes in the fair value of the hedged position prior to discontinuance of hedge accounting but have not been recognised in income, such changes in the value of the hedging instrument should be recognised in income when the corresponding changes in the value of the hedged position are recognised.

111.   Continued application of hedge accounting is based on actual correlation of changes in the fair value of the hedged position and the hedging instrument, rather than on the basis of expectations formed at inception of the hedge as to the probability of a high degree of correlation.   If the actual changes in the value of a hedging instrument do not indicate a high degree of correlation with those of the hedged position, the hedging instrument is reclassified as either operating or, in uncommon circumstances, investing or financing and accounted for accordingly.   Similarly, a financial instrument previously designated as a hedge may cease to qualify as a hedge because the original exposure to price risk no longer exists or, in the case of a hedge of a contractual commitment, the expected future exposure is no longer likely to materialise.   In these circumstances also, hedge accounting is discontinued.

112.   Upon discontinuance of hedge accounting, an enterprise ceases to match recognition in income of gains and losses on the hedging instrument and the hedged position, and determines the appropriate treatment of any previously deferred gains and losses.   Previously reported income is not restated to reflect the discontinuance of hedge accounting.

113.   When a hedged position comprises financial instruments classified as operating, except in the case of a hedge of a contractual commitment, all gains and losses from changes in fair value of the hedged position and the hedging instrument prior to discontinuance of hedge accounting have been recognised in income as they occurred, regardless of the extent to which the hedge was effective.   At the date of discontinuance of a hedge of a contractual commitment, an enterprise may continue to expect the future position to materialise and changes in its fair value to result in

a gain or loss to be recognised in the future, in which case a previously recognised but deferred loss or gain on the instrument hedging that position continues to be carried forward. If the future position has failed to materialise or the original exposure to price risk no longer exists, however, there is no basis for continuing to carry forward the previously recognised loss or gain on the hedging instrument. Accordingly, this loss or gain is recognised in income.

114. When a hedged position comprises financial instruments classified as investing or financing, in some circumstances an unrecognised gain or loss on the hedged position equals or exceeds the unrecognised loss or gain on the hedging instrument. In this case, the unrecognised loss or gain on the hedging instrument is carried forward and recognised in income when the hedged position is disposed of or settled or, in the case of a hedged position that is remeasured in accordance with paragraphs 63, 72 or 73, when such remeasurements occur. In other circumstances, the previously unrecognised loss or gain on the hedging instrument exceeds the unrecognised gain or loss on the hedged position because of an imperfect correlation of values or, in the case of some hedges of contractual commitments, failure of the hedged position to materialise. When a hedging instrument is reclassified as investing or financing, the unrecognised loss or gain that will not be matched in income in future against a gain or loss on the hedged position is recognised in income on settlement, disposal or remeasurement of the instrument in accordance with paragraphs 63, 72 or 73. When the hedging instrument is reclassified as operating, the unrecognised loss or gain that will not be matched in income in future against a gain or loss on the hedged position is recognised in income immediately.

Reclassification

115. In unusual circumstances, when a substantive event occurs that causes management of an enterprise to change its intention with respect to a financial asset or financial liability after initial classification, the asset or liability should be reclassified and the measurement basis changed in accordance with management's revised intention. Except as provided otherwise by paragraph 110, any gain or loss resulting from a change in the measurement basis should be recognised in income in the period of the reclassification and disclosed separately.

116. When a substantive event occurs that changes management's intention with respect to a financial instrument, an enterprise is justified in changing the initial classification of the instrument as operating, investing and financing, or hedging. For example, management may change its business policies with respect to a portfolio of instruments from a relatively passive holding strategy to an active trading strategy or determine that it will retain an instrument previously held in a trading portfolio as a hedge of a financing instrument. In the first instance, the instruments are reclassified from investing to operating and in the second instance

from operating to hedging, reflecting management's revised intention in response to changed business conditions. Such reclassifications, which are relatively uncommon, are made only as a result of a substantive change in circumstances that is reflected in management's subsequent actions in dealing with the instrument.

117. A reclassification may involve a change in the basis of measurement of a financial asset or financial liability from measurement at fair value to measurement on the cost basis, or vice versa. When a financial asset or financial liability previously measured at fair value is reclassified so that it will be carried on the cost basis in the future, fair value at the date of reclassification becomes the cost amount. Changes in fair value prior to reclassification will have been included in income and are not restated. The carrying amount of a financial asset or financial liability previously measured on the cost basis but reclassified so that it will be carried at fair value in the future is adjusted to fair value upon reclassification. The gain or loss from the change in carrying amount is recognised in income except when the reclassification results from the discontinuance of hedge accounting. The treatment of gains and losses arising on discontinuance of hedge accounting is described in paragraphs 113 and 114. When reclassification does not result in a change in the basis of measurement of an asset or liability, it also does not result in recognition of any gain or loss.

Interest income and interest expense

118.   Interest income or interest expense arising from a financial asset or a financial liability should be recognised and measured on a basis that reflects the effective yield on the instrument.

119.   When fees charged or credited in connection with a financial instrument are in substance an integral part of the effective yield on the resulting financial asset or financial liability, the fees should be accounted for on a basis that reflects the effective yield in accordance with paragraph 118.

120.   With respect to interest income, International Accounting Standard 18, Revenue Recognition, provides guidance as to the general principles of recognition and illustrates their application.

121.   An enterprise may be required to capitalise borrowing costs in accordance with International Accounting Standard 23, Capitalisation of Borrowing Costs, in which case interest expense is first determined in accordance with paragraphs 118 and 119 and then reduced by the amount capitalised.

122.   Some financial instruments are issued initially or acquired at a discount or premium (for example, zero coupon bonds) or have fees associated with their issuance or acquisition. For a financial asset or financial liability classified as

investing or financing and accounted for on the cost basis, such fees and discount or premium are accounted for as yield adjustments on a basis that produces a level effective yield on the asset or liability over its life.

123. In the case of an interest-bearing financial instrument classified as investing or financing, the effective yield inherent in its value on initial recognition is the rate of interest that, when used to determine the present value of the stream of future cash receipts or payments from the date of recognition to the maturity date, results in the carrying amount (including any deferred fees) recognised initially. When the financial instrument provides for redemption prior to maturity, the effective yield calculation is based on the assumption that redemption occurs at the earliest contractually provided date rather than at the maturity date. For any financial reporting period, applying the effective yield to the carrying amount of a financial asset or financial liability determines the amount of interest income or interest expense. Interest includes amortisation of any initial premium to or discount from the maturity amount. For purposes of recognition and measurement, interest also includes dividends and similar distributions in respect of a financial instrument that, while taking the legal form of a share or other equity instrument, is classified as a financial liability.

124. Various types of fees may arise in connection with the origination, restructuring or settlement of a financial instrument. These fees have varying labels and are intended to recover costs incurred in implementing the transaction, to compensate for a particular collateral service provided, or to enhance the yield on the instrument. Fees are considered to be cost recoveries only when they clearly relate to incremental direct costs of the lender, including costs associated with evaluating the borrower's financial condition, evaluating and recording guarantees, collateral and other security arrangements, negotiating terms of the instrument, preparing and processing documents and closing the transaction.

125. The purpose for which a fee is assessed, rather than its descriptive label, and the accounting for the associated financial instrument determine the basis for the recognition of the fee in income. Some fees relate to a service provided over the life of the financial instrument or are directly related to the decision to invest in a financial asset or incur a financial liability. When the financial instrument results from investing or financing activities and the fee is part of an ongoing involvement with the instrument or relates to an activity that extends over the expected life of the instrument, the fee is properly deferred and amortised over the life of the instrument. The amortisation is an adjustment to the stated interest rate on the financial instrument in arriving at its effective yield.

126. In some circumstances, the activities giving rise to a fee do not relate solely to a financial instrument retained by the recipient of the fee. For example, activities performed by lead lenders in syndicating and arranging large loan packages may

result in retention of only part (or none) of the resulting financial instruments by the lead lenders. When no instruments are retained or when those retained bear the same yield for comparable risk as that applying to other holders of the instruments, any fee in excess of that accruing to other instrument holders relates to syndication services performed. Such fees are recognised in income in accordance with the provisions of International Accounting Standard 18, Revenue Recognition, relating to rendering of services.

127.   When a financial instrument accounted for after initial recognition on the cost basis is redeemed or refinanced prior to its expected maturity or termination date and the associated financial asset or financial liability is removed from the balance sheet, any unamortised discount, premium or fee is included in income or expense at that time.

128.   The focus of accounting for a financial asset or financial liability classified as operating is on reporting the effects of fair value changes in each period rather than reporting the yield over time until maturity. In any reporting period, the adjustments to carrying amount from marking a financial asset or financial liability to market and the accrued entitlement to receive, or obligation to make, periodic interest payments together reflect the effective yield at prevailing market interest rates. The periodic remeasurement of the asset or liability incorporates an implicit amortisation of the fair value of any discount or premium existing from time to time.

129.   Interest on a financial asset or financial liability classified as operating comprises the periodic cash payments that are recognised as the entitlement to receive them or the obligation to pay them accrues over time. Changes in the carrying amount of a financial asset or financial liability resulting from changes in its fair value, whether due to changes in the general level of interest rates or other economic factors, are not included in interest for purposes of disclosing interest income or interest expense in accordance with International Accounting Standard 5, Information to be Disclosed in Financial Statements.

130.   In the case of a financial instrument that includes an obligation of the issuer to pay on inception fees representing yield adjustments, the stated interest rate on the face amount of the instrument is below its market rate of interest. On initial recognition and immediately after payment of the fees, the fair value of the financial asset or financial liability is, therefore, less than the face value of the instrument. If the instrument results from operating activities, the fees are included in income or expense in the period of initial recognition and offset the effect of reducing the carrying amount of the financial asset or financial liability to fair value from the issue price (including fees) initially recorded in accordance with paragraph 57.

ALLOWED ALTERNATIVE MEASUREMENT STANDARDS

131. Two different bases exist by which financial assets and financial liabilities may be measured subsequent to initial recognition - "cost" and "fair value". Each basis has a number of variations and some accounting methods (such as "lower of cost and market") combine elements of the two bases. The basis adopted for measuring assets and liabilities also has implications for income recognition, particularly with respect to the timing of recognition of gains and losses from changes in fair value. In addition to the benchmark measurement standards, which encompass both bases of measurement, this Statement includes an allowed alternative requiring application of the fair value basis of measurement to all financial assets and financial liabilities. The allowed alternative standards for measurement of financial assets and financial liabilities subsequent to their initial recognition, together with related guidance on applying the standards in the recognition of interest income and interest expense, are set out in paragraphs 137 to 144.

132. The existence of an alternative set of measurement standards makes it particularly important for enterprises to disclose their accounting policies for measurement of financial instruments in sufficient detail to provide financial statement users with adequate information about the measurement standards adopted and the manner in which they are applied. An enterprise applies the selected set of measurement standards consistently from period to period unless a change in accounting policies is made in accordance with International Accounting Standard 8, Unusual and Prior Period Items and Changes in Accounting Policies.

133. A choice of measurement standards is not available for all financial instruments in all circumstances. International Accounting Standard 26, Accounting and Reporting by Retirement Benefit Plans, requires that retirement benefit plans follow the allowed alternative standards in measuring their investments in financial instruments.

134. To assist enterprises in choosing between the benchmark measurement standards and the allowed alternative, the features and advantages of each are summarised below.

135. The principal features of the benchmark measurement standards and the reasons commonly put forward for adopting them are:

(a) They permit the enterprise's purpose in acquiring an asset or assuming a liability and continuing to hold or maintain it to be reflected in the measurement basis.

(b) By not recognising changes in the fair value of assets and liabilities that are considered unlikely to be realised, the benchmark standards avoid volatility

507

in reported earnings that may be misunderstood and an undue emphasis on short-term fluctuations in value that may tend to reverse over time.

(c)   They use carrying amounts that are reliable and avoid the need to make estimates of fair values in circumstances in which such values may not be determinable on a sufficiently precise and accurate basis.

(d)   They incorporate a reasonable degree of prudence in requiring recognition of certain unrealised declines in fair values of assets but not permitting recognition of unrealised increases in fair values unless it is probable they will be realised.

(e)   They approximate practices found in many countries. These practices, which have evolved over time based on experience, are well known, supported by various types of financial statement users and, in some cases, are embedded in existing national standards or legal requirements. The benchmark standards are therefore relatively easy for enterprises to adopt and apply and for financial statement users to understand.

136.   The principal features of the allowed alternative measurement standards and the reasons commonly put forward for adopting them are:

(a)   They result in presentation of an enterprise's financial position using valuation approaches in routine use in financial markets for pricing many types of financial instruments, and more closely reflect the present value of the enterprise's expected future net cash flows on a basis that is comparable between enterprises, regardless of the length of time for which assets and liabilities have been held.

(b)   They minimise the application of judgment by management in determining financial statement amounts, and result in reported financial position and performance that reflect the marketplace rather than the intent of management.

(c)   They require that assets and liabilities having the same economic characteristics (for example, financial risks and rewards) be accounted for in the same fashion, regardless of management's intentions.

(d)   They better reflect the effects of management stewardship by including in net income of each period the effects of decisions made in the period to buy, sell or hold assets and to incur, maintain or discharge liabilities.

(e)   They apply a measurement basis (fair value) that has attracted considerable support, is viewed by some as a long-term goal for improved financial reporting, has been applied in practice to certain classes of financial assets and financial liabilities, and is being considered in some countries for wider application.

Measurement of a financial asset or financial liability

137.   Subsequent to initial recognition, a financial asset or financial liability should be remeasured at each balance sheet date and reported at its fair value.

138.   When adopting the allowed alternative measurement standards, an enterprise applies the fair value measurement basis to all financial assets and financial liabilities, regardless of their characteristics or classification for accounting purposes. This results in measurement of all financial assets and financial liabilities on a consistent and comparable basis.

139.   In some cases, it may be particularly difficult to determine the fair value of a financial asset or a financial liability with an acceptable level of reliability within practical constraints of timeliness or cost. For example, in the case of a shareholding in a private, development-stage enterprise, there is no established market for the shares and the future of the enterprise may be subject to significant uncertainty. In such circumstances, management makes its best estimate of fair value, taking into account all available information and using a discount rate that is commensurate with the risk attached to the estimated future cash flows. The nature of the uncertainties associated with the determination of the fair value and the assumptions made are disclosed.

Gain and loss recognition

140.   A gain or loss from a change in the fair value of a financial asset or financial liability should be recognised in income as it arises, except when the financial asset or financial liability is accounted for as a hedge of a contractual commitment.

141.   A change in the fair value of a financial asset or financial liability may result from a wide variety of different causes, including bad debts on trade accounts receivable, loan losses, fluctuations in prices of listed shares, foreign exchange rate changes and changes in prevailing market interest rates. In general, it is desirable for an enterprise to disclose separately its income and expenses by source or type, and it is common practice to do so. Certain such disclosures are required by International Accounting Standards. For example, International Accounting Standard 5, Information to be Disclosed in Financial Statements, requires separate disclosure in the income statement of income from investments, interest income, interest expense, unusual charges, unusual credits and certain other items. Also, International Accounting Standard 30, Disclosures in the Financial Statements of Banks and Similar Financial Institutions, requires separate disclosure of certain income and expense items arising from financial instruments. In some cases, however, the complex interrelationships of factors affecting fair value may make it difficult to segregate the different factors causing an overall change in the fair value of an asset or liability.

142.   It is desirable to disclose separately the amounts of realised and unrealised gains and losses. Such disclosure is common practice in some countries and may assist financial statement users in assessing the amount of cash flows generated and understanding the relative reliability of the components of net income.

143.   When an enterprise adopts the fair value balance sheet measurement and income recognition standards in paragraphs 137 and 140, changes in the fair value of recognised hedged positions and related hedging instruments are included in income as they arise, thus properly reflecting the substance of the hedging arrangement. In the case of a recognised instrument that hedges an unrecognised contractual commitment, however, immediate recognition in income of changes in fair value would not reflect the substance of the hedging relationship. In these circumstances, provided that the criteria for identification of a hedge described in paragraphs 92 to 103 are met, changes in the fair value of the hedging instrument are accounted for in accordance with the provisions of paragraphs 104 to 114 as they relate to hedges of contractual commitments.

Interest income and interest expense

144.   Those portions of the standards on interest income and interest expense and associated explanatory material in paragraphs 118 to 130 applicable to financial instruments classified as operating and carried at fair value under the benchmark measurement standards are equally applicable to instruments carried at fair value under the allowed alternative measurement standards.

Disclosure

General disclosure requirements

145.   **For each class of financial asset, financial liability and equity instrument, whether recognised or unrecognised, an enterprise should disclose information about factors that may affect the amount, timing and certainty of future cash flows, including the extent and nature of the instruments and their significant terms and conditions. Information should be presented in a manner that distinguishes between investing and financing items, hedging items and operating items.**

146.   Information in financial statements assists users in evaluating the ability of an enterprise to generate cash and the timing and certainty of its generation. To assess the overall ability of an enterprise to generate a net increase in cash, a user of financial statements requires information about transactions, events, resources and obligations that may give rise to significant future cash flows.

147.   The purpose of disclosure is to provide significant information, either through the balance sheet, income statement or other financial statement (such as a cash flow statement) or through notes and supplementary schedules, that:

(a)   describes both recognised and unrecognised financial instruments;

(b)   provides a useful measurement of unrecognised financial instruments and, in some cases, an additional measurement of recognised instruments; and

(c)   provides information to assist users in assessing the risks and rewards associated with both recognised and unrecognised financial instruments.

148.   Some financial assets and financial liabilities are not recognised in the balance sheet because they do not meet the recognition criteria at inception of the financial instrument. For example, the financial instrument that would be acquired on exercise of an option is not recognised because the risks and rewards associated with the instrument are not transferred until exercise of the option. The entitlement to the rewards and exposure to the risks of the instrument are contingent on exercise of the option. In some circumstances, disclosures in notes or supplementary schedules are necessary to inform financial statement users about the potentially significant effects of unrecognised financial instruments on the enterprise's future cash flows.

149.   Disclosure is not an alternative to or substitute for the proper application of standards for recognition, measurement and classification of financial assets, financial liabilities and equity instruments. Furthermore, proper application of these other standards does not obviate the need to apply the disclosure standards in this Statement. In particular, full disclosure is necessary in respect of financial assets and

financial liabilities that have been offset in accordance with paragraph 51, because they are recognised assets and liabilities of the enterprise and certain of their terms and conditions may have an effect on the future cash flows of the enterprise.

150. The extent of information disclosed varies according to the nature of an enterprise's activities and the relative importance and complexity of transactions involving financial instruments. When an enterprise is a party to many individual financial instruments or types of instruments, financial assets, financial liabilities and equity instruments are grouped for disclosure purposes into appropriately determined classes to avoid excessive detail in the financial statements. Classes represent groupings established in accordance with generally accepted practices that have evolved for presentation of information about financial statement items having similar characteristics. Certain groupings for disclosure purposes are required by other International Accounting Standards, particularly International Accounting Standard 5, Information to be Disclosed in Financial Statements. In the absence of standards requiring certain groupings, management of an enterprise applies its judgment to establish classes that most appropriately present financial information.

151. Although transactions in financial instruments have the potential to generate significant gains, some users of financial statements are more concerned about risk of loss resulting from each of the different types of financial risk described in paragraph 19. The nature and extent of some risks, particularly risks associated with recognised assets and liabilities, may be clearly evident from disclosures required by other International Accounting Standards. In the case of liquidity risk, for example, an enterprise's potential liquidity problem may be signalled by an imbalance between cash and liquid assets on one hand and current liabilities on the other hand, as presented on its balance sheet. In other cases, the nature and extent of a risk, such as credit risk, may not be fully evident to financial statement users without additional disclosures.

152. Financial instruments incorporate a number of terms and conditions, some of which affect the amount, timing and certainty of future cash receipts and payments by the parties to the instrument. The effects on cash flows may be direct, as in the case of the contractually determined cash repayment of a bond payable, or indirect, as in the case of an option to exchange one financial instrument for another. Terms and conditions of financial instruments that have a significant effect on the current financial position or may have a significant effect on future operating results of an enterprise are disclosed, regardless of whether financial assets or financial liabilities arising from the instruments are recognised in the financial statements.

153. The specific information to be disclosed in particular circumstances, including the extent to which it is appropriate to group information rather than present it on an instrument by instrument basis, is a matter requiring the exercise of judgment by management of an enterprise. Examples of terms and conditions of financial

instruments that are disclosed if they have a potentially significant effect on the future cash flows of the enterprise include:

(a)   the principal, stated, face or other similar amount;

(b)   the date of maturity, expiry or execution;

(c)   redemption options held by either party to the instrument, including the period in which, or date at which, the options may be exercised and the redemption price or range of prices;

(d)   options of either party to the instrument to convert the instrument into, or exchange it for, another financial instrument or some other asset or liability, including the period in which, or date at which, the options may be exercised and the conversion or exchange ratio(s);

(e)   scheduled future cash receipts or payments of the principal amount of the instrument, including instalment repayments and any sinking fund or similar requirements;

(f)   stated rate or amount of interest, dividend or other periodic return on principal;

(g)   collateral (either held, in the case of a financial asset, or pledged, in the case of a financial liability); and

(h)   in the case of an instrument that provides for an exchange, information described in items (a) to (g) for the instrument to be acquired in the exchange.

154.   When applicable, other significant matters not listed in paragraph 153 may also warrant disclosure. For example, when significant contractual amounts are denominated in a foreign currency, an enterprise discloses the foreign currency amounts. Also, in the case of financial instruments that require a future exchange, there may be more than one contractual amount to disclose in respect of item (a) in paragraph 153. For example, an interest rate swap may require disclosure of payment by one party of a stream of future interest payments that can be defined only by reference to a notional principal amount to which a particular interest rate index (LIBOR, for example) applies, as well as payment by the other party of fixed interest amounts.

155.   It is important for enterprises to present hedging instruments in their financial statements or notes in a fashion that highlights hedging relationships with other financial instruments, so that the extent of hedged risk exposures can be understood by financial statement users.

Disclosures concerning interest rate risk

156.   For each class of financial asset and financial liability, whether recognised or unrecognised, an enterprise should disclose information about its exposure to interest rate risk, including:

(a)   contractual repricing or maturity dates, whichever dates are earlier; and

(b)   effective interest rates.

157.   Information about repricing or maturity dates indicates the length of time for which interest rates are fixed and information about effective interest rates indicates the levels at which they are fixed. Disclosure of this information provides financial statement users with a basis for evaluating the interest rate risk to which an enterprise is exposed. While knowledge of the remaining term to maturity may assist in evaluating interest rate risk when an enterprise issues or holds fixed rate instruments, many instruments reprice to a market rate of interest before maturity. For such instruments, the period until the next repricing is of primary importance.

158.   The period of exposure to interest rate risk from an interest-bearing financial instrument is established primarily by the contractual maturity date of the instrument or the earlier date at which the interest rate is reset at a current market rate. Management of an enterprise may expect the interest rate on a financial instrument to remain fixed for a period shorter than the contractually set period, however, altering the enterprise's exposure to interest rate risk. A financial institution may find, for example, that a predictable portion of fixed rate mortgage loans is repaid by borrowers prior to maturity. To provide a more complete picture of the way in which interest rate risk is managed, an enterprise may elect to disclose additional information about expected repricing or maturity dates when they differ significantly from the contractual dates. The additional disclosure would make clear that the expected dates are based on management's estimates and explain how the estimate is determined and why it differs from the contractual dates.

159.   At any financial reporting date, the effective interest rate of an interest-bearing financial instrument is the rate that, when used in a present value calculation, results in the carrying amount of the instrument. The present value calculation applies the interest rate to the stream of future cash receipts or payments from the reporting date to the next repricing (maturity) date and to the expected carrying amount (principal amount) at that repricing (maturity) date. The rate is a historical rate when the instrument is carried at amortised cost and a current market rate when the instrument is carried at fair value. The effective interest rate to be disclosed is sometimes termed the level yield to maturity or repricing date, and is the internal rate of return of the instrument for that period.

160.   Depending upon the nature of its business and the extent of its activity in financial instruments, an enterprise may choose to disclose information about interest rate risk in narrative form, in tables or by using a combination of the two. At a minimum, however, the carrying amounts of financial instruments are usually grouped by those that are contracted to mature or reprice (i) within one year of the

balance sheet date, (ii) more than one year and less than five years from the balance sheet date, and (iii) five years or more from the balance sheet date. When the performance of an enterprise is significantly affected by the level of its exposure to interest rate risk or changes in that exposure, more detailed information is desirable, including separate groupings of the carrying amounts of financial instruments contracted to mature or reprice (i) within one month of the balance sheet date, (ii) more than one and less than three months from the balance sheet date, and (iii) more than three and less than twelve months from the balance sheet date. Interest rate information may be disclosed for individual financial instruments or weighted average rates may be presented for each class of financial instrument. Exposure to interest rate risk may be disclosed by way of a table showing the difference between interest-bearing financial assets and financial liabilities repricing within various future time periods.

Disclosures concerning credit risk

161. **For each class of financial asset, whether recognised or unrecognised, an enterprise should disclose information about its exposure to credit risk, including:**

(a) **the amount that best represents its maximum credit risk exposure, without taking account of the value of any collateral, in the event other parties fail to perform their obligations under financial instruments;**

(b) **the enterprise's policy with respect to obtaining collateral; and**

(c) **significant concentrations of credit risk.**

162. The purpose of disclosing the total amount exposed to credit risk (an enterprise's "maximum credit risk exposure") is:

(a) to ensure that the users of financial statements have a consistent measure of the amount exposed to that risk for all financial assets, whether the assets are recognised or not; and

(b) to take into account the possibility that the exposure to loss may differ from the carrying amount or the unrecognised contractual amount that is otherwise disclosed in the financial statements.

163. In the case of a recognised financial asset, the maximum credit risk exposure is the expense that would be recognised in the event of a default, determined without regard to the likelihood of default and without taking into account the value of any collateral held. Because this expense would equal the carrying amount of the asset in the balance sheet, net of any applicable provisions for loss, no disclosure beyond that provided by the balance sheet would usually be necessary. The carrying amount

of some recognised financial assets is smaller than the principal, stated, face or other similar contractual amount in the associated financial instrument. In the case of an interest rate swap, for example, the notional principal amount and the total amount of future periodic interest swap payments usually exceed the carrying amount of the contract and the maximum amount that could be lost through default by the other party. The maximum credit risk of an interest rate swap carried at fair value is measured by the cost, at current market rates, of replacing the swap in the event of default.

164.   When the maximum credit risk exposure associated with an unrecognised financial asset is equal to the principal, stated, face or other similar contractual amount of the instrument disclosed in accordance with paragraph 145, no additional disclosure is required. However, with some unrecognised financial assets, the maximum expense that would be recognised upon default by the other party to the underlying instrument may differ substantially from the amount disclosed in accordance with paragraph 145. In other circumstances, an enterprise may have a right of set-off of an unrecognised financial asset against an unrecognised financial liability that would mitigate the maximum possible loss. In such cases, paragraph 161 requires disclosure in addition to that provided in accordance with paragraph 145.

165.   In addition to its maximum credit risk exposure, an enterprise also discloses its policy with respect to obtaining collateral from counterparties as a means of mitigating losses from defaults. In some cases, it may also be desirable to disclose the nature and a brief description of collateral held and management's assessment of its adequacy in the event of default, including its fair value when reliably measurable.

166.   Concentrations of credit risk are disclosed separately when they are not inherent in the business of an enterprise, are not apparent from other disclosures concerning the nature and financial position of the business and may result in significant losses in the event of default by other parties.

167.   Disclosure of concentrations of credit risk includes a description of the shared characteristic that identifies each concentration and the amount of the maximum possible exposure to loss associated with all recognised and unrecognised financial assets sharing that characteristic. Disclosure may be made of concentrations of recognised and unrecognised assets either separately or in aggregate, whichever is considered most informative by management of an enterprise in the circumstances.

168.   Concentrations of credit risk may arise from exposures to a single debtor or to groups of debtors having a similar characteristic such that their ability to meet their obligations is expected to be affected similarly by changes in economic or other conditions. Characteristics that may give rise to a concentration of risk include the nature of the activities undertaken by debtors, such as the industry in which they

operate, and the geographic area in which activities are undertaken. For example, a manufacturer of equipment for the oil and gas industry will normally have trade accounts receivable from sale of its products for which the risk of non-payment is affected by economic changes in the oil and gas industry. A bank that normally lends on an international scale may have a significant amount of loans outstanding to less developed nations and the bank's ability to recover those loans may be adversely affected by local economic conditions. Identification of significant concentrations is a matter for the exercise of judgment by management taking into account the circumstances of the enterprise and its debtors.

169. International Accounting Standard 14, Reporting Financial Information by Segment, provides useful guidance in identifying the types of credit risk concentrations that may arise and determining the appropriate degree of disaggregation in general purpose financial statements.

Disclosures concerning fair value

170. For each class of financial asset and financial liability, whether recognised or unrecognised, an enterprise should disclose information about fair value, identifying separately investing and financing items, hedging items and operating items. When it is not practicable within constraints of timeliness or cost to determine the fair value of a financial asset or financial liability with sufficient reliability, that fact should be disclosed together with information about the principal characteristics of the underlying financial instrument that are pertinent to its fair value.

171. As discussed in paragraphs 23 and 24, the fair value of a financial asset or financial liability may be determined by one of several generally accepted methods. Disclosure of fair value information includes disclosure of the method adopted and any significant assumptions made in its application. Such disclosure is of particular importance in the case of an enterprise that has financial assets or financial liabilities carried in the balance sheet at fair value under either of the alternative measurement standards.

172. When determination of fair value is not practicable, disclosure of fair value information may be omitted provided that the reason for the omission is explained and the principal characteristics of the underlying financial instruments that are pertinent to their fair value are disclosed. Such characteristics include the principal terms and conditions of the instruments that are normally disclosed in accordance with paragraph 145, together with other information about the market for the instruments. This information assists users of the financial statements in making their own judgments concerning the extent of any possible difference between the carrying amount of financial assets and financial liabilities and their fair value.

Provided it has a reasonable basis for doing so, management may also indicate its opinion as to the relationship between fair value and the carrying value of financial assets and financial liabilities for which it is unable to determine fair value. In normal circumstances, receivables and payables subject to the usual trade credit terms would not be adjusted from their historical cost carrying amount since that amount would usually be considered to approximate fair value.

Additional disclosures

173.   Additional disclosures are encouraged when they are likely to enhance financial statement users' understanding of financial instruments. For example, it may be desirable to disclose the amount of the change in the fair value of financial assets and financial liabilities that has been recognised in income. Disclosures might also include an explanation of the nature and extent of an enterprise's use of financial instruments, the risks associated with them and the business purposes that they serve. A discussion of management's policies for controlling the risks associated with financial instruments provides a useful perspective that is independent of the specific instruments outstanding at a particular time.   Policies for controlling financial instrument risks may include such matters as management's requirements for collateral (or other security), hedging of certain risk exposures and avoidance of undue concentrations of certain types of risk.   Some enterprises provide these types of information in a commentary that accompanies their financial statements (sometimes referred to as "management's discussion and analysis of financial condition and operating results").

Effective Date

174.   This Statement becomes operative for financial statements covering periods beginning on or after _____ .

Appendix

This Appendix is illustrative only and does not form part of the accounting standards set forth in this Statement. The purpose of the Appendix is to illustrate the application of the definitions and the recognition and measurement standards to a number of common business situations.

A1.   This Appendix explains how the standards in this Statement can be applied to recognition and measurement of the financial assets and financial liabilities resulting from various common financial instruments. Because the benchmark measurement standards encompass measurement of financial assets and financial liabilities on both the cost basis and the fair value basis, the examples assume application of the benchmark standards. However, fair value measurement is applied to all financial assets and financial liabilities under the allowed alternative measurement standards in the same manner as it is applied to operating financial assets and financial liabilities under the benchmark standards.

Application of the definitions

A2.   Currency (cash) is a financial asset because it represents the medium of exchange and is therefore the basis on which all transactions are measured and reported in financial statements. Cash represents the issuing government's promise to pay, even though generally the only obligation placed on the issuing government is that it accept the currency as legal tender for payments due to it. Governments also require that others within their jurisdiction accept the currency in satisfaction of debts. A deposit of cash with a bank or similar financial institution[1] is a financial asset because it represents the contractual right of the depositor to obtain cash from the institution or to draw a cheque or similar instrument against the balance in favour of a creditor in payment of a financial liability.

A3.   Commonly encountered examples of financial assets representing a contractual right to receive cash in the future and corresponding financial liabilities representing a contractual obligation to deliver cash in the future are:

(a)   trade accounts receivable and payable;

(b)   notes receivable and payable;

(c)   loans receivable and payable; and

(d)   bonds receivable and payable.

---

[1]   A bank or similar financial institution is described in International Accounting Standard 30, Disclosures in the Financial Statements of Banks and Similar Financial Institutions, as an institution "...one of whose principal activities is to take deposits and borrow with the objective of lending and investing...within the scope of banking or similar legislation."

In each case, the examples of financial assets and liabilities are matched, illustrating that a contractual right to receive (obligation to pay) cash must always be matched by a corresponding obligation to pay (right to receive) cash on the part of another party.

A4.   Another type of financial instrument is one for which the future economic benefit (sacrifice) is the receipt (delivery) of a financial asset other than cash. For example, a note payable in government bonds gives the holder the contractual right to receive and the issuer the contractual obligation to deliver government bonds, not cash. The bonds are financial assets because they represent obligations of the issuing government to pay cash. The note is, therefore, a financial asset of the note holder and a financial liability of the note issuer.

A5.   Physical assets such as inventories or property, plant and equipment are not financial assets, as discussed in paragraph 10 of this Statement. A right of one party to a contract to receive a physical asset is also not a financial asset and, consequently, such a contract cannot be a financial instrument even when the other party has a right to receive cash for the physical asset. A financial instrument, in the form of an obligation to deliver and a right to receive cash, arises only when the physical asset that is the subject of the contract has been delivered, giving rise to a receivable for the seller and a payable for the purchaser.

A6.   Under International Accounting Standard 17, Accounting for Leases, a finance lease is accounted for as a sale with delayed payment terms because of the degree to which the risks and rewards associated with the leased asset have been transferred from lessor to lessee. The lease contract is considered to be primarily an entitlement of the lessor to receive, and an obligation of the lessee to pay, a stream of payments that are substantially the same as blended payments of principal and interest under a loan agreement. The lessor accounts for its investment in the amount receivable under the lease contract rather than the leased asset itself. An operating lease, on the other hand, is considered to be primarily an uncompleted contract committing the lessor to provide the use of an asset in future periods in exchange for consideration similar to a fee for a service. Substantially all of the risks and rewards associated with the leased asset have not been transferred and the lessor continues to account for the leased asset itself rather than any amount receivable in future under the contract. Accordingly, a finance lease is considered to be a financial instrument and an operating lease is considered not to be a financial instrument.

A7.   Income tax liabilities or assets, whether current or deferred, are not financial liabilities or financial assets. They result from statutory requirements imposed by governments rather than contracts (financial instruments) between enterprises. Tax accounting issues are dealt with in International Accounting Standard 12, Accounting for Taxes on Income.

A8.　Examples of equity instruments include common shares, certain types of preferred shares, and warrants or options to subscribe for or purchase common shares in the issuing enterprise. Since the only obligation undertaken by the issuer of such a warrant or option is to issue its own shares, exercise of the rights granted by the warrant or option does not result in an outflow from the enterprise of resources embodying economic benefits. Warrants and options of this type do not, therefore, meet the definition of a liability. They represent a right to obtain a residual interest in the enterprise and qualify as equity instruments.

A9.　Derivative financial instruments give an enterprise a contractual right to exchange financial assets with another enterprise under conditions that are potentially favourable, or a contractual obligation to exchange financial assets with another enterprise under conditions that are potentially unfavourable. Some instruments embody both a right and an obligation to make an exchange. Types of financial instruments that may embody such a right or obligation include put and call options, forward contracts, interest rate and currency swaps, interest rate caps, collars and floors, loan commitments, note issuance facilities and letters of credit.

Investments in common shares

A10.　A purchase of common shares results in recognition of a financial asset (the shares) and a financial liability (the payable to the seller) in the investor's financial statements as of the date that the risks and rewards associated with the shares are transferred to the investor. The date of transfer may be either the trade date or the settlement date, depending upon the terms of the transfer. The asset and the liability are measured at the amount of the consideration agreed to be exchanged between the two parties to the transaction. As of the transfer date, the rights and obligations under the contract of sale are usually firm, the risks and rewards associated with the shares that are the subject of the contract have been assumed by the investor and the cost of the shares can be measured reliably.

A11.　The basis of measurement used at subsequent reporting dates depends on management's intentions in purchasing the shares. If the purchase was made for investment purposes, the shares continue to be carried at cost unless a write-down becomes necessary to reflect a decline in fair value. Any gains or losses, other than those resulting from a write-down or reversal of a write-down, are recognised only when realised. If the purchase was made as part of operating activities, the carrying amount of the shares is adjusted at reporting dates subsequent to initial recognition to reflect current fair value. Any unrealised gain or loss is reported in income for the period.

Compound commodity-linked instruments

A12. A compound commodity-linked instrument gives rise to non-financial assets and liabilities as well as financial assets and liabilities, generally by giving the holder an option to exchange a financial asset for a non-financial asset. An oil-linked bond, for example, usually gives the holder the right to receive a fixed amount of cash on maturity or earlier redemption, with a stream of fixed periodic interest payments, and the option to exchange the principal amount for a fixed quantity of oil on maturity or redemption. Since oil is a commodity, its price is subject to fluctuation on commodity markets based on supply and demand factors specific to oil. The desirability of exchanging the principal amount of an oil-linked bond will vary from time to time based on the fair value of oil and the exchange ratio of cash to oil inherent in the bond.

A13. Normally, a commodity-linked instrument is issued at a price and exchange ratio such that the value of the option at inception is small. The option is "out of the money" and has no intrinsic value because the exercise or strike price for the option is above the prevailing market price for the commodity. The option consequently has a time value only. As long as the market price of the commodity remains below the strike price inherent in the instrument, the instrument will not be exchanged and the financial liability of the issuer to pay periodic interest and to repay the principal in cash on maturity or earlier redemption remains. Even if the commodity's market price increases and the option under the instrument is "in the money", the financial liability continues to exist as long as the option is not exercised by the holder of the instrument. Until the option is exercised, the issuer's obligation to repay in cash is not extinguished and the possibility exists of the commodity price dropping so that the option no longer remains "in the money".

Option contracts

A14. The financial instrument underlying an option contract may be any financial asset, including foreign currency, shares or interest-bearing money market instruments. An option to buy or sell an asset other than a financial asset (such as a commodity) does not give rise to a financial asset or financial liability because it does not fit the requirements of the definitions for the receipt or delivery of financial assets or exchange of financial instruments.

A15. In the case of either a put or call option, the holder's right to exchange financial assets under potentially favourable conditions and the writer's obligation to exchange financial assets under potentially unfavourable conditions are distinct from the underlying financial asset to be acquired or financial liability to be assumed upon exercise of the option. The risks and rewards pertaining to the underlying instrument remain with the holder of the instrument unless the option is exercised.

Recognition of the transfer of the underlying instrument coincides with, and is contingent on, transfer of the associated risks and rewards upon exercise of the option. Accordingly, there is no basis for the parties to an option to recognise a transfer of the instrument until the option is exercised.

A16.   For example, a call option to purchase $1,000,000 face value of government bonds in six months time for cash is a financial asset to its holder because the holder has the right to exchange cash for the underlying financial instrument (bonds) under conditions that are potentially favourable. If the market value of the bonds exceeds $1,000,000 in six months time, the conditions will be favourable to the holder and the option would normally be exercised. The writer of the call option has a financial liability because the writer has an obligation to exchange the bonds for cash under conditions that are potentially unfavourable. The writer is usually compensated by the holder for assuming that liability by way of a premium. A put option to sell government bonds has similar but opposite effects.

A17.   The commitments made at inception of an option contract are usually firm and result in the holder of the option acquiring a right to obtain potential future economic benefits associated with changes in the fair value of the financial instrument underlying the contract. Conversely, the writer of a call option assumes an obligation reflecting the fact that certain potential future economic benefits associated with changes in the fair value of the underlying financial instrument have been forgone. The fair value of the holder's right and the writer's obligation at inception of the contract can usually be measured reliably by reference to the value of the consideration exchanged between the parties to the contract. This consideration usually takes the form of a premium paid to the writer of the option. The fair value may also be determined by reference to the financial markets or by use of an option pricing model. The contractual right of the holder and obligation of the writer therefore meet the recognition criteria for a financial asset and a financial liability, respectively.

A18.   In the case of both a put and a call option, the right acquired by the holder and the obligation assumed by the writer are measured initially at the amount of the consideration agreed to be exchanged. The basis used for subsequent measurement of the asset acquired by the holder and the liability assumed by the writer of an option contract depends on management's intentions in entering into the contract. If the contract is entered into as part of operating activities, it is carried at fair value at subsequent reporting dates with gains and losses being included in current income. If the contract is entered into as a hedge, the basis on which the asset or liability is carried and gains and losses are recognised in income will depend on the measurement basis adopted for the hedged item.

A19.   The fair value of an option contract at any time during its life is determined in part by the intrinsic value and in part by the time value. The fair value of the right is not equal to the fair value of the underlying instrument because exercise of the right requires additional consideration to be given up in exchange for the underlying instrument upon exercise of the option.

A20.   Once recognised on an enterprise's balance sheet, an option contract remains as an asset or liability until it is transferred to another party, exercised or expires. Any carrying amount in the balance sheet at the date of a transfer or expiry is written off to income and, in the case of a transfer, offset against any consideration received or paid to determine a gain or loss.

A21.   On exercise of a call option, the writer delivers the underlying financial instrument, receives the exercise price, usually in cash, and is relieved of any further obligation under the option contract. On exercise of a put option, the holder delivers the underlying financial instrument, receives the exercise price, usually in cash, and has no further rights under the option contract. In accordance with paragraph 29 of this Statement, both the holder and writer of an exercised option remove from their balance sheet the carrying amounts of the option contract and the consideration given up and, in accordance with paragraph 57, record the fair value of the consideration received, any difference being recognised as a gain or loss. Because it is normally to their disadvantage, option holders normally do not exercise an option while it retains any time value. Exercise of an option contract carried at fair value results in recognition of a gain or loss to the extent of any change in fair value since the last reporting date. When an option contract is accounted for as a hedge of an investing asset or a financing liability, any gain or loss is recognised in income in a fashion that matches it with income recognition of the corresponding loss or gain on the hedged position.

Forward contracts

A22.   As with option contracts, some forward contracts are financial instruments because they involve the transfer of another underlying financial instrument, such as foreign currency, shares or an interest-bearing money market instrument. Some forward contracts are not financial instruments because they involve the transfer of a non-financial asset, such as metals, oil or gas.

A23.   An example of a financial instrument is a forward contract in which one party promises to deliver $1,000,000 cash in exchange for $1,000,000 face value of fixed rate government bonds, and the other party promises to deliver $1,000,000 face value of fixed rate government bonds in exchange for $1,000,000 cash six months later. During the six-month period, both parties have a contractual right and a contractual obligation to exchange financial instruments. If the market price of the government bonds rises above $1,000,000, the conditions will be favourable to the purchaser and unfavourable to the seller; if the market price falls below $1,000,000, the effect will be the opposite. The purchaser has both a contractual right (a financial asset) similar to the right under a call option held and a contractual obligation (a financial liability) similar to the obligation under a put option written; the seller has a contractual right (a financial asset) similar to the right under a put option held and a contractual obligation (a financial liability) similar to the obligation under a call option written. As with options, these contractual rights and obligations constitute financial assets and financial liabilities separate and distinct from the underlying financial instruments (the bonds and cash to be exchanged). A forward contract differs from an option contract to the extent that future performance of obligations is contingent only on the passage of time, rather than on exercise of an option by one of the parties.

A24. At inception of a forward contract, the rights acquired and obligations assumed are usually of equivalent value and no cash or other assets are exchanged between the parties[2]. The right and the obligation meet the recognition criteria in that the associated risks and rewards are assumed at inception of the contract and the cost or value can be measured reliably. Only the right and the obligation to make an exchange in the future are recognised and not the underlying financial instruments to be exchanged. The amounts that are to be exchanged in the future on maturity of the contract are known, but they are not the measure of the financial asset and financial liability assumed at inception of the contract. The risks and rewards associated with the underlying instruments remain with the holders until the instruments are exchanged on settlement of the contract. Under some circumstances, on inception of a forward contract, one of the parties may not possess the underlying instrument it is obliged to deliver but it plans to acquire that instrument prior to settlement of the contract. If the fair value of the underlying instrument increases before it can be acquired by the party obliged to deliver it on settlement, the higher cost (i.e., the loss from exposure to price risk) is borne by that party.

A25. The right and the obligation under a forward contract normally meet the criteria for offsetting because they result from the same financial instrument and, in general, are extinguished only on simultaneous completion of the contract by both parties on maturity (except in the unusual circumstances in which one party is bound to deliver on maturity of the contract regardless of whether the other party delivers). Accordingly, the net amount reported initially by both parties to a forward contract is usually zero, which is the amount of the cash or other assets exchanged between the parties at inception of the contract.

---

[2]   In some circumstances, one party to a forward contract may require the other party to pay a deposit, similar in some respects to the margin deposit on a futures contract, to safeguard against the economic consequences of a default. This deposit is accounted for as such and does not represent the cost or value of the rights and obligations exchanged on inception of the forward contract.

A26. At reporting dates subsequent to inception of a forward contract, the amounts at which the financial asset acquired and financial liability assumed are measured depend on management's intentions in entering into the contract. As explained in paragraph A18 in respect of option contracts, the basis of measurement applied to the financial asset and financial liability associated with a forward contract subsequent to its initial recognition depends on its classification as between operating, investing and financing, and hedging.

A27. Accounting for a forward contract on maturity is similar to accounting for exercise of an option contract. Upon maturity of a forward contract, the parties exchange the underlying financial assets specified in the contract, remove from their balance sheets the carrying amount of the contract and the cash or other underlying financial instrument given up and recognise the fair value of the cash or underlying financial instrument received. Immediately before maturity, the fair value of the contract is equal to the difference between the fair values of the underlying assets to be exchanged. Settlement of the contract constitutes an exchange transaction that may result in current recognition of a gain or loss in income. For example, maturity of a contract carried at fair value results in recognition of a gain or loss to the extent of any change in fair value since the last reporting date. However, if a contract is accounted for as a hedge of an investing asset or a financing liability, any gain or loss arising over the term of the contract is recognised in income in a fashion that matches it with income recognition of the corresponding loss or gain on the hedged position.

A28. A forward contract for receipt or delivery of foreign currency is accounted for in accordance with International Accounting Standard 21, Accounting for the Effects of Changes in Foreign Exchange Rates, which requires that the difference between the amount of the contract at the forward rate and the amount of the contract at the spot exchange rate on inception of the contract (i.e., the time value of the contract) be recognised in income over the life of the contract. Amortisation of this discount or premium inherent in a contract accounted for on the cost basis is consistent with the measurement standard in paragraph 63 of this Statement.

Futures contracts

A29. A futures contract that is a financial instrument gives the purchaser both a right and an obligation to exchange cash for a specified amount of another financial instrument on the agreed settlement date and the seller a corresponding right and obligation to exchange the underlying instrument for cash. These rights and obligations are substantially the same as those created under a forward contract. Futures contracts differ from forward contracts, however, primarily in that the contracts are standardised and traded on an exchange. These features facilitate opening and closing of positions without the need to deliver or take delivery of the underlying instrument. Indeed, in some cases, the nature of the underlying instrument may be such that it is not possible for it to be delivered, as in the case of a share price index. An additional feature of a futures contract is that, at inception, a margin deposit with the futures exchange is required. The amount of the required margin deposit is adjusted daily during the life of the contract to reflect changes in the fair value of the underlying financial instrument.

A30. The discussion of accounting for forward contracts applies equally to futures contracts, with the following additional considerations. On inception of a futures contract, there is an exchange of cash or other assets in the form of the required margin deposit with the futures exchange. The margin deposit is recorded as an amount due from the exchange but it does not reflect the fair value of the financial asset acquired and the financial liability assumed under the futures contract. At reporting dates subsequent to inception of the contract, changes in the fair value of the futures contract result in daily adjustments to the required margin deposit. The corresponding changes in fair value of the contract itself may or may not be reflected in the balance sheet and income statement, depending on the basis of measurement applied to the contract.

Interest rate swaps

A31. Interest rate and currency swaps are further examples of financial assets and financial liabilities in the form of rights and obligations to exchange financial instruments. A currency swap may be viewed as a variation of a forward contract, in which the parties agree to exchange specified amounts of two different currencies at an agreed future date. Similarly, an interest rate swap may be viewed as a series of forward contracts to exchange, for example, variable cash receipts based on a specified floating-rate market index (for example, LIBOR) for fixed cash payments, both calculated with reference to an agreed notional principal amount. At inception, the currency or interest rate swap has the potential to be favourable or unfavourable to either party, the ultimate outcome depending on movements in the currency exchange rate or interest rate index subsequent to inception of the contract. The swap is, therefore, both a financial asset and a financial liability to both parties.

A32. The accounting for a swap follows that for a forward contract. As with a forward contract, at inception of a swap agreement the financial asset and financial liability assumed by the parties are normally reported at a zero net amount. When a swap is undertaken at other than a market rate current on inception, an asset is recognised by one party and a liability by the other, measured in both cases by reference to the amount of any compensating payment made at inception of the swap. In the relatively uncommon situation in which a party to a swap is required to deliver a financial asset regardless of whether it receives an asset in return from the other party to the agreement, there is no right of set-off of rights and obligations under the agreement and each party recognises its financial asset and financial liability under the agreement on a gross basis.

A33. Each future exchange of interest payments under an interest rate swap is viewed as a separate forward contract and settlement is considered in that context. The benefit or cost of having entered into the contract is realised as the entitlement to each swap receipt and the obligation to make each swap payment accrues over the interest period covered. This benefit or cost is treated as a component of interest cost for the period.

Guarantee of a financial liability

A34. A guarantee of a financial liability results in the guarantor assuming an obligation to pay an amount up to a set maximum, contingent upon occurrence of a specified event of default by the party primarily liable for the guaranteed debt. The guarantee normally terminates on a date that is fixed or determinable or upon occurrence of an event, such as repayment of the debt. In the event the guarantor is called upon to honour the guarantee, the guarantor assumes the rights of the creditor against the primary debtor under the debt agreement. The guarantor receives some form of benefit, often a cash fee, to compensate for the risk undertaken.

A35. Under a financial guarantee, the guarantor has an obligation to pay some or all of the principal amount of the debt plus accrued interest if the creditor demands payment subsequent to a default by the debtor. The guarantor has a receivable from the debtor contingent on having to honour the guarantee, possibly collateralised by specific security pledged by the debtor. The guarantee is a financial liability because it is a contractual liability of the guarantor to exchange one financial instrument (usually cash) for another financial instrument (a receivable from the defaulted debtor) under conditions that are unfavourable. The creditor has a corresponding contractual right to make that exchange at its option.

A36. On inception of the guarantee, the guarantor assumes the risks and rewards of the obligation to honour the guarantee if called. The risks and rewards relating to the debt guaranteed and the entitlements under the right of recourse against the debtor have not been assumed, however, and will only be assumed in the event the guarantee is honoured in the future. As consideration for taking on the risks of the obligation assumed, the guarantor receives a benefit of some kind, which may be an entitlement to a fee to be paid on inception or subsequently in a lump sum or by instalments. The guarantee agreement results on inception in an exchange of consideration between the debtor and the guarantor, each of which is assumed to obtain and give up consideration having equal value. Because the rights and obligations obtained by each party arise from the guarantee agreement, they ordinarily qualify for offsetting and are initially recognised at their nil net value.

A37. Subsequent to initial recognition, the fair value of a guarantee fluctuates over time in relation to the likelihood of default by the debtor, the amount of loss that would result and the fair value of any fee payments remaining to be paid by the debtor. If the guarantee results from investing or financing activities, the guarantor carries the offsetting financial asset and financial liability at its initially recognised carrying amount in accordance with paragraph 62 in this Statement. In the relatively uncommon circumstances in which the guarantee results from operating activities, changes in its fair value are recognised in income as they occur.

A38. As a result of changing circumstances during the term of the guarantee, the guarantor may determine that it will probably be called upon to honour its guarantee. When a contingent loss from having to honour the guarantee satisfies the criteria for recognition in International Accounting Standard 10, Contingencies and Events Occurring After the Balance Sheet Date, a loss and corresponding liability is recognised in accordance with that Statement.

A39. If the guarantor is called upon to honour the guarantee, it assumes the risks and rewards of the underlying debt and the related rights of recourse against the debtor and accords them initial recognition. Assumption of this financial liability and financial asset result in the removal from the balance sheet of the carrying values, if any, of the guarantee itself and any previously recognised contingent liability.

Proposed Revised
International
Accounting Standards

Statement of Intent

Comparability of Financial Statements

Contents

Appendices

1.   Issues on which the Board has agreed to incorporate the proposals in E32, Comparability of Financial Statements, in revised International Accounting Standards without substantive change

2.   Issues on which the Board has agreed to make substantive changes to the proposals in E32, comparability of Financial Statements

3.   Issues on which the Board has deferred consideration pending further work

Comparability of Financial Statements

Introduction

1.   This Statement of Intent sets out the Board's decisions following its review of the comments received on Exposure Draft 32, Comparability of Financial Statements (E32). It describes how the decisions will be implemented and the further efforts of the Board in seeking the improvement and harmonisation of accounting standards and other requirements relating to the presentation of financial statements. The Statement of Intent does not alter the status of existing International Accounting Standards; the changes will take effect after further work on existing Standards, which is described in paragraphs 12 and 13, has been carried out.

E32, Comparability of Financial Statements

2.   E32 was published on 1st January 1989. It dealt with twenty nine accounting issues where the choice of alternative accounting treatments permitted by International Accounting Standards may have a material effect on the definition, recognition, measurement and display of income, expenses, assets, liabilities and equity in the financial statements of an enterprise.

3.   The objectives of the proposals in E32 were to:

(a)   eliminate all but one accounting treatment where the alternative treatments represent a free choice for like transactions and events; and

(b)   ensure that the appropriate treatment is used where the alternatives represent different treatments which should be applied in different circumstances.

4.   In some cases, E32 proposed the retention of two accounting treatments for like transactions and events particularly when the application of the different criteria in paragraph 5 below supports the use of different treatments. In these circumstances, E32 identified one treatment as the preferred treatment and the other as an allowed alternative. E32 proposed that an enterprise that presents financial statements which use allowed alternative treatments and which purport to conform with International Accounting Standards should reconcile its reported net income and shareholders' interests to those amounts determined using the preferred treatments.

535

5.   In E32, the Board used the following criteria in deciding which alternative treatments should be required, preferred or eliminated:

(a)   current worldwide practice and trends in national accounting standards, law and generally accepted accounting principles;

(b)   conformity with the Framework for the Preparation and Presentation of Financial Statements (which was in Exposure Draft form at the time E32 was issued);

(c)   the views of regulators and their representative organisations, such as the International Organisation of Securities Commissions (IOSCO); and

(d)   consistency within an International Accounting Standard and with other International Accounting Standards.

Comments on E32

6.   IASC received over 160 comment letters on the proposals in E32. Many of these comment letters were the result of extensive consultation within national standard setting bodies, accountancy bodies, international accounting firms and other organisations. In addition, representatives of IASC discussed the proposals with standard setting bodies, representatives of preparers and users of financial statements, the accountancy profession, stock exchanges and securities regulators in over twenty countries.

7.   The comment letters were virtually unanimous in supporting the objective of greater comparability of financial statements and the Exposure Draft as a whole. Inevitably, however, many respondents disagreed with one or more of the detailed proposals in E32.

Revised Proposals

8.   The Board has reconsidered the proposals in E32 in the light of the comment letters and its discussions around the world. It has decided that it should continue with the Comparability project in substantially the same form as envisaged in E32 although certain changes will be made on some accounting issues, to the terminology used when a free choice is retained and to the reconciliation requirement.

9.　　The Board has decided that:

(a)　twenty one of the twenty nine proposals in E32 should be incorporated in revised International Accounting Standards without substantive change (see appendix 1);

(b)　three of the proposals in E32 require substantive change and should be reexposed (see appendix 2); and

(c)　reconsideration of five of the proposals should be deferred pending further work (see appendix 3).

10.　　The Board has concluded that it should use the term "benchmark" instead of the proposed term "preferred" in those few cases where it continues to allow a choice of accounting treatment for like transactions and events. The term "benchmark" more closely reflects the Board's intention of identifying a point of reference when making its choice between alternatives.

11.　　A substantial number of comment letters indicated disagreement with the proposed reconciliation requirement in E32 for those enterprises that present financial statements which use allowed alternative treatments and which purport to conform with International Accounting Standards (see paragraph 4 above). The Board has been convinced by the commentators' arguments and does not intend to require the reconciliation requirement proposed in E32. However, it will encourage enterprises to publis' such a reconciliation as part of their financial statements. Furthermore, individual Standards may, as at present, require disclosure of the effects of using accounting treatments which are different from the benchmark treatments.

Implementation of the Changes

12.　　Drafts of revised Standards 8, 11, 16, 18, 19, 21, 22 and 25 will be exposed for comment; the exposure drafts will indicate that the Board does not intend to reconsider the issues described in Appendix 1 which were exposed for comment in E32 and subsequently approved by the Board without substantive change. Drafts of revised Standards 2, 9 and 23 will be exposed for comment and, because the Board has changed its position concerning the issues described in Appendix 2, the Board will reconsider these issues in light of comments received. The Board has deferred consideration of the issues listed in Appendix 3 but once the necessary work on these issues is complete, the Board intends to reexpose and reconsider subsequently only those issues on which it has changed its position from that exposed in E32.

13.   Before the Board implements the agreed changes, it will make other improvements to existing International Accounting Standards. The purpose of this Improvements project is to ensure that International Accounting Standards are sufficiently detailed and complete and contain adequate disclosure requirements to meet the needs of capital markets and the international business community.

14.   As more information becomes available on the likely progress on the revised Standards, the Board will publish further details of its implementation programme. It is intended, however, that the implementation work on existing International Accounting Standards will be completed by the beginning of 1993.

15.   The revisions to existing International Accounting Standards will not take effect until the Board has approved and issued the revised Standards.

16.   The Board will also develop new Standards where it is necessary to fill the gaps in the existing set of International Accounting Standards in order to meet the needs of capital markets and the international business community.   Current projects include Joint Ventures, Financial Instruments, Cash Flow Statements, Long Term Intangible Assets and Earnings per Share.

Further Consultations and Improvements

17.   The Board recognises that it is both impracticable and inappropriate to remove some of the remaining alternative accounting treatments permitted by International Accounting Standards in the foreseeable future - for example, the choice between historical cost and revaluation based carrying amounts for property, plant and equipment and some investments. The Board also recognises that future developments in accounting and the business environment may result in a requirement for a treatment other than that presently identified as the benchmark.

18.   The Board will continue to consult national standard setting bodies, accountancy bodies and others who are interested in the improvement and harmonisation of financial reporting practices.   The purpose of such consultations will be to seek ways of eliminating the remaining free choices in International Accounting Standards and encouraging national standard setting bodies to adopt the required treatments and the benchmark treatments in the revised International Accounting Standards.

19.   The International Organisation of Securities Commissions (IOSCO) has emphasised the need for mutually acceptable accounting standards for use in multinational securities offerings and other foreign issues of equity and debt securities. The Board believes that the Comparability project is an important first step towards meeting this need. The Board will continue to support the efforts of IOSCO which are to encourage individual securities regulators to allow or require each foreign issuer to present:

(a)   a reconciliation of its financial statements prepared in conformity with its domestic requirements to the required treatments and, where a choice remains, the benchmark treatments in International Accounting Standards. Such a reconciliation would replace the reconciliation to the required treatments in national accounting requirements in each country in which the issuer's securities are traded; or

(b)   financial statements prepared in conformity with the required treatments and, where a choice remains, the benchmark treatments in International Accounting Standards.

20.   As a longer term objective, the Board will seek to encourage all issuers of securities to present their financial statements in conformity with the required treatments and benchmark treatments in International Accounting Standards.

Appendix 1

Issues on which the Board has agreed to incorporate the proposals in E32, Comparability of Financial Statements, in revised International Accounting Standards without substantive change

ISSUES	Required or Benchmark Treatment	Allowed Alternative Treatment	Treatment Eliminated
Correction of fundamental errors and omissions, and adjustments resulting from accounting policy changes	Adjust opening retained earnings (subject to certain exceptions)	Include in income of the current period	
	Amend comparative information	Present amended pro forma comparative information	
Recognition of revenue and net income on construction contracts	Percentage of completion method		Completed contract method
	When the conditions for profit recognition are not met, recognise revenue to the extent of costs incurred that are recoverable		
Measurement of property, plant and equipment	Measure at cost	Measure at revalued amounts	
Measurement of property, plant and equipment acquired in exchange for another asset	Fair value for dissimilar assets acquired		Net carrying amount of asset given up for dissimilar assets acquired
	Net carrying amount of asset given up for similar assets acquired		Fair value for similar assets acquired
Recognition of a revaluation increase relating to a revaluation decrease previously charged to income	Recognise in income of the current period		Recognise in shareholders' interests
Recognition of revenue on transactions involving the rendering of services	Percentage of completion method		Completed contract method
	When the outcome of the contract cannot be reliably estimated, recognise revenue to the extent of costs incurred that are recoverable		
Determining the cost of retirement benefits	Accrued benefit valuation methods	Projected benefit valuation methods	
Use of projected salaries in determining the cost of retirement benefits	Incorporate an assumption about projected salaries		Do not incorporate an assumption about projected salaries
Recognition of past service costs, experience adjustments and the effects of changes in actuarial assumptions	Recognise systematically over a period approximating the average of the expected remaining working lives of participating employees (subject to certain exceptions)		Recognise in income of the current period as they arise

ISSUES	Required or Benchmark Treatment	Allowed Alternative Treatment	Treatment Eliminated
Recognition of foreign exchange gains and losses on long-term monetary items	Recognise in income of the current period unless hedged		Defer and recognise in income of current and future periods
Recognition of foreign exchange losses on the acquisition of an asset that result from a severe devaluation against which there is no practical means of hedging	Recognise in income of the current period	Recognise as part of the cost of the asset	
Exchange rate for use in translating income statement items of foreign entities	Exchange rates at the dates of the transactions (or average rate)		Closing exchange rates
Treatment of differences on income statement items translated at other than the closing rate	Recognise in shareholders' interests		Recognise in income of the current period
Subsidiaries operating in hyperinflationary economies	Restate financial statements in accordance with IAS 29, Financial Reporting in Hyperinflationary Economies, before translation		Translate financial statements without prior restatement
Exchange differences on foreign operations integral to those of the parent	Recognise in income of the period unless hedged	Recognise as part of the cost of an asset when they result from a severe devaluation against which there is no practical means of hedging	Defer and recognise in income of current and future periods
Accounting for business combinations	Purchase method for acquisitions		Pooling of interests method for acquisitions
	Pooling of interests method for uniting of interests		Purchase method for uniting of interests
Positive goodwill	Recognise as an asset and amortise to income on a systematic basis over its useful life. The amortisation period should not exceed 5 years unless a longer period can be justified which should not, in any case, exceed 20 years		Adjust immediately to shareholders' interests
Negative goodwill	Allocate over individual non-monetary assets. After such an allocation, if negative goodwill remains, treat as deferred income and recognise in income on a systematic basis as for positive goodwill	Treat as deferred income and recognise in income on a systematic basis as for positive goodwill	Adjust immediately to shareholders' interests
Measurement of minority interest arising on a business combination	Measure at pre-acquisition carrying amounts	Measure at post-acquisition fair values	
Measurement of investment properties	Measure at cost with depreciation	Measure at revalued amounts	Measure at cost without depreciation
Recognition of a realised gain previously recognised in revaluation surplus	Transfer to retained earnings		Recognise in income of the current period

IAS 8, Unusual and Prior Period Items and Changes in Accounting Policies

Correction of fundamental errors and omissions, and adjustments resulting from accounting policy changes

Benchmark treatment - subject to the exception below, prior period items and the amount of any adjustments resulting from changes in accounting policies should be reported by adjusting opening retained earnings. The comparative information in respect of prior years which is included in the financial statements should be amended unless it is impracticable to do so and that fact is disclosed. As an exception to this general requirement, the revised Standard will require that adjustments resulting from changes in accounting policies should be applied prospectively in the limited situations where the amount of any adjustment to opening retained earnings is not reasonably determinable or where prospective application is required by a national accounting standard or an International Accounting Standard.

Allowed alternative treatment - prior period items and the amount of any adjustments resulting from changes in accounting policies should be included in net income for the current period. Comparative information in respect of prior years should be presented on a pro forma basis unless it is impracticable to do so and that fact is disclosed.

The revised Standard will also require:

(a) the disclosure of the nature and amount of prior period items and the amount of any adjustments resulting from changes in accounting policies; and

(b) that the amount of any adjustments resulting from changes in accounting policies resulting from the implementation of a requirement in an International Accounting Standard should be accounted for in accordance with any specific transitional provisions in that Standard.

IAS 11, Accounting for Construction Contracts

Recognition of revenue and net income on construction contracts

Required treatment - revenue and net income should be recognised using the percentage of completion method. The revised Standard will make clear that the percentage of completion method requires the following:

(a) when the outcome of the contract can be reliably estimated, revenue should be recognised by reference to the stage of completion of the contract activity at the end of each accounting period. The conditions that must be satisfied before such a degree of reliability can be obtained are set out in existing paragraph 43 of IAS 11;

(b)   when the outcome of the contract cannot be reliably estimated, revenue should be recognised only to the extent of costs incurred that are recoverable; and

(c)   when the outcome of the contract and the recoverability of the costs already incurred cannot be reliably estimated, revenue should not be recognised.

IAS 16, Accounting for Property, Plant and Equipment

Measurement of property, plant and equipment

Benchmark treatment - the gross carrying amount of an asset included in property, plant and equipment should be its historical cost.

Allowed alternative treatment - the gross carrying amount of an asset included in property, plant and equipment should be determined by reference to revaluations.

Measurement of property, plant and equipment acquired in exchange for another asset

Required treatment - when an item of property, plant and equipment is acquired in exchange or in part exchange for a dissimilar asset, the cost of the asset acquired should be measured at fair value. When the item is acquired in exchange for a similar asset which has a similar use in the same line of business and which has a similar fair value, the cost of the asset acquired should be measured at the net carrying amount of the asset given up, adjusted for any balancing payment or receipt of cash or other consideration.

The revised Standard will include guidance on the identification of similar and dissimilar assets.

Recognition of a revaluation increase relating to a revaluation decrease previously charged to income

Required treatment - an increase in net carrying amount arising on the revaluation of property, plant and equipment should be credited to income to the extent that the increase is related to and not greater than a decrease arising on revaluation previously recorded as a charge to income.

IAS 18, Revenue Recognition

Recognition of revenue on transactions involving the rendering of services

Required treatment - revenue should be recognised using the percentage of completion method.

The revised Standard will make clear that the percentage of completion method requires the following:

(a) when no significant uncertainty exists regarding the consideration that will be derived from rendering the service and the associated costs incurred or to be incurred in rendering the service, revenue should be recognised by reference to the work accomplished at the end of each accounting period;

(b) when the outcome of the contract cannot be reliably estimated, revenue should be recognised only to the extent of costs incurred that are recoverable; and

(c) when the outcome of the contract and the recoverability of the costs already incurred cannot be reliably estimated, revenue should not be recognised.

IAS 19, Accounting for Retirement Benefits in the Financial Statements of Employers

Determination of the cost of retirement benefits

Benchmark treatment - in a defined benefit plan, the cost of retirement benefits should be determined using an accrued benefit valuation method.

Allowed alternative treatment - in a defined benefit plan, the cost of retirement benefits should be determined using a projected benefit valuation method.

The costs which would be involved in undertaking a second actuarial valuation may be substantial and may not be justified. E32 proposed that enterprises which use the allowed alternative treatment need only disclose the amounts based on the accrued benefit methods to the extent practicable. The Board intends to encourage securities regulators to adopt the same approach in any reconciliations which they may require.

Use of projected salaries in determining the cost of retirement benefits

Required treatment - an enterprise should use appropriate and compatible assumptions, including those regarding projected salary levels to date of retirement, in making an actuarial valuation.

Recognition of past service costs, experience adjustments and the effects of changes in actuarial assumptions

Required treatment - subject to the exception below, past service costs, experience adjustments and the effects of changes in actuarial assumptions on retirement benefit costs should be allocated to income systematically over a period approximating the average of the expected remaining working lives of the participating employees. As an exception to the general requirement, the revised Standard will require the immediate write off or the use of shorter amortisation periods for certain adjustments such as curtailments, settlements, some plan amendments and similar items.

IAS 21, Accounting for the Effects of Changes in Foreign Exchange Rates

Recognition of foreign exchange gains and losses on long-term monetary items

Required treatment - exchange differences arising on reporting long-term foreign currency monetary items at rates different from those at which they were recorded during the period or presented in the previous financial statements should be recognised in income for the period except for those differences:

(a) arising in the circumstances set out in the existing paragraph 29 of IAS 21 which should be dealt with in accordance with that paragraph; and

(b) relating to a hedged liability which should, to the extent of the hedge, be deferred until the liability is settled and the asset sold.

It is intended that the definition of a hedge will be dealt with in the Financial Instruments project.

Recognition of foreign exchange losses on the acquisition of an asset that result from a severe devaluation against which there is no practical means of hedging

Benchmark treatment - exchange differences arising on reporting long-term foreign currency monetary items at rates different from those at which they were recorded during the period or presented in the previous financial statements should be recognised in income for the period.

Allowed alternative treatment - exchange differences resulting from a severe devaluation or from depreciation of a currency against which there is no practical means of hedging and that affects liabilities arising directly on the recent acquisition of assets invoiced in a foreign currency should be included in the carrying amount of the related assets provided that the adjusted carrying amount does not exceed the lower of the replacement cost and the amount recoverable from the sale or use of the asset.

Exchange rate for use in translating income statement items of foreign entities and treatment of differences on income statement items translated at other than the closing rate

Required treatment - income statement items should be translated at the exchange rates at the dates of the transactions (or at a rate that approximates the actual rates). Differences resulting from the translation of income statement items at the dates of transactions and balance sheet items at the closing rate should be taken to shareholders' interests.

Subsidiaries operating in hyperinflationary economies

Required treatment - the financial statements of a subsidiary that reports in the currency of a hyperinflationary economy should be restated in accordance with International Accounting Standard 29, Financial Reporting in Hyperinflationary Economies, before they are translated into the reporting currency of the parent.

Procedures applied in translating the financial statements of a foreign operation that is integral to the operations of the parent

Benchmark treatment - exchange differences arising on the translation of the financial statements of a foreign operation that is integral to the operations of the parent should be included in income except that those differences relating to a hedged liability should, to the extent of the hedge, be deferred until the liability is settled and the asset sold.

Allowed alternative treatment - exchange differences resulting from a severe devaluation or from depreciation of a currency against which there is no practical means of hedging and that affects liabilities arising directly on the recent acquisition of assets invoiced in a foreign currency should be included in the carrying amount of the related assets provided that the adjusted carrying amount does not exceed the lower of the replacement cost and the amount recoverable from the sale or use of the asset.

It is intended that the definition of a hedge will be dealt with in the Financial Instruments project.

IAS 22, Accounting for Business Combinations

Acquisitions and mergers

Required treatment - an acquisition should be accounted for using the purchase method. A uniting of interests should be accounted for using the pooling of interests method.

E32 proposed that a uniting of interests should only arise when, among other things, an acquirer cannot be identified. The revised Standard will include guidance on when an acquirer cannot be identified.

Positive goodwill

Required treatment - the excess of the cost of acquisition over the fair values of the net identifiable assets acquired should be recognised as an asset as goodwill arising on acquisition. This goodwill should be amortised to income on a systematic basis over its useful life. The amortisation period should not exceed five years unless a longer useful life can be justified and is explained in the financial statements. The longer period chosen should not exceed twenty years.

Negative goodwill

Benchmark treatment - the amount by which the aggregate fair value of net identifiable assets exceeds the cost of acquisition should be allocated over individual non monetary assets acquired in proportion to their fair values. After making this allocation, in the rare circumstances in which any negative goodwill remains, it should be treated as deferred income and recognised in income on a systematic basis over a period that does not exceed five years unless a longer period can be justified and is explained in the financial statements and which, in any case, does not exceed twenty years.

Allowed alternative treatment - the amount by which the aggregate fair value of net identifiable assets exceeds the cost of acquisition should be treated as deferred income and recognised in income on a systematic basis over a period that does not exceed five years unless a longer period can be justified and is explained in the financial statements and which, in any case, does not exceed twenty years.

Measurement of minority interests arising on a business combination

Benchmark treatment - a minority interest that arises on a business combination should be stated at the appropriate proportion of the pre-acquisition carrying amounts of the net assets of the subsidiary.

Allowed alternative treatment - a minority interest that arises on a business combination should be stated at the appropriate proportion of the fair values of the net assets of the subsidiary.

IAS 25, Accounting for Investments

Measurement of investment properties

Benchmark treatment - investment properties should be carried at cost and depreciated in accordance with International Accounting Standard 4, Depreciation Accounting.

Allowed alternative treatment - investment properties should be carried in the balance sheet at revalued amounts.

Recognition of a realised gain previously recognised in revaluation surplus

Required treatment - on disposal of an investment which was previously revalued and on which an increase in carrying amount was transferred to revaluation surplus, any remaining revalued amount should be credited directly to retained earnings and disclosed.

Appendix 2

Issues on which the Board has agreed to make substantive changes to the proposals in E32, Comparability of Financial Statements; these issues will be reexposed and reconsidered in the light of comments received

ISSUES	Required or Benchmark Treatment	Allowed Alternative Treatment	Treatment Eliminated
Assignment of cost to inventories	FIFO and Weighted Average Cost formulas		LIFO and Base Stock formulas
Development costs	Recognise as assets when they meet specified criteria and as expenses when they do not meet criteria		Recognise development costs that meet specified criteria as expenses
Borrowing costs	Recognise as part of the cost of an asset if it takes a substantial period of time to get it ready for its intended use or sale; recognise as expense in other circumstances		Recognise borrowing costs that meet criteria for capitalisation as expenses

IAS 2, Valuation and Presentation of Inventories in the Context of the Historical Cost System

Assignment of costs to inventories

Required treatment - inventories that are not ordinarily interchangeable or goods manufactured and segregated for specific projects should be accounted for using specific identification of their individual costs. The FIFO formula or a weighted average cost formula should be used for assigning costs to all other inventories.

Eliminated treatments - the Exposure Draft will propose that the use of the LIFO formula and the Base Stock method should not be permitted.

IAS 9, Accounting for Research and Development Activities

Recognition of development costs

Required treatment - development costs should be recognised as an asset when they meet the criteria in paragraph 17 of IAS 9 and it is probable that these costs will be recovered. Such costs should be allocated on a systematic basis to future periods in accordance with paragraph 20 of IAS 9.

Eliminated treatment - the Exposure Draft will propose that development costs which meet the criteria in paragraph 17 of IAS 9 should not be charged as an expense in the period in which they are incurred.

IAS 23 - Capitalisation of Borrowing Costs

Recognition of borrowing costs

Required treatment - borrowing costs should be recognised as an asset when they meet certain criteria which will be developed as part of the Improvements project. The criteria will be based on the procedures set out in paragraphs 22 to 27 of IAS 23.

Eliminated treatment - the Exposure Draft will propose that borrowing costs which meet the criteria should not be charged as an expense in the period in which they are incurred.

Appendix 3

Issues on which the Board has deferred consideration pending further work

IAS 17, Accounting for Leases

Recognition of finance income on finance leases

The Board believes that further study is required on the recognition of finance income on those leases on which the lessor's net investment outstanding is materially affected by income tax factors. It plans to develop an internationally acceptable definition of such a lease and delete the use of the term "leveraged lease".

IAS 25, Accounting for Investments

Measurement of long-term investments

Measurement of marketable equity securities held as long-term investments

Measurement of current investments

Recognition of increases and decreases in market values of current investments

Consideration of all these issues has been deferred pending further work on the Financial Instruments project.

Exposure Drafts

Research and Development Activities

IAS 9 allows a free choice between the capitalisation and expensing for those development costs that meet certain criteria. E32 proposed that all development costs should be expensed (benchmark treatment) with capitalisation as the allowed alternative when certain criteria were met.

After considering the comments on E32, the Board decided that it should require the capitalisation of development costs when the criteria were met and require the expensing of development costs in other circumstances. This position was reflected in the Statement of Intent on the Comparability of Financial Statements.

E37 incorporates the treatment of development costs set out in the Statement of Intent on the Comparability of Financial Statements. It also proposes other improvements to IAS 9 to ensure that the Standard is sufficiently detailed and complete and contains adequate disclosure requirements to meet the needs of capital markets and the international business community.

At its meeting in October 1992, following its review of the comments on E37 and its reconsideration of the issue, the Board confirmed the approach adopted in the Statement of Intent; this approach will be reflected in a revised IAS 9.

The Board is dealing with the Statement of Intent as a package. Therefore, its approval of the revised Standards is subject to its later approval of the revised Standards incorporating the other changes in the Statement of Intent. All the revised Standards will come into effect on the same date.

Exposure Draft

Contents

International Accounting Standard --
Research and Development Activities

International Accounting Standard --

Research and Development Activities

The standards, which have been set in bold type, should be read in the context of the background material and implementation guidance and in the context of the Preface to International Accounting Standards. International Accounting Standards are not intended to apply to immaterial items (see paragraph 12 of the Preface).

Introduction

The primary issue in accounting for the costs of research and development activities is whether such costs meet the criteria to be recognised as an asset or whether the costs are recognised as an expense when incurred. It is often difficult to be reasonably certain that the intended economic benefits of research and development activities will flow to the enterprise. Therefore, in such circumstances the costs of research and development activities are recognised as an expense in the period in which they are incurred.

Scope

1.   **This Statement deals with the accounting for and disclosure of research and development activities.**

2.   This Statement does not deal with activities in the extractive industries for the exploration for oil, gas and mineral deposits. However, it does apply to those research and development activities in the extractive industries which are comparable in nature to the research and development activities of other enterprises.

3.   This Statement does not deal with research and development activities of development stage enterprises. An enterprise is a development stage enterprise if it is devoting substantially all of its efforts to the establishment of a new business and either of the following conditions exists:

(a)   its planned principal operations have not commenced; or

(b)   its planned principal operations have commenced but there has been no significant revenue there from.

4.   An enterprise may carry out research and development activities for others under contract. When the substance of the arrangement is such that the risks and rewards associated with the research and development

activities are, or will be, transferred to others, the costs of the activities are accounted for in accordance with International Accounting Standard 2, Inventories. When the substance of the arrangement is such that the risks and rewards associated with the research and development activities are not, or will not be, transferred to others, for example when the contract is a means of financing the costs of research and development activities of the enterprise itself, the costs are dealt with in accordance with this Statement. Factors to be considered in determining if a contract is a means of financing include:

(a)   whether the enterprise is contractually obligated, or could be required at the option of the other party, to repay any of the funds provided, regardless of the outcome of the research and development; and

(b)   whether, even though the contract does not require the enterprise to repay any of the funds provided, surrounding conditions indicate that repayment is probable.

Definitions

5.   **The following terms are used in this Statement with the meanings specified:**

Research is original and planned investigation undertaken with the prospect of gaining new scientific or technical knowledge and understanding.

Development is the translation of research findings or other knowledge into a plan or design for the production of new or substantially improved materials, devices, products, processes, systems or services prior to the commencement of commercial production or use.

6.   Although the nature of activities encompassed by research and development is generally understood, it may be difficult in practice to identify those activities in particular instances. While the above definitions should assist enterprises in this regard, the identification of research and development activities often depends on the type of business, how the business is organised and the type of projects undertaken.

7.   The following are examples of activities that are typically included in research:

(a)   activities aimed at the discovery of new knowledge;

(b)   the search for applications of new research findings or other knowledge;

(c)   the formulation and design of possible new or improved product or process alternatives; and

(d)   the search for product or process alternatives.

8.   The following are examples of activities that are typically included in development:

(a)   the evaluation of product or process alternatives;

(b)   the design, construction and testing of pre-production prototypes and models;

(c)   the design of tools, jigs, moulds and dies involving new technology; and

(d)   the design, construction and operation of a pilot plant that is not of a scale economically feasible for commercial production.

9.   The following are examples of activities that may be closely associated with research and development activities but that are not research and development:

(a)   engineering follow-through in an early phase of commercial production;

(b)   quality control during commercial production, including routine testing of products;

(c)   trouble-shooting in connection with breakdowns during commercial production;

(d)   routine efforts to refine, enrich or otherwise improve upon the qualities of an existing product;

(e)   adaptation of an existing capability to a particular requirement or customer's need as part of a continuing commercial activity;

(f)   seasonal or other periodic design changes to existing products;

(g)   routine design of tools, jigs, moulds and dies; and

(h)   activities, including design and construction engineering, related to the construction, relocation, rearrangement, or start-up of facilities or equipment other than facilities or equipment whose sole use is for a particular research and development project.

Components of Costs

10.   Research and development costs should include, where applicable:

(a)   the salaries, wages and other employment related costs of personnel engaged in research and development activities;

(b)   the costs of materials and services consumed in research and development activities;

(c)   the depreciation of property, plant and equipment to the extent that they are used for research and development activities;

(d)   overhead costs related to research and development activities; and

(e)   other costs, such as the amortisation of patents and licences to the extent that they are used for research and development activities.

11.   There can be practical difficulties in deciding the amounts of the costs specifically attributable to research and development activities. In order to achieve a reasonable degree of comparability among enterprises, and among accounting periods of the same enterprise, it is necessary to identify the components of research and development costs.

12.   The allocation of overhead costs related to research and development activities is made on bases similar to those used in allocating overhead costs of inventories (see International Accounting Standard 2, Inventories). Selling expenses and general administrative overheads are not allocated. The extent to which borrowing costs are included in the costs of research and development activities is determined in accordance with International Accounting Standard 23, Capitalisation of Borrowing Costs.

Recognition

13.   The allocation of costs of research and development activities to different accounting periods is determined by the relationship between the costs and the economic benefits which are expected to be derived from these activities. When, as a result of undertaking these activities, it is probable that the related costs will give rise to future economic benefits and the costs can be measured reliably, the costs qualify for recognition as an asset. This Statement identifies the criteria which need to be met before these recognition tests are satisfied.

Research Costs

14.   **Research costs should be recognised as an expense of the period in which they are incurred and should not be subsequently recognised as an asset.**

15.   It is not usually possible to identify specific economic benefits as a result of having undertaken research activities. Accordingly, all the costs of research activities are recognised as an expense in the period in which they are incurred.

Development Costs

16.   **The development costs of a project should be recognised as an asset when: (a) the product or process is clearly defined and the costs attributable to the product or process can be separately identified and measured reliably; and (b).all the following criteria are satisfied:**

(i)   **the technical feasibility of the product or process is reasonably assured;**

(ii)   **the enterprise intends to produce and market, or use, the product or process;**

(iii)   **the existence of a market for the product or process or, if it is to be used internally rather than sold, its usefulness to the enterprise, is reasonably assured; and**

(iv)   **adequate resources exist, or are reasonably assured to be available, to complete the project and market or use the product or process.**

17.   **The development costs of a project recognised as an asset in accordance with paragraph 16 should be limited to the amount that, taken together with further development costs, related production costs, and selling and administrative costs directly incurred in marketing the product, is probable of being recovered from related future revenues.**

18.   **To the extent that development costs are not recognised as an asset in accordance with paragraphs 16 and 17, they should be recognised as an expense of the period in which they are incurred and should not be subsequently recognised as an asset.**

19.   In the case of development activities, while an asset might be readily identifiable, the asset recognition criteria may not be met because there is a high degree of uncertainty of future economic benefits. In such cases.

development costs are recognised as an expense in the period in which they are incurred.

20.   The economic benefits derived from development activities include revenue from the sale of the product or process and cost savings resulting from the use of the product or process by the enterprise itself. Estimates of these revenues and cost savings and further development and other costs are based on prices or conditions prevailing at the balance sheet date. However, estimates of future revenues are based on lower future prices when it is probable that the reduction in these future prices will not be fully offset by reductions in related costs.

21.   Application of asset recognition criteria for development costs involves an assessment of the uncertainties that inevitably surround development activities. Such uncertainties are recognised by the exercise of prudence when making the judgements needed in determining the amount of development costs which should be recognised as an asset. This exercise of prudence does not permit the deliberate understatement of assets.

Amortisation of Development Costs

22.   **The development costs of a project recognised as an asset should be allocated on a systematic and rational basis to current and future accounting periods by reference either to the sale or use of the product or process or to the time period over which the product or process is expected to be sold or used.**

23.   The association of costs of development activities with future economic benefits can usually only be broadly and indirectly determined because of the nature of the activities. Therefore, allocation procedures are used to recognise these costs as expenses in the accounting periods in which the economic benefits are recognised.

24.   Technological and economic obsolescence creates uncertainties that restrict the number of units and the time period over which development costs recognised as an asset are to be allocated. Furthermore, it is usually difficult to estimate the further costs and related future revenues of a new product or process beyond a short period. For these reasons, development costs are normally amortised over a period that does not exceed five years. Amortisation commences when the product or process is available for sale or use.

Impairment of Development Costs

25.   **When the criteria in paragraph 16, which previously justified the recognition of the development costs as an asset, no longer apply, the unamortised balance should be recognised as an expense immediately. When the criteria for recognition as an asset continue to be met but the amount of development costs (and other relevant costs as set out in paragraph 17) that is probable of being recovered from related future revenues is exceeded by the unamortised balance of such costs, the excess should be recognised immediately as an expense.**

26.   **When the uncertainties which had led to the recognition of development costs as an expense in accordance with paragraph 25 no longer exist, such costs should not be reinstated as an asset.**

27.   The unamortised balance of development costs of a project recognised as an asset is reviewed at the end of each accounting period. Circumstances or events may indicate that the unamortised balance no longer meets the criteria for recognition as an asset or that it exceeds the expected future economic benefits. In such cases, the unamortised balance is recognised as an expense in the current period to the extent that it cannot be recovered from the expected future economic benefits.

Disclosure

28.   **The following should be disclosed:**

(a)   **the accounting policies adopted for the costs of research and development activities;**

(b)   **the amortisation methods used;**

(c)   **the useful lives or amortisation rates used;**

(d)   **the amount of research and development costs recognised as an expense in the period; and**

(e)   **the movements in, and the balance of, unamortised development costs.**

29.   It is important that users of financial statements have information to enable them to assess the nature and significance of research and development activities to the enterprise itself and in relation to the research and development activities of other enterprises.

30.   The amount disclosed in accordance with paragraph 28(d) includes:

(a)   research and development costs recognised as an expense in accordance with paragraphs 14 and 18;

(b)   amortisation of development costs in accordance with paragraph 22; and

(c)   development costs recognised as an expense in accordance with paragraph 25.

31.   The disclosure described in paragraph 28(e) consists of a reconciliation of the amounts of unamortised development costs at the beginning and end of an accounting period showing development costs recognised as an asset, development costs recognised as an expense (in accordance with paragraphs 22 and 25) and other changes.

32.   Further information which might usefully be provided is a description of the research and development activities of the enterprise.

Transitional Provisions

33.   **When the adoption of this Statement constitutes a change in accounting policy, an enterprise is encouraged to adjust its financial statements in accordance with International Accounting Standard 8, Unusual and Prior Period Items and Changes in Accounting Policies. Alternatively, enterprises should recognise as an asset only those development costs incurred after the effective date of the Statement which meet the criteria in paragraphs 16 and 17.**

Effective Date

34.   **This Statement becomes operative for financial statements covering periods beginning on or after _____.**

Inventories

IAS 2 allows a free choice between the use of FIFO, weighted average cost, LIFO and the base stock method for the assignment of costs to inventories. E32 proposed that the base stock method should be eliminated, and that FIFO and the weighted average cost should be the benchmark treatment and LIFO an allowed alternative treatment.

After considering the comments on E32, the Board decided that it should require the use of FIFO or weighted average cost and eliminate both LIFO and the base stock method. This position was reflected in the Statement of Intent on the Comparability of Financial Statements.

E38 incorporates the elimination of the use of the LIFO and Base Stock formulas of assigning costs to inventories set out in the Statement of Intent on the Comparability of Financial Statements. It also proposes other improvements to IAS 2 to ensure that the Standard is sufficiently detailed and complete and contains adequate disclosure requirements to meet the needs of capital markets and the international business community.

At its meeting in October 1992, following its review of the comments on E38 and its reconsideration of the issue, the Board decided to require the use of FIFO or weighted average cost (benchmark treatment), with the LIFO as the allowed alternative. This is the same approach as that proposed in E32 and will be reflected in the revised IAS 2.

The Board is dealing with the Statement of Intent as a package. Therefore, its approval of the revised Standards is subject to its later approval of the revised Standards incorporating the other changes in the Statement of Intent. All the revised Standards will come into effect on the same date.

Exposure Draft

Contents

International Accounting Standard -- Inventories

International Accounting Standard --

Inventories

The standards, which have been set in bold type, should be read in the context of the background material and implementation guidance and in the context of the Preface to International Accounting Standards. International Accounting Standards are not intended to apply to immaterial items (see paragraph 12 of the Preface).

Introduction

A primary issue in accounting for inventories is the nature and extent of costs to be recognised as an asset and carried forward until the related revenues are recognised. The cost of inventories includes all costs incurred in bringing them to the location and condition necessary for their intended use or sale. The amount recognised as an asset is reduced to the extent it exceeds net realisable value.

Scope

1. This Statement deals with the accounting for and disclosure of inventories in financial statements in the context of the historical cost system.

2. This Statement does not deal with:

(a) costs incurred under construction contracts in progress including directly related service contracts (see International Accounting Standard 11, Accounting for Construction Contracts);

(b) producers' inventories of agricultural products and of mineral ores, certain aspects of which are dealt with in International Accounting Standard 18, Revenue Recognition; and

(c) financial instruments (see Exposure Draft 40, Financial Instruments).

Definitions

3.　　The following terms are used in this Statement with the meanings specified.

<u>Inventories</u> are assets in the form of goods, property or services (a) held for sale in the ordinary course of business, (b) in the process of production for such sale, or (c) to be consumed in the production of goods for sale or in the rendering of services.

<u>Historical cost</u> of inventories is the aggregate of costs of purchase, costs of conversion and other costs incurred in bringing the inventories to their present location and condition.

<u>Net realisable value</u> is the estimated selling price in the ordinary course of business less the costs of completion and the costs which it is necessary to incur in order to make the sale.

4.　　The definition of inventories encompasses the work in progress of an enterprise. In the case of a service provider, inventories include the element of partially completed services rendered for which the enterprise has yet to recognise related service revenue in accordance with International Accounting Standard 18, Revenue Recognition.

Measurement

5.　　Inventories should be measured at the lower of historical cost and net realisable value.

6.　　The historical cost of inventories of goods or property may not be realisable if their selling prices have declined, if they are damaged, or if they have become wholly or partially obsolete. The historical cost of inventories of a service provider is not realisable if it exceeds the related consideration to be received for the services being rendered. The practice of writing inventories down below historical cost to net realisable value accords with the view that current assets should not be carried in excess of amounts expected to be realised from their sale or use.

7.　　Inventories are written down to net realisable value item by item or by groups of similar or related items; whichever method is used is consistently applied. Service providers generally accumulate costs in respect of each service for which a separate selling price will be charged. Therefore, each such service is treated as a separate item. Items of inventory relating to the same product line that have similar purposes or end uses, are produced and marketed in the same geographical area, and cannot be practicably evaluated separately from other items in that product line are an example of those that are written down on a group basis. The practice of writing inventories down based on a classification of inventory, for example, finished goods, or all the inventories of an industry or a geographical segment, is not appropriate.

8.   When circumstances which previously caused inventories to be written down below cost no longer exist, the cost of the inventories is reinstated to the extent that it is realisable.   An example of such circumstances is when an item of inventory is carried at net realisable value because its selling price has declined and, in a subsequent accounting period, that item is still on hand and its selling price has increased. A new assessment is made of net realisable value in the subsequent period. The new carrying amount is the lower of the historical cost and the revised net realisable value.

Historical Cost of Inventories

9.   The costs of purchase of inventories comprise the purchase price, import duties and other taxes (other than those subsequently recoverable), transport and handling costs, and any other costs directly attributable to the acquisition of materials and services. Trade discounts, rebates and subsidies are deducted in determining the costs of purchase.

10.   Advance payments on the purchase of inventories may be included in the costs of purchase.   The costs of purchase of inventories invoiced in a foreign currency may also include foreign exchange differences resulting from a severe devaluation or from depreciation of a currency against which there is no practical means of hedging in accordance with an allowed alternative treatment in International Accounting Standard 21, Accounting for the Effects of Changes in Foreign Exchange Rates.

11.   The costs of conversion of inventories include costs directly related to the units of production, such as direct labour.   They also include a systematic allocation of fixed and variable production overheads that relate to bringing the inventories to their present location and condition.   Fixed production overheads are those indirect costs of production that remain relatively constant regardless of the volume of production, such as depreciation and maintenance of factory buildings and equipment, and the cost of factory management and administration.   Variable production overheads are those indirect costs of production that vary directly, or nearly directly, with the volume of production, such as indirect materials and labour.

12.   The allocation of fixed production overheads to the costs of conversion is based on the normal capacity of the production facilities. Normal capacity is the production expected to be achieved on average over a number of periods or seasons. The actual level of production may be used if it approximates normal capacity. The proportion of overhead allocated

to a unit of production is not increased as a consequence of low production or idle plant. Overheads which are not allocated, are recognised as an expense in the period incurred. In periods of abnormally high production, the proportion of overhead allocated to a unit of production is decreased so that inventories are not measured above historical cost.

13.   Overheads other than production overheads are included in the cost of inventories only to the extent that they clearly contribute to bringing the inventories to their present location and condition. For example, it may be appropriate to include costs incurred in designing products for specific customers or a proportion of the overhead costs of a manager who is involved in both production and non-production functions.

14.   The extent to which borrowing costs are included in the cost of inventories is determined in accordance with International Accounting Standard 23, Capitalisation of Borrowing Costs.

15.   The cost of inventories of a service provider consists primarily of the labour and other costs of personnel directly engaged in providing the service, including supervisory personnel and attributable overheads. Labour and other costs relating to sales and general administrative personnel are not included. Personnel engaged in providing services often share the same premises as sales and administrative personnel. In these circumstances, overhead costs are apportioned between those attributable to service, which are included in the cost of inventories, and those attributable to sales and administration, which are recognised as an expense in the period incurred.

16.   The following are examples of items that are excluded from the cost of inventories:

(a)   abnormal amounts of wasted material, labour, or other expenses;

(b)   storage costs, unless those costs are necessary in the production process prior to a further production stage;

(c)   administrative overheads that are not related to production; and

(d)   selling expenses.

17.   Techniques for measuring the cost of inventories, such as the standard cost method or the retail method, may be used for convenience if the results obtained approximate historical cost. Standard costs take into account normal levels of efficiency and of capacity utilisation. They are

regularly reviewed and, if necessary, revised in the light of current conditions.

18.   The retail method is often used in the retail industry for measuring inventories of large numbers of rapidly changing items, when margins are similar and other costing methods are impracticable. The cost of the inventory is determined by reducing the sales value of the inventory by the appropriate percentage gross margin. The percentage used takes into consideration inventory which has been marked down to below its original selling price. An average percentage for each retail department is often used.

Cost Formulas

19.   Inventories of items that are not ordinarily interchangeable and goods or services produced and segregated for specific projects should be accounted for by using specific identification of their individual costs. The first-in, first-out (FIFO) or weighted average cost formulas should be used for assigning costs to all other inventories.

20.   Specific identification is a formula that attributes specific costs to identified items of inventory. This is an appropriate treatment for goods or services that have been bought or produced and are segregated for a specific project. However, when there are large numbers of items of inventory which are ordinarily interchangeable, the formula is not appropriate because the selection of items could be made in such a way as to obtain predetermined effects on profit.

21.   The FIFO and weighted average cost formulas make specific assumptions about the flow of interchangeable items, and their associated costs, through inventory. The FIFO formula assumes that the items of inventory which were purchased first are sold first, and consequently the items remaining in inventory at the balance sheet date are those most recently acquired or produced. Under the weighted average cost formula, the cost of each item is determined from the weighted average of the cost of similar items at the beginning of a period and the cost of similar items acquired during the period. The average may be calculated on a periodic basis, or as each additional shipment is received, depending upon the circumstances of the business.

Net Realisable Value

22.   Estimates of net realisable value are based on the most reliable evidence available at the time the estimates are made as to the amount of cash or cash equivalents the inventories are expected to realise. They do not reflect temporary fluctuations of price or cost. However, they do take into consideration fluctuations of price or cost occurring subsequent to the

balance sheet date to the extent that such fluctuations confirm conditions existing at the balance sheet date.

23.   Estimates of net realisable value also take into consideration the purpose for which the inventory is held. The net realisable value of the quantity of inventory held to satisfy firm sales or service contracts is based on the contract price. If the sales contracts are for less than the inventory quantities held, the net realisable value of the excess is based on general market prices. Contingent losses on firm sales contracts in excess of inventory quantities held and contingent losses on firm purchase contracts are dealt with in accordance with International Accounting Standard 10, Contingencies and Events Occurring After the Balance Sheet Date.

24.   Normal quantities of materials and other supplies held for incorporation in the production of goods are not written down below cost if the finished products in which they will be incorporated are expected to be realised at or above cost. Nevertheless, when a decline in the price of materials is an indication that the cost of the finished products will exceed net realisable value, the materials inventories are written down.   In some circumstances, replacement cost may be the best available measure of the net realisable value of those materials.

Recognition as an Expense

25.   The carrying amount of inventories sold should be recognised as an expense in the period in which the related revenue is recognised. The amount of any writedown of inventories to net realisable value and all other losses of inventories should be recognised as an expense in the period the writedown or loss occurs. The amount of any reinstatement of cost of inventories, arising from an increase in net realisable value, should be recognised as a reduction of expense in the period the reinstatement occurs.

26.   The process of recognising as an expense the amount of inventories sold is usually referred to as the matching of costs with revenues. Some inventories may be allocated to other asset accounts, for example, inventory used as a component of self-constructed property, plant or equipment. Inventories allocated to other asset accounts in this way are recognised as an expense during the useful life of the asset.

Disclosure

27.   The following should be disclosed:

(a)   **the accounting policies adopted for the purpose of measuring inventories, including the cost formulas used;**

(b) the total amount of inventories and the amounts in classifications appropriate to the business;

(c) the amount of inventories pledged as security for liabilities;

(d) the amount recognised as an expense or as income during the period in respect of inventories written down to net realisable value, net of reinstatements of cost; and

(e) either:

   (i) the cost of inventories sold during the period, or

   (ii) the operating costs, applicable to revenues, recognised as an expense during the period, classified by their nature.

28. Information about the amounts held in different classifications of inventories and the extent of the changes from period to period is useful to financial statement users. Common classifications of inventories are raw materials, work in progress, finished goods, merchandise, and production supplies. The inventories of a service provider may simply be described as work in progress.

29. The cost of inventories sold includes those costs previously included in the measurement of the items of inventory sold. It also includes unallocated production overheads and abnormal amounts of production costs of inventories. The circumstances of the enterprise may warrant the inclusion of other costs, such as distribution costs.

30. Instead of disclosing the cost of inventories sold, some enterprises disclose the amounts of operating costs, applicable to revenues for the period, classified by their nature. In this case, the enterprise discloses the amounts of costs incurred for materials, labour and other expenses together with the amount of the net change in inventories for the period.

Effective Date

31. This Statement becomes operative for financial statements covering periods beginning on or after _____.

Capitalisation of Borrowing Costs

IAS 23 allows a free choice between the capitalisation and expensing for those borrowing costs that relate to expenditures on assets that take a substantial period to get ready for their intended use or sale. E32 proposed the expensing of all such costs (benchmark treatment), with capitalisation as the allowed alternative.

After considering the comments on E32, the Board decided that it should require the capitalisation of these borrowing costs. This position was reflected in the Statement of Intent.

E39 incorporates the treatment of borrowing costs set out in the Statement of Intent. It also proposes other improvements to IAS 23 to ensure that the Standard is sufficiently detailed and complete and contains adequate disclosure requirements to meet the needs of capital markets and the international business community.

At its meeting in October 1992, following its review of the comments on E39, and its reconsideration of the issue, the Board decided to require the expensing of all borrowing costs (benchmark treatment) and the capitalisation of borrowing costs in certain circumstances (allowed alternative treatment). This is the same approach as that proposed in E32 and will be reflected in the revised IAS 23.

The Board is dealing with the Statement of Intent as a package. Therefore, its approval of the revised Standards is subject to its later approval of the revised Standards incorporating the other changes in the Statement of Intent. All the revised Standards will come into effect on the same date.

Contents

International Accounting Standard --
Capitalisation of Borrowing Costs

International Accounting Standard --

Capitalisation of Borrowing Costs

The standards, which have been set in bold type, should be read in the context of the background material and implementation guidance and in the context of the Preface to International Accounting Standards. International Accounting Standards are not intended to apply to immaterial items (see paragraph 12 of the Preface).

Introduction

The primary issue in accounting for borrowing costs is the extent to which such costs form part of the historical cost of an asset or are to be recognised as an expense when incurred. The historical cost of an asset includes all costs incurred in bringing it to the condition and location necessary for its intended use or sale. Therefore, borrowing costs incurred during the acquisition, construction or production of an asset are part of the historical cost of the asset. However, when there is only a short period of time between the commencement of incurrence of costs and when the asset is ready for sale or use, capitalisation of borrowing costs does not significantly enhance the comparability or usefulness of information.

Scope

1.   This Statement deals with the capitalisation of borrowing costs as a part of the historical cost of acquiring, producing or constructing certain assets.

2.   This Statement does not deal with the capitalisation of actual or imputed costs of equity, including preferred capital that is not classified as a liability.

Definitions

3.   The following terms are used in this Statement with the meanings specified:

Borrowing costs are interest and other costs incurred by an enterprise in connection with the borrowing of funds.

A qualifying asset is an asset that necessarily takes a substantial period of time to get ready for its intended use or sale.

4.   Borrowing costs include:

(a)   interest on bank overdrafts and short and long-term borrowings;

(b)   amortisation of discount or premium relating to borrowings;

(c)   amortisation of ancillary costs incurred in connection with the arrangement of borrowings;

(d)   finance charges in respect of finance leases recognised in accordance with International Accounting Standard 17, Accounting for Leases; and

(e)   exchange differences arising from foreign currency borrowings to the extent that they are regarded as an adjustment to interest costs.

5.   Examples of qualifying assets include manufacturing plants, power generation facilities, investment properties and inventories that require a substantial period of time to bring them to saleable condition such as ships. Other investments, and those inventories that are routinely manufactured or otherwise produced in large quantities on a repetitive basis over a short period of time, are not qualifying assets.

Recognition

6.   An enterprise that has incurred borrowing costs and incurred expenditures on a qualifying asset should capitalise borrowing costs as part of the cost of that asset. The amount of borrowing costs capitalised should be determined by applying a capitalisation rate to expenditures on the acquisition, construction or production of the qualifying asset, subject to the overall limit established in paragraph 22.

7.   Borrowing costs should be recognised as an expense of the period in which they are incurred, except to the extent that they are capitalised in accordance with paragraph 6.

8.   The amount of borrowing costs to be capitalised is in principle that part of the borrowing costs incurred by an enterprise that would have been avoided if expenditures on a qualifying asset had not been made.

9.   Expenditures on a qualifying asset include only those expenditures that have resulted in payments of cash, transfers of other assets or incurrences of interest-bearing liabilities. The average carrying amount of the asset during the period, including borrowing costs previously capitalised,

is normally a reasonable approximation of such expenditures. Expenditures on a qualifying asset are reduced by any progress payments received and grants (see International Accounting Standard 20, Accounting for Government Grants and Disclosure of Government Assistance) received in connection with the asset.

10.   Capitalisation of borrowing costs continues throughout the period of acquisition, production or construction. When the carrying amount or the expected ultimate cost of the qualifying asset exceeds its recoverable amount or net realisable value, an adjustment is made to reduce the carrying amount in accordance with International Accounting Standard 2, Inventories, or International Accounting Standard 16, Property, Plant and Equipment. This treatment is followed in order to be consistent with the treatment of other costs capitalised as part of the carrying amount of the asset.

Commencement of Capitalisation

11.   The capitalisation of borrowing costs as part of the cost of a qualifying asset should commence when:

(a)   expenditures for the asset are being incurred;

(b)   borrowing costs are being incurred; and

(c)   activities that are necessary to prepare the asset for its intended use or sale are in progress.

12.   The activities necessary to prepare the asset for its intended use or sale are wide in scope. They encompass more than physical construction of the asset. They also include technical and administrative work prior to the commencement of physical construction, for example, activities to obtain permits. However, such activities exclude the holding of an asset when no process of production or development that changes the asset's condition, is taking place. For example, borrowing costs incurred while land is under development are capitalised during the period in which activities related to the development are being undertaken. However, borrowing costs incurred while land acquired for building purposes is held, without any associated development activity, do not qualify for capitalisation.

Suspension of Capitalisation

13.   Capitalisation of borrowing costs should be suspended during extended periods in which active development is interrupted.

14.   Borrowing costs incurred during an extended period when the activities that are necessary to prepare an asset for its intended use or sale are interrupted are costs of holding partially completed assets. Such costs do not qualify for capitalisation. However, capitalisation of borrowing costs is not normally suspended during a period when substantial technical and administrative work is being carried out. Capitalisation of borrowing costs is also not suspended when a delay is a necessary part of the process of getting an asset ready for its intended use or sale or is otherwise unavoidable. For example, capitalisation continues during the extended period needed for a product to mature or the extended period during which high water levels delay construction of a bridge.

Cessation of Period for Capitalisation

15.   Capitalisation of borrowing costs should cease when the qualifying asset is ready for its intended use or sale.

16.   An asset is ready for its intended use or sale when substantially all the activities necessary to prepare it for use or sale are complete. Such activities include, where appropriate, technical and administrative work necessary after completion of physical construction. The capitalisation period ceases at the earlier of the actual or intended date of achieving a commercial level of use. Thus, for example, borrowing costs are capitalised during a reasonable initial period to lease an investment property to a minimum occupancy level. However, capitalisation of borrowing costs does not continue merely because the enterprise has yet to undertake minor works which cannot be carried out until use is about to begin or sale is about to take place, such as the decoration of a property to the purchaser's specification.

17.   When the construction of a qualifying asset is completed in parts and each part is capable of being used while construction continues on other parts, capitalisation of borrowing costs should cease on each part as it is completed.

18.   An example of a part that is usable while construction continues on other parts of an asset is a business park comprising several buildings that can be used individually. An example of an asset that needs to be complete before it can be used is an industrial plant involving several processes which are carried out in sequence at different units within the same site, such as a steel mill.

Determination of Capitalisation Rate

19.   The capitalisation rate should be determined by relating the borrowing costs incurred during a period to the borrowings outstanding during that period. When a new borrowing is associated with expenditures on the acquisition, construction or production of a specific qualifying asset, the capitalisation rate should be determined on the basis of the actual borrowing costs incurred on that borrowing.

20.   When a new borrowing is associated with a specific qualifying asset and the amount of the expenditures on the asset exceeds the amount of the associated borrowings, the capitalisation rate applied to the excess is the weighted average of the rates applicable to the other borrowings of the enterprise.

21.   In a group of companies various problems may exist in identifying the borrowings from which the capitalisation rate is determined. Such problems can arise from the complexities of borrowing money in different countries at varying rates of interest and lending that money on various bases throughout the group. Other complications arise through loans denominated in or linked to foreign currencies, by group operations in highly inflationary economies, or by fluctuating exchange rates. In some circumstances, it may be appropriate to include all borrowings of the parent and its consolidated subsidiaries when computing a weighted average rate; in other circumstances, it may be appropriate for each subsidiary to use a weighted average of the rates applicable to its own borrowings. Selection of a capitalisation rate requires judgement to determine a reasonable measure of the cost of borrowing in terms of costs incurred that could otherwise have been avoided.

Overall Limit on the Amount Capitalised

22.   The amount of borrowing costs capitalised during a period should not exceed the total amount of borrowing costs incurred, less interest income earned, by the enterprise in that period. In consolidated financial statements, the amount should not exceed the consolidated amount of borrowing costs less interest income.

Disclosure

23.   The amount of borrowing costs that have been capitalised during the period should be disclosed.

Transitional Provisions

24. When the adoption of this Statement constitutes a change in accounting policy, an enterprise is encouraged to adjust its financial statements in accordance with International Accounting Standard 8, Unusual and Prior Period Items and Changes in Accounting Policies. Alternatively, enterprises should capitalise only those borrowing costs incurred after the effective date of the Statement which meet the criteria for capitalisation.

Effective Date

25. This Statement becomes operative for financial statements covering periods beginning on or after _____.

Revenue Recognition

This draft incorporates the changes to International Accounting Standard 18 as set out in the Statement of Intent on the Comparability of Financial Statements. It also proposes other improvements to IAS 18 to ensure that the Standard is sufficiently detailed and complete and contains adequate disclosure requirements to meet the needs of capital markets and the international business community.

As indicated in the Statement of Intent the Board does not intend to reconsider the issues which were exposed for comment in E32 and subsequently approved by the Board without substantive change.

The Board is expected to approve a revised International Accounting Standard 8, Revenue Recognition, in March 1993.

Contents

International Accounting Standard -- Revenue Recognition

International Accounting Standard --

Revenue Recogntion

The standards, which have been set in bold italic type, should be read in the context of the background material and implementation guidance and in the context of the Preface to International Accounting Standards. International Accounting Standards are not intended to apply to immaterial items (see paragraph 12 of the Preface).

Introduction

The primary issue in accounting for revenue is determining when to recognise revenue. Revenue is recognised when it is probable that future economic benefits will flow to the enterprise and the revenue can be measured reliably. This Statement identifies the circumstances in which these criteria will be met and, therefore, revenue will be recognised.

Scope

1. This Statement should be applied in the recognition of revenue arising from:

- *the sale of goods held for resale;*

- *the rendering of services; and*

- *the use by others of enterprise resources yielding interest, royalties and dividends.*

2. This Statement does not deal with revenue arising from:

(a) construction contracts (see Proposed International Accounting Standard, E42, Construction Contracts);

(b) lease agreements (see International Accounting Standard 17, Accounting for Leases);

(c) dividends arising from investments which are accounted for under the equity method (see International Accounting Standard 28, Accounting for Investments in Associates);

(d) insurance contracts of insurance companies;

(e) changes in the fair value of financial assets and financial liabilities (see Proposed International Accounting Standard, E40, Financial Instruments);

(f) changes in the value of other current assets;

(g)   natural increases in herds, and agricultural and forest products; and

(h)   the extraction of mineral ores.

Definitions

3.   The following terms are used in this Statement with the meanings specified:

Revenue is the inflow of cash, cash equivalents, receivables or other consideration, or decreases in liabilities, arising in the course of the ordinary activities of an enterprise and on its own account.

Fair value is the amount for which an asset could be exchanged, or a liability settled, between knowledgeable, willing parties in an arm's length transaction.

4.   Income encompasses both revenue and gains. Revenue arises in the course of the ordinary activities of an enterprise and is referred to by a variety of different names including sales, fees, interest, dividends, royalties and rent.

5.   This Statement does not deal with income arising from:

(a)   the disposal of subsidiaries, lines of business, or industry segments;

(b)   the disposal of, and changes in the value of, noncurrent assets;

(c)   changes in foreign exchange rates and adjustments arising on the translation of foreign currency financial statements (see Proposed International Accounting Standard, E44, The Effects of Changes in Foreign Exchange Rates);

(d)   the discharge of a liability at less than its carrying amount;

(e)   the restatement of the carrying amount of a liability; and

(f)   government grants and other similar subsidies (see International Accounting Standard 20, Accounting for Government Grants and Disclosure of Government Assistance).

6.   The amount of revenue arising on a transaction is usually determined by agreement between the enterprise and the buyer. It is measured at the fair value of the consideration received or receivable by the enterprise less the amount of any trade discounts and volume rebates allowed by the enterprise. In most cases, the consideration is cash or cash equivalents and the amount of revenue is the amount of cash or cash equivalents received or receivable.

7. When the inflow of the cash or cash equivalents is deferred the fair value of the consideration is less than the nominal amount of cash or cash equivalents. For example, an enterprise may provide interest free credit or may accept a note receivable bearing a below-market interest rate as consideration for the sale of goods. In such circumstances, the fair value of the consideration may be determined by discounting all future receipts using an imputed rate of interest. The imputed rate of interest is:

(a) the prevailing rate for a similar instrument of an issuer with a similar credit rating; or

(b) a rate of interest that discounts the nominal amount of the instrument to the current cash sales price of the goods or services, whichever is the more clearly determinable.

The difference between the fair value and the nominal amount of the consideration is recognised as interest revenue in accordance with paragraphs 25 and 26 .

8. In some cases, the consideration is non-monetary assets or services. When goods or services are exchanged or swapped for similar goods or services in the same line of business and they have a similar value the exchange is not regarded as a transaction which generates revenue. However, in all other cases when goods are sold or services are rendered in exchange for dissimilar goods or services the amount of revenue is the fair value of the goods or services given up or the fair value of the goods or services received, whichever is more clearly evident.

9. Revenue includes only those amounts received by the enterprise on its own account. Amounts collected on behalf of third parties such as sales taxes, goods and services taxes and value added taxes are not economic benefits which flow to the enterprise. Therefore, they are excluded from revenue. Similarly, in an agency relationship, the gross inflows of cash, cash equivalents, receivables or other consideration, or decreases in liabilities, are not economic benefits which flow to the enterprise. Instead, revenue is the amount of commission.

Identification of the Transaction

10. The timing of revenue recognition reflects the substance of the transaction. To achieve this it may be necessary to apply the recognition criteria to the separately identifiable components of a single transaction. For example, a financial institution may charge a fee which is intended both to recover loan origination costs incurred and to compensate for a below market interest rate on the loan; in such a case, each component of the fee may need to be accounted for separately. Conversely, it may be necessary to apply the recognition criteria to two or more transactions together. For example, an enterprise may sell goods and, at the same time, enter into a separate agreement to repurchase the goods at a later date, thus negating the substantive effect of the transaction; in such a case, the two transactions are dealt with together.

Sale of Goods Held for Resale

11.   Revenue should be recognised when the following conditions have been fulfilled:

(a)   the enterprise has transferred to the buyer the significant risks and rewards of ownership of the goods;

(b)   the enterprise retains no continuing managerial involvement in, or effective control over, the goods transferred;

(c)   the amount of revenue that will be derived from the sale of the goods can be measured reliably;

(d)   it is probable that, at the time of the sale, the enterprise will receive the revenue; and

(e)   the costs incurred or to be incurred in respect of the transaction can be measured reliably.

12. The assessment of when an enterprise has transferred the significant risks and rewards of ownership to the buyer requires an examination of the circumstances of the transaction. In most cases, the transfer of the risks and rewards coincides with the transfer of the legal title or the passing of possession to the buyer. This is the case for most retail sales. In other cases, the transfer of risks and rewards of ownership occurs at a different time from the transfer of legal title or the passing of possession.

13.   If the enterprise retains significant risks of ownership, the transaction is not a sale and revenue is not recognised. An enterprise may retain a significant risk of ownership in a number of ways. For example, it may retain an obligation for unsatisfactory performance not covered by normal warranty provisions. It may give the buyer an unlimited right to return the goods. Alternatively, the receipt of the revenue may be contingent on the derivation of revenue by the buyer from its sale of the goods.

14.   An enterprise may retain only an insignificant risk of ownership. For example, a seller may retain the legal title to the goods solely to protect the collectability of the amount due. If the enterprise has transferred the significant risks and rewards of ownership, the transaction is a sale and revenue is recognised.

15.   Revenue is recognised only when it is probable that the enterprise will receive the revenue. In some cases, it may not be probable until the cash is received or when an uncertainty is removed, for example, when permission is granted by a foreign governmental authority to remit the proceeds from a transaction in a foreign country. However, when an uncertainty about the receipt of the revenue arises after the revenue has been recognised, the uncollectable amount is recognised as an expense, rather than as a reduction of the amount of revenue originally recognised.

16.   Revenue and expenses that result from the same transaction or other event are recognised simultaneously; this process is commonly referred to as the matching of revenues and expenses. The costs incurred or to be incurred, including warranties and other costs to be incurred after the shipment of the goods, from most transactions can be measured reliably when the revenue otherwise qualifies for recognition. However, when the costs cannot be measured reliably, revenue cannot be recognised; in such circumstances, any consideration already received is recognised as a liability.

Rendering of Services

17. When the outcome of a transaction involving the rendering of services can be reliably estimated, revenue should be recognised by reference to the stage of completion of the transaction at the balance sheet date. The outcome of a transaction can be reliably estimated when all the following conditions are satisfied:

(a) the amount of the revenue that will be derived from the transaction can be measured reliably;

(b) it is probable that the enterprise will receive the revenue that will be derived from the transaction;

(c) both the costs to complete and stage of completion of the transaction at the balance sheet date can be measured reliably; and

(d) the costs incurred for the transaction can be clearly identified so that actual experience can be compared with prior estimates.

18. The recognition of revenue by reference to the stage of completion of a transaction is often referred to as the percentage of completion method. The recognition of revenue on this basis provides useful information on the extent of service activity and performance of an enterprise in a period. Proposed International Accounting Standard, E42, Construction Contracts, also requires the recognition of revenue on this basis. The procedures set out in that proposed Standard are generally applicable to the recognition of revenue for a transaction involving the rendering of services.

19. The assessment of the outcome of the transaction usually involves the use of estimates. An enterprise is generally able to make reliable estimates only when it has agreed the following with the other parties to the transaction:

(a) each party's enforceable rights regarding the service to be provided and received by the parties;

(b) the consideration to be exchanged; and

(c) the manner and terms of settlement.

In order to make reliable estimates, it is often necessary for the enterprise to have an effective internal financial budgeting and reporting system in order that it make reliable estimates. These estimates are revised as the service is performed; however, the fact that circumstances may necessitate periodic revision of estimates does not indicate that the outcome of the contract cannot be measured reliably.

20. The stage of completion of a transaction may be determined in a variety of ways. They include:

(a) surveys work performed;

(b) the proportion that associated costs incurred to date bear to estimated total costs of the transaction;

(c) the proportion of the number of acts completed to the total number of acts to complete the transaction; or

(d) by a combination of different ways.

For practical purposes, when services are provided by an indeterminate number of acts over a specified period of time, revenue is recognised on a straight line basis over the specified period unless there is evidence that some other method better represents the stage of completion. When a specific act is much more significant than any other acts, the recognition of revenue is postponed until the significant act is executed.

21. *When the outcome of the transaction involving the rendering of services cannot be reliably estimated, revenue should be recognised only to the extent of the expenses recognised that are recoverable.*

22. Although the outcome of a transaction cannot be measured reliably, it may be probable that the enterprise will recover the costs incurred. This is often the case, for example, during the early stages of a transaction. In such circumstances, revenue is recognised to the extent of costs incurred that are recoverable.

23. When the outcome of a transaction cannot be reliably estimated and the recoverability of the costs incurred is not probable, revenue is not recognised. When the uncertainties that prevented the recognition of revenue no longer exist, revenue is recognised in accordance with paragraph 17.

Interest, Royalties and Dividends

24. The use by others of enterprise resources gives rise to:

(a) interest - charges for the use of cash resources or for amounts due to the enterprise;

(b) royalties - charges for the use of long-term assets held by the enterprise, for example, patents, trademarks, copyrights and computer software; and

(c) dividends - distributions of earnings to holders of equity investments in proportion to their holdings of a particular class of capital.

25. Revenue arising from the use by others of enterprise resources yielding interest, royalties and dividends should be recognised on the bases set out in paragraph 28 when:

(a) it is probable that the amount of revenue will be received; and

(b) the amount of the revenue can be measured reliably.

26. Interest should be recognised on a time proportion basis that takes into account the effective yield on the asset. Royalties should be recognised on an accrual basis in accordance with the substance of the relevant agreement. Dividends should be recognised when the shareholder's right to receive payment is established.

27.   The effective yield on an asset carried at historical cost is the rate of interest required to discount the stream of future cash receipts expected over the life of the asset to equate to the initial carrying amount of the asset. Interest revenue includes the amount of amortisation of any discount, premium or other difference between the initial carrying amount of a debt security and its amount at maturity.

28.   When an asset is carried at fair value, the focus of reporting is on the changes in fair value rather than on the asset's effective yield. In each reporting period, the adjustments to carrying amount from marking the asset to market and the accrued entitlement to receive interest together reflect the effective yield for the period. The periodic remeasurement of the asset incorporates an implicit amortisation of the fair value of any discount or premium. For purposes of this Statement, interest revenue comprises only the periodic cash receipts that are recognised as the entitlement to receive them accrues over time.

29.   When unpaid interest has accrued before the acquisition of an interest-bearing investment, the subsequent receipt of interest is allocated between pre-acquisition and post-acquisition periods; only the post-acquisition portion is recognised as revenue. When dividends on equity securities are declared from pre-acquisition net income, those dividends are deducted from the cost of the securities. If it is difficult to make such an allocation except on an arbitrary basis, dividends are recognised as revenue unless they clearly represent a recovery of part of the cost of the equity securities.

30.   Royalties accrue in accordance with the terms of the relevant agreement and are usually recognised on that basis unless, having regard to the substance of the agreement, it is more appropriate to recognise revenue on some other systematic and rational basis.

Disclosure

31.   The following should be disclosed:

(a)   the accounting policies adopted for the recognition of revenue; and

(b)   the amount of each significant category of revenue recognised during the period.

32.   The following should be disclosed for transactions involving the rendering of services:

(a)   the nature of the major components of revenues and costs;

(b)   the methods used to determine revenue, including the methods to determine the stage of completion of transactions in progress; and

(c)   each of the following relating to transactions in progress:

(i)   the aggregate amount of expenses recognised and estimated profits (less estimated losses) to date;

(ii)   the amount of progress billings to date;

(iii)   the net amount of costs incurred plus estimated profits less the sum of estimated losses and progress billings for all transactions for which costs incurred plus estimated profits (less estimated losses) exceed progress billings;

(iv)   the net amount of costs incurred plus estimated profits less the sum of estimated losses and progress billings for all transactions for which progress billings exceed costs incurred plus estimated profits (less estimated losses);

(v)   the amount of advances received; and

(vi)   the amount of retentions.

Effective Date

33.   This International Accounting Standard becomes operative for financial statements covering periods beginning on or after_____.

Appendix

The examples in this appendix illustrate the application of the International Accounting Standard to a number of commercial situations to assist in clarifying application of the International Accounting Standard. The examples focus on particular aspects of a transaction and are not a comprehensive discussion of all the relevant factors which might influence revenue recognition. Unless specifically referred to in the analysis of each situation, the examples assume that there is no significant uncertainty about the amount or collectability of the consideration to be received, the costs incurred or to be incurred or the extent to which goods may be returned. The examples do not modify or override the standards in the International Accounting Standard.

Sale of Goods Held for Resale

1. 'Bill and hold' sales, in which delivery is delayed at the buyer's request but the buyer takes title and accepts billing.

Revenue is recognised when the buyer takes title, provided:

(a)   it is probable that delivery will be made; and

(b)   the item is on hand, identified and ready for delivery to the buyer at the time the sale is recognised.

Revenue is not recognised when there is simply an intention to acquire or manufacture the goods in time for delivery.

2.   Goods shipped subject to conditions

(a)   installation and inspection

Revenue is normally recognised when the buyer accepts delivery, and installation and inspection are complete. However, revenue is recognised immediately the buyer accepts delivery when:

(i)   the installation process is simple in nature, for example the installation of a factory tested television receiver which only requires unpacking and connection of power and antennae; or

(ii)   the inspection is performed only for purposes of final determination of contract prices, for example, shipments of iron ore, sugar or soya beans.

(b)   on approval when, the buyer has negotiated a limited right of return

Revenue is recognised when the shipment has been formally accepted by the buyer or the goods have been delivered and the time period for rejection has elapsed.

(c)   guaranteed sales in which the seller has granted all buyers an unlimited right of return

In the case of normal retail sales (for example a chain store offering 'money back if not completely satisfied'), revenue is recognised at the time of sale provided the seller can reasonably estimate future returns and recognises a liability for returns based on previous experience and other relevant factors.

In other cases, the substance of the agreement may amount to a sale on consignment, in which case it should be treated as indicated below.

(d)   consignment sales under which the recipient (buyer) undertakes to sell the goods on behalf of the shipper (seller).

Revenue is recognised by the shipper when the goods are sold by the recipient to a third party.

(e)   cash on delivery sales

Revenue is recognised when delivery is made and cash is received by the seller or its agent.

3.   Lay away sales, under which the goods are delivered only when the buyer makes the final payment in a series of instalments.

Revenue from such sales is recognised when the goods are delivered. However, when experience indicates that most such sales are consumated, revenue may be recognised when a significant deposit is received provided the goods are on hand, identified and ready for delivery to the buyer.

4.   Orders when payment (or partial payment) is received in advance of delivery for goods not presently held in inventory, for example, the goods are still to be manufactured or will be delivered directly to the customer from a third party.

Revenue is recognised when the goods are delivered to the buyer.

5.   Sale and repurchase agreements (other than swap transactions) under which the seller concurrently agrees to repurchase the same goods at a later date, or when the seller has a call option to repurchase, or the buyer has a put option to require the repurchase, by the seller, of the goods.

The terms of the agreement need to be analysed to ascertain whether, in substance, the seller has transferred the risks and rewards of ownership to the buyer and hence revenue is recognised. When the seller has retained the risks and rewards of ownership, even though legal title has been transferred, the transaction is a financing arrangement and does not give rise to revenue.

6.   *Sales to intermediate parties, such as distributors, dealers or others for resale.*

Revenue from such sales is generally recognised when the risks and rewards of ownership have passed. However, when the buyer is acting, in substance as an agent, the sale is treated as a consignment sale.

7.   *Publication and other similar subscriptions.*

When the items involved are of similar value in each time period, revenue is recognised on a straight line basis over time. When the items vary in value from period to period, revenue is recognised on the basis of the sales value of the item despatched in relation to the total estimated sales value of all items covered by the subscription.

8.   *Instalment sales, under* which the consideration is receivable in instalments.

Revenue attributable to the sales price, exclusive of interest, is recognised at the date of sale. The sale price is the present value of the consideration, determined by discounting the instalments receivable at the imputed rate of interest. The interest element is recognised as revenue as it is earned, on a time proportion basis that takes into account the imputed rate of interest.

9.   *Real estate sales.*

Revenue is normally recognised when legal title passes to the buyer. However, in some jurisdictions the equitable interest in a property may vest in the buyer before legal title passes and therefore the risks and rewards of ownership have been transferred at that stage. In such cases, provided that the seller has no further substantial acts to complete under the contract, it may be appropriate to recognise revenue. In either case, if the seller is obliged to perform any significant acts after the transfer of the equitable and/or legal title, revenue is recognised as the acts are performed. An example is a building or other facility on which construction has not been completed.

In some cases, real estate may be sold with a degree of continuing involvement by the seller such that the risks and rewards of ownership have not been transferred. Examples are sale/repurchase agreements (including put and call options), and agreements whereby the seller guarantees occupancy of the property for a specified period, or guarantees a return on the buyer's investment for a specified period. In such cases, the nature and extent of the seller's continuing involvement determines how the transaction is accounted for. This may be as a sale, or as a financing, leasing or some other profit sharing arrangement. If it is treated as a sale, the continuing involvement may affect the timing of revenue recognition.

A seller must also consider the means of payment and evidence of the buyer's commitment to complete payment. For example, when the aggregate of the payments received, including the buyer's initial down payment, or continuing payments by the buyer, provide insufficient evidence of the buyer's commitment to complete payment, revenue is recognised only to the extent cash is received.

Rendering of Services

1.   Installation fees.

Installation fees are recognised as revenue by reference to the stage of completion of the installation, unless they are incidental to the sale of a product

2.   Servicing fees included in the price of the product.

When the selling price of a product includes an identifiable amount for subsequent servicing (for example, after sales support and product enhancement on the sale of software), that amount is deferred and recognised as revenue over the period during which the service is performed. The amount deferred is that which will cover the expected costs of the services under the agreement, together with a reasonable profit on those services.

3.   Advertising commissions.

Media commissions are recognised when the related advertisement or commercial appears before the public. Production commissions are recognised by reference to the stage of completion of the project.

4.   Insurance Agency Commissions

Insurance agency brokerage and commissions are recognised on the effective commencement or renewal dates of the related policies. Commission adjustments resulting from claims experience, policy cancellations, changes in premiums or changes in the coverage of policies written by the agent are recognised when they can be reliably estimated. When it is probable that the policy will need servicing during its life, the commission, or part thereof, is deferred and recognised as revenue over the period during which the servicing is performed.

5. *Financial service fees.*

The recognition of revenue for financial services fees depends on the purposes for which the fees are assessed and the basis of accounting for any associated financial instrument (see proposed International Accounting Standard E40, Financial Instruments). The description of fees for financial services may not be indicative of the nature and substance of the services provided. Therefore, it is necessary to distinguish between fees which are an integral part of the effective yield of a financial instrument, fees which are earned as services are provided, and fees which are earned on the execution of a significant act.

(a)   Fees which are an integral part of the effective yield of a financial instrument.

Such fees are generally treated as an adjustment to the effective yield. However, when the financial instrument is measured at fair value subsequent to its initial recognition the fees are recognised as revenue when the instrument is initially recognised.

(i)   Origination fees received by the enterprise relating to the creation or acquisition of a financial instrument which is held by the enterprise as an investment

Such fees may include compensation for activities such as evaluating the borrower's financial condition, evaluating and recording guarantees, collateral and other security arrangements, negotiating the terms of the instrument, preparing and processing documents and closing the transaction. These fees are an integral part of generating an ongoing involvement with the resultant financial instrument and, together with the related direct costs, are deferred and recognised as an adjustment to the effective yield.

(ii)   Commitment fees received by the enterprise to originate or purchase a loan.

If it is probable that the enterprise will enter into a specific lending arrangement, the commitment fee received is regarded as compensation for an ongoing involvement with the acquisition of a financial instrument and, together with the related direct costs, is deferred and recognised as an adjustment to the effective yield. If the commitment expires without the enterprise making the loan, the fee is recognised as revenue immediately.

(b)   Fees earned as services are provided

(i)   Fees charged for servicing a loan

Fees charged by an enterprise for servicing a loan are recognised as revenue as the services are provided. If the enterprise sells a loan but retains the servicing of that loan at a fee which is lower than a normal fee for such services, part of the sales price of the loan is deferred and recognised as revenue as the servicing is provided.

> (ii)   *Commitment fees to originate or purchase a loan*

If it is unlikely that a specific lending arrangement will be entered into, the commitment fee is recognised as revenue on a time proportion basis over the commitment period.

(c)   *Fees earned on the execution of a significant act, which is much more significant than any other acts*

The fees are recognised as revenue when the significant act has been completed, as in the examples below.

> (i)   *Commission on the allotment of shares to a client*

The commission is recognised as revenue when the shares have been allotted.

> (ii)   *Placement fees for arranging a loan between a borrower and an investor*

The fee is recognised as revenue when the loan has been arranged.

> (iii)   *Loan syndication fees*

It is necessary to distinguish between fees earned on completion of a significant act and fees related to future performance or risk retained. A syndication fee received by an enterprise which arranges a loan and which retains no part of the loan package for itself (or retains a part at the same effective yield for comparable risk as other participants) is compensation for the service of syndication. Such a fee is recognised as revenue when the syndication has been completed. However, when a syndicator retains a portion of the loan package at an effective yield for comparable risk which is lower than that earned by other participants in the syndicate, part of the syndication fee received relates to the risk retained. The relevant portion of the fee is deferred and recognised as revenue as an adjustment to the effective yield of the investment, as in 5 (a) above.

6.   *Admission fees.*

Revenue from artistic performances, banquets and other special events is recognised when the event takes place. When a subscription to a number of events is sold, the fee is allocated to each event on a basis which reflects the extent to which services are performed at each event.

7.   *Tuition fees.*

Revenue is recognised over the period of instruction.

8. *Initiation, entrance and membership fees.*

Revenue recognition depends on the nature of the services provided. If the fee permits only membership, and all other services or products are paid for separately, or if there is a separate annual subscription, the fee is recognised as revenue when no significant uncertainty as to its collectability exists. If the fee entitles the member to services or publications to be provided during the membership period, or to purchase goods or services at prices lower than those charged to nonmembers, it is recognised on a basis that reflects the timing, nature and value of the benefits provided.

9. *Franchise fees.*

Franchise fees may cover the supply of initial and subsequent services, equipment and other tangible assets, and knowhow. Accordingly, franchise fees are recognised as revenue on a basis that reflects the purpose for which the fees were charged. The following methods of franchise fee recognition are appropriate:

(a) *Supplies of equipment and other tangible assets*

The amount, based on the fair value of the assets sold, is recognised as revenue when the items are delivered or title passes.

(b) *Supplies of initial and subsequent services.*

Fees for the provision of continuing services, whether part of the initial fee or a separate fee are recognised as revenue as the services are rendered. When the separate fee does not cover the cost of continuing services together with a reasonable profit, part of the initial fee, sufficient to cover the costs of continuing services and to provide a reasonable profit on those services, is deferred and recognised as revenue for the continuing services.

The franchise agreement may provide for the franchisor to supply equipment, inventories, or other tangible assets, at a price lower than that charged to others or a price that does not provide a reasonable profit on those sales. In these circumstances, part of the initial fee, sufficient to cover estimated costs in excess of that price and to provide a reasonable profit on those sales, is deferred and recognised over the period the goods are likely to be sold to the franchisee. The balance of an initial fee is recognised as revenue when performance of all the initial services and other obligations required of the franchisor (such as assistance with site selection, staff training, financing and advertising) has been substantially accomplished.

The initial services and other obligations under an area franchise agreement may depend on the number of individual outlets established in the area. In this case, the fees attributable to the initial services are recognised as revenue in proportion to the number of outlets for which the initial services have been substantially completed.

If the initial fee is collectable over an extended period and there is a significant uncertainty that it will be collected in full, the fee is recognised as cash instalments are received.

(c)   Continuing Franchise Fees

Fees charged for the use of continuing rights granted by the agreement, or for other services provided during the period of the agreement, are recognised as revenue as the services are provided or the rights used.

(d)   Agency Transactions

Transactions may take place between the franchisor and the franchisee which, in substance, involve the franchisor acting as agent for the franchisee. For example, the franchisor may order supplies and arrange for their delivery to the franchisee at no profit. Such transactions do not give rise to revenue.

(e)   Option to Purchase Franchisee's Business

The franchise agreement may contain an option for the franchisor to purchase the business of the franchisee. If at the time of the agreement it is probable that the option will be exercised, the initial franchise fee is deferred. When the option is exercised the initial fee is deducted from the cost of the repurchase. The fee is not recognised as revenue.

10.   Fees from the development of customised software.

Fees from the development of customised software are recognised as revenue by reference to the stage of completion of the development, including completion of services provided for post delivery service support.

Interest, Royalties and Dividends

Licence fees and royalties

Fees and royalties paid for the use of an enterprise's assets (such as trademarks, patents, software, music copyright, record masters and motion picture films) are normally recognised in accordance with the substance of the agreement. As a practical matter, this may be on a straight line basis over the life of the agreement, for example, when a licensee has the right to use certain technology for a specified period of time.

An assignment of rights for a fixed fee or nonrefundable guarantee under a noncancellable contract which permits the licensee to exploit those rights freely and the licensor has no remaining obligations to perform is, in substance, a sale. An example is a licensing agreement for the use of software when the licensor has no obligations subsequent to delivery. Another example is the granting of rights to exhibit a motion picture film in markets where the licensor has no control over the distributor and expects to receive no further revenues from the box office receipts. In such cases, revenue is recognised at the time of sale.

In some cases, whether or not a licence fee or royalty will be received is contingent on the occurrence of a future event. In such cases, revenue is recognised only when it is reasonably assured that the fee or royalty will be received, which is normally when the event has occurred.

Construction Contracts

This draft incorporates the changes to International Accounting Standard 11 as set out in the Statement of Intent on the Comparability of Financial Statements. It also proposes other improvements to IAS 11 to ensure that the Standard is sufficiently detailed and complete and contains adequate disclosure requirements to meet the needs of capital markets and the international business community.

As indicated in the Statement of Intent the Board does not intend to reconsider the issues which were exposed for comment in E32 and subsequently approved by the Board without substantive change.

The Board is expected to approve a revised International Accounting Standard 11, Construction Contracts, in March 1993.

Exposure Draft

Contents

International Accounting Standard -- Construction Contracts

International Accounting Standard --

Construction Contracts

The standards, which have been set in bold italic type, should be read in the context of the background material and implementation guidance and in the context of the Preface to International Accounting Standards. International Accounting Standards are not intended to apply to immaterial items (see paragraph 12 of the Preface).

Introduction

The primary issue in accounting for construction contracts is the allocation of contract revenue and related costs to accounting periods over the duration of the contract. This Statement requires revenue and expenses to be recognised when it is probable that future economic benefits will flow to or from the enterprise and the amounts can be measured reliably. This will occur as contract activity progresses and will depend on whether the outcome of the contract can be reliably measured and the extent to which costs are recoverable.

Scope

1.   This Statement should be applied in accounting for construction contracts in the financial statements of contractors.

Definitions

2.   The following terms are used in this Statement with the meanings specified:

A construction contract is a contract specifically negotiated for the construction of an asset or a combination of assets that are closely interrelated or interdependent in terms of their design, technology and function or their ultimate purpose or use.

A fixed price contract is a construction contract in which the contractor agrees to a fixed contract price, or a fixed rate per unit of output, which in some cases is subject to cost escalation clauses.

A cost plus contract is a construction contract in which the contractor is reimbursed for allowable or otherwise defined costs, plus a percentage of these costs or a fixed fee.

3.   Examples of construction contracts are contracts for the construction of single assets such as bridges, buildings, dams, pipelines, roads, ships and tunnels. Construction contracts may also deal with the construction of a number of assets which are closely interrelated or interdependent in terms of their design, technology and function or their ultimate purpose or use. This includes, for example, the construction of refineries and other complex pieces of plant or equipment.

4.   Because of the nature of the activity undertaken, the date at which the contract activity is entered into and the date when the contract activity is completed usually fall into different accounting periods. The specific duration of the contract performance is not important in identifying a construction contract.

5.   For the purposes of this Statement, construction contracts includes contracts for the rendering of services which are directly related to the construction of the asset, for example, those for the services of project managers and architects.

Combining and Segmenting Construction Contracts

6.   The recognition of revenue and expenses relating to construction contracts needs to reflect the substance of the transaction. In order to achieve this, it may be necessary to apply the recognition criteria in this Statement to the separately identifiable components of a single contract or to two or more contracts together. For example, when a contract covers a number of projects, each subject to separate negotiation and the costs and revenues of each project can be identified, each project is treated as a separate contract. Alternatively, when a series of contracts, possibly with several customers, are negotiated as a package, the whole project is treated as a single construction contract.

7.   A contract may provide for the construction of an additional asset at the option of the customer. Alternatively, a contract may be amended to include the construction of an additional asset. The construction of the additional asset is treated as a separate construction contract if:

(a)   the asset differs significantly in design, technology or function from the asset or assets covered by the original contract; or

(b)   the price of the asset is negotiated without regard to the original contract price.

Construction Contract Revenue

8. *Construction contract revenue comprises:*

(a) *the initially agreed contract price; and*

(b) *variations in contract work approved by the customer, other claims made by the contractor, and incentive payments:*

  (i) *to the extent that it is probable that they will result in revenue; and*

  (ii) *they are capable of being reliably measured.*

9.   Variations in contract work approved by the customer, claims made by the contractor and incentive payments will probably result in revenue and be capable of reliable measurement when:

(a)   there is evidence of a legal basis of acceptability by the customer of the amount of the variation, claim or payment; and

(b)   with respect to claims, there is evidence that the amount of the claim is reasonable and the associated costs were unforeseen at the inception of the contract.

10.   A variation is an instruction by the customer for a change in the scope of the work to be performed under the contract. Examples of variations are changes in the specifications or design of the asset and changes in the duration of the contract.

11.   A claim made by a contractor is an amount which the contractor seeks to collect from the customer or another party as reimbursement for costs not included in the contract price. A claim may arise from, for example, disputed variations in contract work.

12.   Incentive payments are additional amounts paid to the contractor if specified performance standards are met or exceeded. For example, a contract may allow for an additional payment to the contractor for early completion of the contract.

Contract Costs

13.   The costs of a construction contract comprise:

(a)   costs that relate directly to the specific contract;

(b)   costs that are attributable to the contract activity in general and can be allocated to the contract; and

(c)   such other costs as are specifically chargeable to the customer under the terms of the contract.

14.   Costs which relate directly to a contract include:

(a)   site labour costs, including supervision;

(b)   materials used in construction;

(c)   depreciation of plant and equipment used on the contract; and

(d)   costs of moving plant and equipment to and from the contract site.

Costs which relate directly to a contract also include expected warranty costs and claims from third parties (for example, subcontractors) or penalties against the contractor arising from delays in the completion of the contract or from other causes.

15.   Costs that may be attributable to the contract activity in general and can be allocated to specific contracts include:

(a)   insurance;

(b)   borrowing costs;

(c)   design and technical assistance; and

(d)   construction overheads.

Such costs are allocated using methods that are systematic and rational and are applied consistently to all costs having similar characteristics. The extent to which borrowing costs are included in accumulated contract costs is determined in accordance with Proposed International Accounting Standard, E39 Capitalisation of Borrowing Costs. Construction overheads include costs such as the preparation and processing of construction personnel payroll.

16.   Costs which are specifically chargeable to the customer under the terms of the contract may include some general administration costs and development costs for which reimbursement is specified in the terms of the contract.

17. General costs that cannot be attributed to the contract activity or cannot be allocated to a contract are excluded from the accumulated contract costs. Such costs include:

(a) general administration and selling costs;

(b) research and development costs; and

(c) depreciation of idle plant and equipment that is not used on a particular contract.

18. Contract costs include the costs attributable to a contract for the period from the date of securing the contract to the completion of the contract. However, costs incurred in securing the contract are also included as part of the contract costs if they can be separately identified and measured reliably and it is probable that the contract will be obtained.

Recognition of Contract Revenue and Expenses

19. When the outcome of a construction contract can be estimated reliably as set out in paragraphs 20 or 21, revenue and expenses associated with the construction contract should be recognised by reference to the stage of completion of the contract activity at the balance sheet date.

20. In the case of a fixed price contract, the outcome of a construction contract can be estimated reliably when all of the following conditions are satisfied:

(a) total contract revenue can be measured reliably;

(b) it is probable that the enterprise will receive the contract revenue;

(c) both the costs to complete the contract and the stage of contract completion at the balance sheet date can be measured reliably; and

(d) the costs attributable to the contract can be clearly identified so that actual costs incurred can be compared with prior estimates.

21. In the case of a cost plus contract, the outcome of a construction contract can be estimated reliably when all of the following conditions are satisfied:

(a) it is probable that the enterprise will receive the contract revenue; and

(b) the costs attributable to the contract, whether or not specifically reimbursable, can be clearly identified and measured reliably.

22.   In order to recognise construction contract revenue and expenses by reference to the stage of completion of the contract, an enterprise must be able to estimate the outcome of the contract reliably. An enterprise is generally able to make reliable estimates when it has agreed a contract which establishes the following:

(a)   each party's enforceable rights regarding the asset to be constructed;

(b)   the consideration to be exchanged; and

(c)   the manner and terms of settlement.

Therefore, it is often necessary for the enterprise to have an effective internal financial budgeting and reporting system in order that it can make reliable estimates. These estimates are reviewed and when necessary revised as the contract progresses; however, the fact that circumstances may necessitate periodic revision of estimates does not necessarily indicate that the outcome of the contract cannot be estimated reliably.

23.   The recognition of construction contract revenue and expenses by reference to the stage of completion of a contract is often referred to as the percentage of completion method. The costs incurred in reaching the stage of completion are matched with the revenue, resulting in the reporting of a profit or loss which can be attributed to the proportion of work completed. In most cases under this method, contract costs are recognised as an expense in the period when incurred. Contract costs are considered incurred when they reflect work performed. They include the cost of materials that have been installed, used or applied during the performance and the cost of materials as work specially made for the contract. The use of this method provides useful information on the extent of contract activity and performance during a period.

24.   The stage of completion of a contract may be determined in a variety of ways. These include:

(a)   the proportion that costs incurred for work performed to date bear to the estimated total costs of the contract;

(b)   by surveys of work performed;

(c)   completion of a physical proportion of the contract work; or

(d)   a combination of the above-mentioned ways.

The method used is the one that most closely approximates the stage of completion. Progress payments and advances received from customers do not necessarily reflect the stage of completion.

25. When the stage of completion is determined by reference to the costs incurred to date, only those costs that reflect work performed are included. Examples of costs which are excluded are:

(a) costs of materials that have been delivered to a contract site or set aside for use in a contract but not yet installed, used or applied during contract performance, unless the materials have been made specially for the contract;

(b) payments made to subcontractors in advance of work performed under the subcontract; and

(c) penalties incurred by the contractor.

26. A change in an estimate of contract revenue, contract costs or the outcome of a contract is accounted for as part of income from the ordinary activities of the enterprise.

27. When the outcome of a construction contract cannot be measured reliably:

(a) revenue should be recognised only to the extent of costs incurred that are recoverable; and

(b) contract costs should be recognised as an expense in the period when incurred.

28. During the early stages of a contract it will often be the case that the outcome of the contract will not be able to be estimated reliably. Nevertheless, it may be probable that the enterprise will recover the costs incurred.

29. Contract revenue is recognised only when it is probable that, at the time revenue would otherwise be recognised, the enterprise will receive the revenue. When an uncertainty relating to collectability of the contract revenue arises subsequent to the recognition of revenue on a contract, the estimated uncollectable amount is recognised as an expense rather than as an adjustment of the amount of revenue originally recognised.

30. Examples of circumstances in which the recoverability of costs incurred is not probable are:

(a) contracts which are not fully enforceable, that is, their validity is seriously in question;

(b) contracts the completion of which is subject to the outcome of pending litigation or legislation; or

(c) contracts relating to properties that are likely to be condemned or expropriated.

31. When the uncertainties that prevented reliable measurement no longer exist, revenue and expenses should be recognised in accordance with paragraph 19.

Recognition of Foreseeable Losses

32. When it is probable that total contract costs will exceed total contract revenues, the excess contract costs should be recognised as an expense immediately.

33. The amount of such a loss is determined irrespective of:

(a) whether or not work has commenced on the contract;

(b) the stage of completion of contract activity; or

(c) the amount of profits expected to arise on other unrelated contracts.

Disclosure

34. An enterprise should disclose:

(a) the nature of the major components of contract revenues and costs (paragraphs 8 to 18);

(b) the methods used to determine the contract revenue recognised in the period;

(c) the methods used to determine the stage of completion of contracts in progress (paragraph 24); and

(d) each of the following for contracts in progress at the balance sheet date:

(i) the aggregate of the amount of costs incurred and estimated profits (less estimated losses) to date;

(ii) the amount of progress billings to date;

(iii) the net amount of costs incurred plus estimated profits less the sum of estimated losses and progress billings for all contracts in progress for which costs incurred plus estimated profits (less estimated losses) exceed progress billings;

(iv) *the net amount of costs incurred plus estimated profits less the sum of estimated losses and progress billings for all contracts in progress for which progress billings exceed costs incurred plus estimated profits (less estimated losses);*

(v) *the amount of advances received; and*

(vi) *the amount of retentions.*

35. Progress billings are amounts billed for work performed on a contract whether or not they have been paid by the customer. Retentions are amounts of progress billings which are not paid until the satisfaction of conditions specified in the contract for the payment of such amounts. Advances are amounts received by the enterprise before the related work is performed.

36. An enterprise discloses any contingent gains and losses in accordance with International Accounting Standard 10, Contingencies and Events Occurring After the Balance Sheet Date. Such contingent gains and contingent losses may arise from such items such as warranty costs, claims, penalties or foreseeable losses.

Effective Date

37. *This International Accounting Standard becomes operative for financial statements covering periods beginning on or after_____.*

Appendix

The examples in this Appendix are included in order to assist in clarifying the application of the International Accounting Standard. They do not deal comprehensively with all the factors which affect the accounting for and disclosure of construction contracts. The examples do not modify or override the standards in the International Accounting Standard.

Disclosure of Accounting Policies

The following are examples of accounting policy disclosures;

Revenue from fixed price construction contracts is recognised on the percentage of completion method, measured by reference to the percentage of labour hours incurred to date to estimated total labour hours for each contract.

Revenue from cost plus contracts is recognised by reference to the recoverable costs incurred during the period plus the fee earned, measured by the proportion that costs incurred to date bear to the estimated total costs of the contract.

Incentives are included in revenue when it is probable that they will be received. An amount equal to contract costs attributable to claims is included in revenue when realisation is probable and the amount can be reliably estimated.

Contract costs include all direct material and labour costs and those indirect costs that are attributable to contract activity, including indirect labour, supplies, repairs and depreciation. Selling, general and administrative costs are recognised as an expense as incurred. Estimated losses on uncompleted contracts are recognised as an expense in the year in which such losses are determined. Changes in job performance, job conditions and estimated profitability, including those arising from contract penalty provisions, and final contract settlements may result in revisions to costs and are recognised in the year in which the costs are incurred.

The Determination of Revenue and Expenses

The following example illustrates one method of determining the stage of completion of a contract and the timing of the recognition of contract costs as an expense.

A construction contractor has a fixed price contract for 9,000 to build a bridge at an estimated total cost of 8,000. It will take 3 years to build the bridge. In year 1, high water levels in the river resulted in delays in construction activity and the contractor incurred 50 in unexpected costs of labour overtime. In year 2, the customer approved a variation in the contract terms resulting in an increase of the contract price of 200 and estimated additional costs of 150. At the end of year 2, costs incurred to date included 100 of standard materials stored at the site to be used in year 3 to complete the project. The contractor determines the stage of completion of the contract by calculating the proportion that costs incurred to date bear to the latest estimated total costs of the contract. A summary of the financial data during the construction period is as follows:

	Year 1	Year 2	Year 3
Total estimated revenue	9,000	9,200	9,200
Costs incurred to date	2,093	6168	8,200
Estimated costs to complete	5,957	2,032	-
Total estimated cost	8,050	8,200	8,200
Estimated profit	950	1,000	1,000
Progress to date	26%	74%	100%

The amount of revenue, expenses and profit recognised in the income statement in the three years would be as follows:

	To date	Recognised in Prior Years	Current Year
Year 1			
Revenue (9,000 x 26%)	2,340		2,340
Expenses	2,093		2,093
Profit	247		247
Year 2			
Revenue (9,200 x 74%)	6,808	2,340	4,468
Expenses (6,168 - 100)	6,068	2,093	3,975
Profit	740	247	493
Year 3			
Revenue (9,200 x 100%)	9,200	6,808	2,392
Expenses	8,200	6,068	2,132
Profit	1,000	740	260

Disclosure

A contractor has reached the end of its first year of operations and all its contract activity has been paid for and received in cash (except for foreseeable losses). Costs incurred for contracts B, C and E include the cost of materials that have been purchased for the contract but have not been used in contract performance to date. The following is the status of its five contracts in progress:

	Contract				
	A	B	C	D	E
Revenue	145	520	380	200	55
Cost of revenue (excluding foreseeable losses)	110	450	350	250	55
Progress billings	100	600	400	150	80
Costs incurred	110	510	450	250	100
Foreseeable losses	-	-	-	40	30

The amounts in the following disclosures are determined as follows:

	Contract					
	A	B	C	D	E	Totals
Costs incurred	110	510	450	250	100	1,420
Estimated profits (revenue-cost of sales-foreseeable losses)	35	70	30	(90)	(30)	15
	145	580	480	160	70	1,435
Progress billings	100	600	400	150	80	1,330
	45		80	10		135
		(20)			(10)	(30)
						105

The following disclosures are required by paragraph 35 (d) (i) to (iv) of the International Accounting Standard:

Costs incurred and estimated profits on uncompleted contracts	1,435
Progress billings	1,330
	105
Costs and estimated profits in excess of billings on uncompleted contracts	135
Billings in excess of costs and estimated profits on uncompleted contracts	(30)
	105

Property, Plant and Equipment

This draft incorporates the changes to International Accounting Standard 16 as set out in the Statement of Intent on the Comparability of Financial Statements. It also incorporates the text of the related International Accounting Standard 4, Depreciation Accounting. The draft proposes other improvements to ensure that the Standard is sufficiently detailed and complete and contains adequate disclosure requirements to meet the needs of capital markets and the international business community.

As indicated in the Statement of Intent the Board does not intend to reconsider the issues which were exposed for comment in E32 and subsequently approved by the Board without substantive change.

The Board is expected to approve a revised International Accounting Standard 16, Property, Plant and Equipment, in March 1993.

Contents

International Accounting Standard -- Property, Plant and Equipment

International Accounting Standard --
Property, Plant and Equipment

The standards, which have been set in bold italic type, should be read in the context of the background material and implementation guidance and in the context of the Preface to International Accounting Standards. International Accounting Standards are not intended to apply to immaterial items (see paragraph 12 of the Preface).

Introduction

The principal issues in accounting for property, plant and equipment are the timing of recognition of the assets, the determination of their carrying amounts and the depreciation charges to be recognised in relation to them, and the determination and accounting treatment of other impairments to the carrying amounts.

This Statement requires an item of property, plant and equipment to be recognised as an asset when it satisfies the definition and recognition criteria for assets as set down in the Framework for the Preparation and Presentation of Financial Statements.

The benchmark treatment in this Statement requires and item of property, plant and equipment to be carried at its acquisition cost less any depreciation or at a lower amount, being the asset's recoverable amount, where its earning power is impaired.

An allowed alternative treatment in this Statement is the revaluation to fair value of property, plant and equipment and the use of this revalued amount as the basis for determining the depreciation charge.

Scope

1.   This Statement should be applied in accounting for all property, plant and equipment except when another International Accounting Standard requires or permits a different accounting treatment.

2.   This Statement replaces International Accounting Standards, IAS 4, Depreciation Accounting, and IAS 16, Accounting for Property, Plant and Equipment, to the extent that they apply to property, plant and equipment. While application of the principles contained in this Statement may also be appropriate for other assets like long-term intangible assets, IAS 4, Depreciation Accounting, continues to apply to such assets.

3.   This Statement does not deal with:

(a)   forests and similar regenerative natural resources;

(b)   expenditures on mineral rights, the exploration for and extraction of minerals, oil, natural gas and similar non-regenerative resources; and

(c)   expenditures on real estate development.

However, expenditures on individual items of property, plant and equipment used to develop or maintain the activities or assets covered in (a), (b) or (c), but separable from those activities or assets, are to be accounted for in accordance with this Statement.

4.   In some circumstances International Accounting Standards permit the carrying amount of property, plant and equipment to be determined using an approach different from that prescribed in this Statement. For instance, under the allowed alternative treatment for negative goodwill, Proposed International Accounting Standard, E45, Business Combinations, permits property, plant and equipment acquired in a business combination to be accounted for at fair value even when it exceeds cost. However, in such cases all other aspects of the accounting treatment for these assets, including depreciation, is determined by the requirements of this Statement.

5.   International Accounting Standard, IAS 25, Accounting for Investments, permits an enterprise to treat investment properties as property, in accordance with this Statement, or as long-term investments. When investment properties are accounted for as long-term investments they are carried at cost or a revalued amount, without depreciation.

6.   This Statement does not deal with certain aspects of the application of a comprehensive system reflecting the effects of changing prices (see International Accounting Standards, IAS 15, Information Reflecting the Effects of Changing Prices, and IAS 29, Financial Reporting in Hyperinflationary Economies). However, enterprises applying such a system are required to comply with all aspects of this Statement, except for those that deal with the determination of the measurement of property, plant and equipment subsequent to its initial recognition.

Definitions

7.   *The following terms are used in this Statement with the meanings specified:*

Property, plant and equipment are tangible assets that:

(a)   are held by an enterprise for use in the production or supply of goods or services, for rental to others, or for administrative purposes; and

(b)   are expected to be used during more than one period.

Depreciation is the systematic allocation of the depreciable amount of an asset over its useful life.

Depreciable amount is the cost of an asset, or other amount substituted for cost in the financial statements, less its residual value.

Useful life is either:

(a)   the period of time over which an asset is expected to be used by the enterprise; or

(b)   the number of production or similar units expected to be obtained from the asset by the enterprise.

Cost is the amount of cash or cash equivalents paid or the fair value of the consideration given to acquire an asset at the time of its acquisition or construction.

Residual value is the net amount which the enterprise expects to obtain for an asset at the end of its useful life after deducting the expected costs of disposal.

Fair value is the amount for which an asset could be exchanged between a knowledgeable, willing buyer and a knowledgeable, willing seller in an arm's length transaction.

Carrying amount is the amount at which an asset is included in the balance sheet after deducting any accumulated depreciation thereon.

Recoverable amount is the amount which the enterprise expects to recover from the future use of an asset, including its residual value on disposal.

Recognition of Property, Plant and Equipment

8.   An item of property, plant and equipment should be recognised as an asset when:

(a)   it is probable that future economic benefits associated with the asset will flow to the enterprise; and

(b)   the cost of the asset to the enterprise can be measured reliably.

9.   Property, plant and equipment is often a major portion of the total assets of an enterprise, and therefore is significant in the presentation of financial position. Furthermore, the determination of whether an expenditure represents an asset or an expense can have a significant effect on an enterprise's reported results of operations.

10.   In determining whether an item satisfies the first criterion for recognition, an enterprise needs to assess the degree of certainty attaching to the flow of future economic benefits on the basis of the available evidence at the time of initial recognition. Existence of sufficient certainty that the future economic benefits will flow to the enterprise necessitates an assurance that the enterprise will receive the rewards attaching to the asset and will undertake the associated risks. This assurance is usually only available when the risks and rewards have passed to the enterprise. Before this occurs, the transaction to acquire the asset can usually be cancelled without significant penalty and, therefore, the asset is not recognised.

11.   The second criterion for recognition is usually readily satisfied because the exchange transaction evidencing the purchase of the asset identifies its cost. In the case of a self-constructed asset, a reliable measurement of the cost can be made from the transactions with parties external to the enterprise for the acquisition of the materials, labour and other inputs used during the construction process.

12.   In identifying what constitutes a separate item of property, plant and equipment, judgement is required in applying the criteria in the definition to specific circumstances or specific types of enterprises. It may be appropriate to aggregate individually insignificant items, such as moulds, tools and dies, and to apply the criteria to the aggregate value. Most spare parts and servicing equipment are usually carried as inventory and recognised as an expense as consumed. However, major spare parts and stand-by equipment qualify as property, plant and equipment when the enterprise expects to use them during more than one period. Similarly, if the spare parts and servicing equipment can be used only in connection with an item of property, plant and equipment and their use is expected to be irregular, they are accounted for as property, plant and equipment; they are depreciated over a time period not exceeding the useful life of the related asset.

13. In certain circumstances, it is appropriate to allocate the total expenditure on an asset to its component parts and account for each component separately. This is the case when the component assets have different useful lives or provide benefits to the enterprise in a different pattern thus necessitating use of different depreciation rates and methods. For example, an aircraft and its engines need to be treated as separate depreciable assets if they have different useful lives.

14. Expenditure on property, plant and equipment may be made for safety or environmental reasons. This expenditure, while not directly increasing the future economic benefits of any particular individual item of property, plant and equipment may be necessary in order for the enterprise to obtain the future economic benefits from its other assets. When this is the case, such expenditure qualifies for recognition as an asset in that its outlay enables future economic benefits from the related assets to be derived by the enterprise in excess of what it could derive if the expenditure were not to be made. However, such expenditure can be recognised only to the extent that the amounts capitalised do not exceed the recoverable amount of that asset and related items of property, plant and equipment. For example, a chemical manufacturer may have to install certain new chemical handling processes in order to comply with environmental requirements on the production and storage of dangerous chemicals; related plant enhancements are recognised as an asset to the extent they are recoverable because, without them, the enterprise is unable to manufacture and sell chemicals.

Initial Measurement of Property, Plant and Equipment

15. An item of property, plant and equipment which qualifies for recognition as an asset under paragraph 8 should initially be measured at its cost.

Components of Cost

16. The cost of an item of property, plant and equipment comprises its purchase price, including import duties and non refundable purchase taxes, and any directly attributable costs of bringing the asset to working condition for its intended use; any trade discounts and rebates are deducted in arriving at the purchase price. Examples of directly attributable costs are:

(a)   the cost of site preparation;

(b)   initial delivery and handling costs;

(c)   installation costs; and

(d)   professional fees such as for architects, legal advisers and engineers.

17.   When payment for an item of property, plant and equipment is deferred beyond normal credit terms, its cost is the cash price equivalent; the difference between this amount and the total payments is recognised as interest expense over the period of credit unless required to be capitalised by Proposed International Accounting Standard, E39, Capitalisation of Borrowing Costs.

18.   Administration and other general overhead costs are not a component of the cost of property, plant and equipment unless they can be directly attributed to the acquisition of the asset or bringing the asset to its working condition. Similarly, start-up and similar pre-production costs do not form part of the cost of an asset unless they are necessary to bring the asset to its working condition.

19.   The cost of a self-constructed asset is determined using the same principles as for an acquired asset. If an enterprise makes similar assets for sale in the normal course of business, the cost of the asset is usually the same as the cost of producing the assets for sale (see Proposed International Accounting Standard, E38, Inventories). Therefore, any internal profits are eliminated in arriving at such costs. Similarly, the cost of abnormal amounts of wasted material, labour, or other resources incurred in the production of a self-constructed asset is not included in the cost of the asset.

Exchanges of Assets

20.   An item of property, plant and equipment may be acquired in exchange or part exchange for a dissimilar asset or securities. The cost of such an item is the fair value of the asset or securities given up or the fair value of the item acquired, whichever is the more clearly evident.

21.   An item of property, plant and equipment may be acquired in exchange for a similar asset that has a similar use in the same line of business and which has a similar fair value. An item of property, plant and equipment may also be sold in exchange for an equity interest in a similar asset. In both cases, since the earning process is incomplete, no gain or loss is recognised on the transaction. Instead, the cost of the new asset is the carrying amount of the asset given up, adjusted for any balancing payment or receipt of cash or other consideration. Examples of exchanges of similar assets include the exchange of hotels, service stations and other real estate properties.

Subsequent Expenditure

22.   Subsequent expenditure relating to an item of property, plant and equipment should be added to the carrying amount of the asset to the extent that the expenditure increases the future economic benefits that an enterprise can expect from the originally assessed standard of performance of the existing asset. All other subsequent expenditure should be recognised as an expense in the period in which it is incurred.

23. Expenditure increases the probable future economic benefits from an asset only if it improves the condition of the asset beyond its originally assessed standard of performance. Examples of improvements which may result in increased future economic benefits include:

(a)   modification of an item of plant to extend its useful life, including an increase in its capacity;

(b)   upgrading machine parts to achieve a substantial improvement in the quality of output;

(c)   adoption of new production processes enabling a substantial reduction in previously assessed operating costs; and

(d)   an improvement in the safety or environmental efficiency of an asset.

24. Expenditure on repairs or maintenance of property, plant and equipment is made to restore or maintain the future economic benefits that an enterprise can expect from the originally assessed standard of performance of the asset. As such, it is usually recognised as an expense when incurred. For instance, the cost of servicing or overhauling plant and equipment is usually an expense since it restores, rather than increases, the originally assessed standard of performance. Similarly, the costs of cleaning the environment and the payment of fines for breaches of environmental regulations resulting from the operation of plant and equipment are recognised as expenses when incurred and are not deferred as an item of property, plant and equipment. This is because they do not increase the future economic benefits arising from the related assets. The removal of contamination is also an expense except to the extent that the removal process results in an improvement in the originally assessed standard of safety or environmental efficiency of the asset.

25. The appropriate accounting treatment for expenditure incurred subsequent to the acquisition of an item of property, plant and equipment depends on the circumstances which were taken into account on the initial measurement and recognition of the related item of property, plant and equipment and whether the subsequent expenditure is recoverable. For instance, when the carrying amount of the item of property, plant and equipment already takes into account a loss in economic benefits, the subsequent expenditure to restore the future economic benefits expected from the asset is capitalised provided that the carrying amount does not exceed the recoverable amount of the asset. This is also the case when the purchase price of an asset already reflects the enterprise's obligation to incur expenditure in the future which is necessary to bring the asset to its working condition. An example of this might be the acquisition of a building known to require renovation. In such circumstances, the subsequent expenditure is added to the carrying amount of the asset to the extent that it can be recovered from future use of the asset.

26.   Major components of some items of property, plant and equipment may require replacement at regular intervals. For instance, a furnace may require relining after a specified number of hours of usage or a building might require refurbishment every ten to fifteen years. The components are accounted for as separate assets because they have useful lives different from those of the items of property, plant and equipment to which they relate. Therefore, provided the recognition criteria in paragraph 8 are satisfied, the expenditure incurred in replacing or renewing the component is accounted for as the acquisition of a separate asset and the replaced asset is written off.

Measurement Subsequent to Initial Recognition

Benchmark Treatment

27.   *Subsequent to initial recognition as an asset, an item of property, plant and equipment should be carried at its cost less any accumulated depreciation, subject to the requirements in paragraph 54.*

Allowed Alternative Treatment

28.   *Subsequent to initial recognition as an asset, an item of property, plant and equipment should be carried at a revalued amount, being its fair value at the date of the revaluation less any subsequent accumulated depreciation, subject to the requirements in paragraph 54. Revaluations should be made with sufficient regularity such that the carrying amount does not differ materially from that which would be determined using fair value at the balance sheet date.*

Revaluations

29.   The fair value of land is usually its open market value for existing use which presupposes continued use of the asset in the same or a similar business. This value is usually determined by appraisal normally undertaken by professionally qualified valuers.

30.   The fair value of items of plant and equipment, is usually their market value determined by appraisal by reference to current values. When there is no evidence of market value, as may be the case for items of a specialised nature that are rarely sold, they are valued at their depreciated replacement cost.

31.   In determining fair value, items of property, plant and equipment are valued on the basis of their existing use. However, assets for which a change in use is probable are valued on the same basis as other similar assets held for the same intended use. For example, it is inappropriate to value a factory and the equipment within it at their value in use, while valuing the factory site at the open market value of the land for redevelopment as a shopping centre.

32. The frequency of revaluations depends upon the movements in the fair values of the items of property, plant and equipment being revalued. When the fair value of a revalued asset differs materially from its carrying amount, a further revaluation is necessary. Some items of property, plant and equipment may experience significant and volatile movements in fair value thus necessitating annual revaluation. Such frequent revaluations are unnecessary for items of property, plant and equipment with only insignificant movements in fair value. Instead, revaluation every three or five years may be sufficient.

33. When an item of property, plant and equipment is revalued, any accumulated depreciation at the date of the revaluation is either:

(a) restated proportionately with the change in the gross carrying amount of the asset so that the carrying amount of the asset after revaluation equals its revalued amount. This method is often used when an asset is revalued, by means of an index, to its depreciated replacement cost; or

(b) eliminated against the gross carrying amount of the asset and the net amount restated to the revalued amount of the asset. This method is usually used for buildings which are revalued to their open market value.

The amounts of the adjustments arising on the restatement or elimination of accumulated depreciation form part of the increase or decrease in carrying amount which is dealt with in accordance with paragraphs 37 and 38.

34. When an item of property, plant and equipment is revalued, the entire class of property, plant and equipment to which that asset belongs should be revalued.

35. The classes of assets which must be revalued at the same time are the classes which are presented in the financial statements in accordance with paragraph 60. Therefore, they usually include some or all of the following classes:

(a) land;

(b) land and buildings;

(c) machinery;

(d) ships;

(e) aircraft;

(f) motor vehicles; and

(g) furniture and fixtures.

Other classes may be revalued separately provided that the same classes are used for the purposes of disclosing information under paragraph 60.

36. The items within a class of property, plant and equipment are revalued simultaneously in order to avoid selective revaluation of assets and the reporting of amounts in the financial statements which are a mixture of costs and values as at different dates. However, a class of assets may be revalued on a rolling basis provided revaluation of the class of assets is completed within a short period of time and provided the revaluations are kept up to date.

37. *When an asset's carrying amount is increased as a result of a revaluation, the increase should be credited to equity under the heading of revaluation surplus, except in the circumstances specified by paragraph 38. When an asset's carrying amount is decreased as a result of a subsequent revaluation, the decrease should be charged to equity under the heading of revaluation surplus, to the extent that the decrease does not exceed the amount held in the revaluation surplus in respect of that asset.*

38. *When an asset's carrying amount is decreased as a result of a revaluation, the decrease should be recognised as an expense, except in the circumstances required by paragraph 37. When an asset's carrying amount is increased as a result of a subsequent revaluation, the increase should be recognised as income to the extent that it relates to and is not greater than the decrease recognised as an expense in respect of that asset.*

39. The revaluation surplus included in equity may be transferred to retained earnings when the surplus is realised. The whole surplus may be realised on the retirement or disposal of the asset. However, some of the surplus may be realised as the asset is used by the enterprise; in such a case, the amount of the surplus realised is the difference between depreciation based on the revalued carrying amount of the asset and depreciation based on the asset's original cost.

40. The effects on taxes on income, if any, resulting from the revaluation of property, plant and equipment are dealt with in Proposed International Accounting Standard, E33, Accounting for Taxes on Income.

Depreciation

41. *The depreciable amount of an item of property, plant and equipment should be allocated on a systematic basis over its useful life. The depreciation method used should reflect the pattern in which the asset's economic benefits are consumed by the enterprise. The depreciation charge for each period should be recognised as an expense unless it is included in the carrying amount of another asset.*

42.   As the economic benefits embodied in an asset are consumed by the enterprise, the carrying amount of the asset is reduced to reflect this consumption, normally by charging an expense for depreciation. Such depreciation is required even if the value of the asset exceeds its carrying amount.

43.   The economic benefits embodied in an item of property, plant and equipment are consumed by the enterprise principally through the use of the asset. However, other factors such as technical obsolescence and wear and tear while an asset remains idle often result in the diminution of the economic benefits that might have been expected to be available from the asset. Consequently, all of the following factors need to be considered in determining the useful life of an asset:

(a)   the expected usage of the asset by the enterprise. Usage is assessed by reference to the asset's expected capacity or physical output;

(b)   the expected physical wear and tear, which depends on operational factors such as the number of shifts for which the asset is to be used and the repair and maintenance programme of the enterprise, and the care and maintenance of the asset while idle;

(c)   technical obsolescence arising from changes or improvements in production, or from a change in the market demand for the product or service output of the asset; and

(d)   legal or similar limits on the use of the asset, such as the expiry dates of related leases.

44.   The useful life of an asset is defined in this Statement in terms of the asset's expected utility to the enterprise. The asset management policy of an enterprise may involve the disposal of assets after a specified time or after consumption of a certain proportion of the economic benefits embodied in the asset. Therefore, the useful life of an asset may be shorter than its economic life. The estimation of the useful life of an item of property, plant and equipment is a matter of judgement based on the experience of the enterprise with similar assets. For an asset using new technology or used in the production of a new product or service, estimation of the useful life is more difficult.

45.   Land and buildings are separable assets and are dealt with separately for accounting purposes, even when they are acquired together. Land normally has an unlimited life and therefore is not depreciated. Land which has a limited life, such as certain agricultural land or land acquired for extractive purposes, is depreciated over its useful life. Buildings have a limited life and, therefore, are depreciable assets. An increase in the value of the land on which a building stands does not affect the determination of the useful life of the building.

46.   In this Statement, the depreciable amount of an asset is determined after deducting the residual value of the asset. In practice, the residual value of an asset is often insignificant and therefore is immaterial in the calculation of the depreciable amount. However, if the residual value is likely to be significant, it is estimated at the date of acquisition. A new estimate is made at the date of any subsequent revaluation of the asset. The estimate is based on the residual value prevailing at the date of the estimate for similar assets which have reached the end of their useful lives and which have operated under conditions similar to those in which the asset will be used. The use of an item of property, plant and equipment may involve dismantling and removal costs at the end of the asset's useful life. In such circumstances, the estimated costs are deducted in determining the residual value.

47.   When the purchase of an asset involves the enterprise in significant restoration costs at the end of the asset's useful life, an expense is usually recognised over the life of the asset. Similarly, when an item of property, plant and equipment involves the enterprise in significant dismantling and removal costs at the end of the asset's useful life which would result in a negative residual value, the excess is reported as a liability.

48.   A variety of depreciation methods can be used to allocate the depreciable amount of an asset on a systematic basis over its useful life. These methods include the straight-line method, the diminishing balance method and the sum-of-the-units method. Straight-line depreciation results in a constant charge over the useful life of the asset. The diminishing balance method results in a decreasing charge over the useful life of the asset. The sum-of-the-units method results in a charge based on the expected use or output of the asset. The method used for an asset is applied consistently from period to period unless altered circumstances justify a change.

49.   The depreciation charge for a period is usually recognised as an expense. However, in some circumstances, the economic benefits embodied in an asset are absorbed by the enterprise in producing other assets rather than giving rise to an expense. In this case the depreciation charge comprises part of the cost of the other asset and is included in its carrying amount. For example, the depreciation of manufacturing plant and equipment is included in the costs of conversion of inventories (see Proposed International Accounting Standard, E38, Inventories). Similarly, depreciation of property, plant and equipment used for development activities may be included in development costs which are capitalised in accordance with Proposed International Accounting Standard, E37, Research and Development Activities.

Review of Useful Life

50. The useful life of an item of property, plant and equipment should be reviewed periodically and, if expectations are significantly different from previous estimates, the depreciation charge for the current and future periods should be adjusted.

51. During the life of an asset it may become apparent that the estimate of the useful life is inappropriate. For example, the useful life may be extended by subsequent expenditure on the asset which improves the condition of the asset beyond its originally assessed standard of performance. Alternatively, technological changes or changes in the market for the products may reduce the useful life of the asset. In such cases, the useful life and, therefore, the depreciation rate is adjusted for the current and future periods.

52. The repair and maintenance policy of the enterprise may also affect the useful life of an asset. The policy may result in an extension of the useful life of the asset or an increase in its residual value. However, the adoption of such a policy does not negate the need to charge depreciation.

Review of Depreciation Method

53. The depreciation method used should be reviewed periodically. When a change in depreciation method is necessary, it should be accounted for as a change in accounting policy in accordance with the accounting treatment proposed in the Statement of Intent, Comparability of Financial Statements.

Recovery of the Carrying Amount

54. The carrying amount of an item or a group of identical items of property, plant and equipment should be reviewed periodically in order to assess whether the recoverable amount has declined below the carrying amount. When such a decline has occurred, the carrying amount should be reduced to the recoverable amount. The amount of the reduction should be recognised as an expense immediately, unless it reverses a previous revaluation in which case it is charged to equity in accordance with paragraph 37. A subsequent increase in the recoverable amount of the asset should be recognised as income, to the extent of the previous decline.

55. The cost or revalued amount of an item of property, plant and equipment is normally recovered on a systematic basis over the useful life of the asset. If the usefulness of an item or a group of identical items is impaired, for example by damage or technological obsolescence or other economic factors, the recoverable amount may be less than the carrying amount of the asset. In such circumstances, a write-down of the asset is necessary. A write-down may also be necessary when an item of property, plant and equipment remains idle for a considerable period either prior to commencement of it being depreciated or during its useful life.

56. Individual assets are usually accounted for separately. However, it is often necessary to assess the recoverable amount for groups of assets rather than individual assets, for example when all of the plant and equipment in a factory is used for the same purpose. In such circumstances, the carrying amount of all of the relevant assets is reduced in proportion to any overall decline in recoverable amount, to the extent that declines in value of individual assets cannot be specifically identified.

Retirements and Disposals

57. An item of property, plant and equipment should be eliminated from the balance sheet on disposal or when no future economic benefits are expected from its use and disposal.

58. Gains or losses arising from the retirement or disposal of an item of property, plant and equipment should be determined as the difference between the net disposal proceeds and the carrying amount of the asset and should be recognised as income or expenses in the income statement.

59. When an item of property, plant and equipment is exchanged for a similar asset under circumstances described in paragraph 21, the net disposal proceeds are measured by reference to the similar asset acquired. Since the cost of the acquired asset is equal to the carrying amount of the asset disposed of, no gain or loss results.

Disclosure

60. The financial statements should disclose, in respect of each class of property, plant and equipment:

(a)   the measurement bases used for determining the gross carrying amount. When more than one basis has been used, the gross carrying amount for that basis in each category should be disclosed;

(b)   the gross carrying amount and the accumulated depreciation at the beginning and end of the period;

(c)   a reconciliation of the carrying amount at the beginning and end of the period showing:

(i)   additions;

(ii)   disposals;

(iii)   acquisitions through business combinations;

(iv)   increases or decreases resulting from revaluations in accordance with paragraph 28;

(v)   reductions in carrying amount in accordance with paragraph 54;

(vi)   increases resulting from reinstatement of the carrying amount in accordance with paragraph 54;

(vii)   depreciation; and

(viii) other movements.

(d)   the amount of payments on account of property, plant and equipment in the course of construction; and

(e)   the amount of commitments for the acquisition of property, plant and equipment.

61.   The financial statements should also disclose:

(a)   the depreciation methods used;

(b)   the useful lives or the depreciation rates used;

(c)   whether, in determining the recoverable amount of items of property, plant and equipment, expected future cash flows have been discounted to their present values;

(d)   the existence and amounts of restrictions on title, and property, plant and equipment pledged as security for liabilities; and

(e)   the accounting policy for restoration costs relating to items of property, plant and equipment.

62.   The selection of the depreciation method and the estimation of the useful life of assets are matters of judgement. Therefore, disclosure of the methods adopted and the estimated useful lives or depreciation rates provides users of financial statements with information which allows them to review the policies selected by management and enables comparisons to be made with other enterprises. For similar reasons, it is necessary to disclose the depreciable amount allocated in a period and the accumulated depreciation at the end of that period.

63. When items of property, plant and equipment are stated at revalued amounts the following should be disclosed:

(a)   the basis used to revalue the assets;

(b)   the effective date of the revaluation;

(c)   whether an independent valuer was involved;

(d)   the nature of any indices used to determine replacement cost;

(e)   the carrying amount of each class of property, plant and equipment that would have been included in the financial statements had the assets been carried at cost less depreciation; and

(f)   the revaluation surplus, indicating the movement for the period and any restrictions on the distribution of the balance to shareholders.

64.   Financial statement users also find the following information relevant to their needs:

(a)   the carrying amount of temporarily idle property, plant and equipment;

(b)   the gross carrying amount of any fully depreciated property, plant and equipment that is still in use; and

(c)   the carrying amount of property, plant and equipment retired from active use and held for disposal.

Therefore, enterprises are encouraged to disclose these amounts.

Effective Date

65.   This International Accounting Standard becomes operative for financial statements covering periods beginning on or after_____.

Exposure Draft E44   **May 1992**

The Effects of Changes in Foreign Exchange Rates

This draft incorporates the changes to International Accounting Standard 21 as set out in the Statement of Intent on the Comparability of Financial Statements. It also proposes other improvements to IAS 21 to ensure that the Standard is sufficiently detailed and complete and contains adequate disclosure requirements to meet the needs of capital markets and the international business community.

As indicated in the Statement of Intent the Board does not intend to reconsider the issues which were exposed for comment in E32 and subsequently approved by the Board without substantive change.

The Board is expected to approve a revised International Accounting Standard 21, The Effects of Changes in Foreign Exchange Rates, in November 1993.

Exposure Draft

Contents

International Accounting Standard--
The Effects of Changes in Foreign Exchange Rates

International Accounting Standard -- The Effects of Changes in Foreign Exchange Rates

The standards, which have been set in bold italic type, should be read in the context of the background material and implementation guidance and in the context of the Preface to International Accounting Standards. International Accounting Standards are not intended to apply to immaterial items (see paragraph 12 of the Preface).

Introduction

An enterprise may carry on foreign activities in two ways. It may have transactions in foreign currencies or it may have foreign operations. In order to include foreign currency transactions and foreign operations in the financial statements of an enterprise, transactions must be expressed in the enterprise's reporting currency and the financial statements of foreign operations must be translated into the enterprise's reporting currency.

The principal issues in accounting for foreign currency transactions and foreign operations are to decide which exchange rate to use and how to recognise in the financial statements the financial effect of changes in exchange rates.

Scope

1. *This Statement should be applied by an enterprise:*

(a) *in accounting for transactions in foreign currencies; and*

(b) *in translating the financial statements of foreign operations for inclusion in the financial statements of the enterprise.*

2. This Statement does not specify the currency in which an enterprise presents its financial statements. However, an enterprise normally uses the currency of the country in which it is domiciled. If it uses another currency, this Statement requires the disclosure of the reason for using that currency.

3. This Statement does not deal with the restatement of an enterprise's financial statements from its reporting currency into another currency for the convenience of users accustomed to that currency or for similar purposes.

4.   This Statement does not deal with the presentation in a cash flow statement of cash flows arising from transactions in a foreign currency and the translation of cash flows of a foreign operation (see Proposed International Accounting Standard, E36, Cash Flow Statements).

Definitions

5.   *The following terms are used in this Statement with the meanings specified:*

Foreign operation is a subsidiary, associate, joint venture or branch, the activities of which are based or conducted in a country other than the country of the reporting enterprise.

Foreign entity is a foreign operation, the activities of which are not an integral part of those of the reporting enterprise.

Reporting currency is the currency used in presenting the financial statements.

Foreign currency is a currency other than the reporting currency of an enterprise.

Exchange rate is the ratio for exchange of two currencies.

Forward rate is the exchange rate established by the terms of an agreement for exchange of two currencies at a specified future date.

Closing rate is the exchange rate at the balance sheet date.

Net investment in a foreign entity is the reporting enterprise's share in the net assets of that entity.

Monetary items are money held and assets and liabilities to be received or paid in fixed or determinable amounts of money.

Settlement date is the date at which a receivable is due to be collected or a payable is due to be paid.

Foreign Currency Transactions

Recording Transactions on Initial Recognition

6.   A transaction in a foreign currency should be recorded in the reporting currency by applying to the foreign currency amount the exchange rate between the reporting currency and the foreign currency at the date of the transaction.

7.   A transaction in a foreign currency is recorded in the financial records of an enterprise as at the date on which the transaction occurs, normally using the exchange rate at that date. This exchange rate is often referred to as the spot rate. For practical reasons, a rate that approximates the actual rate is often used, for example, an average rate for all transactions during the week or month in which the transactions occur. However, if exchange 'rates fluctuate significantly, the use of the average rate for a period is unreliable.

8.   The carrying amount of an item is determined in accordance with the relevant International Accounting Standards. For example, Proposed International Accounting Standard, E40, Financial Instruments requires that certain financial instruments are measured at fair value. Whether the carrying amount of an item is determined based on historical cost or fair value, denominated in a foreign currency, the amounts so determined are then expressed in the reporting currency of the reporting enterprise in accordance with the provisions of this Standard.

Reporting Effects of Changes in Exchange Rates Subsequent to Initial Recognition

9.   At each balance sheet date:

(a)   foreign currency monetary items should be reported using the closing rate;

(b)   non - monetary items which are carried in terms of historical cost denominated in a foreign currency should be reported using the exchange rate at the date of the transaction; and

(c)   non - monetary items which are carried at fair value denominated in a foreign currency should be reported using the exchange rates that existed when the values were determined.

Recognition of Exchange Differences

10.   Paragraphs 11 to 29 set out the accounting treatment required by this Statement in respect of exchange differences on foreign currency transactions. They also include the benchmark treatment for exchange differences that result from a severe devaluation or from depreciation of a currency against which there is no practical means of hedging and that affects liabilities arising directly on the recent acquisition of assets invoiced in a foreign currency. The allowed alternative treatment for such exchange differences is set out in paragraphs 31 and 32.

11.   Exchange differences arising on foreign currency transactions should be recognised as income or as expenses in the period in which they arise, with the exception of exchange differences dealt with in accordance with paragraphs 13 and 23.

12.   An exchange difference results when there is a change in the exchange rate between the transaction date and the date of settlement of any monetary items arising from a foreign currency transaction. When the transaction is settled within the same accounting period as that in which it occurred, all the exchange difference is recognised in that period. However, when the transaction is not settled in the same accounting period as that in which it occurred, the exchange difference is recognised in more than one period.

13.   Exchange differences arising on a monetary item that, in substance, forms part of an enterprise's net investment in a foreign entity should be classified as equity in the enterprise's financial statements until the disposal of the net investment at which time they should be recognised as income or as expense.

14.   An enterprise may have a monetary item that is receivable from, or payable to, a foreign entity. An item for which settlement is neither planned nor likely to occur in the foreseeable future is, in substance, an extension to, or deduction from, the enterprise's net investment in that foreign entity. Such monetary items may include long-term receivables or loans but do not include trade receivables or trade payables.

Foreign Currency Hedging Transactions

15.   With respect to foreign currency hedging transactions, this Statement deals with:

(a)   a foreign currency monetary asset accounted for as a hedge of an unrecognised foreign currency commitment;

(b)   a foreign currency liability accounted for as a hedge of a net investment in a foreign entity; and

(c)   a foreign currency liability accounted for as a hedge of non-monetary assets which are not financial instruments.

16.   Proposed International Accounting Standard, E40, Financial Instruments, deals generally with the hedging of financial instruments, including foreign currency monetary items. However, E40, Financial Instruments, does not deal with the accounting treatment of exchange differences arising from the application of this Statement to foreign currency monetary items accounted for as a hedge.

17.   An effective foreign currency hedge eliminates or reduces substantially the risk of loss from changes in exchange rates on the position being hedged. This is achieved by taking a foreign currency position exposed to exchange differences (the "hedge") that will offset exchange differences arising from the position being hedged. A foreign currency hedge may involve the use of financial instruments, such as foreign currency loans or deposits, forward exchange contracts, options, currency swaps, futures contracts, or a combination of such financial instruments.

18.   A foreign currency item should be accounted for as a hedge when all of the following criteria are met:

(a)   the position to be hedged is specifically identified and exposes the enterprise to a risk of loss from changes in exchange rates;

(b)   it is highly probable that the effect of changes in exchange rates on that foreign currency item and the opposite effect of changes in exchange rates on the hedged position will have a high degree of correlation so that the foreign currency item will be effective as a hedge; and

(c)   in the event that the hedged position is a non-monetary asset, it is probable that the hedged asset will be converted into the necessary foreign currency funds by the date of settlement of the liability being used as the hedge.

When a foreign currency item is accounted for as a hedge, it should be designated as such.

19.   A foreign currency item may be accounted for as a hedge only when the position to be hedged is exposed to risk of loss from changes in exchange rates. If the exposed position is already hedged by other foreign currency items or commitments, a further transaction increases the currency exposure of the enterprise and the resulting foreign currency item does not qualify as a hedge.

20.   A foreign currency item may be accounted for as a hedge if it offsets the risk of loss from changes in exchange rates for only part of the hedged position. In such a case, part of the position is considered hedged and the remainder is fully exposed. Similarly, a foreign currency item may be accounted for as a hedge if it offsets the risk of loss from changes in exchange rates for only part of the life of the hedged position. In such a case, the position is considered hedged for the life of the foreign currency item.

21.   When a hedge is denominated in the same currency as that of the hedged position, it is effective as a hedge because changes in the exchange rate have an equal and offsetting effect on the hedging item and the hedged position. However, a foreign currency item denominated in another currency, or group of currencies, may be effective as a hedge provided that it is highly probable that changes in the exchange rates of that currency or currencies will have a high degree of correlation with those of the currency in which the hedged position is denominated. Changes in the exchange rates between two currencies may have a high degree of correlation as a result of a formal arrangement in one or both of the countries to adjust interest rates in order to maintain the exchange rate between the currencies.

22.   A foreign currency liability may be accounted for as a hedge of a non-monetary asset provided that it satisfies all three criteria in paragraph 18. For such a hedge to be effective, it must be probable that the non-monetary asset will generate foreign currency funds at the date of settlement of the liability. Furthermore, the necessary high degree of correlation between changes in exchange rates is only likely to be achieved when the liability is expressed in the same functional currency as the non-monetary asset.

Recognition of Exchange Differences on Hedging Transactions

23. Exchange differences on a foreign currency item accounted for as a hedge should be recognised as income or as expenses as follows:

(a) for a foreign currency liability accounted for as a hedge of a net investment in a foreign entity, on the disposal of the net investment in the foreign entity (see paragraph 45);

(b) for a foreign currency monetary item accounted for as a hedge of an unrecognised foreign currency monetary item, when the exchange differences on the unrecognised item are recognised as income or expenses; and

(c) for a foreign currency liability accounted for as a hedge of a non-monetary asset, when the asset is sold.

Discontinuance of Hedge Accounting

24. A foreign currency item should cease to be accounted for as a hedge when it ceases to meet the criteria in paragraph 18. Any exchange differences relating to the foreign currency item which have been deferred should continue to be dealt with in accordance with paragraph 23 to the extent that it is probable that the corresponding exchange differences on the hedged position will be recognised as income or expenses.

25. A foreign currency item ceases to be accounted for as a hedge when the position to be hedged is no longer identifiable or it is unlikely to expose the enterprise to risk of loss from changes in exchange rate. For example, commitments may fail to materialise or a liability may be waived. In such circumstances, there is no basis for continuing to defer the foreign currency item and, therefore, the exchange differences are immediately recognised as income or expenses.

26. A foreign currency monetary item ceases to be accounted for as a hedge when the item is denominated in a different currency or group of currencies from that of the hedged position and the currencies do not achieve the expected high degree of correlation or it is no longer highly probable that they will achieve the high degree of correlation in the future. Exchange differences on the hedging item which were deferred while the hedge was effective remain deferred to the extent that it is probable that the corresponding exchange differences on the former hedged position will be recognised as income or expenses.

27. A foreign currency liability also ceases to be accounted for as a hedge of a non-monetary asset when it is no longer probable that the asset will be converted into the necessary foreign currency funds at the date of the settlement of the liability. For example, the enterprise may decide not to sell the asset or to settle the liability. In such circumstances, there is no basis for continuing to defer the exchange differences on the foreign currency liability. Therefore, the exchange differences on the liability are immediately recognised as income or expenses.

Forward Exchange Contracts

28. An enterprise may enter into a forward exchange contract, or another financial instrument that is in substance a forward exchange contract, to establish the amount of the reporting currency required or available at the settlement date of a transaction. The income or expense arising from the difference between the forward rate and the exchange rate at inception of the forward exchange contract should be recognised as interest income or expense over the life of the contract.

29. The difference between the forward rate and the exchange rate at the inception of a forward exchange contract represents a premium or discount that reflects the relationship between market interest rates for each of the two currencies concerned. Therefore this premium or discount is recognised as interest income or expense over the life of the contract.

Recognition of Exchange Differences - Allowed Alternative Treatment

30. The benchmark treatment for exchange differences that result from a severe devaluation or from depreciation of a currency against which there is no practical means of hedging and that affects liabilities arising directly on the recent acquisition of assets invoiced in a foreign currency is set out in paragraph 11.

31. Exchange differences may result from a severe devaluation or depreciation of a currency against which there is no practical means of hedging and that affects liabilities which cannot be settled and which arise directly on the recent acquisition of an asset invoiced in a foreign currency. Such exchange differences should be included in the carrying amount of the related asset, provided that the adjusted carrying amount does not exceed the lower of the replacement cost and the amount recoverable from the sale or use of the asset.

32.   Exchange differences are not included in the carrying amount of an asset when the enterprise is able to settle or hedge the foreign currency liability arising on the acquisition of the asset. However, exchange losses are part of the directly attributable costs of the asset when the liability cannot be settled and there is no practical means of hedging, for example when, as a result of exchange controls, there is a delay in obtaining foreign currency. Therefore under the allowed alternative treatment, the cost of an asset invoiced in a foreign currency is regarded as the amount of reporting currency that the enterprise ultimately has to pay to settle its liabilities arising directly on the recent acquisition of the asset.

Translation of the Financial Statements of Foreign Operations

Classification of Foreign Operations

33.   The method used to translate the financial statements of a foreign operation depends on the way in which it is financed and operates in relation to the reporting enterprise. For this purpose, foreign operations are classified as either "foreign operations that are integral to the operations of the reporting enterprise" or "foreign entities".

34.   A foreign operation that is integral to the operations of the reporting enterprise carries on its business as if it was an extension of the reporting enterprise's operations. For example, such a foreign operation might only sell goods imported from the reporting enterprise and remit the proceeds to the reporting enterprise. In such cases, a change in the exchange rate between the reporting currency and the currency in the country of foreign operation has an almost immediate effect on the reporting enterprise's cash flow from operations. Therefore, the change in the exchange rate affects the individual monetary items held by the foreign operation rather than the reporting enterprise's net investment in that operation.

35.   In contrast, a foreign entity accumulates cash and other monetary items, incurs expenses, realises revenues and perhaps arranges borrowings, all substantially in its local currency. It may also enter into transactions in foreign currencies, including transactions in the currency of the reporting enterprise. When there is a change in the exchange rate between the currencies of the reporting enterprise and the foreign entity, there is little or no direct effect on the present and future cash flows from operations of either the foreign entity or the reporting enterprise. The change in the exchange rate affects the reporting enterprise's net investment in the foreign entity rather than the individual monetary and non-monetary items held by the foreign entity.

36.   The following are indications that a foreign operation is a foreign entity rather than an operation that is integral to the operations of the reporting enterprise:

(a)   while the reporting enterprise may control the foreign operation, the activities of the foreign operation are carried out with a significant degree of autonomy from those of the reporting enterprise;

(b)   transactions with the reporting enterprise are not a high proportion of the foreign operation's activities;

(c)   the activities of the foreign operation are financed mainly from its own operations or local borrowings rather than from the reporting enterprise;

(d) costs of labour, material and other components of the foreign operation's products or services are primarily local costs rather than costs of products and services obtained from the country in which the reporting enterprise is located;

(e) the foreign operation's market is mainly outside the reporting enterprise's country; and

(f) cash flows of the reporting enterprise are insulated from the daytoday activities of the foreign operation rather than being directly affected by the activities of the foreign operation.

Foreign Operations that are Integral to the Operations of the Reporting Enterprise

37. The financial statements of a foreign operation that is integral to the operations of the reporting enterprise should be translated using the procedures in paragraphs 6 to 32 of this Statement as if the transactions of the foreign operation had been those of the reporting enterprise itself.

38. The individual items in the financial statements of the foreign operation are translated as if all its transactions had been entered into by the reporting enterprise itself. For example, the cost and depreciation of property, plant and equipment is translated using the exchange rate at the date of purchase of the asset or, if the asset is carried at fair value, using the rate that existed on the date of the revaluation. Likewise, the cost of inventories is translated at the exchange rates that existed when those costs were incurred. However, when an adjustment is made to reflect a lower recoverable amount or realisable value, the amount is translated using the exchange rate that existed when the recoverable amount or net realisable value was determined.

Foreign Entities

39. In translating the financial statements of a foreign entity for incorporation in its financial statements, the reporting enterprise should use the following procedures:

(a) the assets and liabilities, both monetary and nonmonetary, of the foreign entity should be translated at the closing rate;

(b) income and expense items of the foreign entity should be translated at exchange rates at the dates of the transactions, except where the foreign entity reports in the currency of a hyperinflationary economy, in which case income and expense items should be translated at the closing rate; and

(c) all resulting exchange differences should be classified as equity until the disposal of the net investment.

40.   The financial statements of a foreign entity are translated in a manner that preserves, as far as possible, the results and the interrelationships of amounts appearing in the foreign entity's financial statements. This provides the most meaningful indicator of the performance and financial position of the foreign entity for inclusion in the financial statements of the reporting enterprise.

41.   The translation of the financial statements of a foreign entity results in the recognition of exchange differences arising from:

(a)   translating income and expense items at the exchange rates at the dates of transactions and balance sheet items at the closing rate;

(b)   translating the opening net investment in the foreign entity at an exchange rate different from that at which it was previously reported; and

(c)   other changes to equity in the foreign entity.

These exchange differences are not recognised as income or expenses for the period because the changes in the exchange rates have little or no direct effect on the present and future cash flows from operations of either the foreign entity or the reporting enterprise.

42.   The incorporation of the financial statements of a foreign entity in those of the reporting enterprise follows normal procedures, such as the elimination of intragroup balances and intragroup transactions of a subsidiary (see International Accounting Standards, IAS 27, Consolidated Financial Statements and Accounting for Investments in Subsidiaries, IAS 28, Accounting for Investments in Associates and IAS 31, Financial Reporting of Interests in Joint Ventures). However, an exchange difference arising on an intragroup monetary item, whether short-term or long-term, cannot be eliminated because the monetary item represents a commitment to convert one currency into another and exposes the reporting enterprise to a gain or loss through currency fluctuations.   Accordingly, in the consolidated financial statements of the reporting enterprise, such an exchange difference continues to be recognised as income or as an expense or, if it arises from the circumstances described in paragraph 13, it is classified as equity until the disposal of the net investment.

43. When the financial statements of a foreign entity are drawn up to a different reporting date from that of the reporting enterprise, the foreign entity often prepares, for purposes of incorporation in the financial statements of the reporting enterprise, statements as at the same date as the reporting enterprise. When it is impracticable to do this, International Accounting Standard IAS 27, Consolidated Financial Statements and Accounting for Investments in Subsidiaries, allows the use of financial statements drawn up to a different reporting date provided that the difference is no greater than three months. In such a case, the assets and liabilities of the foreign entity are translated at the exchange rate at the balance sheet date of the foreign entity.

44. The financial statements of a foreign entity that reports in the currency of a hyperinflationary economy should be restated in accordance with International Accounting Standard, IAS 29, Financial Reporting in Hyperinflationary Economies, before they are translated into the reporting currency of the reporting enterprise. When the economy ceases to be hyperinflationary and the foreign entity discontinues the preparation and presentation of financial statements prepared in accordance with IAS 29, it should use the amounts expressed in the measuring unit current at the date of discontinuation as the historical costs in translating into the reporting currency of the reporting enterprise.

Disposal of a Foreign Entity

45. On the disposal of a foreign entity, the cumulative amount of the exchange differences which have been deferred and which relate to that foreign entity should be included as part of the gain or loss on disposal and recognised in net profit or loss.

46. An enterprise may dispose of its interest in a foreign entity through sale, liquidation, repayment of share capital, abandonment of all, or part of, that entity. The payment of a dividend forms part of a disposal only when it constitutes a return of the investment. In the case of a partial disposal, only the proportionate share of the related accumulated exchange differences is included in the gain or loss. A write-down of the carrying amount of a foreign entity does not constitute a partial disposal. Accordingly, no part of the deferred foreign exchange gain or loss is recognised at the time of a write-down.

Change in the Classification of a Foreign Operation

47.   When there is a change in the classification of a foreign operation, the translation procedures applicable to the revised classification should be applied from the date of the change in the classification.

48.   A change in the way in which a foreign operation is financed and operates in relation to the reporting enterprise may lead to a change in the classification of that foreign operation. When a foreign operation that is integral to the operations of the reporting enterprise is reclassified as a foreign entity, exchange differences arising on the translation of non-monetary assets at the date of the reclassification are classified as equity. When a foreign entity is reclassified as a foreign operation that is integral to the operations of the reporting enterprise, the translated amounts for nonmonetary items at the date of the change are treated as the historical cost for those items in the period of change and subsequent periods. Exchange differences which have been deferred are not recognised as income or expenses until the disposal of the operation.

All Effects of Changes in Foreign Exchange Rates

Tax Effects of Exchange Differences

49.   Gains and losses on foreign currency transactions and exchange differences arising on translation may have associated tax effects which are accounted for in accordance with International Accounting Standard, IAS 12, Accounting for Taxes on Income.

Disclosure

50.   When the reporting currency is not the currency of the country in which the enterprise is domiciled, the reason should be disclosed.

51.   An enterprise should disclose the amount of exchange differences included in the net profit or loss for the period.

52.   Exchange differences classified as equity should be shown as a separate component of equity.   The following movements for the period in the cumulative balance of exchange difference classified as equity should be separately disclosed:

(a)   the net exchange difference arising on monetary items that, in substance, form part of the net investment in a foreign entity;   and

(b)   the net exchange difference arising from the translation of the financial statements of foreign entities.

53.   Deferred exchange differences, other than those dealt with in paragraph 52, should be shown as a separate component of assets or liabilities, as the case may be. The cumulative balance at the beginning and the end of the period should be disclosed together with:

(a)   the amount of exchange differences included during the period in the carrying amount of an asset in accordance with the allowed alternative treatment in paragraph 31; and

(b)   the net exchange difference arising from foreign currency items accounted for as a hedge where such difference has been deferred during the period.

54. An enterprise should disclose the effect on foreign currency monetary items or on the financial statements of a foreign operation of a change in exchange rates occurring after the balance sheet date if the change is of such importance that non-disclosure would affect the ability of users of the financial statements to make proper evaluations and decisions. (See International Accounting Standard, IAS 10, Contingencies and Events Occurring after the Balance Sheet Date).

55. Disclosure is also encouraged of an enterprise's foreign currency risk management policy.

56. When foreign activities involve the use of financial instruments, a reporting enterprise also needs to disclose the information required by Proposed International Accounting Standard, E40, Financial Instruments.

Transitional Provisions

57. On the first occasion that an enterprise applies this Statement, the enterprise is encouraged, but is not required, to classify separately and disclose, the cumulative balance, at the beginning of the period, of exchange differences deferred and classified as equity in previous periods.

Effective Date

58. This International Accounting Standard becomes operative for financial statements covering periods beginning on or after_____ .

Business Combinations

This draft incorporates the changes to International Accounting Standard 22 as set out in the Statement of Intent on the Comparability of Financial Statements. It also proposes other improvements to IAS 22 to ensure that the Standard is sufficiently detailed and complete and contains adequate disclosure requirements to meet the needs of capital markets and the international business community.

As indicated in the Statement of Intent the Board does not intend to reconsider the issues which were exposed for comment in E32 and subsequently approved by the Board without substantive change.

The Board is expected to approve a revised International Accounting Standard 22, Business Combinations, in July 1993.

Contents

International Accounting Standard --
Business Combinations

International Accounting Standard -- Business Combinations

The standards, which have been set in bold italic type, should be read in the context of the background material and implementation guidance and in the context of the Preface to International Accounting Standards. International Accounting Standards are not intended to apply to immaterial items (see paragraph 12 of the Preface).

Introduction

The objective of this Statement is to prescribe the accounting treatment for business combinations. The Statement covers an acquisition of one enterprise by another and also the rare situation of a uniting of interests when an acquirer cannot be identified. Accounting for an acquisition involves determination of the cost of the acquisition, allocation of the cost over the identifiable assets and liabilities of the enterprise being acquired and accounting for the resulting goodwill or negative goodwill, both at acquisition and subsequently. Other accounting issues include the determination of the minority interest amount, accounting for acquisitions which occur over a period of time, subsequent changes in the cost of acquisition or in the identification of assets and liabilities, and the disclosures required.

Scope

1.   This Statement should be applied in accounting for business combinations.

2.   A business combination may be structured in a variety of ways which are determined for legal, taxation or other reasons. It may involve the purchase by an enterprise of the equity of another enterprise or the purchase of the net assets of a business enterprise. It may be effected by the issue of shares or by the transfer of cash, cash equivalents or other assets. The transaction may be between the shareholders of the combining enterprises or between one enterprise and the shareholders of the other enterprise. The business combination may involve the establishment of a new enterprise to have control over the combining enterprises, the transfer

of the net assets of one or more of the combining enterprises to another enterprise or the dissolution of one or more of the combining enterprises.

3.   To the extent that the substance of the transaction is consistent with the definition of a business combination in this Statement, the accounting and disclosure requirements contained herein are appropriate irrespective of the particular structure adopted for the combination.

4.   A business combination often gives rise to a parent and subsidiary relationship. The parent is required to present consolidated financial statements in accordance with International Accounting Standard, IAS 27, Consolidated Financial Statements and Accounting for Investments in Subsidiaries. Accordingly, this Statement is directed principally to consolidated financial statements of incorporated enterprises.

5.   However, certain of the requirements of this Statement apply to financial statements of individual enterprises as, for example, when a business combination is effected by purchasing the net assets, rather than shares, of another enterprise or when a business combination is effected as a legal merger. While the requirements for a legal merger may differ between countries, it usually results in only one enterprise remaining in existence after the business combination.

6.   This Statement does not deal with the separate financial statements of a parent which may be prepared in addition to consolidated financial statements to meet legal or other requirements. In order to meet a variety of needs, these separate financial statements are prepared using different reporting practices in different countries.

7.   This Statement does not cover transfers or exchanges of assets among enterprises under common control.

Definitions

8. *The following terms are used in this Statement with the meanings specified:*

A *business combination* is the bringing together of separate enterprises into one economic entity as a result of one enterprise uniting with or obtaining control over the net assets and operations of another enterprise.

An *acquisition* is a business combination in which one of the enterprises, *the acquirer*, obtains control over the net assets and operations of another enterprise, *the acquiree*, in exchange for the transfer of assets, incurrence of a liability or issue of equity.

A *uniting of interests* is a business combination in which the shareholders of the combining enterprises combine control over the whole, or effectively the whole, of their net assets and operations to achieve a continuing mutual sharing in the risks and benefits attaching to the combined entity such that neither party can be identified as the acquirer.

Control is the power to govern the financial and operating policies of an enterprise so as to obtain benefits from its activities and, in so doing, be exposed to the risks associated with its existence.

A *parent* is an enterprise that has one or more subsidiaries.

A *subsidiary* is an enterprise that is controlled by another enterprise (known as the parent).

Minority interest is that part of the net results of operations and of net assets of a subsidiary attributable to interests which are not owned, directly or indirectly through subsidiaries, by the parent.

Fair value is the amount for which an asset could be exchanged or a liability settled between knowledgeable, willing parties in an arm's length transaction.

Date of acquisition is the date on which control of the net assets and operations of the acquiree is effectively transferred to the acquirer.

Nature of a Business Combination

9.   In this Statement the view taken is that in accounting for a business combination, an acquisition is in substance different from a uniting of interests and the substance of the transaction needs to be reflected in the financial statements.   Accordingly, a different accounting method is prescribed for each.   The principal features of each type of business combination are discussed below.

Acquisitions

10.   In virtually all business combinations one of the combining enterprises obtains control over the other combining enterprises, thereby enabling an acquirer to be identified.   Control is presumed to be obtained when one of the combining enterprises acquires more than one half of the voting power of the other combining enterprises unless, in exceptional circumstances, it can be clearly demonstrated that such ownership does not constitute control.   Even when one of the combining enterprises does not acquire more than one half of the voting power of the other combining enterprises, it may still be possible to identify an acquirer when one of the combining enterprises, as a result of the business combination, acquires:

(a)   power over more than one half of the voting rights of the other enterprises by virtue of an agreement with other investors;

(b)   power to govern the financial and operating policies of the other enterprises under a statute or an agreement;

(c)   power to appoint or remove the majority of the members of the board of directors or equivalent governing body of the other enterprises; or

(d)   power to cast the majority of votes at meetings of the board of directors or equivalent governing body of the other enterprises.

11.   Although it may sometimes be difficult to identify an acquirer, there are usually indications that one exists. For example:

(a)   the fair value of the net assets of one enterprise or its scale of operations is significantly greater than that of the other combining enterprises. In such cases, the larger enterprise is the acquirer; or

(b)   the business combination is effected through an exchange of voting common shares for cash. In such cases, the enterprise giving up cash is the acquirer.

In each case, one enterprise's relative influence on decisions made in respect of the combined entity is reduced thereby enabling the other enterprise to be identified as the acquirer.

Reverse Acquisitions

12.   Occasionally a business combination is effected as a reverse acquisition in which, for example, control of the combined entity passes to the former owners of the target enterprise in the business combination, rather than the owners of the other enterprise. The latter enterprise issues sufficient voting shares as purchase consideration, or other factors described in paragraph 10 exist, to result in control passing to the target enterprise. Consequently, the combination results in the target enterprise enjoying the voting or other powers identified in paragraph 10. For accounting purposes, the enterprise which obtains control is the acquirer, although at law this enterprise might be regarded as the subsidiary. This controlling enterprise accounts for the acquisition by applying the purchase method to its investment in the other enterprise in accordance with the requirements of this Statement.

Unitings of Interests

13.   In exceptional circumstances, it may not be possible to identify an acquirer.   Instead of a dominant party emerging, the shareholders of the combining enterprises join in a substantially equal arrangement to share control over the whole, or effectively the whole, of their net assets and operations.   In addition, the management of the combining enterprises continues to participate in the management of the combined entity.   As a result, the shareholders of the combining enterprises continue to share mutually in the risks and benefits of the combined entity.   Such a business combination is accounted for as a uniting of interests.

14.   A continued mutual sharing of risks and benefits will usually not be possible without a substantially equal exchange of voting common shares between the combining enterprises.   Such an exchange ensures that the relative ownership interests of the combining enterprises, and consequently their relative risks and benefits in the combined enterprise, are maintained and the decision-making powers of the parties are preserved.   However, for an equal share exchange to be effective in this regard there cannot be a significant reduction in the rights attaching to the shares of one of the combining enterprises, otherwise the influence of that party is weakened.

15.   In order to achieve a mutual sharing of the risks and benefits attaching to the combined entity, the substantial majority, if not all, of the voting common shares of the combining enterprises must be exchanged or pooled.   As the relative equality in size of the combining enterprises is reduced and as the percentage of voting common shares exchanged decreases, the influence of one of the combining enterprises becomes dominant and the opportunity for a mutual sharing in the risks and benefits is diminished.   Furthermore, a continued mutual sharing of the risks and benefits does not exist if the owners of each enterprise fail to maintain substantially the same voting rights and interest in the combined entity, relative to each other, after the combination as before.

16.   Financial arrangements which provide a relative advantage to one group of shareholders over the other shareholders may negate a mutual sharing of the risks and benefits and increase the likelihood of an acquirer being able to be identified. Such arrangements may take effect either prior to or after the business combination. Similarly, arrangements whereby one party's share of the equity in the combined entity depends on how the business which it previously controlled performs, subsequent to the business combination, indicate that an acquisition has occurred. This is because such an arrangement precludes risks and benefits of the combined entity from being shared mutually.

Acquisitions

17.	*A business combination which is an acquisition should be accounted for by use of the purchase method of accounting as set down in the standards contained in paragraphs 19 to 61.*

18.	The use of the purchase method results in an acquisition of an enterprise being accounted for similarly to the purchase of other assets. This is appropriate since an acquisition involves a transaction in which assets are transferred, liabilities are incurred or capital is issued in exchange for control of the net assets and operations of another enterprise. The purchase method uses cost as the basis for recording the acquisition and relies on the exchange transaction underlying the acquisition for determination of the cost.

Date of Acquisition

19.	*As from the date of acquisition, an acquirer should:*

(a)	*incorporate into the income statement the results of operations of the acquiree; and*

(b)	*recognise in the balance sheet the assets and liabilities of the acquiree and any goodwill or negative goodwill arising on the acquisition .*

20.	The date of acquisition is the date on which control of the net assets and operations of the acquiree is effectively transferred to the acquirer and the date when application of the purchase method commences. In substance, the date of acquisition is the date from when the acquirer is able to enjoy the benefits and is exposed to the risks associated with the net assets acquired. Control is not deemed to have been transferred to the acquirer until all conditions necessary to protect the interests of the parties involved have been satisfied. However, this does not necessitate a transaction being closed or finalised at law before control effectively passes to the acquirer. In assessing whether control has effectively been transferred the substance of the acquisition needs to be considered.

Cost of Acquisition

21.   An acquisition should be accounted for at its cost, being the amount of cash or cash equivalents paid or the fair value of the other purchase consideration given by the acquirer in exchange for control over the net assets of the other enterprise plus any direct costs relating to the acquisition.

22.   When an acquisition involves more than one exchange transaction the cost of the acquisition is the aggregate cost of the individual transactions. When an acquisition is achieved in stages, the distinction between the date of acquisition and the date of the exchange transaction is important. While accounting for the acquisition commences as from the date of acquisition, it uses cost and fair value information determined as at the date of each exchange transaction.

23.   In determining the amount of the cost of the acquisition, all aspects of the acquisition, including factors entering into the negotiations as well as independent valuations, need to be considered.

24.   Monetary assets given and liabilities incurred are measured at their fair values at the date of the transaction. When settlement of the purchase consideration is deferred, the cost of the acquisition is the present value of the consideration, taking into account any premium or discount likely to be incurred in settlement, and not the nominal value of the payable.

25.   Marketable securities issued by the acquirer are measured at their fair value which is their market price as at the date of the exchange transaction, net of selling costs, provided that undue fluctuations or the narrowness of the market do not make the market price an unreliable indicator. However, in using the market price of the securities, price movements for a reasonable period before and after the announcement of the terms of the acquisition need to be considered. When the market is unreliable or no quotation exists, the fair value of the securities issued by the acquirer is estimated by reference to their proportional interest in the fair value of the acquirer's enterprise or by reference to the proportional interest in the fair value of the enterprise acquired, whichever is the more clearly evident. Purchase consideration which is paid in cash to shareholders of the acquiree as an alternative to securities may also provide evidence of the total fair value given.

26.   In addition to the purchase consideration, the acquirer may incur direct costs relating to the acquisition. These include the costs of registering and issuing equity securities, and professional fees paid to accountants, legal advisers, valuers and other consultants to effect the acquisition. General administrative costs, including the costs of maintaining an acquisitions department, and other costs which cannot be directly attributed to the particular acquisition being accounted for, are not included in the cost of the acquisition but are recognised as an expense as incurred.

Adjustment to Purchase Consideration

27.   *When the acquisition agreement provides for an adjustment to the purchase consideration contingent on one or more future events, the amount of the adjustment should be included in the cost of the acquisition as at the date of acquisition if the adjustment is probable and the amount can be measured reliably.*

28.   Many acquisition agreements allow for adjustments to be made to the purchase consideration in the light of one or more future events. The adjustments may be contingent on a specified level of earnings being maintained or achieved in future periods or on the market price of the securities issued as part of the purchase consideration being maintained.

29.   When initially accounting for the acquisition, it is usually possible to include a reasonable estimate of the amount of the adjustment in the cost of acquisition without impairing the reliability of the information, even though uncertainty exists.

Recognition of Identifiable Assets and Liabilities

30.   *Individual assets and liabilities acquired should be recognised separately as at the date of acquisition when:*

(a)   *it is probable that any associated future economic benefits will flow to or from the acquirer; and*

(b)   *a reliable measure is available of their cost or fair value to the acquirer.*

31.   Assets and liabilities acquired which meet the recognition criteria in paragraph 30 are described in this Statement as identifiable assets and liabilities. To the extent that assets and liabilities are purchased which do not satisfy these recognition criteria there is a resultant impact on the amount of goodwill or negative goodwill arising on the acquisition, because goodwill or negative goodwill is determined as the residual cost of acquisition after recognising the identifiable assets and liabilities.

32.   The identifiable assets and liabilities over which the acquirer obtains control may include assets and liabilities which were not previously recorded in the financial statements of the acquiree. This may be because they did not qualify for recognition prior to the acquisition. This is the case, for example, when a tax benefit arising from tax losses of the acquiree qualifies for recognition as an asset as a result of the acquirer earning sufficient taxable income.

33.   Assets and liabilities requiring recognition at the date of acquisition may also include those arising as a result of the acquisition. For instance, the acquirer, in making the acquisition may have undertaken an obligation to compensate employees of the acquiree for services rendered prior to the acquisition. However, application of the recognition criteria in paragraph 30 does not permit the raising of a provision to cover future operating losses since such losses do not constitute a liability at the date of acquisition.

Allocation of Cost of Acquisition

Benchmark Treatment

34.   The cost of an acquisition should be allocated to the assets and liabilities recognised in accordance with paragraph 30 by reference to their fair values at the date of the exchange transaction. Any difference between the cost of the acquisition and the fair values of the acquirer's interest in the identifiable assets and liabilities acquired as at the date of the exchange transaction should be accounted for as goodwill or negative goodwill in accordance with this Statement. Any minority interest arising on the acquisition should be stated at the minority's proportion of the pre-acquisition carrying amounts of the net assets of the subsidiary.

35.   The cost of the acquisition only relates to the percentage of the identifiable assets and liabilities purchased by the acquirer. Consequently, when an acquirer purchases less than all of the shares of the other enterprise, the resulting minority interest is stated at the minority's proportion of the pre-acquisition carrying amounts of the net assets of the subsidiary. This is because the minority's proportion has not been part of the exchange transaction to effect the acquisition.

Allowed Alternative Treatment

36.   The assets and liabilities recognised in accordance with paragraph 30 should be recognised at their fair values as at the date of acquisition or at their fair values reduced in accordance with paragraph 53. Any difference between the cost of the acquisition and the acquirer's share of the fair values of the identifiable assets and liabilities acquired as at the date of each exchange transaction should be accounted for as goodwill or negative goodwill in accordance with this Statement. Any minority interest arising on the acquisition should be stated at the minority's proportion of the fair values of the assets and liabilities recognised in accordance with paragraph 30 or their fair values reduced in accordance with paragraph 53.

37.   Under this approach, the net identifiable assets over which the acquirer has obtained control are stated at their fair values, regardless of whether the acquirer has acquired all, or only some of the capital of the other enterprise or has acquired the assets directly.   Consequently, any minority interest is stated at the minority's proportion of the fair values of the net identifiable assets of the subsidiary.

Successive Share Purchases

38.   An acquisition may involve more than one exchange transaction, as for example when it is achieved in stages by successive purchases on a stock exchange.   When this occurs, each significant transaction is treated separately for the purpose of determining the fair values of the identifiable assets and liabilities acquired and for determining the amount of any goodwill or negative goodwill on that transaction. This results in a step-by-step comparison of the cost of the individual investments with the acquirer's percentage interest in the fair values of the identifiable assets and liabilities acquired at each significant step.

39.   When an acquisition is achieved by successive purchases the fair values of the identifiable assets and liabilities may vary at the date of each exchange transaction. To the extent that assets and liabilities are restated to reflect these changes and they reflect post-acquisition movements they constitute a revaluation.

40.   Prior to qualifying as an acquisition, a transaction may qualify as an investment in an associate and be accounted for by use of the equity method in accordance with International Accounting Standard IAS 28, Accounting for Investments in Associates. If so, the determination of fair values for the identifiable assets and liabilities acquired and the recognition of goodwill or negative goodwill occurs notionally as from the date when equity accounting is applied. When equity accounting is not used for the investment prior to it becoming an acquisition because the investment does not qualify as an associate, the fair values of the identifiable assets and liabilities are determined as at the date of each significant step and goodwill or negative goodwill is recognised from the date of acquisition.

Determining the Fair Values of Assets and Liabilities Acquired

41.   The fair values of identifiable assets and liabilities acquired in an acquisition are determined by reference to their intended use by the acquirer.

42.   The intended use of an asset is usually the asset's existing use unless it is probable that the asset will be used for some other purpose. If an asset is intended to be used for another purpose and is valued accordingly, related assets must be valued on a consistent basis. When an asset or business segment of the acquiree is to be disposed of, this must be taken into consideration in assigning fair values. To the extent that the cash or cash equivalents expected to be received on disposal of an asset is expected to be reduced by the payment of tax on any gain on the disposal, this needs to be taken into consideration in determining the fair value.

43.   General guidelines for arriving at the fair values of assets and liabilities acquired are as follows:

(a)   marketable securities at their current market values;

(b)   nonmarketable securities, at estimated or appraised values, taking into consideration features such as price earnings ratios, dividend yields and expected growth rates of comparable securities of enterprises with similar characteristics;

(c)   receivables at the present values of the amounts to be received, determined at appropriate current interest rates, less allowances for uncollectability and collection costs, if necessary;

(d)   inventories:

      (i)   finished goods and merchandise at estimated selling prices less the sum of (a) the costs of disposal and (b) a reasonable profit allowance for the selling effort of the acquirer based on profit for similar finished goods;

      (ii)   work in progress at estimated selling prices of finished goods less the sum of (a) costs to complete, (b) costs of disposal and (c) a reasonable profit allowance for the completing and selling effort based on profit for similar finished goods; and

      (iii)   raw materials at current replacement costs;

(e)   land and buildings at appraised values usually established by reference to their current market values if available;

(f)   plant and equipment:

      (i)   to be used, at current replacement costs for similar capacity unless the expected future use of the assets indicates a lower value to the acquirer. When second-hand values are not available the gross replacement cost is determined by reference to suppliers' quotes and list prices and is reduced by an amount of depreciation to reflect useful life of the asset and available government grants or allowances;

      (ii)   to be used temporarily, at the lower of current replacement cost for similar capacity and recoverable amount; and

(iii)   to be sold or held for later sale rather than used, at recoverable amount;

(g)   intangible assets, such as patent rights and licences, at estimated or appraised values;

(h)   other assets including natural resources at estimated or appraised values, taking into consideration features such as current market prices, expected demand, quantity available and where relevant, expected growth rates;

(i)   net pension assets or obligations, in accordance with the requirements of International Accounting Standard IAS 19, Accounting for Retirement Benefits in the Financial Statements of Employers;

(j)   tax assets and liabilities, at the present values of the tax benefit arising from tax losses or the taxes payable in respect of the net profit or loss, assessed from the perspective of the combined entity or group resulting from the acquisition. The tax asset or liability is determined after allowing for the tax effect of restating identifiable assets and liabilities to their fair values;

(k)   accounts and notes payable, long-term debt, and other claims payable at present values of amounts to be disbursed in discharging the liability determined at appropriate current interest rates;

(l)   liabilities and accruals at present values of amounts to be disbursed in discharging the liability determined at appropriate current interest rates; and

(m)   contingent liabilities and commitments which it is probable will result in a liability, for example, some unfavourable leases, contracts, and plant closure expenses incidental to the acquisition, at present values of amounts to be disbursed in discharging the obligation determined at appropriate current interest rates.

Goodwill Arising on Acquisition

44.   Any excess of the cost of the acquisition over the fair values of the identifiable assets and liabilities acquired as at the date of the exchange transaction should be described as goodwill and recognised as an asset.

45.   Goodwill arising on acquisition represents a payment made by the acquirer in anticipation of future economic benefits. The future economic benefits may result from synergy between the identifiable assets acquired or from assets which, individually, do not qualify for recognition in the financial statements but for which the acquirer is prepared to make a payment in the acquisition.

46.   Goodwill should be amortised by recognising it as an expense over its useful life. In amortising goodwill, the straight-line basis should be used unless another amortisation method is more appropriate in the circumstances and produces a more conservative result. The amortisation period should not exceed five years unless a longer period, not exceeding twenty years from the date of acquisition, can be justified.

47.   With the passage of time, goodwill diminishes, reflecting its reduced capacity to contribute to the future income of the enterprise. Therefore, it is appropriate that goodwill is amortised and charged as an expense on a systematic basis over its useful life.

48.   Factors to be considered in estimating the useful life of goodwill include:

(a)   the foreseeable life of the business or industry;

(b)   the effects of product obsolescence, changes in demand and other economic factors;

(c)   the service life expectancies of key individuals or groups of employees;

(d)   expected actions by competitors or potential competitors; and

(e)   legal, regulatory or contractual provisions affecting the useful life.

49.   Because goodwill represents future economic benefits from synergy or assets for which separate recognition is not possible, it is frequently difficult to estimate its useful life.   Therefore, for accounting purposes, an arbitrary limit on the amortisation period is specified.   The presumption in this Statement is that goodwill does not normally have a useful life in excess of five years.   However, there may be circumstances when the goodwill is so clearly related to an identifiable asset that it can reasonably be expected to benefit the acquirer over the useful life of the identifiable asset. This may be the case, for example, when the principal identifiable asset in the acquisition is a broadcasting licence with a term longer than five years.   After recording the fair value of the broadcasting licence as an asset, any goodwill arising on the acquisition is amortised over the period of the broadcasting licence. Nevertheless, since an enterprise's planning horizon with respect to its operations as a whole is unlikely to exceed twenty years, projections as to the life of goodwill beyond this period are not sufficiently reliable to permit an amortisation period of longer than twenty years.

50.   The unamortised balance of goodwill should be reviewed at each balance sheet date and, to the extent that it is not supported by future economic benefits, it should be recognised immediately as an expense. Any write-down of goodwill should not be reversed in a subsequent period.

51.   When initially accounting for the acquisition, there may be circumstances in which goodwill on acquisition does not reflect future economic benefits that are expected to flow to the acquirer. This is the case when the cost of acquisition is excessive or, since negotiating the purchase consideration, there has been a decline in the expected future cash flows from the net identifiable assets being acquired. A discovery that fraud in the accounts of the acquiree existed at the date of acquisition is a further example of when goodwill on acquisition does not reflect future economic benefits. In these circumstances, goodwill is written down and an expense recognised immediately.

52.   An impairment in the value of goodwill may be caused by factors such as unfavourable economic trends, changes in the competitive situation and legal, statutory or contractual proceedings. It may be evidenced by a reduction in the cash flows generated, or reasonably likely to be generated, by the acquiree's business. In these circumstances, the carrying amount of goodwill is written down and an expense recognised.

Negative Goodwill Arising on Acquisition

Benchmark Treatment

*53.   When the cost of the acquisition is less than the fair values of the
identifiable assets and liabilities acquired as at the date of the exchange
transaction, the fair values of the non-monetary assets acquired should be
reduced proportionately until the excess is eliminated. Any excess which
remains should be described as negative goodwill and treated as deferred
income. It should be recognised as income on a systematic basis over a
period not exceeding five years unless a longer period, not exceeding
twenty years from the date of acquisition, can be justified.*

54.   When the aggregate fair values of the identifiable net assets
acquired exceed the cost of the acquisition the net assets acquired have
effectively been acquired at a discount. Accordingly, the fair values of the
non-monetary assets acquired are reduced by the discount to ensure that the
acquisition is not recorded at more than its cost. The total discount, spread
over those assets, will be realised as income as the assets concerned are sold
or as the future economic benefits embodied therein are consumed. In the
case of current assets, such as inventory, the realisation process will be
completed as the inventory is sold. In the case of long-term assets, such as
plant and equipment, the discount is realised through lower depreciation
charges over the useful life of the asset.

Allowed Alternative Treatment

*55.   Any excess, as at the date of the exchange transaction, of the fair
values of the identifiable assets and liabilities acquired over the cost of the
acquisition, should be described as negative goodwill and treated as
deferred income. It should be recognised as income on a systematic basis
over a period not exceeding five years unless a longer period, not
exceeding twenty years from the date of acquisition, can be justified.*

Subsequent Changes in Cost of Acquisition

56.   The cost of the acquisition should be adjusted when a contingency affecting the amount of the purchase consideration is resolved subsequent to the date of the acquisition, so that payment of the amount is probable and a reliable estimate of the amount can be made.

57.   The terms of an acquisition may provide for an adjustment of the purchase consideration if the results from the acquiree's operations exceed or fall short of an agreed level after acquisition. When the adjustment subsequently becomes probable and a reliable estimate can be made of the amount, the acquirer treats the receipt or payment of the additional consideration as an adjustment to the cost of acquisition, with a consequential effect on goodwill, or negative goodwill, as the case may be.

58.   In some circumstances, the acquirer may be required to make subsequent payment to the seller as compensation for a reduction in the value of the purchase consideration. This is the case when the acquirer has guaranteed the market price of securities or debt issued as consideration and has to make a further issue of securities or debt for the purpose of restoring the originally determined cost of acquisition. In such cases, there is no increase in the cost of acquisition and, consequently, no adjustment to goodwill or negative goodwill. Instead, the increase in securities or debt issued represents a reduction in the premium or an increase in the discount on the initial issue.

Subsequent Identification or Changes in Value of Assets and Liabilities

59.   Assets and liabilities acquired in an acquisition which do not satisfy the criteria in paragraph 30 for separate recognition when the acquisition is initially accounted for should be recognised subsequently as and when they satisfy the criteria. The carrying amounts of assets and liabilities acquired should be adjusted when, subsequent to acquisition, additional evidence becomes available to assist with the estimation of the amounts assigned to those assets and liabilities when the acquisition was initially accounted for. The goodwill or negative goodwill amount should also be adjusted, when necessary, provided that such adjustment is made by the end of the first full annual accounting period following the acquisition; otherwise the adjustment should be recognised as income or expense.

60.   Assets and liabilities of an acquiree may not have been recognised at the time of acquisition because they did not meet the recognition criteria for assets and liabilities or the acquirer was unaware of their existence. Similarly, the fair values assigned at the date of acquisition to assets and liabilities acquired may need to be adjusted as additional evidence becomes available to assist with the estimation of the value of the asset or liability at the date of acquisition. When the assets or liabilities are recognised or the carrying amounts are adjusted after the end of the first full annual accounting period following the acquisition, income or expense is recognised rather than an adjustment to goodwill or negative goodwill. This time limit, while arbitrary in its size, prevents goodwill and negative goodwill from being reassessed and adjusted indefinitely.

61.   When, subsequent to acquisition, the acquirer becomes aware of the existence of a liability which had existed at the date of acquisition, goodwill ought not to be increased without firstly assessing whether additional future economic benefits can be expected. If additional future economic benefits cannot be expected the amount is recognised as an expense.

Unitings of Interests

62.   A uniting of interests should be accounted for by use of the pooling of interests method as set down in paragraphs 63, 64 and 68.

63.   In applying the pooling of interests method, the financial statement items of the combining enterprises for the period in which the combination occurs and for any comparative periods disclosed should be included in the financial statements of the combined enterprises as if they had been combined from the beginning of the earliest period presented. The financial statements of an enterprise should not incorporate a uniting of interests to which the enterprise is a party if the date of the uniting of interests is after the date of the most recent balance sheet included in the financial statements.

64.   Any difference between the amount recorded as share capital issued plus any additional consideration in the form of cash or other assets and the amount recorded for the share capital acquired should be adjusted against equity.

65.   The substance of a uniting of interests is that no acquisition has occurred and there has been a continuation of the mutual sharing of risks and benefits that existed prior to the business combination. Use of the pooling of interests method recognises this by accounting for the combined enterprises as though the separate businesses were continuing as before, though now jointly owned and managed. Accordingly, only minimal changes are made in aggregating the individual financial statements.

66.   Since the existing carrying amounts of the assets, liabilities and equity are combined without adjustment there is no recognition of any new goodwill or negative goodwill.

67.   Since a uniting of interests results in a single combined entity, a single uniform set of accounting policies is adopted by that entity and applied consistently for all periods being presented. Similarly, the effects of all transactions between the combining enterprises, whether occurring before or after the uniting of interests, are eliminated in preparing the financial statements of the combined entity.

68.   *Expenditures incurred in relation to a uniting of interests should be recognised as expenses in the period in which they are incurred.*

69.   Expenditures incurred in relation to a uniting of interests include registration fees, costs of furnishing information to shareholders, fees of finders and consultants, and salaries and other expenses related to services of employees involved in achieving the business combination. They also include any costs or losses incurred in combining operations of the previously separate businesses.

All Business Combinations

Taxes on Income

70.   In some countries the accounting treatment for a business combination may differ from that applied under their respective income tax laws. Permanent or timing differences which arise between recognition of income or expenses for financial reporting and for tax purposes are recognised in accordance with International Accounting Standard IAS 12, Accounting for Taxes on Income.

71.   An enterprise entering into a business combination may have potential benefits from tax loss carryforwards which because of uncertainty about the earning of sufficient future taxable income have not been recognised in its financial statements. However, this doubt may be removed as a result of the business combination, thus necessitating recognition of the asset.

Business Combinations after the Balance Sheet Date

72.   *Business combinations which have been effected after the balance sheet date and before the date on which the financial statements of one of the combining enterprises are authorised for issue should be disclosed if they are of such importance that non-disclosure would affect the ability of the users of the financial statements to make proper evaluations and decisions (see International Accounting Standard IAS 10, Contingencies and Events Occurring After the Balance Sheet Date). Disclosure should also be made of the information in paragraphs 74 to 78 of this Statement, to the extent that this can be estimated or, alternatively, a statement should be made that no such estimate can be made.*

73.   In certain circumstances, the effect of the combination may be to allow the going concern assumption to be maintained, when otherwise this might not have been possible.   If this is the case, disclosure of this information in the financial statements is relevant.

Disclosure

74.   For all business combinations the following disclosures should be made in the financial statements for the period during which the combination has taken place:

(a)   the names and descriptions of the combining enterprises;

(b)   whether the combination is an acquisition or a uniting of interests and the method of accounting used to reflect the combination;

(c)   the effective date of the combination for accounting purposes; and

(d)   any material operations of which the enterprise has decided to dispose.

75.   For a business combination which is an acquisition, the following additional disclosures should be made in the financial statements for the period during which the acquisition has taken place:

(a)   the percentage of voting shares acquired; and

(b)   the cost of acquisition and a description of the purchase consideration paid or contingently payable.

76.   The following disclosures should be made separately in respect of both goodwill and negative goodwill:

(a)   the gross amount and the accumulated amortisation at the beginning of the period;

(b)   any additional goodwill or negative goodwill arising from acquisitions during the period;

(c)   amortisation charged during the period;

(d)   any other write-offs during the period; and

*(e)   the accounting treatment for goodwill and negative goodwill,
including the period of amortisation.*

*When the useful life of goodwill or the amortisation period for negative
goodwill exceeds five years, justification of the period adopted should be
provided.*

77.   *In an acquisition, if the fair values of the assets and liabilities or
the purchase consideration can only be determined on a provisional basis
at the end of the period in which the acquisition took place, this should be
stated and reasons given. Where there are subsequent adjustments to such
provisional fair values those adjustments should be disclosed and
explained in the financial statements of the period concerned.*

78.   *For a business combination which is a uniting of interests, the
following additional disclosures should be made in the financial
statements for the period during which the uniting of interests has taken
place:*

*(a)   description and number of shares issued, together with the
percentage of each enterprise's voting shares exchanged to effect
the uniting of interests;*

*(b)   amounts of assets and liabilities contributed by each enterprise;
and*

*(c)   sales revenue, other operating revenues, unusual items and the net
profit or loss of each enterprise prior to the date of the
combination that are included in the net profit or loss shown by
the combined enterprise's financial statements.*

79.   General disclosures required to be made in consolidated financial
statements are contained in International Accounting Standard IAS 27,
Consolidated Financial Statements and Accounting for Investments in
Subsidiaries.

Transitional Provisions

80.   Retrospective application of this Statement is encouraged but not required. If the Statement is not applied retrospectively, the balance of any pre-existing goodwill or negative goodwill is deemed to have been properly determined and should be accounted for thereafter in accordance with the provisions of this Statement. The amortisation period for pre-existing goodwill or negative goodwill should be the shorter of the remaining life as specified in the enterprise's amortisation policy and the amortisation period specified in this Statement.

Effective Date

81.   This International Accounting Standard becomes operative for financial statements covering periods beginning on or after_____.

Extraordinary Items, Fundamental Errors and Changes in Accounting Policies

This draft incorporates the changes to International Accounting Standard 8, Unusual and Prior Period Items and Changes in Accounting Policies, as set out in the Statement of Intent on the Comparability of Financial Statements. It also proposes other improvements to IAS 8 to ensure that the Standard is sufficiently detailed and complete and contains adequate disclosure requirements to meet the needs of capital markets and the international business community.

As indicated in the Statement of Intent the Board does not intend to reconsider the issues which were exposed for comment in E32 and subsequently approved by the Board without substantive change.

The Board is expected to approve a revised International Accounting Standard 8, Extraordinary Items, Fundamental Errors and Changes in Accounting Policies, in July 1993.

Exposure Draft

Contents

International Accounting Standard --

Extraordinary Items, Fundamental Errors and Changes in Accounting Policies

International Accounting Standard --

Extraordinary Items, Fundamental Errors and Changes in Accounting Policies

The standards, which have been set in bold italic type, should be read in the context of the background material and implementation guidance and in the context of the Preface to International Accounting Standards. International Accounting Standards are not intended to apply to immaterial items (see paragraph 12 of the Preface).

Introduction

The income statement is the principal statement used to report the performance of an enterprise for a period. Information about the performance of an enterprise, in particular its profitability, is required in order to assess the economic resources that the enterprise is likely to control in the future. It is also frequently used to predict the ability of an enterprise to generate cash and cash equivalents in the future. Information about the variability of performance is also important in this respect.

The objective of this Statement is to prescribe the classification, disclosure and accounting treatment of certain items in the income statement so that all enterprises prepare and present an income statement on a consistent basis. This enhances the comparability of the financial statements of an enterprise through time and with the financial statements of other enterprises. Accordingly, this Statement sets standards in respect of the classification and disclosure of extraordinary items, the disclosure of certain items within profit or loss from ordinary activities and the accounting treatment for changes in accounting estimates and accounting policies and for the correction of fundamental errors.

Scope

1.   This Statement should be applied by all enterprises in presenting profit or loss from ordinary activities and extraordinary items in the income statement, and in accounting for changes in accounting estimates, fundamental errors and changes in accounting policies.

2.   This Statement deals with, among other things, the determination of net profit or loss for the period and the disclosure of certain items included in the net profit or loss. These disclosures are made in addition to any other disclosures that are made in accordance with other International Accounting Standards, including International Accounting Standard IAS 5, Information to be Disclosed in the Financial Statements.

3.   This Statement deals with certain disclosures relating to discontinued operations. However, it does not deal with the recognition and measurement issues related to discontinued operations. These issues may be dealt with in a future project of the International Accounting Standards Committee.

4.   Extraordinary items, fundamental errors and changes in accounting policies may have associated tax effects which are accounted for and disclosed in accordance with International Accounting Standard IAS 12, Accounting for Taxes on Income. When IAS 12 refers to unusual items, this should be read as extraordinary items as defined in this Statement.

Definitions

5.   *The following terms are used in this Statement with the meanings specified:*

Extraordinary items are income or expenses that arise from events or transactions that are clearly distinct from the ordinary activities of the enterprise and therefore are not expected to recur frequently or regularly.

Ordinary activities are any activities which are undertaken by an enterprise as part of its business and such related activities in which the enterprise engages in furtherance of, incidental to, or arising from, these activities.

A discontinued operation results from the sale or abandonment of an operation that represents a separate major line of business of an enterprise and of which the assets, net profit or loss and activities can be distinguished physically, operationally and for financial reporting purposes.

Fundamental errors are errors discovered in the current period that are of such significance that the financial statements of one or more prior periods can no longer be considered to have been reliable at the date of their issue.

Accounting policies are the specific principles, bases, conventions, rules and practices adopted by an enterprise in preparing and presenting financial statements.

Net Profit or Loss for the Period

6.   *All items of income and expense which are recognised in a period should be included in the determination of net profit or loss[1] for the period unless an International Accounting Standard requires or permits otherwise.*

7.   Normally, all items of income and expense which are recognised in a period are included in the determination of the net profit or loss for the period. This includes extraordinary items and the effects of changes in accounting estimates. However, there are circumstances when it may be desirable to exclude certain items from net profit or loss for the current period. This Statement deals with two such circumstances; the correction of fundamental errors and changes in accounting policies. In addition, other International Accounting Standards deal with items which may meet the Framework definitions of income or expense but which are usually excluded from the determination of the net profit or loss. Examples of such items include revaluation surpluses (see International Accounting Standard IAS 16, Property, Plant and Equipment) and gains and losses arising on the translation of the financial statements of a foreign entity (see International Accounting Standard IAS 21, The Effects of Changes in Foreign Exchange Rates).

8.   *The net profit or loss for the period comprises the following components, each of which should be disclosed on the face of the income statement:*

(a)   *profit or loss from ordinary activities; and*

(b)   *extraordinary items.*

---

[1]Terms such as "net income" may also be used.

Extraordinary Items

9.   The nature and the amount of each extraordinary item should be separately disclosed.

10.   Virtually all items of income and expense included in the determination of net profit or loss for the period arise in the course of the ordinary activities of the enterprise.   Therefore, only on rare occasions does an event or transaction give rise to an extraordinary item.

11.   Whether an event or transaction is clearly distinct from the ordinary activities of the enterprise is determined by the nature of the event or transaction in relation to the business ordinarily carried on by the enterprise. Therefore, an event or transaction may be extraordinary for one enterprise but not so for another enterprise because of the differences between their respective ordinary activities.

12.   Examples of events or transactions that generally give rise to extraordinary items for most enterprises are:

* the expropriation of assets; or
* an earthquake.

13.   The disclosure of the nature and amount of each extraordinary item may be made on the face of the income statement or in the notes to the financial statements.

Profit or Loss from Ordinary Activities

14.   The nature and amount of items of income and expense within profit or loss from ordinary activities that are of such size, nature or incidence that their disclosure is relevant to explain the performance of the enterprise for the period should be disclosed separately.

15.   The disclosure of the nature and the amount of income and expenses in accordance with paragraph 14 is relevant to users of financial statements in understanding the financial position and performance of an enterprise and in making projections about financial position and performance. These disclosures are made in addition to the minimum disclosures specified in International Accounting Standard IAS 5, Information to be Disclosed in Financial Statements. They are usually made in the notes to the financial statements.

16.   Circumstances which may give rise to items of income and expense referred to in paragraph 14 include:

*   write-down of inventories to net realisable value;

*   restructuring of the activities of an enterprise;

*   disposals of items of property, plant and equipment;

*   disposals of long-term investments;

*   discontinued operations; and

*   litigation settlements.

17.   While the disposal of investments or other major assets may be sufficiently important to warrant disclosure of the related items of income or expense, occasionally an enterprise discontinues a separate major line of business which is distinguishable from other business activities, for example a segment determined in accordance with International Accounting Standard IAS 14, Reporting Financial Information by Segment.   When this constitutes a discontinued operation as defined in this Statement the disclosures contained in paragraph 18 are relevant to users of financial statements.

18.   The following disclosures should be made for each discontinued operation:

- *the nature of the discontinued operation, and the industry and geographical segments in which it is reported in accordance with International Accounting Standard IAS 14, Reporting Financial Information by Segment;*

- *the effective date of discontinuance for accounting purposes;*

- *the manner of discontinuance (sale or abandonment);*

- *the gain or loss on discontinuance and the accounting policy used to measure that gain or loss; and*

- *the revenue and profit or loss from ordinary activities of the operation for the period, together with the corresponding amounts for prior periods included in the financial statements.*

19.   When it is known at the date on which the financial statements are authorised for issue that an operation has been or will be discontinued after the balance sheet date, the event is dealt with in accordance with International Accounting Standard IAS 10, Contingencies and Events Occurring After the Balance Sheet Date. In addition, the disclosure requirements of paragraph 18 of this Statement are applied to the extent that the information is known and can be reliably estimated.

Changes in Accounting Estimates

20.   As a result of the uncertainties inherent in business activities and the need to prepare periodic financial statements before uncertainties can be resolved, many financial statement items cannot be measured with precision but can only be estimated on the basis of the latest information available. For example, estimates are required of bad debts, inventory obsolescence and the useful lives of depreciable assets.

The use of reasonable estimates is an essential part of the preparation of financial statements and does not undermine their reliability.

21. An estimate may have to be revised in a subsequent period if there is a change in the circumstances on which the estimate was based, or as a result of new information, more experience or subsequent developments. The revision of the estimate, by its nature, does not bring the adjustment within the definitions of an extraordinary item or a fundamental error. However, it is sometimes difficult to distinguish between a change in accounting policy and a change in an accounting estimate. In such cases, the change is treated as a change in an accounting estimate, with appropriate disclosure.

22. *The effect of a change in an accounting estimate should be included in the determination of net profit or loss in:*

(a) *the period of the change, if the change affects the period only; or*

(b) *the period of the change and future periods, if the change affects both.*

23. *The effect of a change in an accounting estimate should be classified using the same income statement classification that was used previously for the estimate.*

24. In order to ensure the comparability of financial statements of different periods, the effect of a change in an accounting estimate that was previously included in the profit or loss from ordinary activities should be included in that component of net profit or loss; the effect of a change in an accounting estimate that was previously included as an extraordinary item should itself be reported as an extraordinary item.

25.   A change in an accounting estimate may affect the current period only or both the current period and future periods. For example, a change in the estimate of the amount of bad debts is recognised immediately and therefore affects only the current period. However, a change in the estimated useful life of a depreciable asset affects the depreciation expense in the current period and in each period during the remaining useful life of the asset. In both cases, the effect of the change relating to the current period is recognised as income or expense in the current period. The effect on future periods, if any, is recognised in future periods.

26.   *The nature and amount of a change in an accounting estimate that has a material effect in the current period, or which is expected to have a material effect in subsequent periods should be disclosed. If it is impracticable to quantify the amount, this fact should be disclosed.*

Fundamental Errors

27.   Errors in the preparation of the financial statements of one or more prior periods may be discovered in the current period. Errors may occur as a result of mathematical mistakes, mistakes in applying accounting policies, misinterpretation of facts, fraud or oversights. The correction of these errors is normally included in the determination of net profit or loss for the current period.

28.   On rare occasions, an error has such a significant effect on the financial statements of one or more prior periods that those financial statements can no longer be considered to have been reliable at the date of their issue. An example of such a fundamental error is the discovery that the financial statements for a previous period include material amounts of work in progress and receivables in respect of fraudulent contracts which cannot be enforced. It is necessary to account for fundamental errors by restating the comparative information to correct the fundamental error or by presenting such information on an additional pro forma basis.

29.   The correction of fundamental errors can be distinguished from changes in accounting estimates which are, by their nature, approximations that may need revision as additional information becomes known in subsequent periods. Similarly, the gain or loss recognised on the outcome of a contingency, which previously could not be estimated accurately, does not constitute the correction of a fundamental error.

30.   This Statement contains two sets of standards for the accounting treatment of fundamental errors. Under the benchmark treatment the opening balance of retained earnings is adjusted and the comparative information is restated. Under the allowed alternative treatment, the correction of the fundamental error is included in the determination of the net profit or loss for the current period and additional comparative information is presented.

Benchmark Treatment

31.   In correcting a fundamental error, the amount of the correction that relates to prior periods should be reported by adjusting the opening balance of retained earnings. Comparative information should be restated, unless it is impracticable to do so and this fact is disclosed.

32.   Under the benchmark treatment, the financial statements, including the comparative information for prior periods, are presented as if the fundamental error had been corrected in the period in which it was made. Therefore, the amount of the correction that relates to each period presented is included within the net profit or loss for that period. The amount of the correction relating to periods prior to those included in the comparative information in the financial statements is adjusted against the opening balance of retained earnings in the earliest period presented. Any other information reported with respect to prior periods, such as historical summaries of financial data, is also restated.

33.   The restatement of comparative information does not necessarily give rise to the amendment of financial statements which have been approved by shareholders or registered or filed with regulatory authorities.   However, national laws may require the amendment of such financial statements.

Allowed Alternative Treatment

34.   In correcting a fundamental error, the amount of the correction should be included in the determination of net profit or loss for the current period. Comparative information should be presented as reported in the financial statements of the prior period and additional pro forma information, prepared in accordance with paragraph 31, should be presented. If it is impracticable to restate the comparative amounts, this fact should be disclosed.

35.   Under the allowed alternative treatment, the correction of the fundamental error is included in the determination of the net profit or loss for the current period.   However, additional information is presented, often as a separate column, to show the net profit or loss of the prior periods as if the fundamental error had been corrected in the period when it was made.   It may be necessary to apply this accounting treatment in countries where the financial statements are required to include comparative information which agrees with the financial statements presented in prior periods.

Disclosure

36.   The nature of the fundamental error and the amount of the correction for each period presented should be separately disclosed.

Changes in Accounting Policies

37.   Users need to be able to compare the financial statements of an enterprise over a period of time in order to identify trends in its financial position, performance and changes in financial position. Therefore, the same accounting policies are normally adopted for similar events or transactions in each period.

38.   A change in accounting policy should be made only if the adoption of a different accounting policy is required by statute, or by an accounting standard setting body, or if it is considered that the change will result in a more appropriate presentation of events or transactions in the financial statements of the enterprise.

39.   A more appropriate presentation of events or transactions in the financial statements occurs when the new accounting policy results in more relevant or reliable information about the financial position, performance or changes in financial position of the enterprise.

40.   The adoption of an accounting policy to deal with events or transactions that are different in substance from those events or transactions previously occurring is not a change in accounting policy. Similarly, the adoption of a new accounting policy to deal with events or transactions which did not occur in the past or that were previously immaterial in their effect is not a change in accounting policy.

41.   A change in accounting policy may be applied retrospectively or prospectively. Retrospective application results in the new accounting policy being applied to events and transactions as if the new accounting policy had always been in use. Therefore, the accounting policy is applied to events and transactions from the date of origin of such times. Prospective application means that the new accounting policy is applied to the events and transactions occurring after the date of the change. No adjustments relating to prior periods are made either to the opening balance of retained earnings or in reporting the net profit or loss for the current period, because existing balances are not recalculated. However, the new accounting policy is applied to existing balances as from the date of the change. For example, an enterprise

may decide to change its accounting policy for development costs and capitalise those costs in conformity with Proposed International Accounting Standard, E37 Research and Development. If the enterprise is unable to determine the development costs which would have been capitalised in prior periods, it applies the new policy only to development costs that are incurred after the date of the change in accounting policy.

Adoption of an International Accounting Standard

42.   A change in accounting policy which is made on the adoption of an International Accounting Standard should be accounted for in accordance with the specific transitional provisions, if any, in that International Accounting Standard.   In the absence of any transitional provisions and for all other changes in accounting policies, the change in accounting policy should be applied in accordance with the benchmark treatment or the allowed alternative treatment prescribed in paragraphs 44 to 50 of this Statement.

43.   The transitional provisions in an International Accounting Standard may require either a retrospective or a prospective application of a change in accounting policy.

Other Changes in Accounting Policies

Benchmark Treatment

44.   A change in accounting policy should be applied retrospectively by reporting the amount of any resulting adjustment that relates to prior periods as an adjustment to the opening balance of retained earnings, unless the amount is not reasonably determinable. Comparative information should be restated unless it is impracticable to do so and this fact is disclosed.

45.   Under the benchmark treatment the financial statements, including the comparative information for prior periods, are presented as if the new accounting policy had always been in use.   Therefore, comparative information is restated in order to reflect the new accounting policy.   The amount of the adjustment relating to periods prior to those included in the financial statements is adjusted against the opening balance of retained earnings of the earliest period presented. Any other information with respect to prior periods, such as historical summaries of financial data, is also restated.

46.   The restatement of comparative information does not necessarily give rise to the amendment of financial statements which have been approved by shareholders or registered or filed with regulatory authorities.   However, national laws may require the amendment of such financial statements.

47.   *The change in accounting policy should be applied prospectively when the amount of the adjustment to the opening balance of retained earnings required by paragraph 44 cannot be reasonably determined.*

Allowed Alternative Treatment

48.   *A change in accounting policy should be applied retrospectively by including the amount of any resulting adjustments in the determination of the net profit or loss for the current period, unless the amount is not reasonably determinable.   Comparative information should be presented as reported in the financial statements of the prior period. Additional pro forma comparative information, prepared in accordance with paragraph 44, should be presented unless it is impracticable to do so and this fact is disclosed.*

49.   Under the allowed alternative, adjustments resulting from a change in accounting policy are included in the determination of the net profit or loss for the period.   However, additional comparative information is presented, often as a separate column, in order to show the net profit or loss and the financial position of prior periods as if the new accounting policy had always been applied. It may be necessary to apply this accounting treatment in countries where the financial statements are required to include comparative information which agrees with the financial statements presented in prior periods.

50.   The change in accounting policy should be applied prospectively when the amount to be included in net profit or loss for the current period required by paragraph 48 cannot be reasonably determined.

Disclosure

51.   When a change in accounting policy has a material effect in the current period, or may have a material effect in subsequent periods, the effect of the change should be quantified and disclosed, together with the reasons for the change. If it is impracticable to quantify the effect, this fact should be disclosed.

52.   When an enterprise has not adopted a new International Accounting Standard which has been published by the International Accounting Standards Committee but which has not yet come into effect, the enterprise is encouraged to disclose the nature of the future change in accounting policy and an estimate of the effect of the change on its net profit or loss and financial position.

Effective Date

53.   This International Accounting Standard becomes operative for financial statements covering periods beginning on or after_____.

Retirement Benefit Costs

This draft incorporates the changes to International Accounting Standard 19, Accounting for Retirement Benefits in the Financial Statements of Employers, as set out in the Statement of Intent on the Comparability of Financial Statements. Other changes to IAS 19 have been limited to the adoption of the new format for International Accounting Standards and any additional guidance that is necessary in order to implement the changes set out in the Statement of Intent on the Comparability of Financial Statements. The Board has recognised that it may have to carry out a more comprehensive review of IAS 19 in the foreseeable future.

As indicated in the Statement of Intent the Board does not intend to reconsider the issues which were exposed for comment in E32 and subsequently approved by the Board without substantive change. However, comments are sought as to the adequacy and appropriateness of other improvements made to IAS 19.

Comments should be submitted in writing so as to be received by **15 March 1993**. All replies will be put on public record unless confidentiality is requested by the commentator. Comments should be addressed to:

The Secretary-General
International Accounting Standards Committee
167 Fleet Street
London EC4A 2ES
England

Telefax: +44 (071) 353-0652.

Exposure Draft

Contents

International Accounting Standard -- Retirement Benefit Costs

International Accounting Standard --

Retirement Benefit Costs

The standards, which have been set in bold italic type, should be read in the context of the background material and implementation guidance in this Standard, and in the context of the Preface to International Accounting Standards. International Accounting Standards are not intended to apply to immaterial items (see paragraph 12 of the Preface).

Objective

In many countries, the provision of retirement benefits is a significant element of an enterprise's remuneration package for its employees. It is important that the cost of providing these retirement benefits is properly accounted for and that appropriate disclosures are made in the financial statements of the enterprise. The objective of this Standard is to prescribe when the cost of providing retirement benefits should be recognised as an expense and the amount that should be recognised. It also prescribes the information to be disclosed in the enterprise's financial statements.

Scope

1.   This Standard should be applied by all enterprises in accounting for the cost of retirement benefit plans.

2.   This Standard applies in respect of all retirement benefits provided under a retirement benefit plan, however described, irrespective of whether the plans are formal or informal, or whether the plans are funded or unfunded. It also applies when an enterprise is required, pursuant to law or industry plans, to contribute to national, state, industry or other multi-employer retirement benefit plans.

3.   Many employers provide other forms of employee remuneration or post-employment benefits including employment termination indemnities, deferred compensation arrangements, long-service leave benefits, health and welfare plans, and bonus plans. These arrangements are not dealt with by this Standard although it is usually appropriate to account for their costs in a similar manner to the costs of retirement benefit plans if the predominant

characteristics of the arrangements are the same as those of retirement benefit plans.

Definitions

4. *The following terms are used in this Standard with the meanings specified:*

Retirement benefit plans *are arrangements whereby an enterprise provides benefits for its employees on or after termination of service (either in the form of an annual income or as a lump sum) when such benefits can be determined or estimated in advance of retirement from the provisions of a document or from the enterprise's practices.*

Defined contribution plans *are retirement benefit plans under which amounts to be paid as retirement benefits are determined by reference to contributions to a fund together with investment earnings thereon.*

Defined benefit plans *are retirement benefit plans under which amounts to be paid as retirement benefits are determined by reference to a formula usually based on employees' earnings and/or years of service.*

Funding *is the transfer of assets to an entity separate from the enterprise ("the fund") to meet future obligations for the payment of retirement benefits.*

Current service cost *is the cost to an enterprise under a retirement benefit plan for the services rendered in the current period by participating employees exclusive of those costs identified as past service costs, experience adjustments, the effects of plan amendments and the effects of changes in actuarial assumptions.*

Past service cost *is the cost to an enterprise arising on:*

(a) *the introduction of a retirement benefit plan;*

(b) *the making of improvements to such a plan; or*

(c)   *the completion of minimum service requirements for eligibility in such a plan;*

all of which give employees credit for benefits for service prior to the occurrence of one or more of those events.

Experience adjustments are adjustments to an enterprise's retirement benefit cost arising from the differences between the previous actuarial assumptions as to future events and what has actually occurred.

Retirement Benefit Plans

5.   Most retirement benefit plans are formal agreements between an enterprise and its employees or their representatives. The plans may be established by the enterprise as a normal part of the remuneration package for its employees. In some countries, the plans may be established by law or through industry arrangements whereby enterprises are required to contribute to national, state, industry or other multi-employer retirement benefit plans. Retirement benefit plans may also be informal arrangements or evidenced only by an enterprise's practices.

Funding

6.   Many retirement benefit plans involve a separate fund into which the enterprise, and sometimes its employees, make contributions and from which retirement benefits are paid. Such funds are separate entities and are often administered by third parties who may be appointed by the enterprise or its employees and who may have total discretion as to the use of the funds. The third parties may undertake the obligation to provide the retirement benefits to the employees.

7.   In some cases, the fund takes the form of an insurance contract. The benefits insured by such a contract need not have a direct or automatic relationship with the enterprise's obligation for retirement benefits. Retirement benefit plans involving insurance contracts are similar to other funded plans and are subject to the same distinction between accounting and funding as other funded plans.

8.   Under some retirement benefits plans, the enterprise retains the obligation for the payment of retirement benefits under the plan without the

establishment of a separate fund. Such retirement benefit plans are described as being unfunded.

Types of Retirement Benefit Plans

9.   For the purposes of this Standard, retirement benefit plans are classified as either defined contribution plans or defined benefit plans.

10.   Under a defined contribution plan, an enterprise's obligation is the amount that it agrees to contribute to cover the payment of retirement benefits to its employees. Defined contribution plans usually involve a separate fund. The amount of a participant's future retirement benefits is determined by the contributions paid to the fund by the enterprise, the employees, or both, and the operating efficiency and investment earnings of that fund. An actuary's advice is not required when accounting for the costs of defined contribution plans but is sometimes used to estimate future retirement benefits that may be achievable based on contribution levels and estimates of investment earnings.

11.   Under a defined benefit plan, the enterprise's obligation is the amount of the expected payments to existing and retired employees, determined by reference to a formula usually based on employees' earnings and/or years of service. The enterprise measures the present value of these promised retirement benefits with the periodic advice of an actuary. The actuary may also assess the financial condition of the plan and recommend the future contribution levels to any fund.

12.   Defined benefit plans may be funded or unfunded. When a plan is funded, the payment of retirement benefits when they fall due depends on the financial position of the fund and the ability of contributors to make future contributions to the fund as well as the investment performance and operating efficiency of the fund. When a plan is unfunded, the payment of retirement benefits depends on the ability of the enterprise to meet the retirement benefit obligations as they fall due.

13.   Retirement benefit plans may contain characteristics of both defined benefit and defined contribution plans. Such hybrid plans are generally considered to be defined benefit plans for the purposes of this Standard. For example, a retirement benefit plan may stipulate the basis of contributions on which the retirement benefits are determined and, because

of this, appear to be a defined contribution plan. However, the plan may make the enterprise responsible for specified retirement benefits or a specified level of retirement benefits. In this case, the plan is, in substance, a defined benefit plan and an enterprise's cost of providing retirement benefits is determined and accounted for accordingly.

14. The payment of retirement benefits under national, state, industry or other multi-employer plans may not be the responsibility of the enterprise and the cost of such plans may be assessed generally for enterprises on a country, state, industry or multi-employer basis. Such plans are generally considered to be defined contribution plans. However, to the extent that the enterprise retains responsibility for retirement benefits, the plan is considered to be a defined benefit plan.

Accounting for Retirement Benefit Costs

15. The cost to an enterprise of providing retirement benefits arises as services are rendered by the employees who are entitled to receive such benefits. Consequently, the cost of retirement benefits is recognised as an expense in the periods during which the services are rendered. The recognition of retirement benefit costs only when employees retire or receive retirement benefits does not allocate those costs to the periods in which the services were rendered. Even when a plan permits an enterprise to terminate its obligation under the plan, it is usually difficult for an employer to cancel a plan if employees are to be retained. Therefore, the cost of retirement benefits is recognised as an expense whether or not it results in a legal liability.

16. The amount funded by an enterprise during a period may be similar to the amount recognised as an expense in the period. However, there is a vital distinction between the funding of retirement benefits and the allocation of the cost of providing those benefits for purposes of recognising the expense. Funding is a financial procedure and, in determining the periodic amounts to be funded, the enterprise may be influenced by such factors as the availability of cash and tax considerations. In contrast, the objective of accounting is to ensure that the cost of retirement benefits is recognised as an expense as services are rendered by the employees who are entitled to receive benefits.

Defined Contribution Plans

Recognition

17.   The enterprise's contributions to a defined contribution plan applicable to a particular period should be recognised as an expense in that period.

18.   The enterprise's contribution to a defined contribution plan is usually determined by a formula stated under the terms of the plan. Therefore, the amount of the expense can be calculated with certainty each period.

19.   An enterprise may agree to make additional contributions under a defined contribution plan. The increased contributions are recognised as an expense in the periods during which the associated services are rendered by employees. For example, when the additional contributions are determined by reference to employee service in prior periods and are in return for services to be rendered by existing employees in the current and future periods, the increased contributions are recognised as an expense systematically over the expected remaining working lives of those employees. When the additional contributions relate to retired employees, the contributions are recognised as an expense in the period in which the promise of additional contributions is made since no further services are expected to be received by the enterprise from those employees.

20.   The contributions agreed by the enterprise determine the amount of the expense recognised and the amount of the enterprise's obligation under a defined contribution plan. Therefore, plan termination does not usually result in any additional obligation requiring recognition as a liability and an expense. However, to the extent that increased contributions have been agreed but not recognised as an expense, an additional obligation needs to be recognised as a liability and expense when it is probable that the plan will be terminated.

Disclosure

21. *The financial statements should disclose the following in respect of a defined contribution plan:*

(a) *a general description of the plan, including employee groups covered;*

(b) *the amount recognised as an expense during the period; and*

(c) *any other significant matters related to retirement benefits that affect comparability with the previous period.*

Defined Benefit Plans

Recognition of Current Service Cost

22.   The current service cost in respect of a defined benefit plan should be recognised as an expense systematically as the employees covered by the retirement benefit plan render services to the enterprise over their expected remaining working lives.

23.   Defined benefit plans, especially those that promise retirement benefits based on remuneration at or near retirement, present significant difficulties in the estimation of costs.   The extent of the enterprise's obligation under such plans is usually uncertain because there are many variables that influence the amount of the ultimate benefits and, hence, the cost of those retirement benefits. This uncertainty is likely to remain so over a long period of time. For example, the amount of future retirement benefits may be determined by employees' earnings at retirement and by their years of service, both of which are uncertain. Moreover, in estimating the obligation, assumptions need to be made regarding future conditions and events which are largely outside the enterprise's control, such as the investment earnings on the assets of any fund and employee turnover. Furthermore, these long-term uncertainties may give rise to changes of estimates that can be very significant in relation to current service cost.

24.   Because of the potentially significant effect of differences between assumptions and experience, it is necessary to determine the cost of retirement benefits by obtaining actuarial valuations at frequent intervals. At least every three years is appropriate.   Additional valuations are appropriate in intervening years when significant changes in the circumstances of the plan are known to have taken place or when events indicate that one or more of the assumptions may have to be modified.

Recognition of Retirement Benefit Cost other than Current Service Cost

Existing Employees

25.   Past service costs, experience adjustments, the effects of changes in actuarial assumptions and the effects of plan amendments in respect of existing employees in a defined benefit plan should be recognised as an expense or as income systematically over the expected remaining working lives of those employees or over a shorter time period to reflect the receipt of benefits by the enterprise.

26.   Past service costs arise on the introduction of a retirement benefit plan, the making of improvements to a plan or when employees complete the minimum service requirements for eligibility to a plan. Employees who have been employed by the enterprise or who have been members of the existing plan for longer than others are promised additional benefits. A plan may be improved to provide additional benefits, for example, when retirement benefits are deemed to be inadequate, because of inflation or for other reasons. Such entitlements to retirement benefits are in return for services to be rendered by those employees in the future. Therefore, the past service cost is usually allocated over the current and future periods during which the services are to be rendered, regardless of the fact that these costs are computed by reference to employee service in previous periods.

27.   Experience adjustments arise because actual events inevitably differ from actuarial assumptions and because actuaries make their assumptions with a long term view. For example, the rate of employee turnover may be different from that assumed in the last actuarial valuation. These experience adjustments may give rise to either expense or income. If costs are adjusted each time there is a difference between actual experience and the previous actuarial assumptions, an erratic retirement benefits expense may result from period to period. The actuarially determined cost is intended to provide a more reliable measure of expense in each period than an expense determined substantially as actual experience to date. Furthermore, in the long term, experience adjustments may offset one another. Therefore, experience adjustments are usually allocated over the expected remaining working lives of existing employees.

28.   Changes in actuarial assumptions are made when actual experience in the long term consistently differs from the original actuarial assumptions. These changes may give rise to expense or income. They are equivalent to changes in accounting estimates arising from new information   (see Proposed International Accounting Standard, E46, Extraordinary Items, Fundamental Errors and Changes in Accounting Policies). Therefore, the effects of changes in actuarial assumptions are usually allocated over the expected remaining working lives of existing employees.

29.   Retirement benefit costs other than current service costs for existing employees may provide an enterprise with benefits over a shorter time period than the expected remaining working lives of the employees concerned.   Such costs are recognised as an expense over that shorter period.   For example, when plan amendments are made regularly, the additional cost is recognised as an expense or income systematically over the period to the next plan amendment.   Another example is when a significant change in the normal level of contributions is necessary to eliminate a deficiency resulting from an impairment in the value of plan assets.

Retired Employees

30.   The effects of plan amendments in respect of retired employees in a defined benefit plan should be measured as the present value of the effect of the amended benefits and should be recognised as an expense or as income in the period in which the plan amendment is made.

31.   The effect of providing amended retirement benefits for retired employees is recognised as an expense or as income in the period in which the plan amendment is made since no further benefits in the nature of future services are expected to be received by the enterprise from those employees.

Plan Terminations, Curtailments and Settlements

32.   When it is probable that a retirement benefit plan that is a defined benefit plan will be terminated or that there will be a curtailment or settlement of the retirement benefits payable under that plan:

(a)   any resulting increase in the enterprise's retirement benefit cost should be recognised as an expense immediately; and

(b)   any resulting gain should be recognised as income in the period in which the termination, curtailment or settlement occurs.

33.   A curtailment occurs when an enterprise reduces benefits available under a retirement benefit plan.   A curtailment may arise from an isolated event, such as the closing of a plant or discontinuation of a segment that results in a significant reduction in the number of employees participating in

a retirement benefit plan. Alternatively, a curtailment may result from termination or suspension of a plan.

34.   A settlement occurs when an enterprise discharges its retirement benefit obligation. This occurs, for example, when a lump-sum cash payment is made to plan participants in exchange for their rights to receive specified retirement benefits.

Actuarial Valuation Methods and Actuarial Assumptions to be Used for Determination of Cost

35.   A number of actuarial valuation methods have been developed to estimate the enterprise's obligation under defined benefit plans. While primarily designed to calculate funding requirements, these methods are frequently used for accounting purposes to determine the cost to the enterprise of providing retirement benefits and to determine the expense to be recognised each period. The Appendix describes these methods.

36.   In allocating the retirement benefit cost over the periods in which employees' services are rendered, it is usually appropriate to determine the actuarial present value of promised retirement benefits on the basis of methods and assumptions that result in annual current service costs that bear a reasonably constant relationship to remuneration. The actuarial present value of promised retirement benefits is the present value of the expected payments by a retirement benefit plan to existing and retired employees, attributable to the service already rendered. The cost recognised as an expense may differ significantly depending on the actuarial valuation method used and the assumptions about the variable elements affecting the computations.

Benchmark Treatment

37.   The cost of providing retirement benefits under a defined benefit plan should be determined using an accrued benefit valuation method.

38.   Accrued benefit valuation methods are actuarial valuation methods that determine the cost of providing retirement benefits on the basis of services rendered by employees to the date of the actuarial valuation. Under accrued benefit methods the annual current service cost applicable to each employee increases as his or her retirement approaches. This increase

occurs because there is less opportunity for investment earnings to accumulate on the contributions and the probability of the employee remaining in the plan to retirement increases. This effect is compounded when retirement benefits are based on final salary and discounted for the impact of inflation on salary levels. However, for a retirement benefit plan as a whole, annual current service cost tends to be approximately the same each period provided the number and age distribution of participating employees remains relatively unchanged.

Allowed Alternative Treatment

39.   The cost of providing retirement benefits under a defined benefit plan should be determined using a projected benefit valuation method.

40.   Projected benefit valuation methods are actuarial valuation methods that determine the present value of the total expected cost of providing retirement benefits on the basis of service both rendered and to be rendered by employees as at the date of the actuarial valuation. These methods spread the cost evenly, either in absolute amounts or as a percentage of salaries, over all periods of service making up the working lives of participating employees. These methods achieve a relatively level annual current service cost.

Actuarial Assumptions

41.   Appropriate and compatible assumptions, including those regarding projected salary levels to the date of retirement, should be used in determining the cost of retirement benefits.

42.   Actuarial assumptions are used to estimate the expected inflow from future contributions under the plan and from investments as well as the expected outflow for retirement benefits. The uncertainty inherent in projecting future trends in rates of inflation, salary levels and earnings on investments are taken into consideration in the actuarial valuations by using a set of compatible assumptions. This may be achieved by actuarial assumptions that reflect the relative relationships between inflation, rates of salary increase, earnings on investments held as plan assets and discount rates, even though the absolute values of these may not accord with current practice or experience. For example, the basis of valuing plan assets needs to be compatible with the interest assumption used for determining the

actuarial obligation. Usually these projections have to be extended until the expected date of death of the last pensioner and are, accordingly, long-term.

43. The following actuarial assumptions are normally appropriate in determining the cost to the enterprise of providing retirement benefits:

(a) the discount rate assumed in determining the actuarial present value of promised benefits in respect of services rendered to the valuation date reflects the long-term rates, or an approximation thereto, at which such obligations are expected to be settled;

(b) plan assets are valued at fair value. When fair values are estimated by discounting future cash flows, the long-term rate of return reflects the average rate of total income (interest, dividends and appreciation in value) expected to be earned on the plan assets during the time period until benefits are paid;

(c) when retirement benefits are based on future salaries, as is the case in final salary and career average plans, salary increases to the date of termination reflect factors such as inflation, promotion and merit awards; and

(d) automatic retirement benefit increases, such as cost of living adjustments, are taken into account. When, in the absence of formal requirements to increase benefits, it is the practice of the enterprise or the plan to grant such increases on a regular basis, it is assumed that the increases will continue.

44. The actuarial assumptions used in determining the cost to the employer of providing retirement benefits are based on long-term considerations. It may be necessary to modify these assumptions from time to time as is the case when salary increases exceed the assumed rate of increase and this trend is expected to continue. On the other hand, the higher salaries may have been due to special circumstances that are not expected to recur so that the initial assumption about salary increases is expected to be valid in the future. In the latter case, the previous salary assumption would not be changed.

Change in Actuarial Valuation Method

45.   The effect of a change in the actuarial valuation method used for the determination of retirement benefit costs, that affects the expense recognised in the current period or may affect the expense to be recognised in subsequent periods, should be accounted for and disclosed as a change in accounting policy in accordance with Proposed International Accounting Standard, E46, Extraordinary Items, Fundamental Errors and Changes in Accounting Policies.

Disclosure

46.   The financial statements should disclose the following in respect of a defined benefit plan:

(a)   a general description of the plan, including employee groups covered;

(b)   the accounting policies adopted for retirement benefit costs, including a general description of the actuarial valuation method or methods used (see International Accounting Standard IAS 1, Disclosure of Accounting Policies);

(c)   whether or not the plan is separately funded;

(d)   the amount recognised as an expense or as income during the period;

(e)   the actuarial present value of promised retirement benefits at the date of the most recent actuarial valuation;

(f)   if the plan is funded, the fair value of the plan assets at the date of the most recent actuarial valuation;

(g)   if the amounts funded since the inception of the plan are different from the amounts recognised as expense or income (or charged or credited to retained earnings on a change in accounting policy) over the same period, the amount of the resulting liability or asset and the funding approach adopted if there is no systematic policy of funding. When an employer has more than one plan and this

results in there being both a liability and an asset, the liability or asset should not be reduced by deducting one from the other;

(h) *the actuarial present value of the vested benefits, the rights to which (under the conditions of the retirement benefit plan) are not conditional on continued employment;*

(i) *the principal actuarial assumptions used in determining the cost of retirement benefits and any significant changes in those assumptions;*

(j) *the date of the most recent actuarial valuation and the frequency with which valuations are made; and*

(k) *any other significant matters related to retirement benefits that affect comparability with the previous period.*

47. When an enterprise has more than one retirement benefit plan, the disclosures in the financial statements summarise the significant and relevant information for all of the enterprise's plans. However, the value of the information is lessened if the amount of an asset in one plan or plans is offset against a liability in another plan or plans.

Transitional Provisions

48.   When the adoption of this Standard constitutes a change in accounting policy, an enterprise should either:

(a)   adjust its financial statements in accordance with Proposed International Accounting Standard, E46, Extraordinary Items, Fundamental Errors and Changes in Accounting Policies, to recognise a liability or an asset for the cumulative effect of the change; or

(b)   disclose the cumulative effect of the change in the period of change and subsequently disclose the amount still unrecognised. The amount unrecognised at the date of introduction of the Standard should be recognised as a liability or as an asset over a period not exceeding the expected remaining working lives of participating employees. The cost of retirement benefits that arises in subsequent periods should be recognised as income or expense in accordance with the requirements of this Standard.

Effective Date

49.   This International Accounting Standard becomes operative for financial statements covering periods beginning on or after _____.

Appendix

Principal Actuarial Valuation Methods

Actuarial valuation methods generally fall into two broad categories: the accrued benefit valuation method and projected benefit valuation methods. These titles are not necessarily those used in all countries.

Accrued Benefit Valuation Method

Under this method:

• current service cost is the present value of retirement benefits payable in the future in respect of service in the current period;

• past service cost is the present value on the introduction of a retirement benefit plan, on the making of improvements to such a plan or on the completion of minimum service requirements for eligibility in such a plan, of the units of benefits payable in the future in respect of services rendered prior to the occurrence of one or more of those events; and

• the accrued actuarial liability is the present value of benefits payable in the future in respect of service to date.

Assuming no inflation or deflation, this method produces a current service cost applicable to an employee that increases each year as the period to retirement shortens, because there is less opportunity for investment earnings on the contributions to accumulate and the probability of the employee remaining in the plan to retirement increases.

For a retirement benefit plan as a whole, annual current service cost tends to be approximately the same each year provided the number and age distribution of participating employees remains relatively unchanged. In a salary-related plan, inflation adds to the rate of increase each year and, accordingly, this method is often modified for final pay plans by introducing salary projections. As a result, employees' final salaries are estimated and the benefits based on these final salaries are allocated to years of service in calculating each year's cost.

Projected Benefit Valuation Methods

Projected benefit valuation methods reflect retirement benefits based on service both rendered and to be rendered by employees as at the date of the actuarial valuation. These methods allocate the cost of employees' retirement benefits evenly (either in absolute amounts or as a percentage of salaries) over the full period of employment.

There are four principal forms of the projected benefit valuation method:

The Entry Age Normal Method

Under this method, each employee is assumed to have entered the plan when first employed or as soon as he or she became eligible. When a new plan is introduced the assumed date of entry is that on which the employee would have become eligible to join if the plan had been in existence at the time.

The current service cost is a level annual amount or a fixed percentage of salary which, when invested at the rate of interest assumed in the actuarial valuation, is sufficient to provide the required retirement benefit at the employee's retirement. Under this method, past service cost is the present value of the excess of projected retirement benefits over the amount expected to be provided by future contributions based on the current service cost.

The application of this method conceptually requires calculations to be made for each individual employee. However, in practice it is often used for groups of employees and the application of the method is often simplified by using one entry date for all employees.

The Individual Level Premium Method

This method is generally used in conjunction with individual annuity insurance policies. It allocates the cost of each employee's retirement benefit over the period from the date of entry into the plan to the date of retirement by level annual amounts or by a fixed percentage of salary. There is no separate calculation of past service cost because the whole cost of the ultimate benefit is spread between the date the employee enters the plan and his retirement date.

Under this method, annual current service costs are higher than those which would result from the use of the entry age normal method. The reason for this is that, under this method, the costs otherwise identified as past service costs are charged as current service costs.

The Aggregate Method

This method uses the same basic principles as the individual level premium method but it is applied to the plan as a whole rather than to individual employees. The cost of benefits is allocated over the average service lives of active employees. The effect of averaging the cost for all employees or groups of employees under this method is that the relatively high annual cost in the early years of the plan is less pronounced than under the individual level premium method.

Past service cost and experience adjustments are not identified but are spread over future periods through regular computations using this method.

The Attained Age Normal Method

This method is similar to the aggregate method and the individual level premium method except that, under this method, the past service cost is calculated and identified using the accrued benefit valuation method. Current service costs are determined using the aggregate method but applied only to retirement benefits in respect of service in the future.

Index

This index is based on the 29 International Accounting Standards that are operative for financial statements covering periods beginning on or after 1 January 1993 and does not include the new revised IAS 7, Cash Flow Statements, or the Exposure Drafts.

Indexing is by Statement number and paragraph number. References to the Framework for the Preparation and Presentation of Financial Statements are preceded by F.

728